Grayarts & Cocovet

Elemental Gelade VIII / Mayumi Azuma

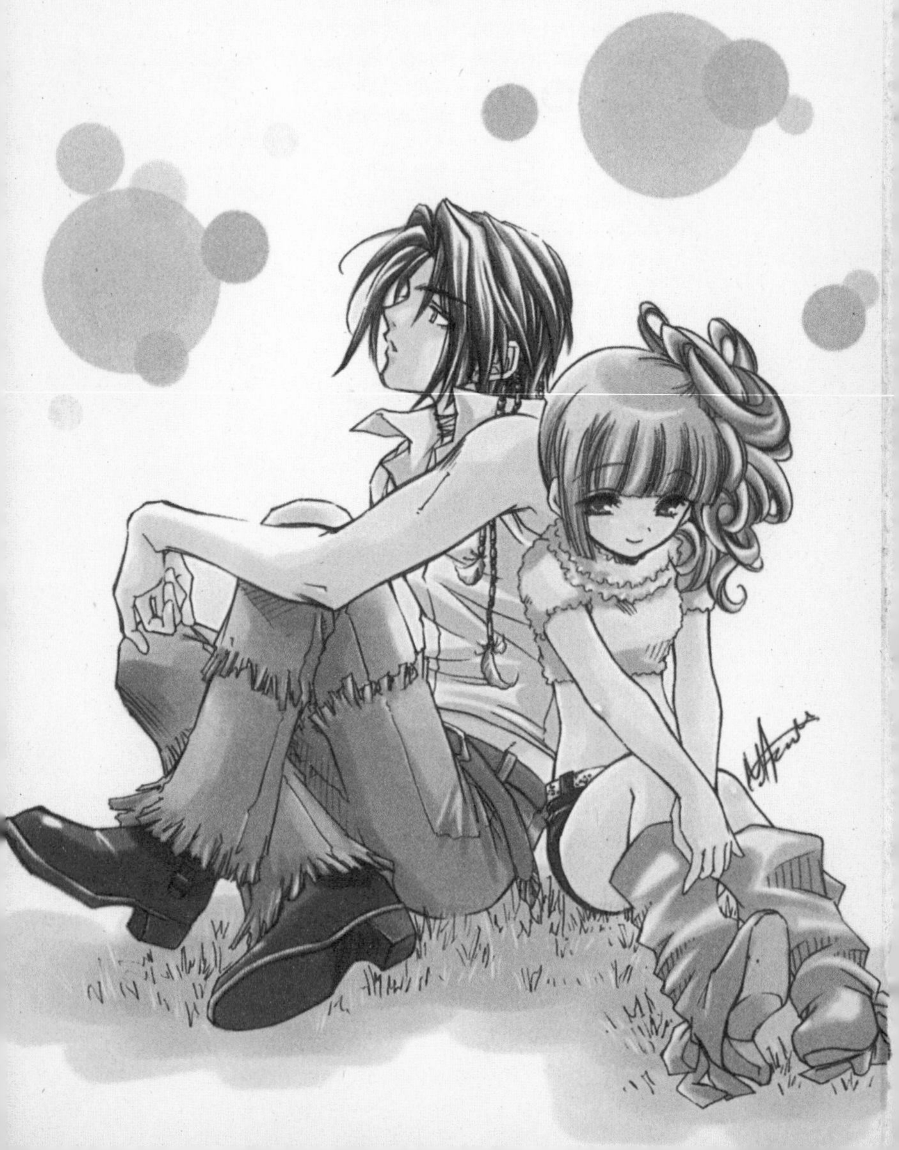

Elemental Gelade Volume 8
Created by Mayumi Azuma

Translation - Alethea & Athena Nibley
English Adaptation - Jordan Capell
Retouch and Lettering - Star Print Brokers
Production Artist - Vicente Rivera, Jr.
Graphic Designer - James Lee
Copy Editor - Jessica Chavez

Editor - Troy Lewter
Digital Imaging Manager - Chris Buford
Pre-Production Supervisor - Lucas Rivera
Production Manager - Elisabeth Brizzi
Managing Editor - Vy Nguyen
Creative Director - Anne Marie Horne
Editor-in-Chief - Rob Tokar
Publisher - Mike Kiley
President and C.O.O. - John Parker
C.E.O. and Chief Creative Officer - Stu Levy

A **TOKYOPOP** Manga

TOKYOPOP and ☁ are trademarks or registered trademarks of TOKYOPOP Inc.

TOKYOPOP Inc.
5900 Wilshire Blvd. Suite 2000
Los Angeles, CA 90036

E-mail: info@TOKYOPOP.com
Come visit us online at www.TOKYOPOP.com

© 2005 MAYUMI AZUMA. All Rights Reserved. All rights reserved. No portion of this book may be
First published in Japan in 2005 by MAG Garden reproduced or transmitted in any form or by any means
Corporation. English translation rights arranged with MAG without written permission from the copyright holders.
Garden Corporation. This manga is a work of fiction. Any resemblance to
actual events or locales or persons, living or dead, is
English text copyright © 2008 TOKYOPOP Inc. entirely coincidental.

ISBN: 978-1-59816-605-7
First TOKYOPOP printing: July 2008
10 9 8 7 6 5 4 3 2 1
Printed in the USA

ELEMENTAL GELADE

Volume 8

by
Mayumi Azuma

HAMBURG // LONDON // LOS ANGELES // TOKYO

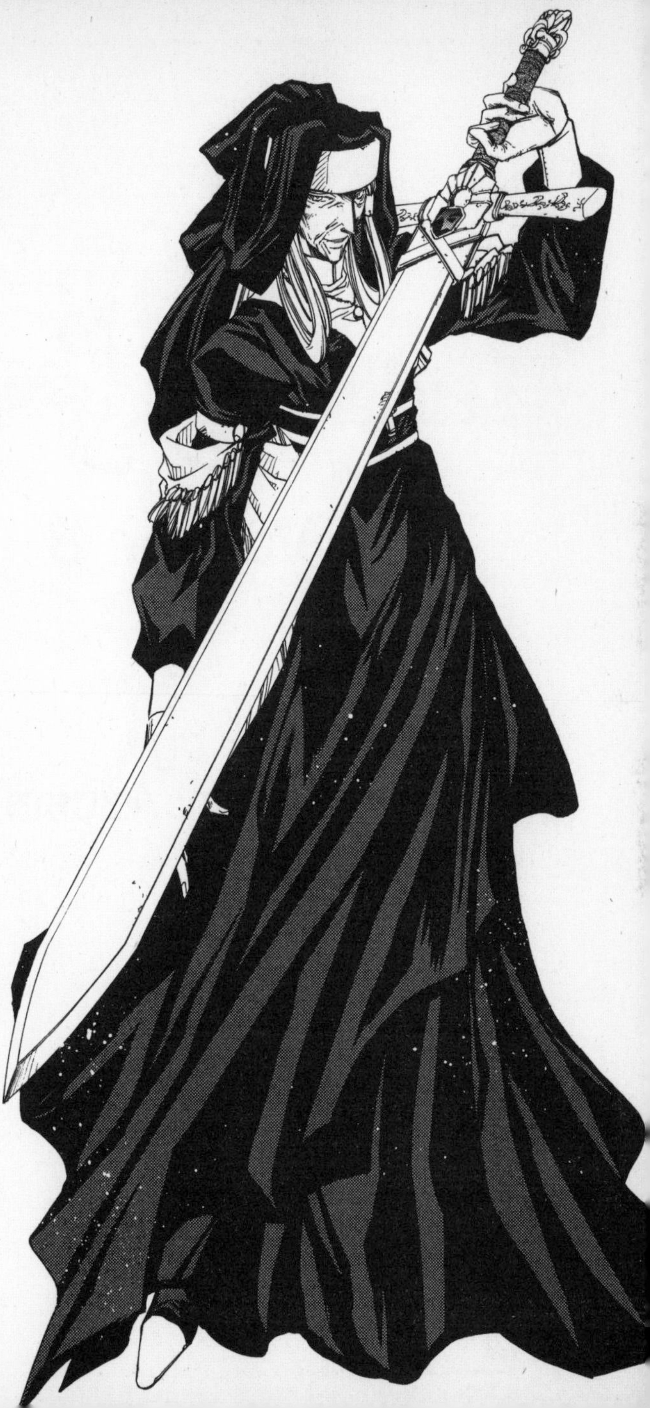

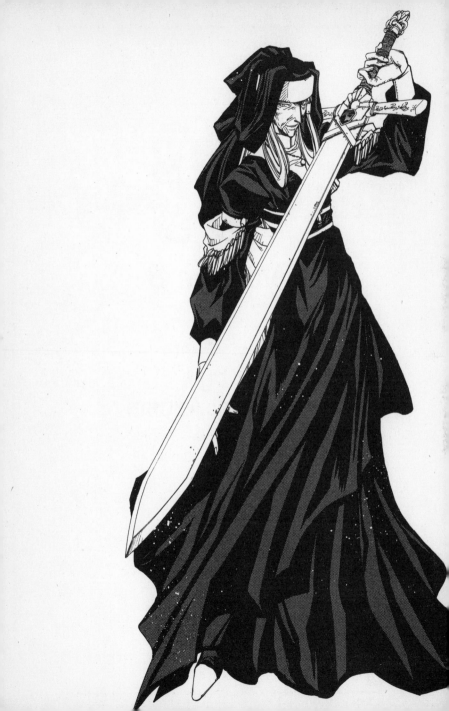

ELEMENTAL GELADE

Story So Far

FOLLOWING A ROUTINE RAID, SKY PIRATE COUD VAN GIRUET DISCOVERS A MOST UNUSUAL BOUNTY--A BEAUTIFUL GIRL IN A BOX NAMED REN, WHO SAYS SHE NEEDS TO GO TO A PLACE CALLED EDEL GARDEN. BUT BEFORE COUD CAN MAKE SENSE OF IT ALL, A GROUP NAMED ARC AILE ARRIVES, STATING THAT THE GIRL IS IN FACT AN EDEL RAID (A LIVING WEAPON WHO REACTS WITH A HUMAN TO BECOME A FIGHTING MACHINE) AND THAT THEY WISH TO BUY HER. A BATTLE BREAKS OUT, DURING THE COURSE OF WHICH REN BONDS WITH COUD, BECOMING HIS WEAPON DURING THE FIGHT. REN IS SO TOUCHED BY COUD'S RESOLVE TO HELP HER THAT SHE DECIDES TO BECOME HIS PERSONAL EDEL RAID.

WITH THE HELP OF CISQUA (LEADER OF THE ARC AILE TEAM), ROWEN (HER SECOND IN COMMAND) AND HIS EDEL RAID KUEA, COUD AND REN SET OUT FOR EDEL GARDEN. BUT THE ROAD THERE IS A TREACHEROUS ONE, IN WHICH THEY FIND THEMSELVES PROTECTING REN FROM BLACK-MARKET EDEL RAID DEALERS, AS WELL AS EDEL RAID BOUNTY HUNTERS. LACK OF MONEY FORCES THEM TO STOP AT THE BETTING GROUND MILLIARD TREY, WHERE THEY HELP TO FREE AN ENSLAVED FIGHTER NAMED RASATI AND HER ADOPTED EDEL RAID SISTER, LILIA.

SOON AFTER, A "FAN" OF COUD'S FROM MILLIARD TREY NAMED VIRO JOINS THEM ON THEIR JOURNEY, BUT CISQUA BEGINS TO SUSPECT THAT VIRO IS HIDING SOMETHING. THE PARTY CLIMBS UP A MOUNTAIN WHERE THEY FIND A BROKEN ROPEWAY STATION THAT COULD HELP THEM CROSS A RAVINE. WHILE COUD REPAIRS THE ROPEWAY CAR, ROWEN NOTICES VIRO BEHAVING STRANGELY, AND THAT REN IS SUDDENLY SLEEPIER THAN USUAL.

AS THEY TRAVEL IN THE ROPEWAY CAR THEY ARE ATTACKED BY VIRO'S BOSS, GLAUDIAS. VIRO THEN REVEALS THAT HER TRUE PURPOSE IS TO KILL COUD AND TAKE REN. (IT IS ALSO REVEALED THAT VIRO IS A TERM FOR MAN-MADE EDEL RAIDS, CREATED BY IMPLANTING ARTIFICIAL GELADES INTO HUMAN WOMEN). THEIR SALIVA IS LIKE POISON TO REAL EDEL RAIDS (VIRO SECRETLY POISONED REN BY LICKING HER GELADE STONE).

ROWN TRIES TO CONVINCE VIRO THAT SHE CAN LIVE A LIFE OTHER THAN THAT OF A WEAPON, BUT SHE REFUSES TO LISTEN--AND HE HAS NO OTHER CHOICE BUT TO DEFEAT HER. GLAUDIAS, SEEING THAT HIS PLANS AREN'T GOING AS SMOOTHLY AS HE'D HOPED, DECIDES IT'S TIME TO RETREAT...BUT BEFORE HE LEAVES, HE DESTROYS VIRO'S GELADE, AND SHE DIES IN ROWEN'S ARMS.

Contents

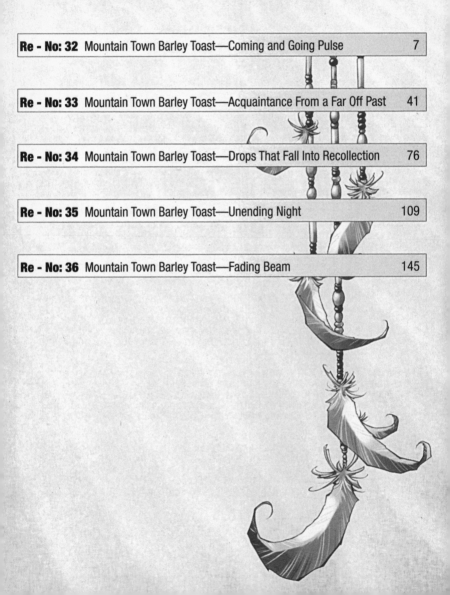

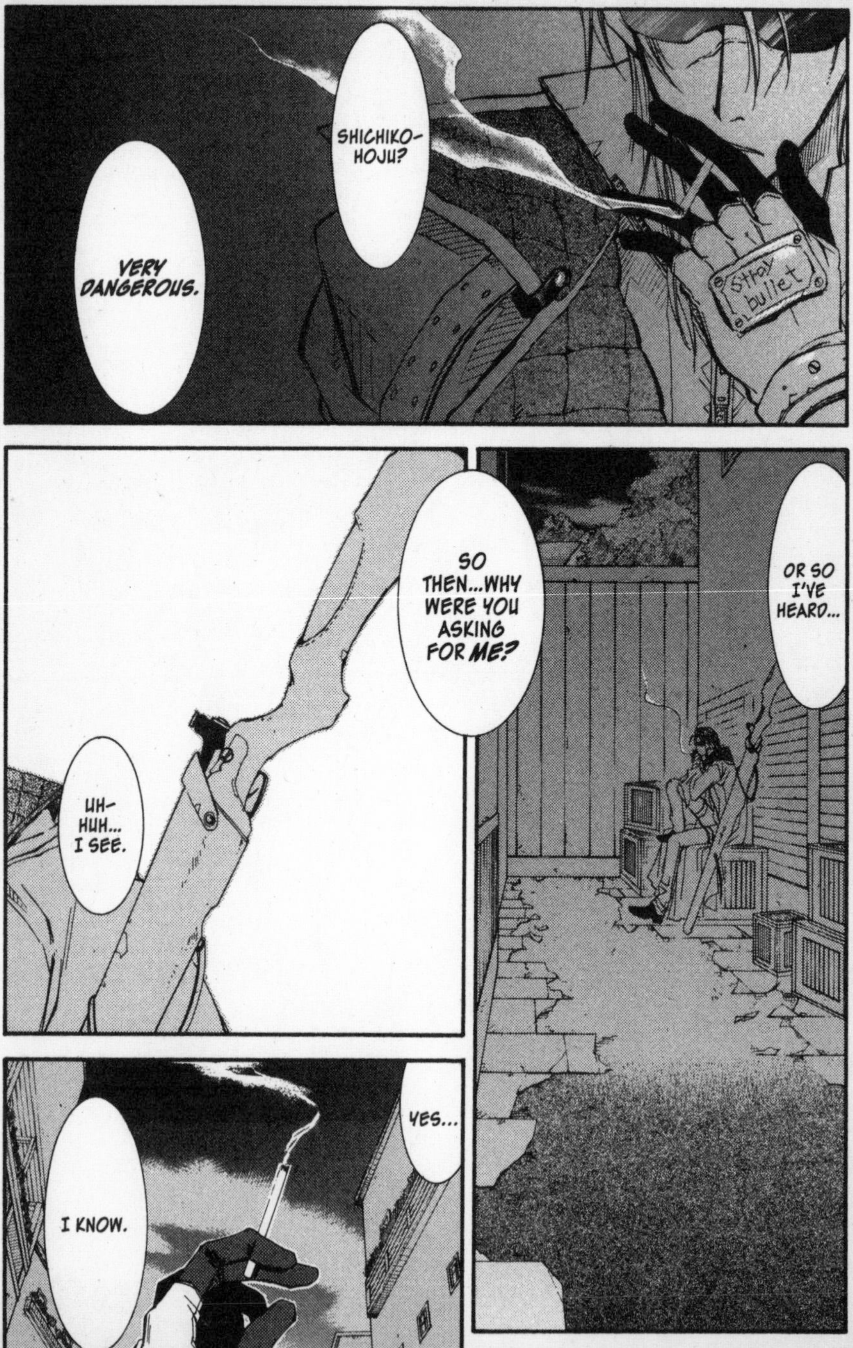
SHICHIKO-HOJU?
VERY DANGEROUS.
Stray bullet
OR SO I'VE HEARD...
SO THEN...WHY WERE YOU ASKING FOR ME?
UH-HUH... I SEE.
YES...
I KNOW.

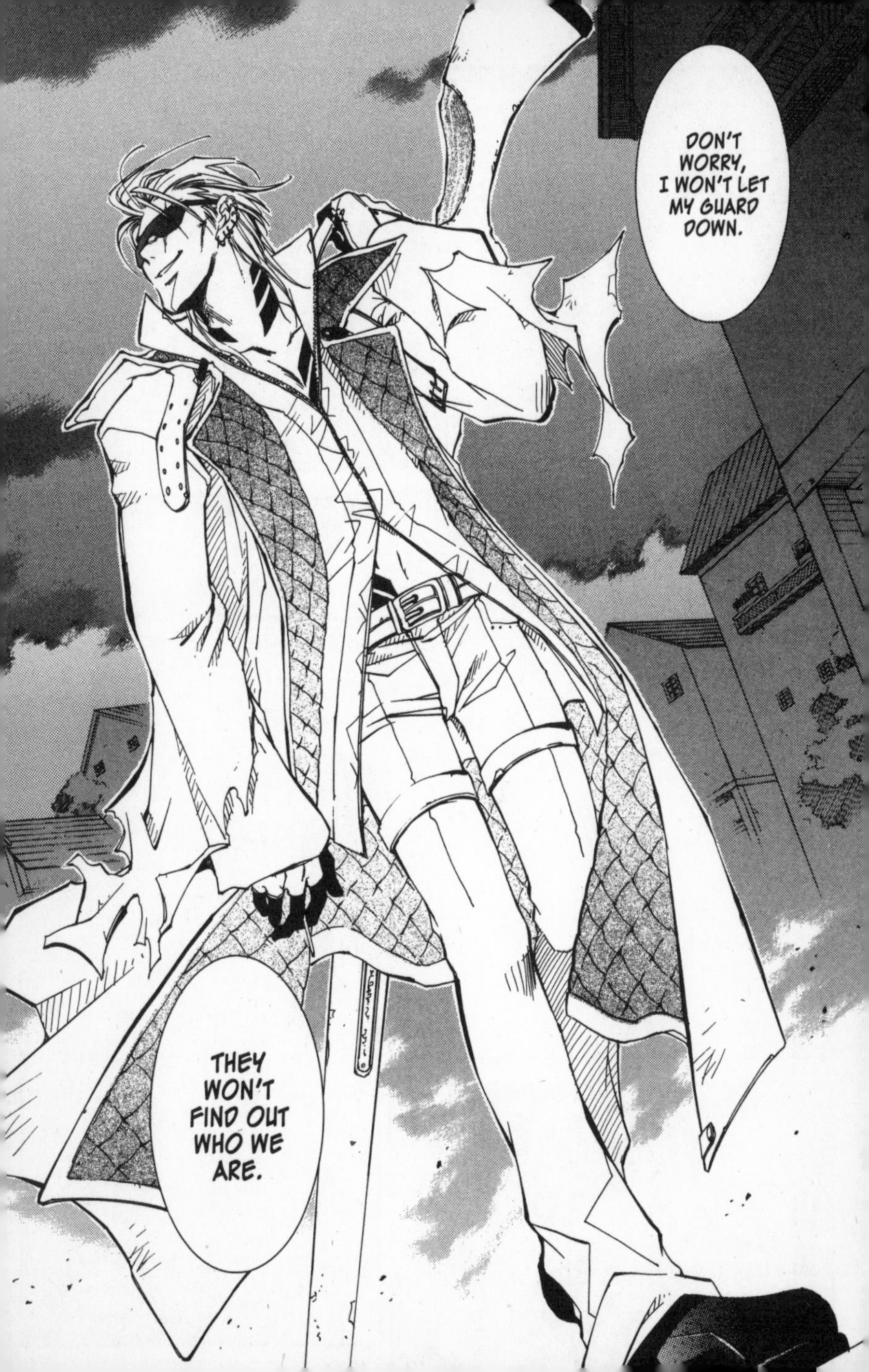
DON'T WORRY, I WON'T LET MY GUARD DOWN.
THEY WON'T FIND OUT WHO WE ARE.

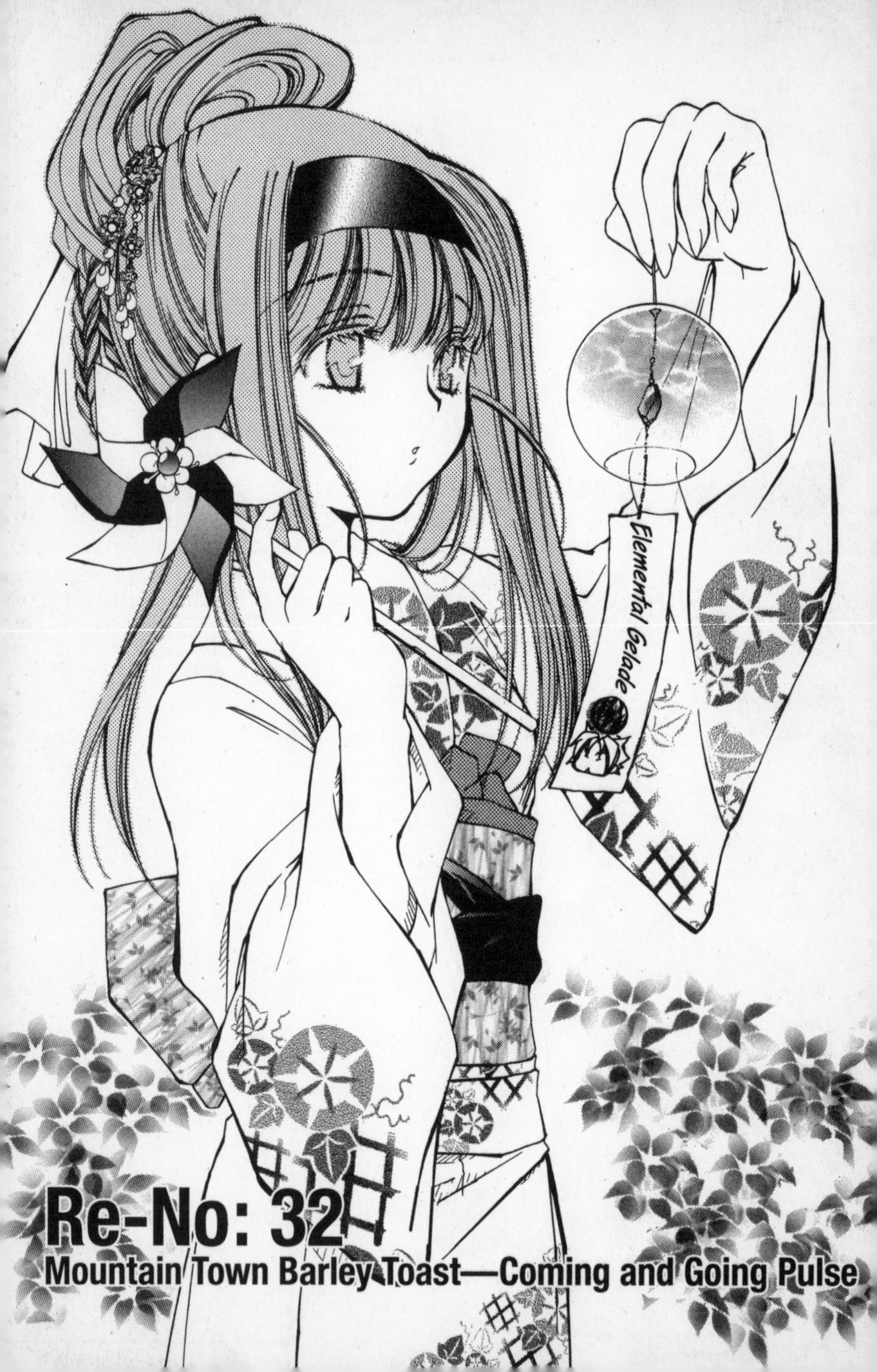
Elemental Gelade

Re-No: 32
Mountain Town Barley Toast—Coming and Going Pulse

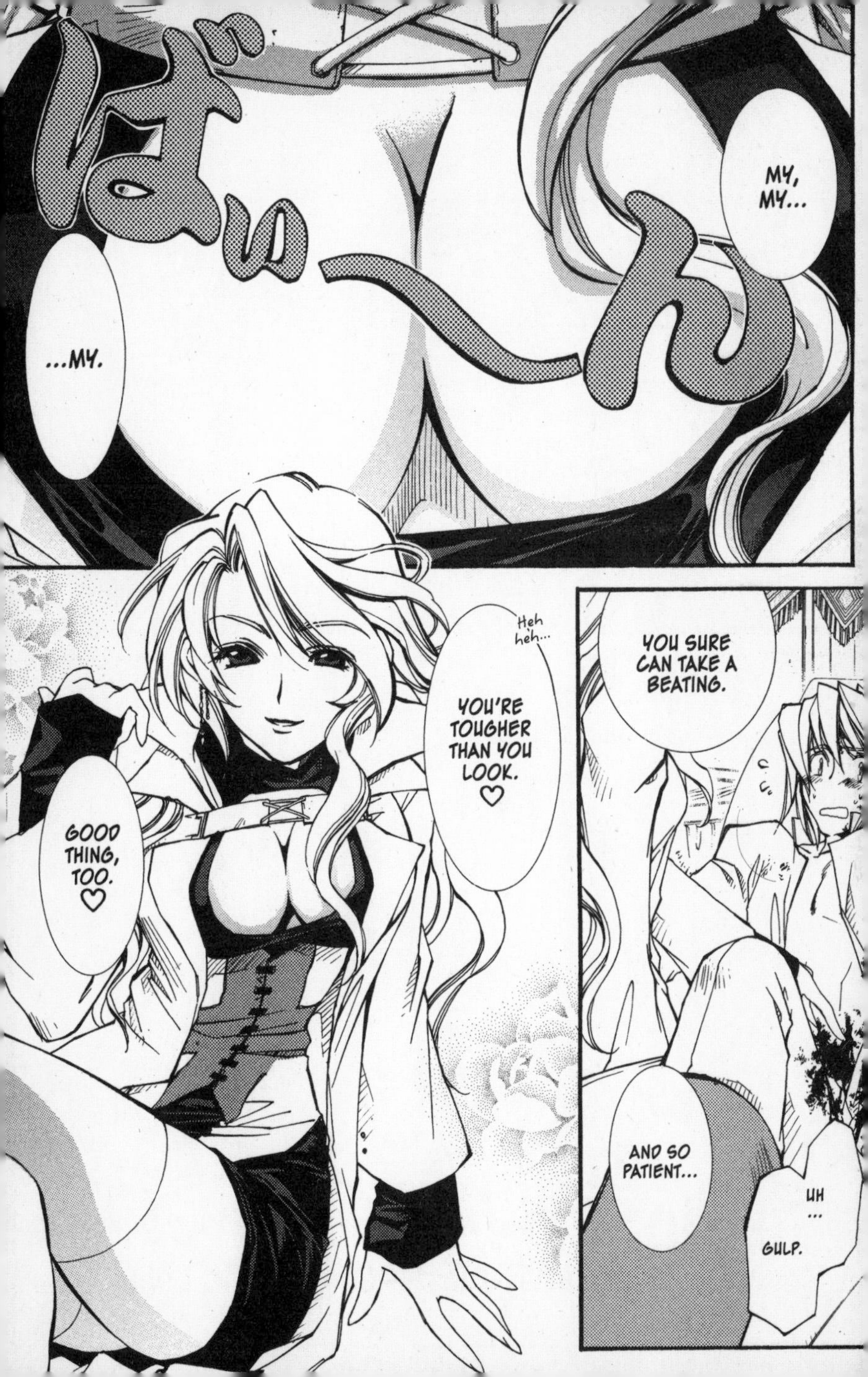
MY, MY...
...MY.
YOU SURE CAN TAKE A BEATING.
AND SO PATIENT...
UH ...
GULP.
Heh heh...
YOU'RE TOUGHER THAN YOU LOOK. ♡
GOOD THING, TOO. ♡

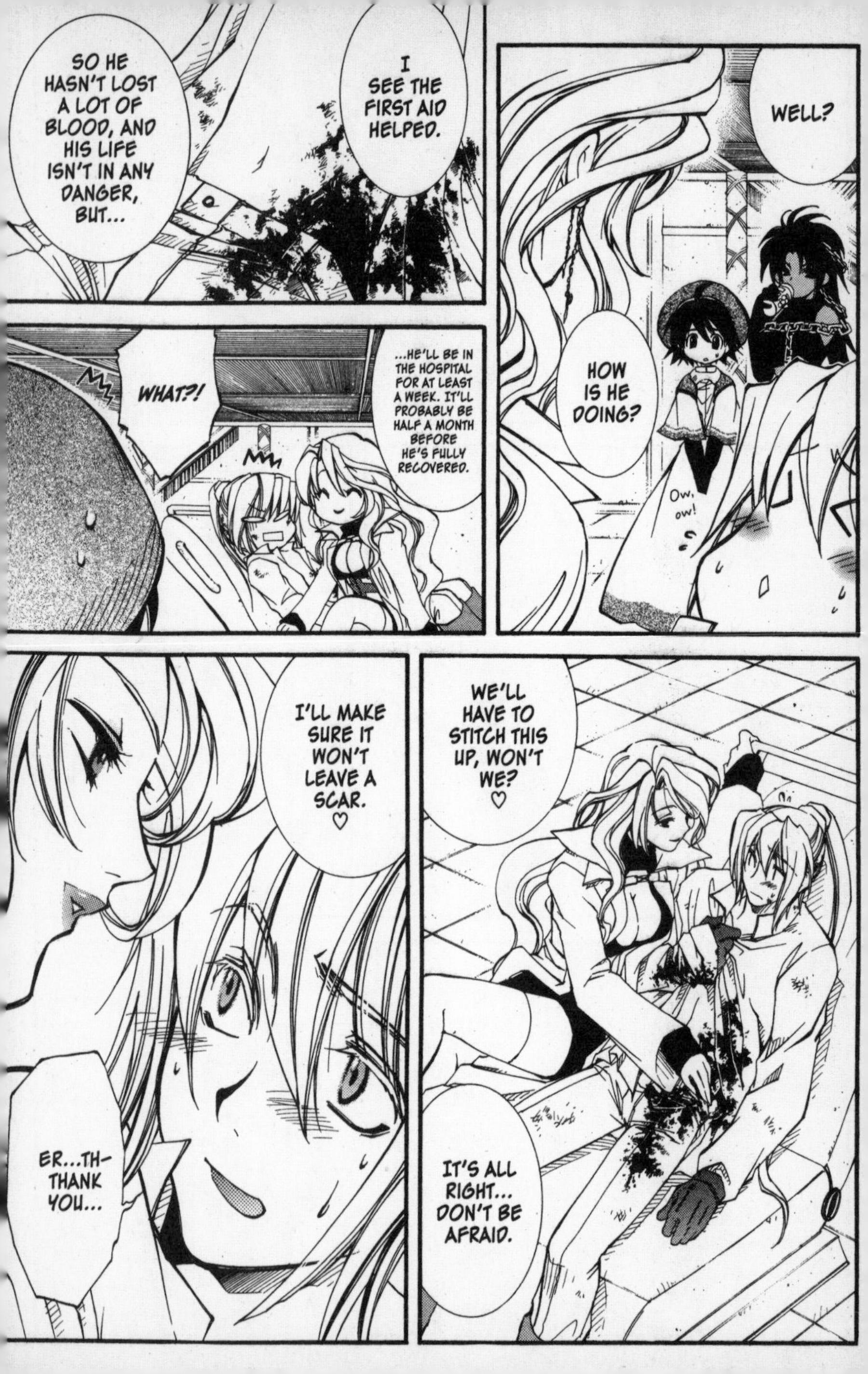
WELL?
HOW IS HE DOING?
Ow, ow!
I SEE THE FIRST AID HELPED.
SO HE HASN'T LOST A LOT OF BLOOD, AND HIS LIFE ISN'T IN ANY DANGER, BUT...
...HE'LL BE IN THE HOSPITAL FOR AT LEAST A WEEK. IT'LL PROBABLY BE HALF A MONTH BEFORE HE'S FULLY RECOVERED.
WHAT?!
WE'LL HAVE TO STITCH THIS UP, WON'T WE? ♡
IT'S ALL RIGHT... DON'T BE AFRAID.
I'LL MAKE SURE IT WON'T LEAVE A SCAR. ♡
ER...TH-THANK YOU...

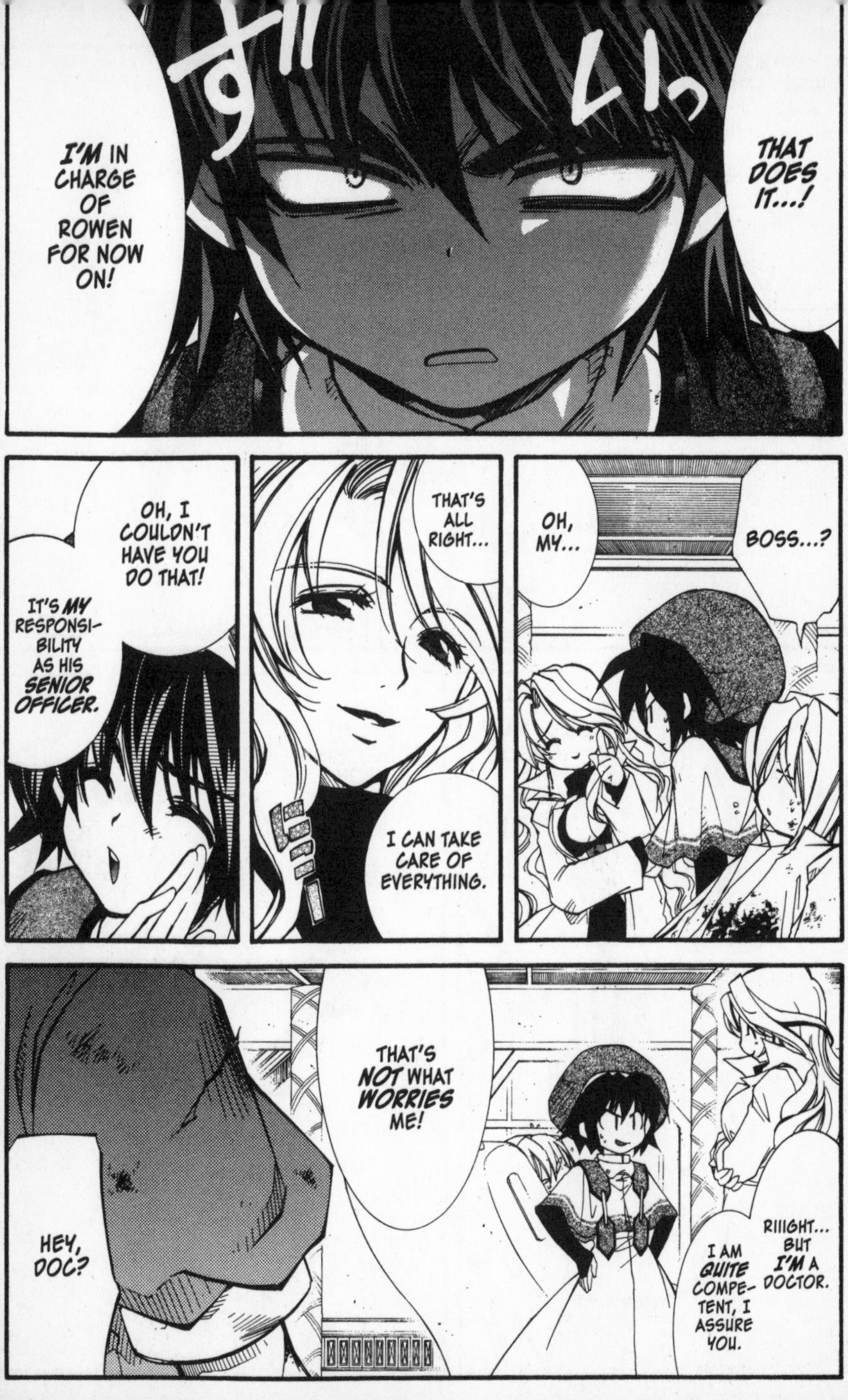
THAT DOES IT...!
I'M IN CHARGE OF ROWEN FOR NOW ON!
BOSS...?
OH, MY...
THAT'S ALL RIGHT...
I CAN TAKE CARE OF EVERYTHING.
OH, I COULDN'T HAVE YOU DO THAT!
IT'S MY RESPONSIBILITY AS HIS SENIOR OFFICER.
THAT'S NOT WHAT WORRIES ME!
RIIIGHT... BUT I'M A DOCTOR.
I AM QUITE COMPETENT, I ASSURE YOU.
HEY, DOC?

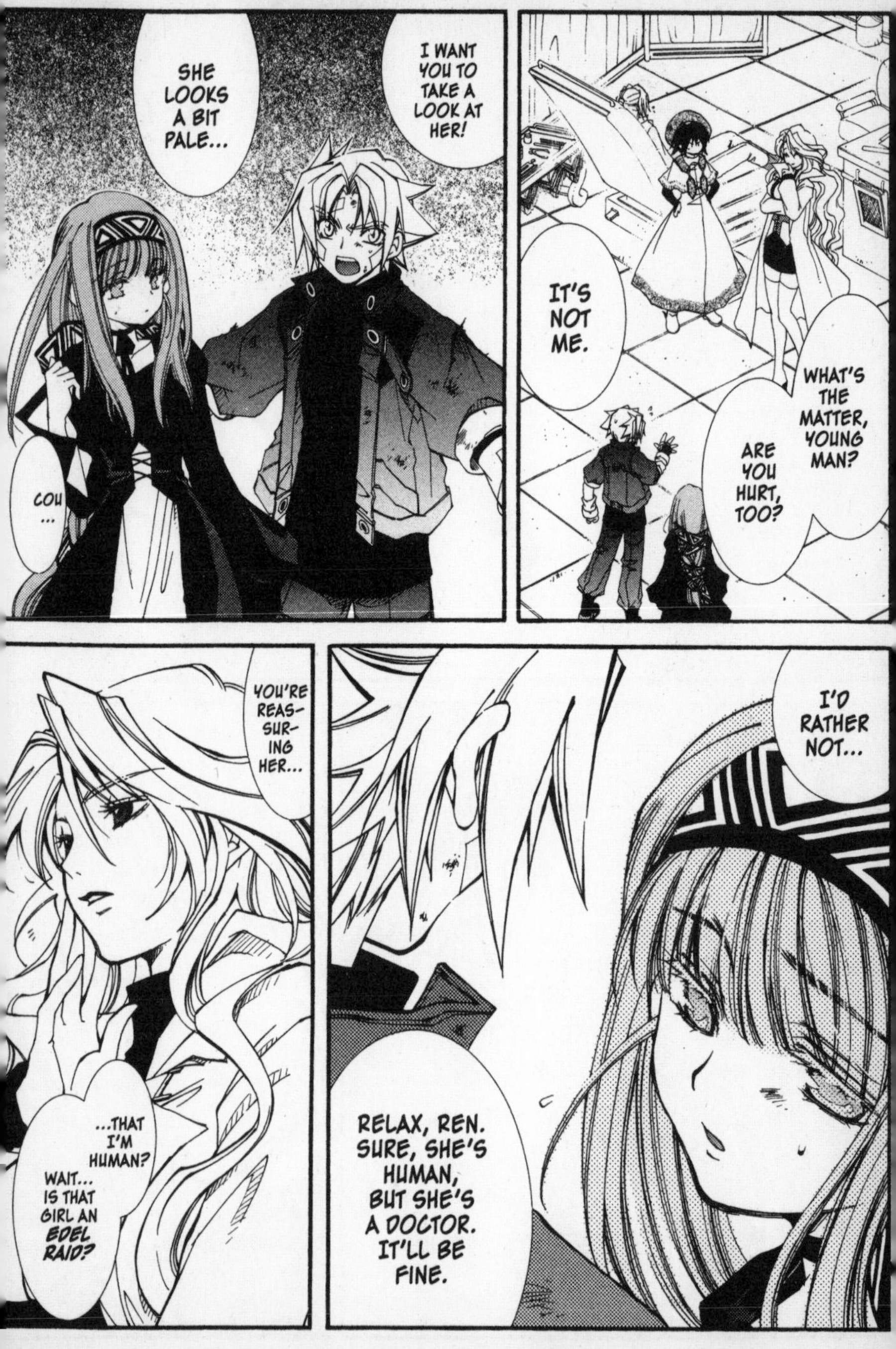
WHAT'S THE MATTER, YOUNG MAN?
ARE YOU HURT, TOO?
IT'S NOT ME.
I WANT YOU TO TAKE A LOOK AT HER!
SHE LOOKS A BIT PALE...
COU...
I'D RATHER NOT...
RELAX, REN. SURE, SHE'S HUMAN, BUT SHE'S A DOCTOR. IT'LL BE FINE.
YOU'RE REAS-SUR-ING HER...
...THAT I'M HUMAN?
WAIT... IS THAT GIRL AN *EDEL RAID*?

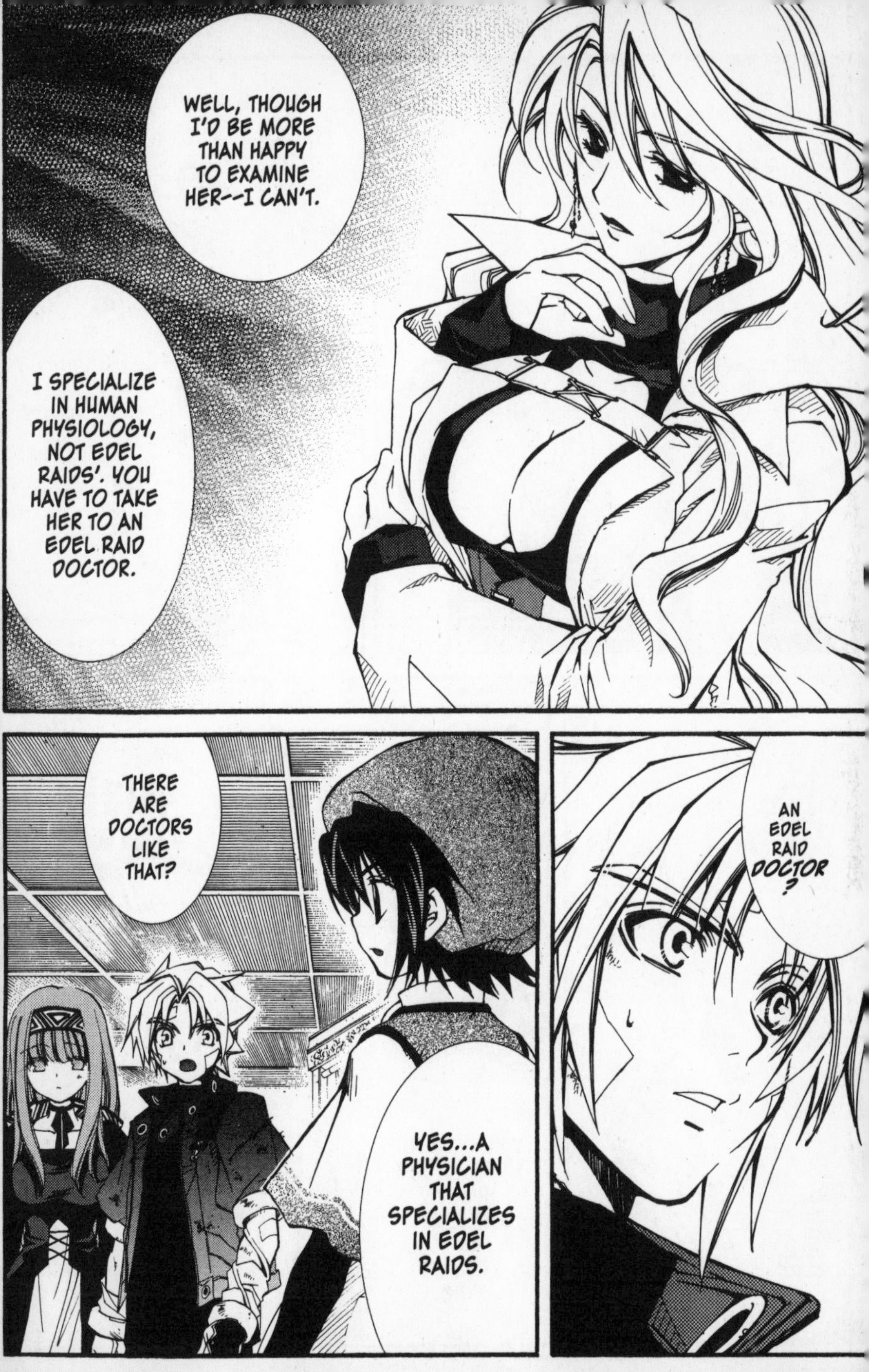
WELL, THOUGH I'D BE MORE THAN HAPPY TO EXAMINE HER--I CAN'T.
I SPECIALIZE IN HUMAN PHYSIOLOGY, NOT EDEL RAIDS'. YOU HAVE TO TAKE HER TO AN EDEL RAID DOCTOR.
AN EDEL RAID DOCTOR?
THERE ARE DOCTORS LIKE THAT?
YES...A PHYSICIAN THAT SPECIALIZES IN EDEL RAIDS.

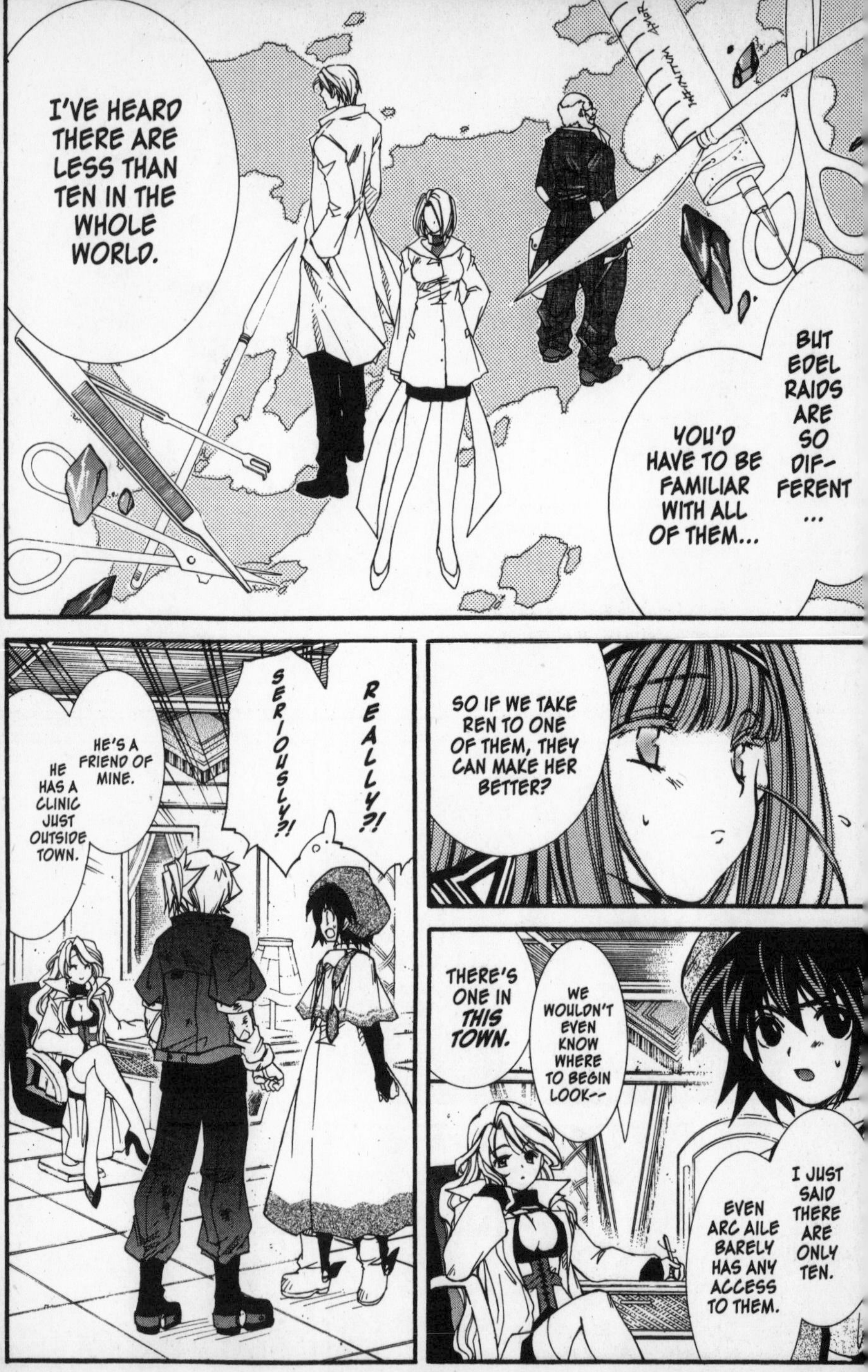
BUT EDEL RAIDS ARE SO DIF-FERENT ...
YOU'D HAVE TO BE FAMILIAR WITH ALL OF THEM...
I'VE HEARD THERE ARE LESS THAN TEN IN THE WHOLE WORLD.
SO IF WE TAKE REN TO ONE OF THEM, THEY CAN MAKE HER BETTER?
I JUST SAID THERE ARE ONLY TEN.
EVEN ARC AILE BARELY HAS ANY ACCESS TO THEM.
WE WOULDN'T EVEN KNOW WHERE TO BEGIN LOOK--
THERE'S ONE IN THIS TOWN.
REALLY?!
SERIOUSLY?!
HE'S A FRIEND OF MINE.
HE HAS A CLINIC JUST OUTSIDE TOWN.

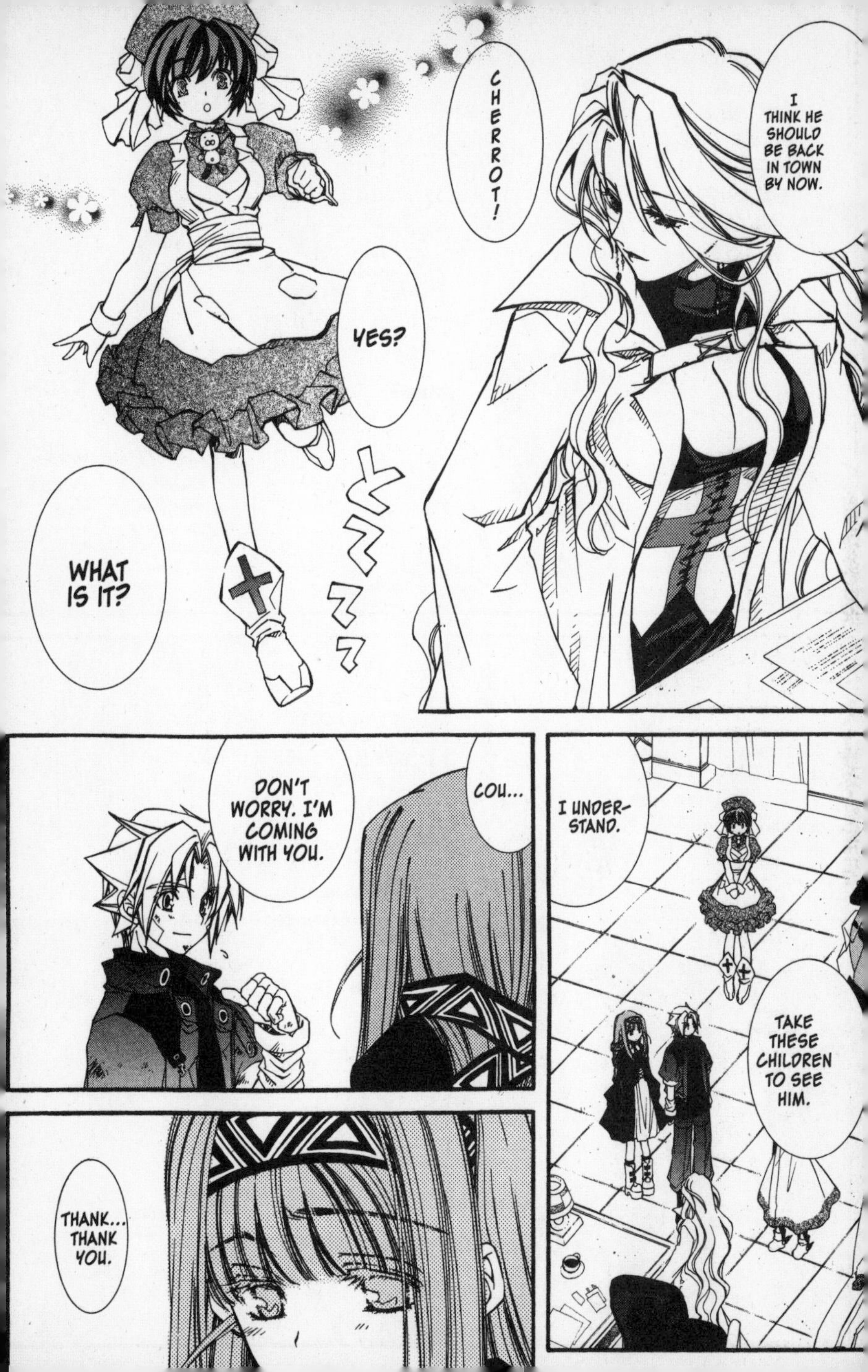
I THINK HE SHOULD BE BACK IN TOWN BY NOW.
CHERROT!
YES?
WHAT IS IT?
TAKE THESE CHILDREN TO SEE HIM.
I UNDER-STAND.
COU...
DON'T WORRY. I'M COMING WITH YOU.
THANK... THANK YOU.

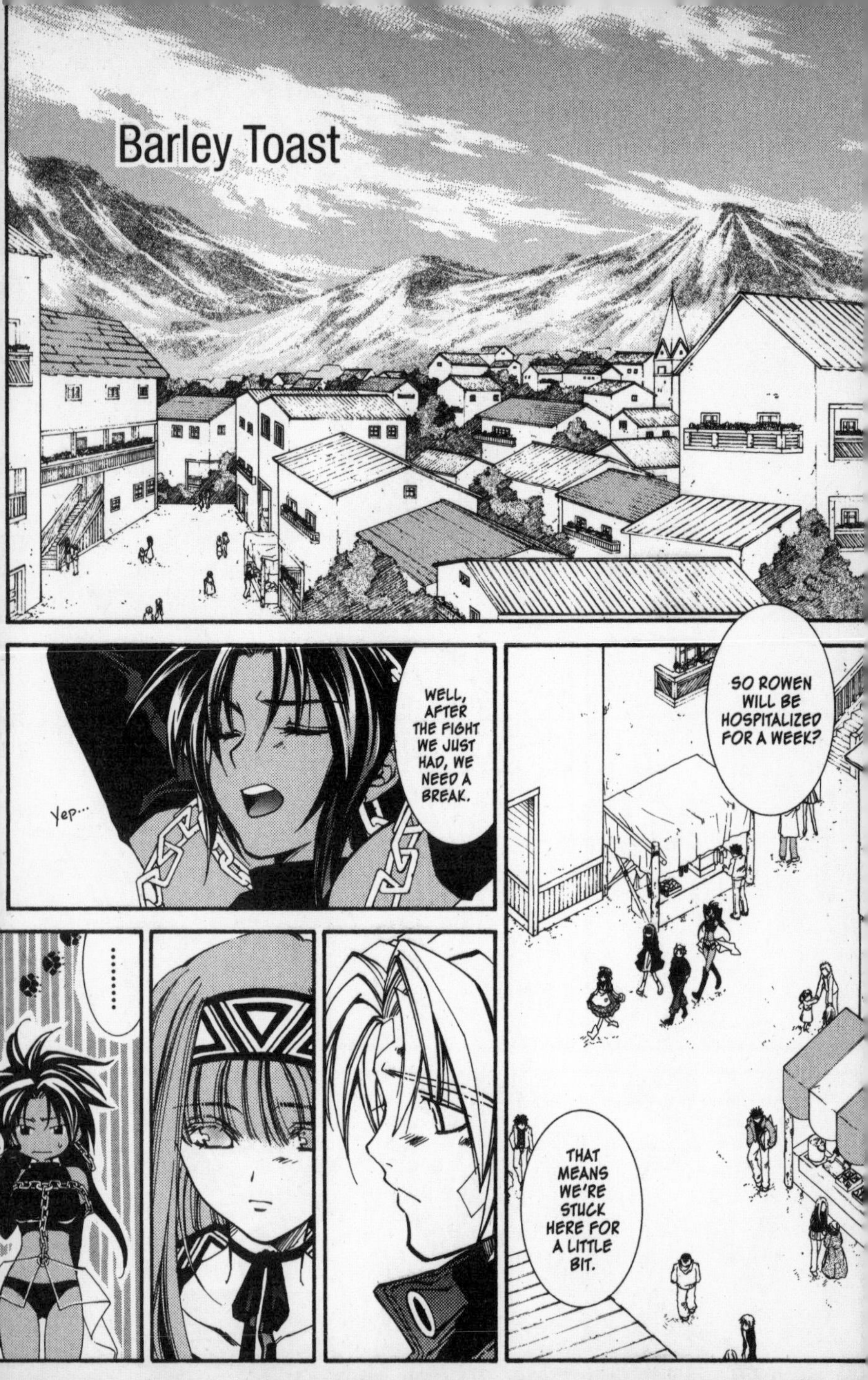
Barley Toast
SO ROWEN WILL BE HOSPITALIZED FOR A WEEK?
THAT MEANS WE'RE STUCK HERE FOR A LITTLE BIT.
WELL, AFTER THE FIGHT WE JUST HAD, WE NEED A BREAK.
Yep...
......

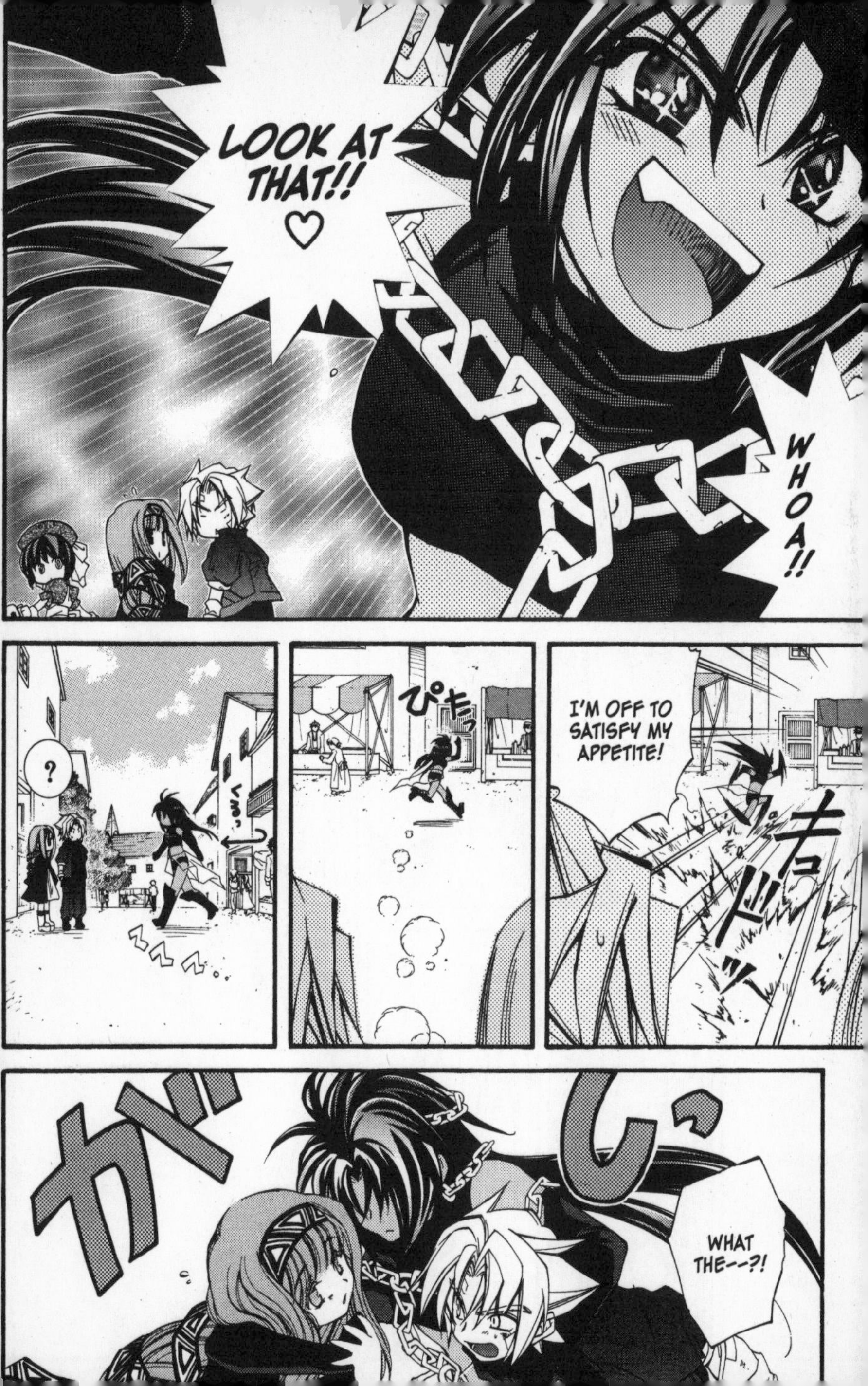
LOOK AT THAT!! ♡
WHOA!!
I'M OFF TO SATISFY MY APPETITE!
?
WHAT THE--?!

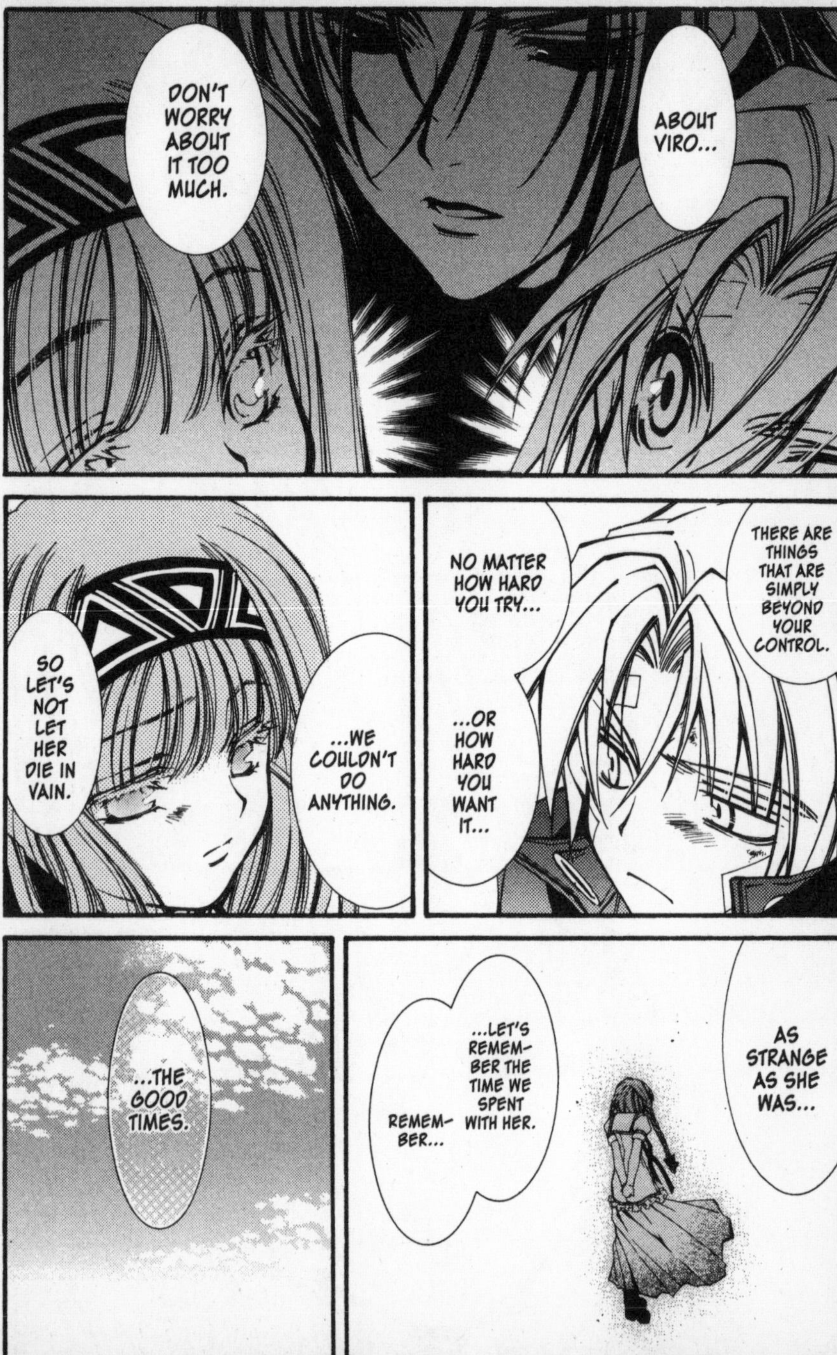
ABOUT VIRO...
DON'T WORRY ABOUT IT TOO MUCH.
THERE ARE THINGS THAT ARE SIMPLY BEYOND YOUR CONTROL.
NO MATTER HOW HARD YOU TRY...
...OR HOW HARD YOU WANT IT...
...WE COULDN'T DO ANYTHING.
SO LET'S NOT LET HER DIE IN VAIN.
AS STRANGE AS SHE WAS...
...LET'S REMEMBER THE TIME WE SPENT WITH HER.
REMEMBER...
...THE GOOD TIMES.

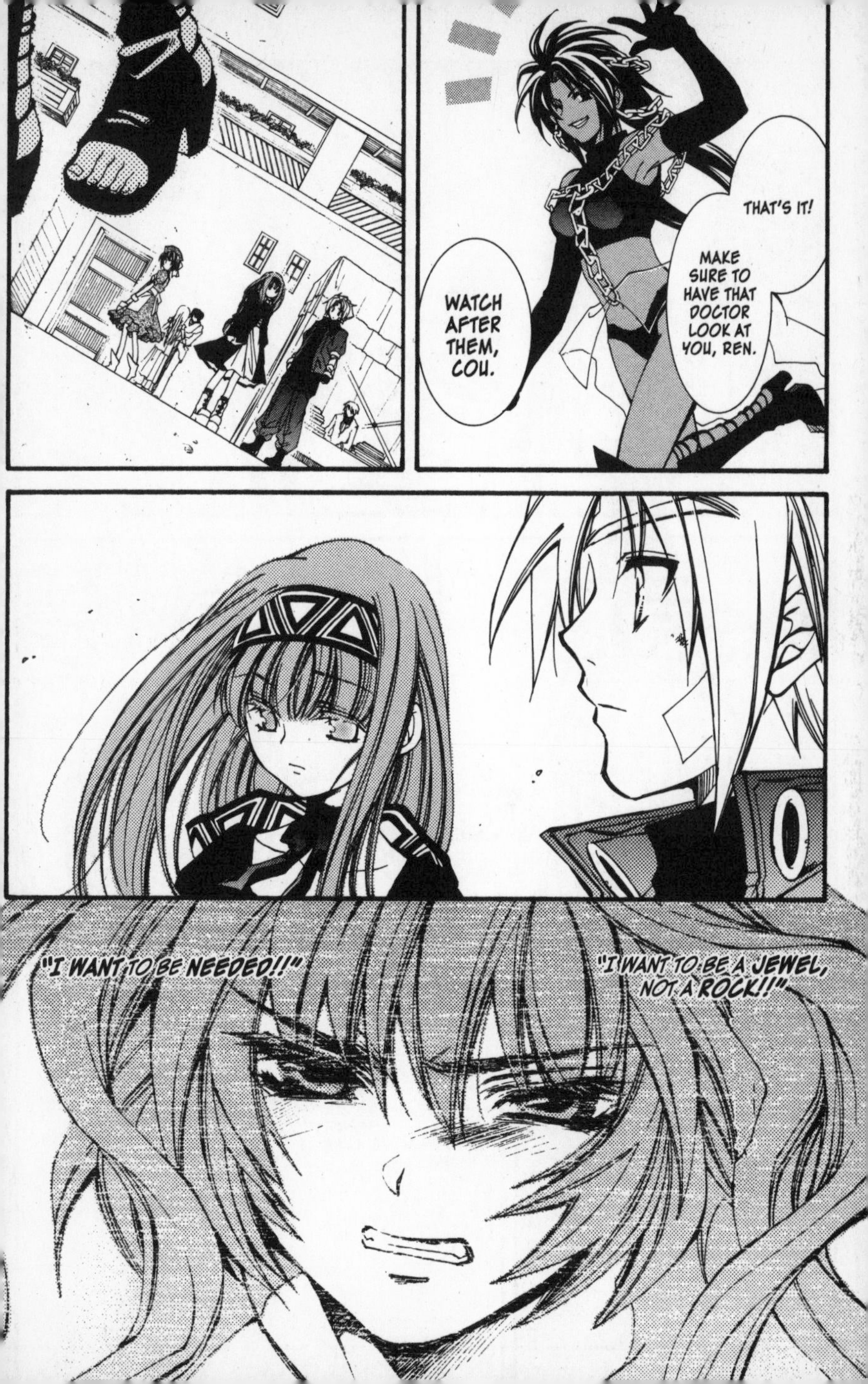
THAT'S IT!
MAKE SURE TO HAVE THAT DOCTOR LOOK AT YOU, REN.
WATCH AFTER THEM, COU.
"I WANT TO BE A JEWEL, NOT A ROCK!!"
"I WANT TO BE NEEDED!!"

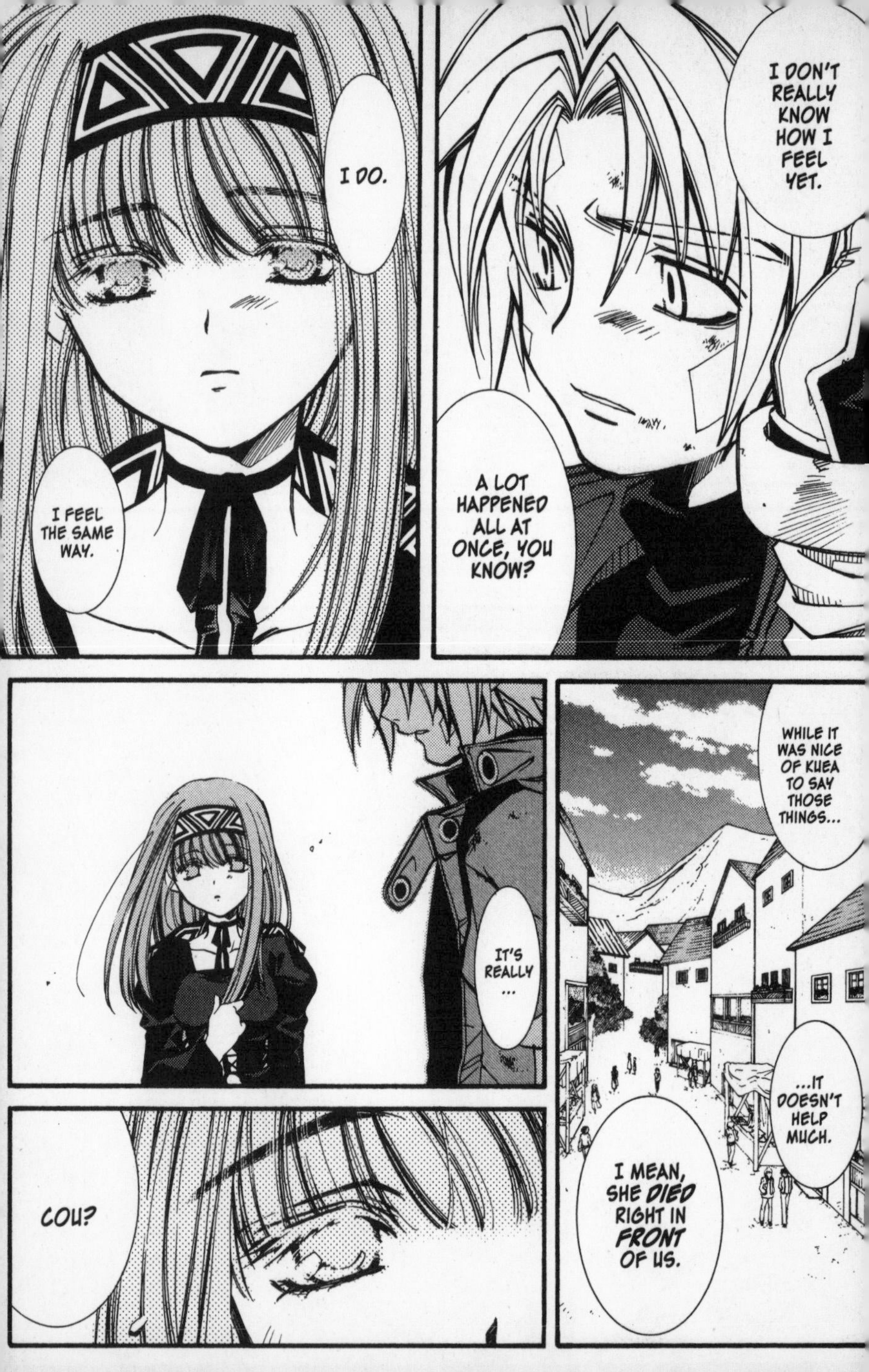
I DON'T REALLY KNOW HOW I FEEL YET.
A LOT HAPPENED ALL AT ONCE, YOU KNOW?
I DO.
I FEEL THE SAME WAY.
WHILE IT WAS NICE OF KUEA TO SAY THOSE THINGS...
...IT DOESN'T HELP MUCH.
I MEAN, SHE *DIED* RIGHT IN *FRONT* OF US.
IT'S REALLY ...
COU?

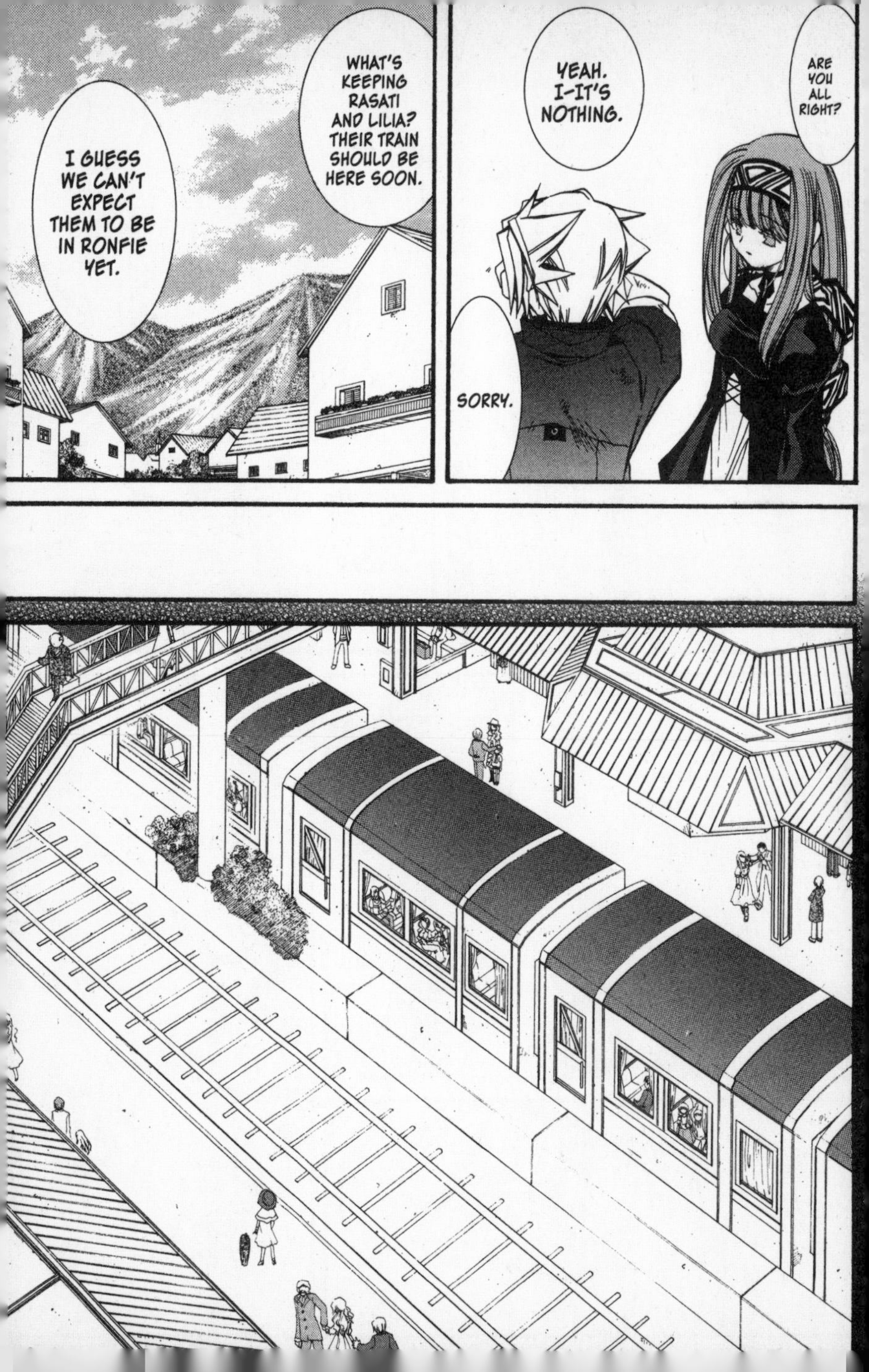
ARE YOU ALL RIGHT?
YEAH. I-IT'S NOTHING.
SORRY.
WHAT'S KEEPING RASATI AND LILIA? THEIR TRAIN SHOULD BE HERE SOON.
I GUESS WE CAN'T EXPECT THEM TO BE IN RONFIE YET.

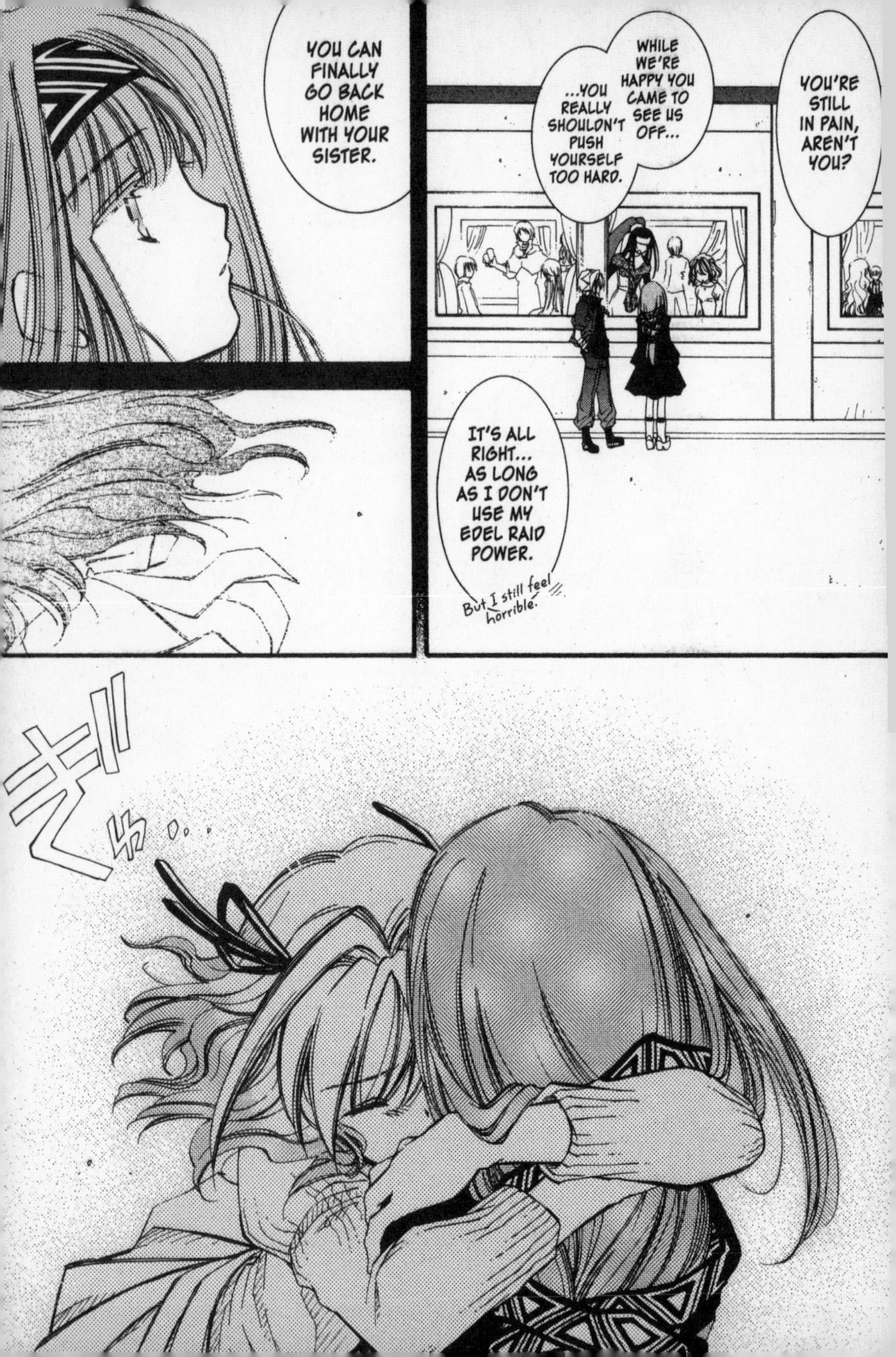
YOU'RE STILL IN PAIN, AREN'T YOU?
WHILE WE'RE HAPPY YOU CAME TO SEE US OFF...
...YOU REALLY SHOULDN'T PUSH YOURSELF TOO HARD.
IT'S ALL RIGHT... AS LONG AS I DON'T USE MY EDEL RAID POWER.
But I still feel horrible.
YOU CAN FINALLY GO BACK HOME WITH YOUR SISTER.
ぎゅ...

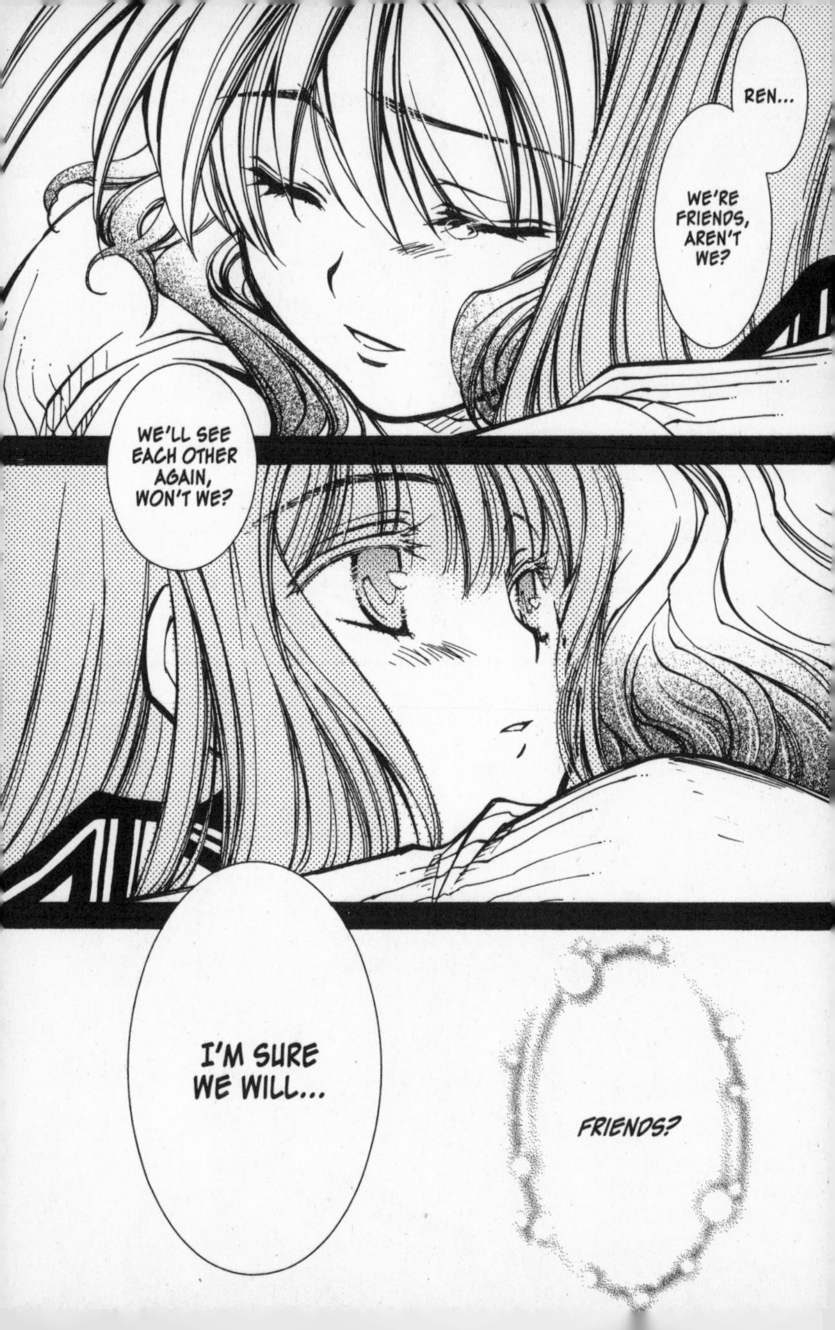
REN...
WE'RE FRIENDS, AREN'T WE?
WE'LL SEE EACH OTHER AGAIN, WON'T WE?
FRIENDS?
I'M SURE WE WILL...

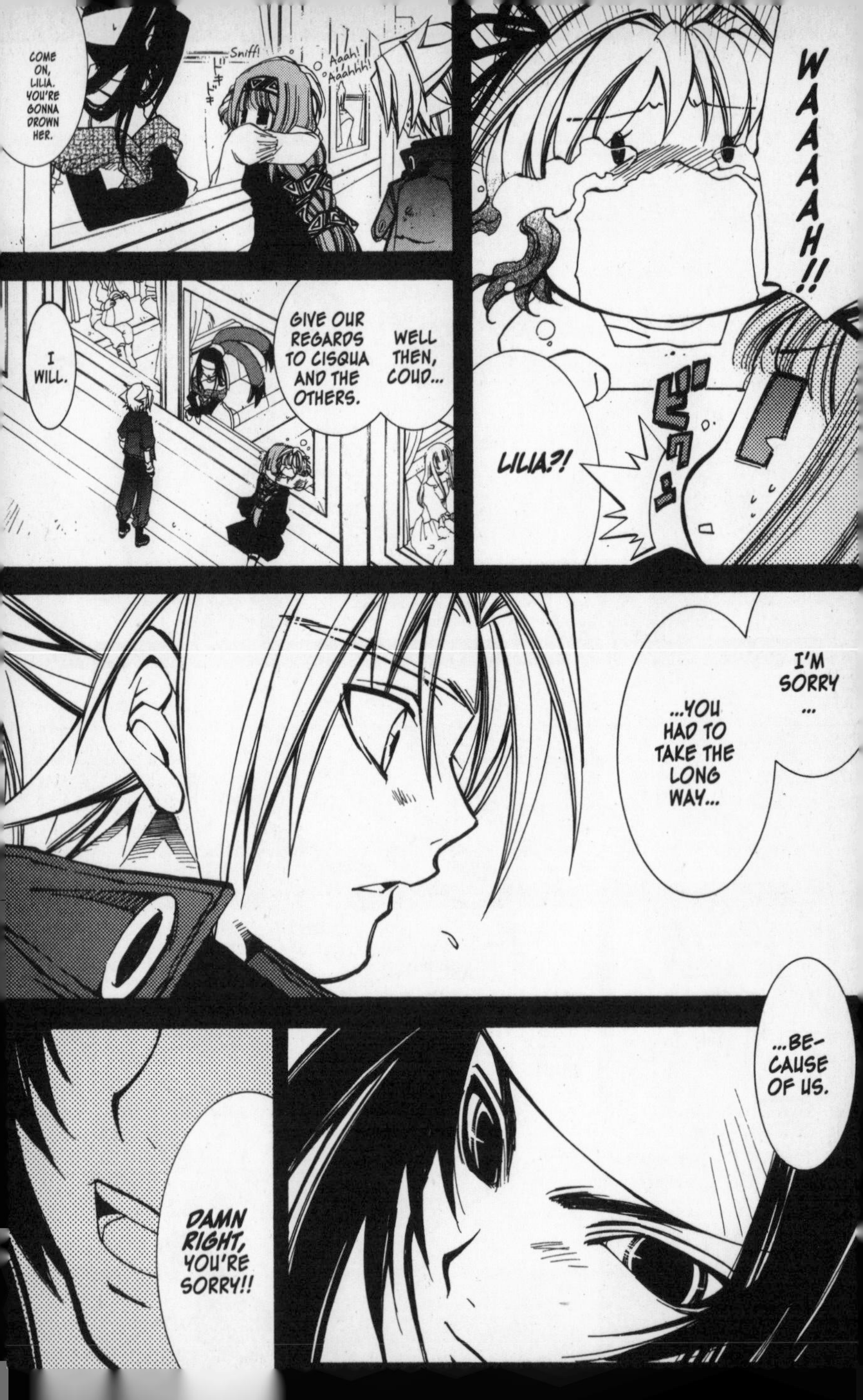
WAAAAAH!!
LILIA?!
Sniff!
Aaah! Aaahhh!
COME ON, LILIA. YOU'RE GONNA DROWN HER.
WELL THEN, COUD...
GIVE OUR REGARDS TO CISQUA AND THE OTHERS.
I WILL.
I'M SORRY...
...YOU HAD TO TAKE THE LONG WAY...
...BE-CAUSE OF US.
DAMN RIGHT, YOU'RE SORRY!!

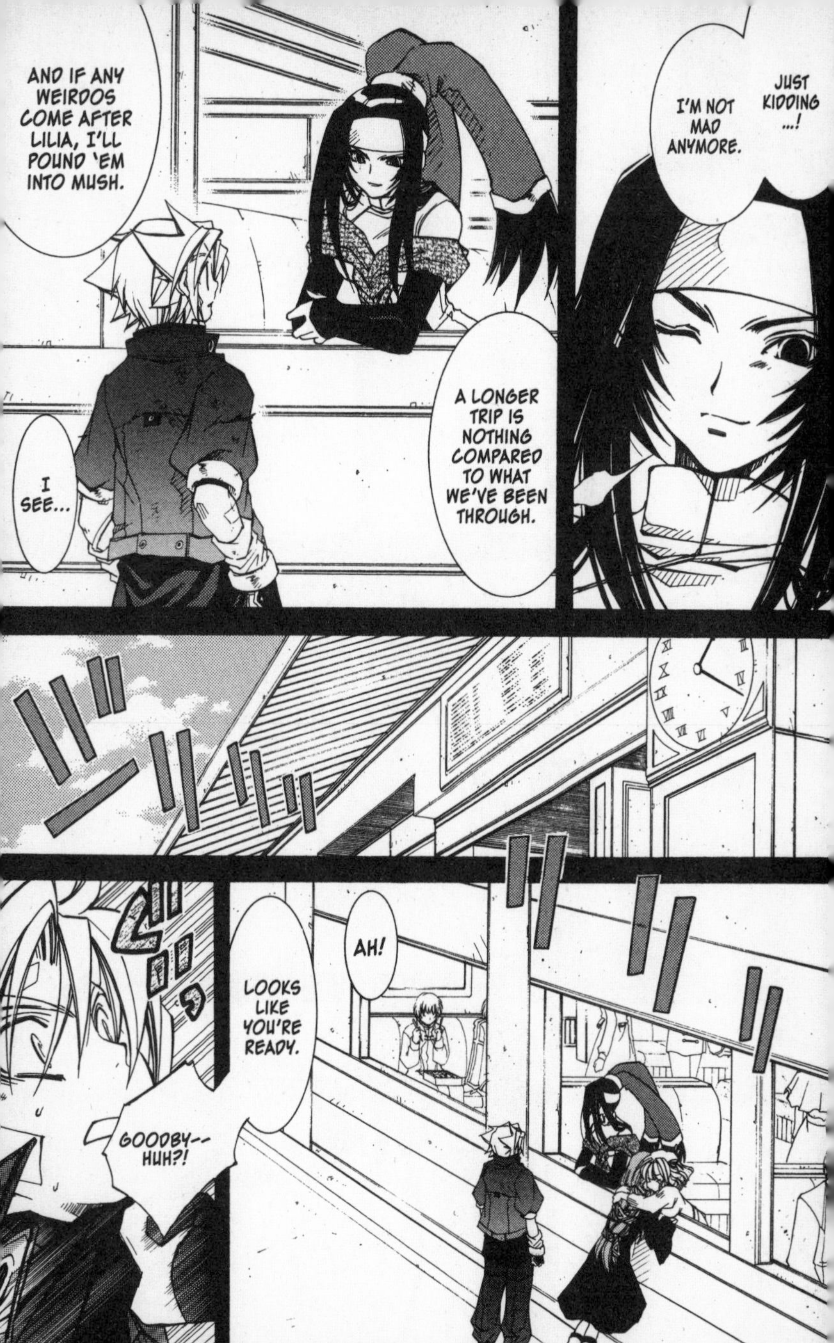
I'M NOT MAD ANYMORE.
JUST KIDDING ...!
AND IF ANY WEIRDOS COME AFTER LILIA, I'LL POUND 'EM INTO MUSH.
A LONGER TRIP IS NOTHING COMPARED TO WHAT WE'VE BEEN THROUGH.
I SEE...
AH!
LOOKS LIKE YOU'RE READY.
GOODBY-- HUH?!

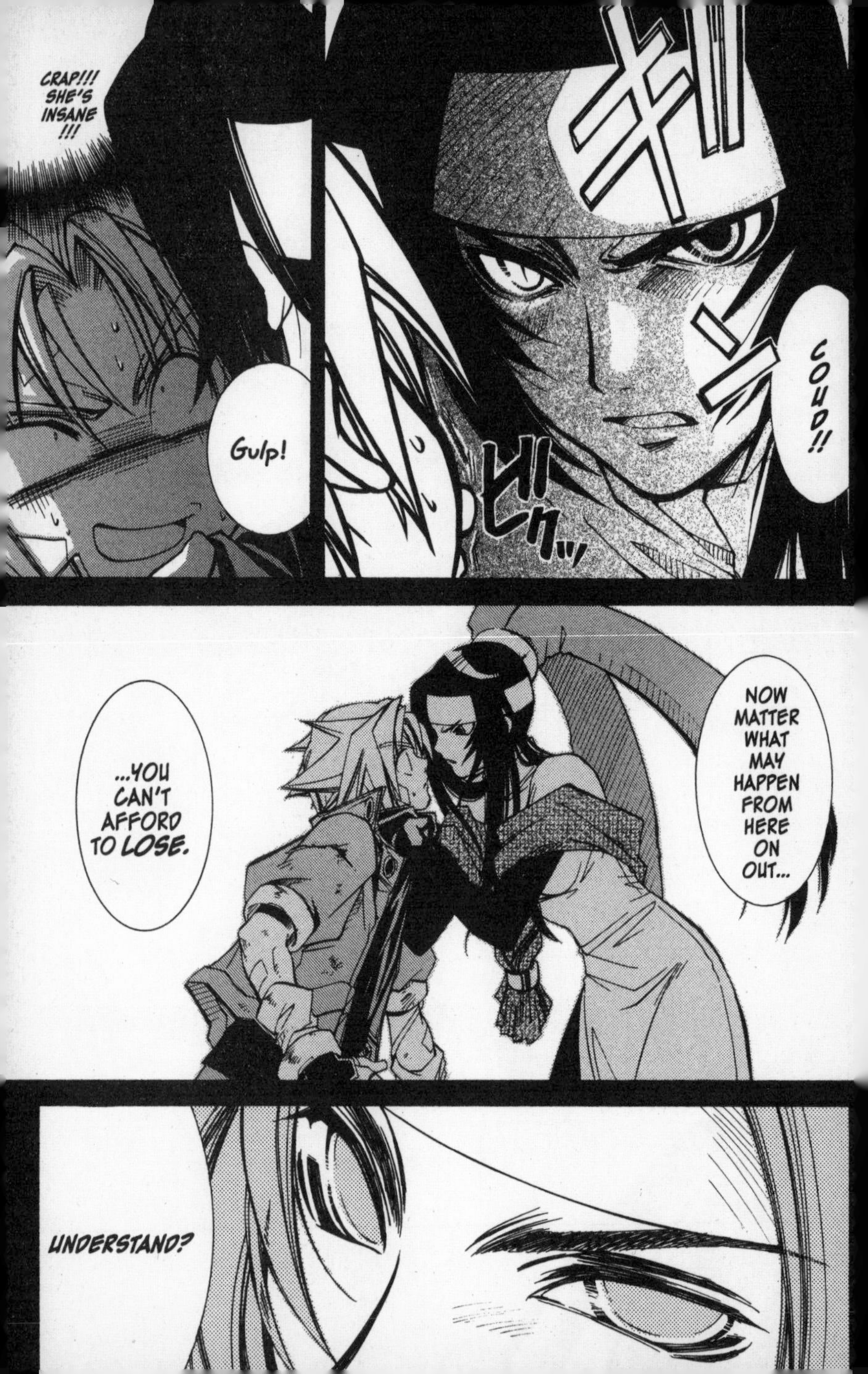
COUGH!!
CRAP!!! SHE'S INSANE !!!
Gulp!
NOW MATTER WHAT MAY HAPPEN FROM HERE ON OUT...
...YOU CAN'T AFFORD TO LOSE.
UNDERSTAND?

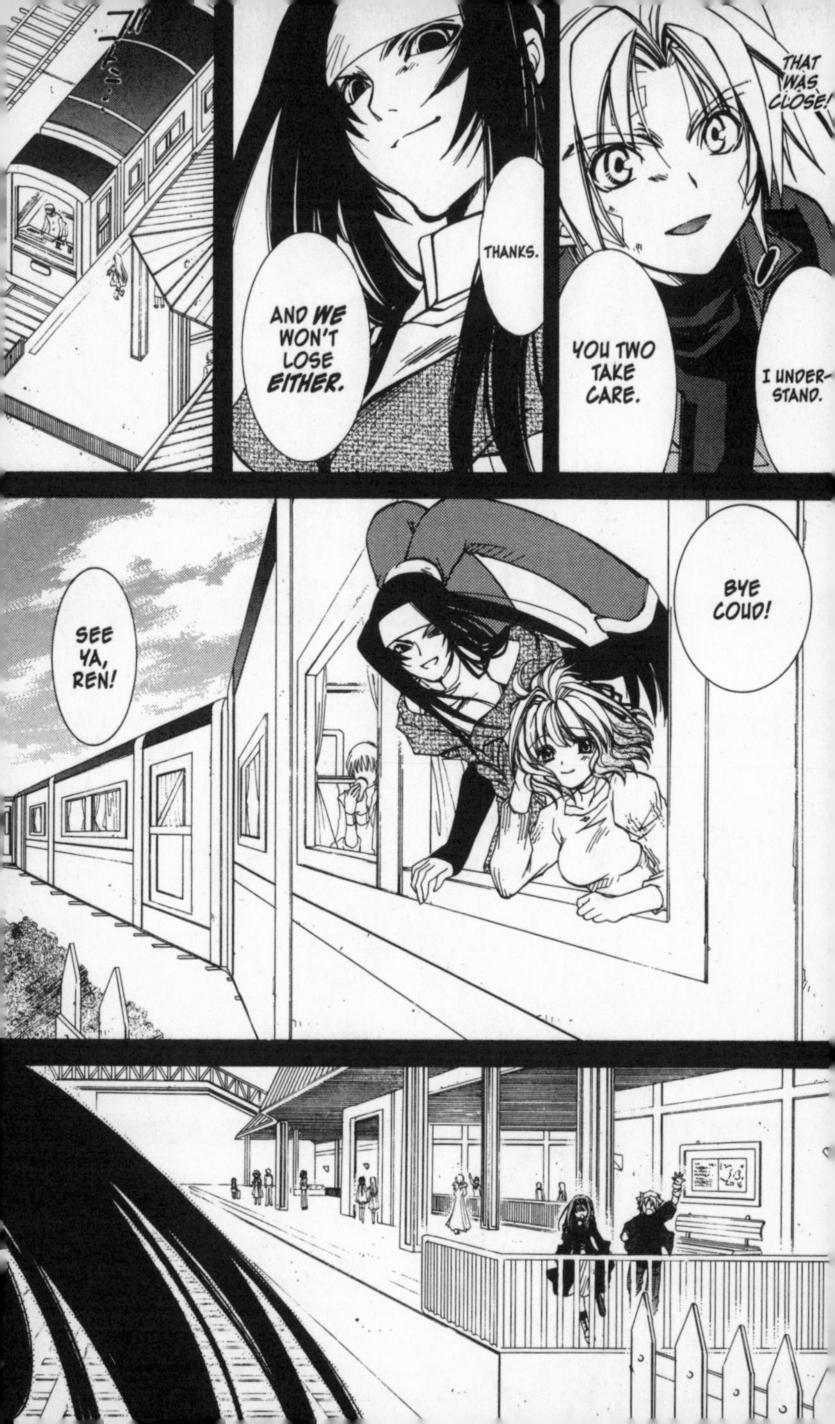
THAT WAS CLOSE!
I UNDER-STAND.
YOU TWO TAKE CARE.
THANKS.
AND WE WON'T LOSE EITHER.
BYE COUD!
SEE YA, REN!

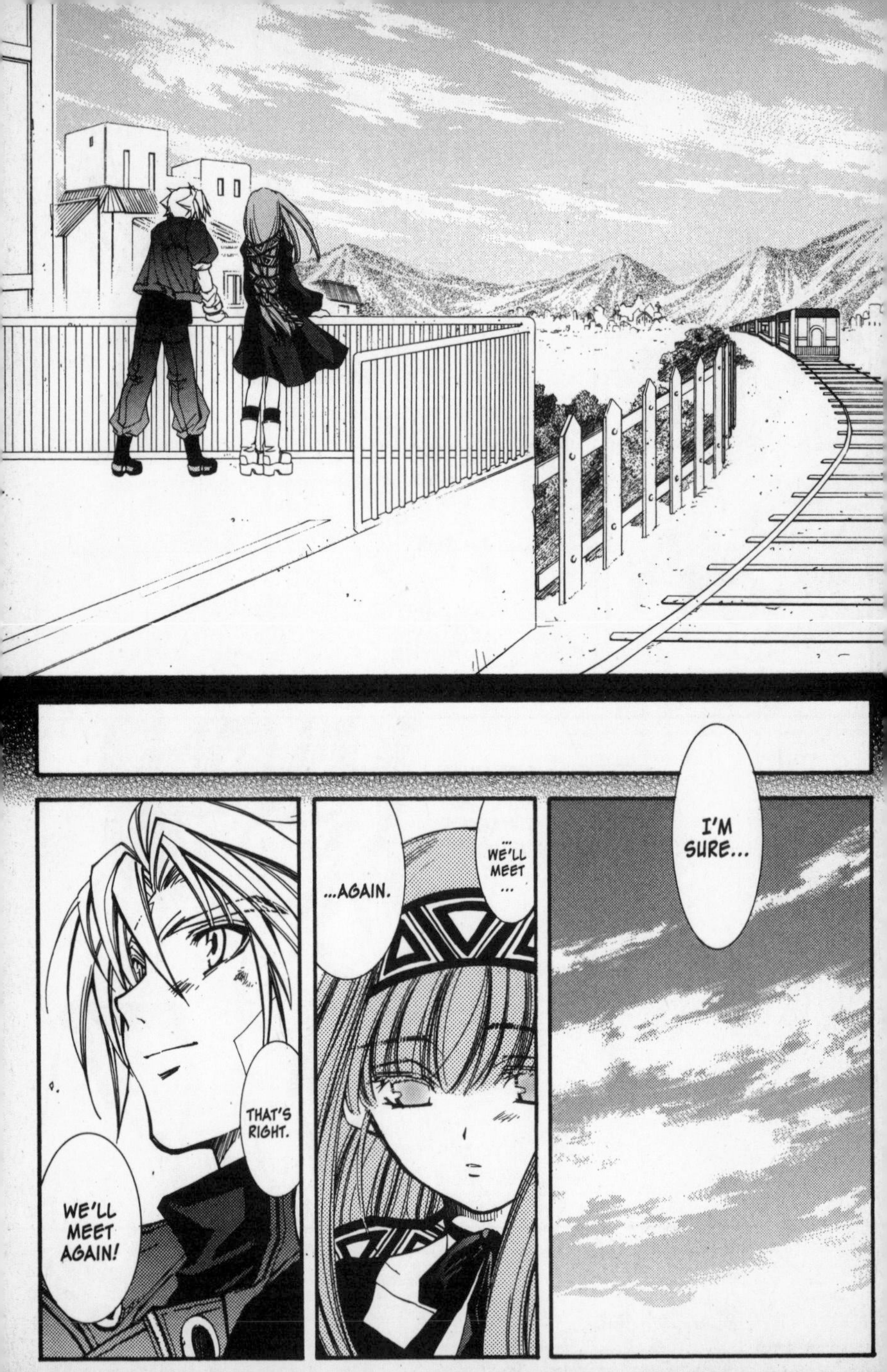
I'M SURE...
...WE'LL MEET...
...AGAIN.
THAT'S RIGHT.
WE'LL MEET AGAIN!

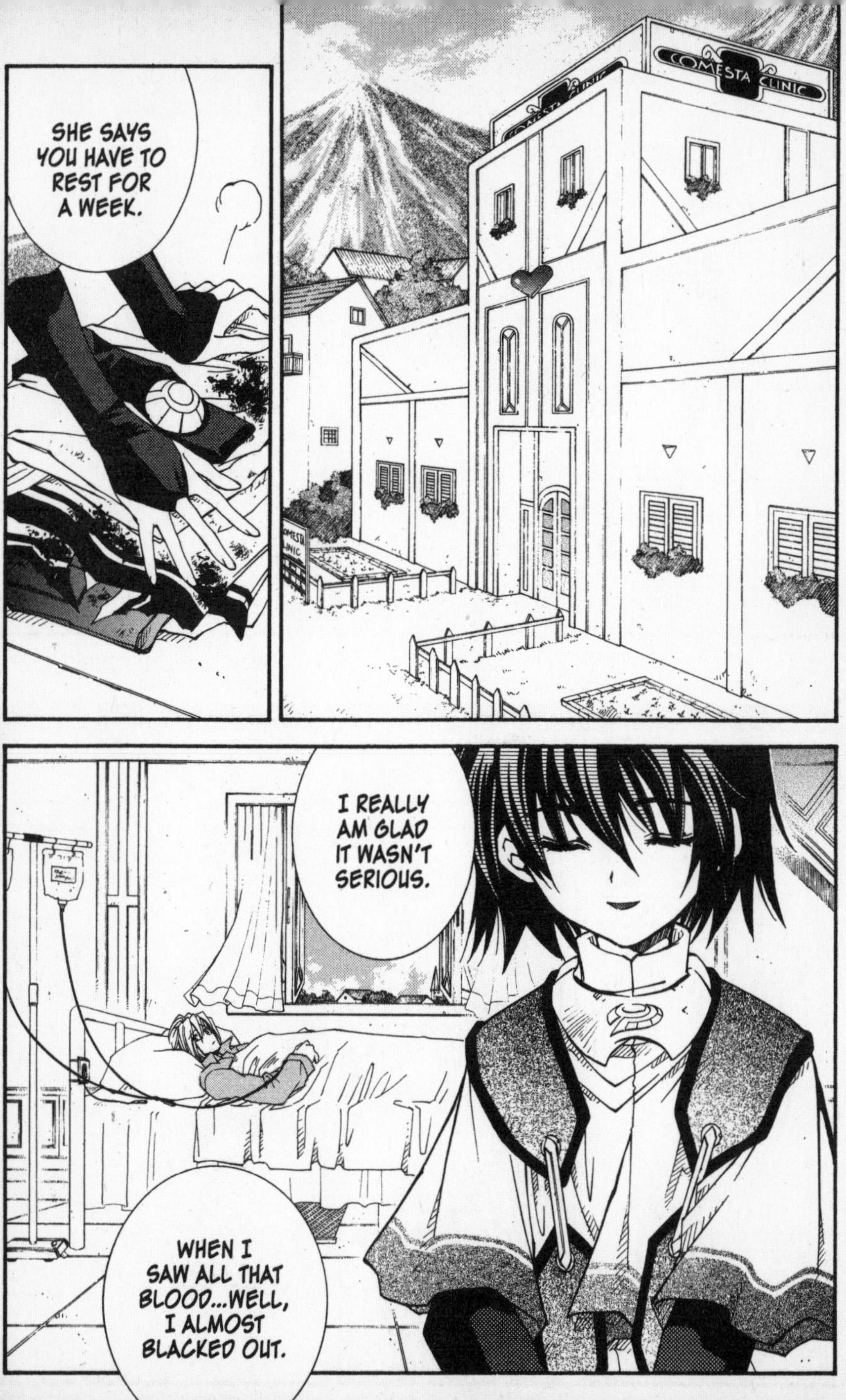
COMESTA CLINIC
SHE SAYS YOU HAVE TO REST FOR A WEEK.
I REALLY AM GLAD IT WASN'T SERIOUS.
WHEN I SAW ALL THAT BLOOD...WELL, I ALMOST BLACKED OUT.

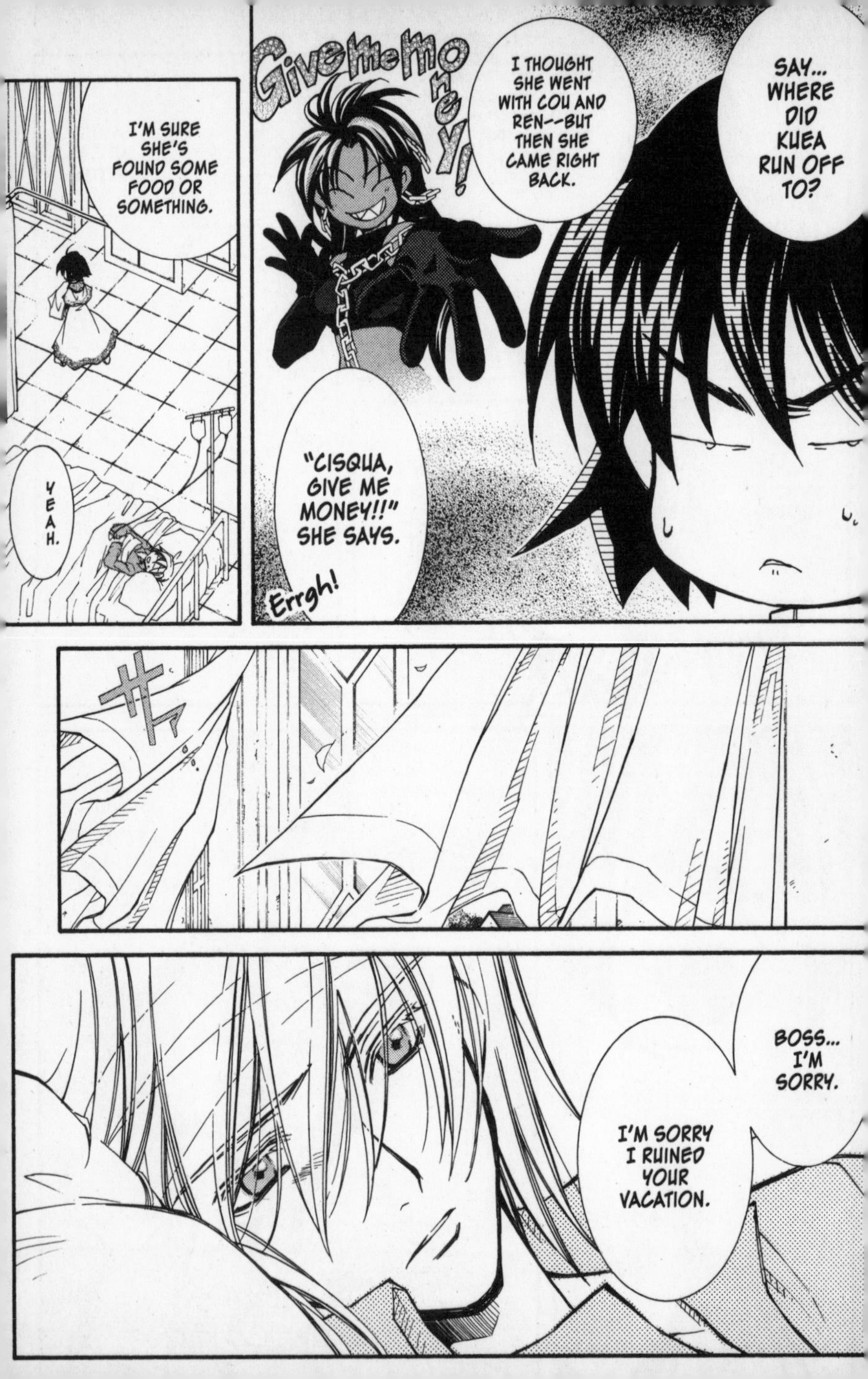
SAY... WHERE DID KUEA RUN OFF TO?
I THOUGHT SHE WENT WITH COU AND REN--BUT THEN SHE CAME RIGHT BACK.
Give me money!
"CISQUA, GIVE ME MONEY!!" SHE SAYS.
Errgh!
I'M SURE SHE'S FOUND SOME FOOD OR SOMETHING.
YEAH.
BOSS... I'M SORRY.
I'M SORRY I RUINED YOUR VACATION.

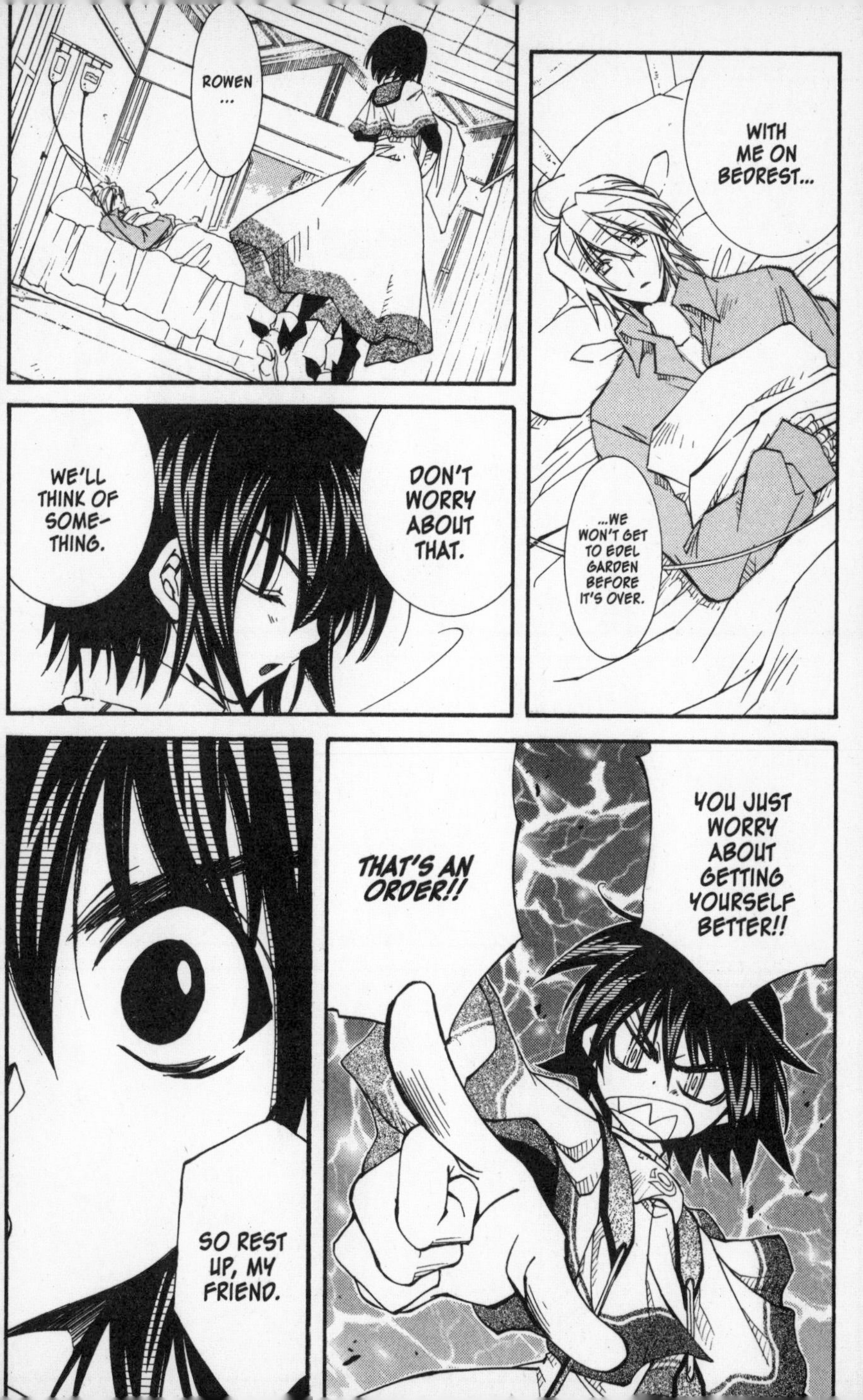
WITH ME ON BEDREST...
...WE WON'T GET TO EDEL GARDEN BEFORE IT'S OVER.
ROWEN ...
DON'T WORRY ABOUT THAT.
WE'LL THINK OF SOME-THING.
YOU JUST WORRY ABOUT GETTING YOURSELF BETTER!!
THAT'S AN ORDER!!
SO REST UP, MY FRIEND.

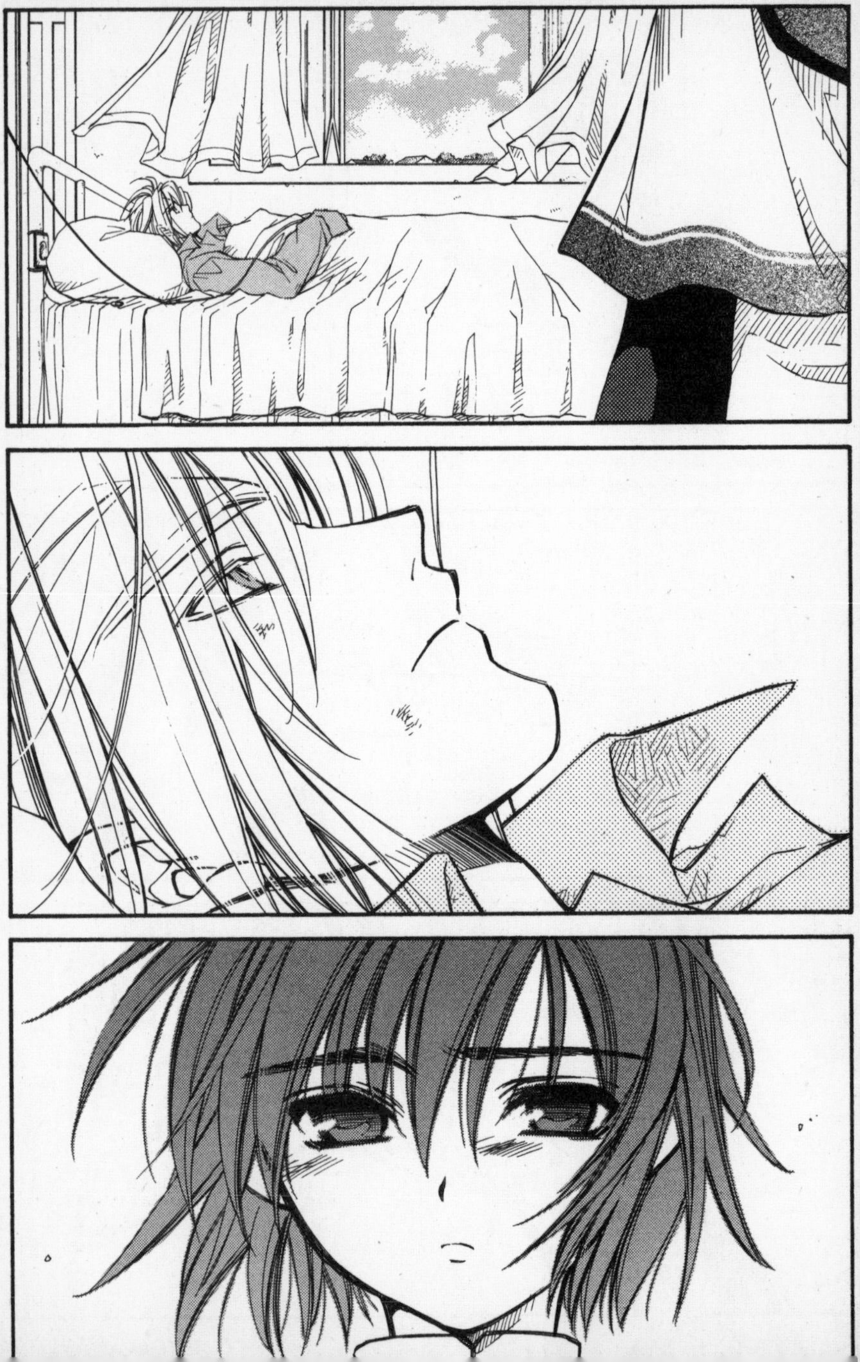

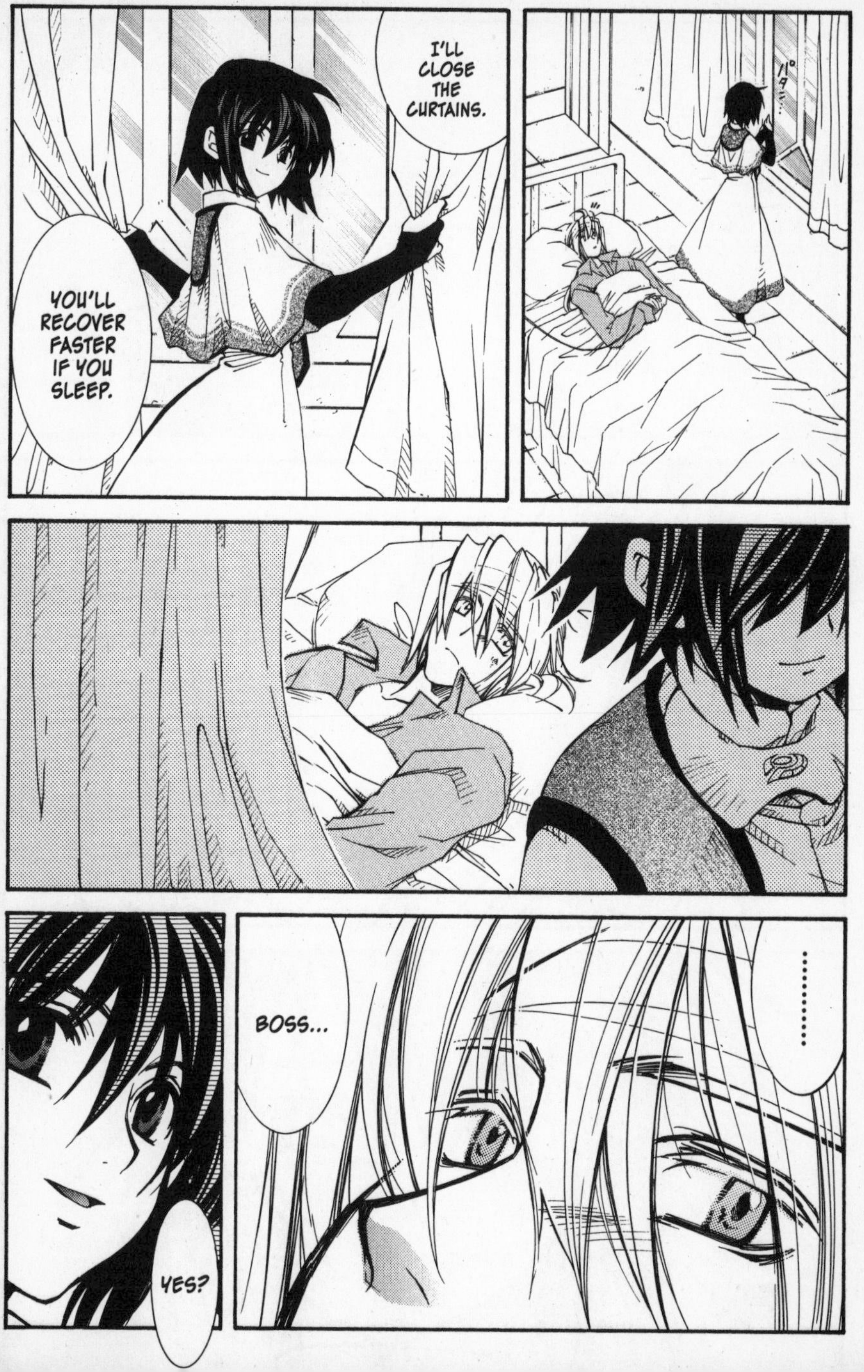
パタ…
I'LL CLOSE THE CURTAINS.
YOU'LL RECOVER FASTER IF YOU SLEEP.
……
BOSS...
YES?

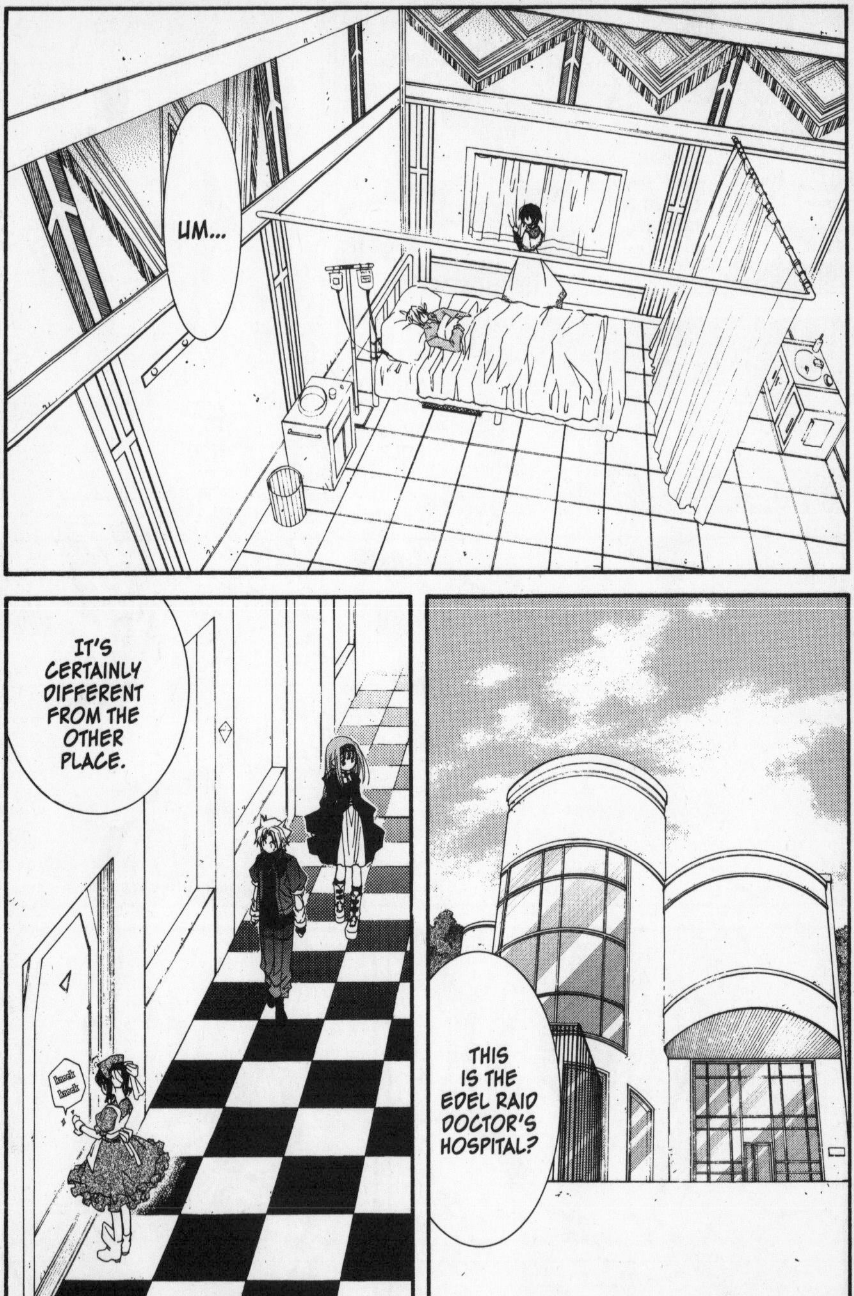
UM...
THIS IS THE EDEL RAID DOCTOR'S HOSPITAL?
IT'S CERTAINLY DIFFERENT FROM THE OTHER PLACE.
knock knock

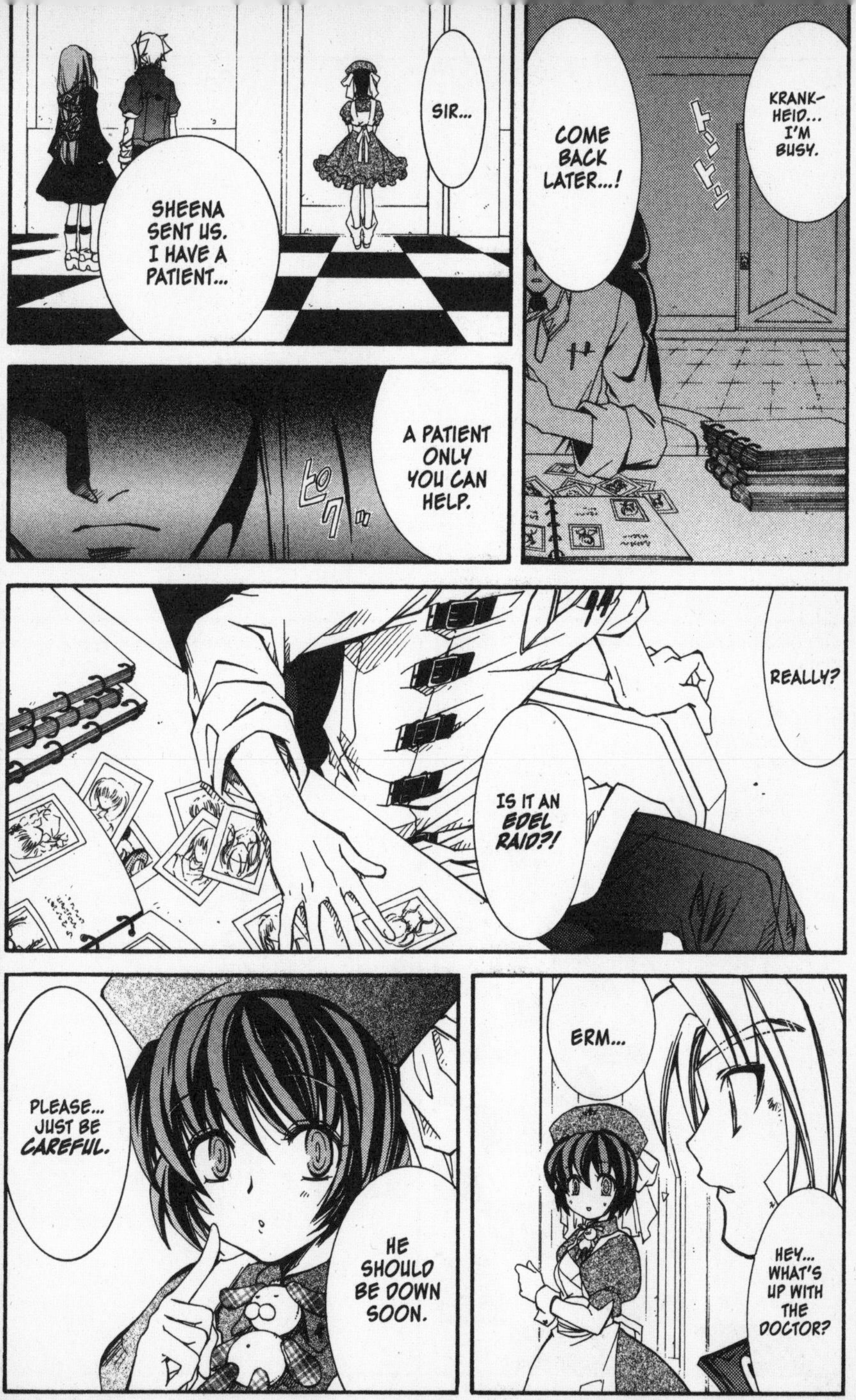
KRANK-HEID... I'M BUSY.
COME BACK LATER...!
SIR...
SHEENA SENT US. I HAVE A PATIENT...
A PATIENT ONLY YOU CAN HELP.
REALLY?
IS IT AN *EDEL RAID?!*
ERM...
HEY... WHAT'S UP WITH THE DOCTOR?
HE SHOULD BE DOWN SOON.
PLEASE... JUST BE *CAREFUL*.

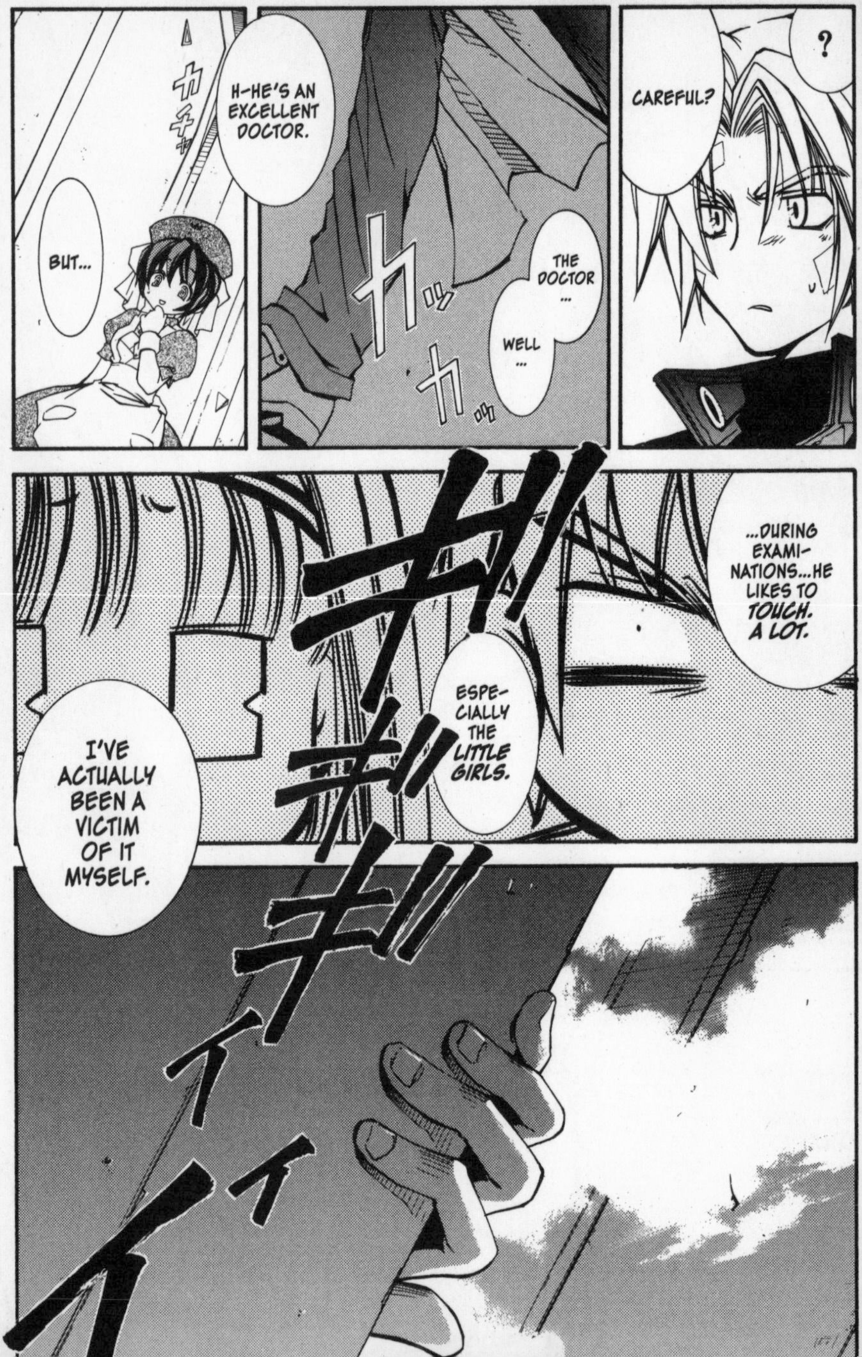
?
CAREFUL?
H-HE'S AN EXCELLENT DOCTOR.
THE DOCTOR ...
WELL ...
BUT...
...DURING EXAMI-NATIONS...HE LIKES TO TOUCH. A LOT.
ESPE-CIALLY THE LITTLE GIRLS.
I'VE ACTUALLY BEEN A VICTIM OF IT MYSELF.

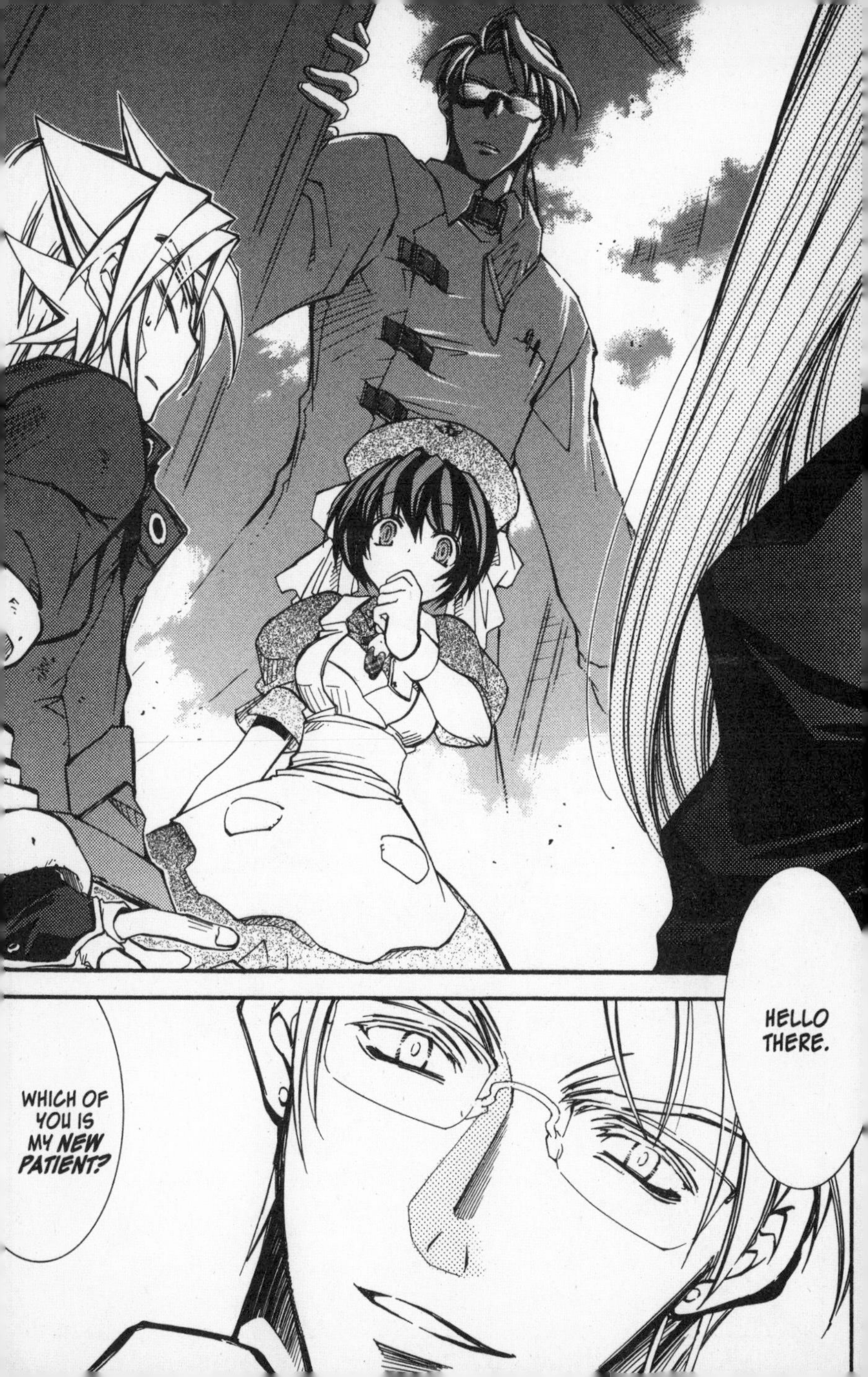
HELLO THERE.
WHICH OF YOU IS MY *NEW PATIENT?*

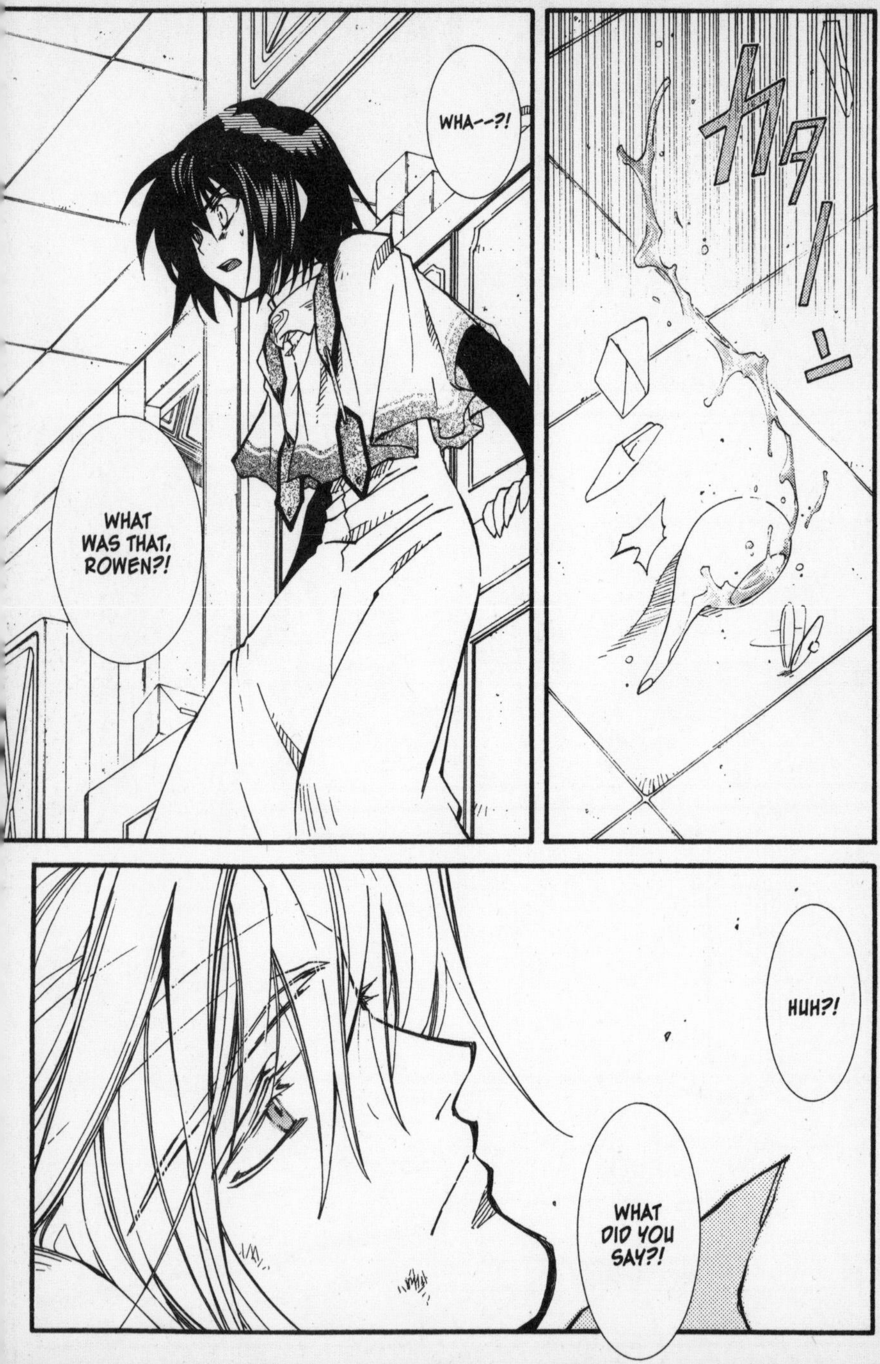
WHA--?!
WHAT WAS THAT, ROWEN?!
HUH?!
WHAT DID YOU SAY?!

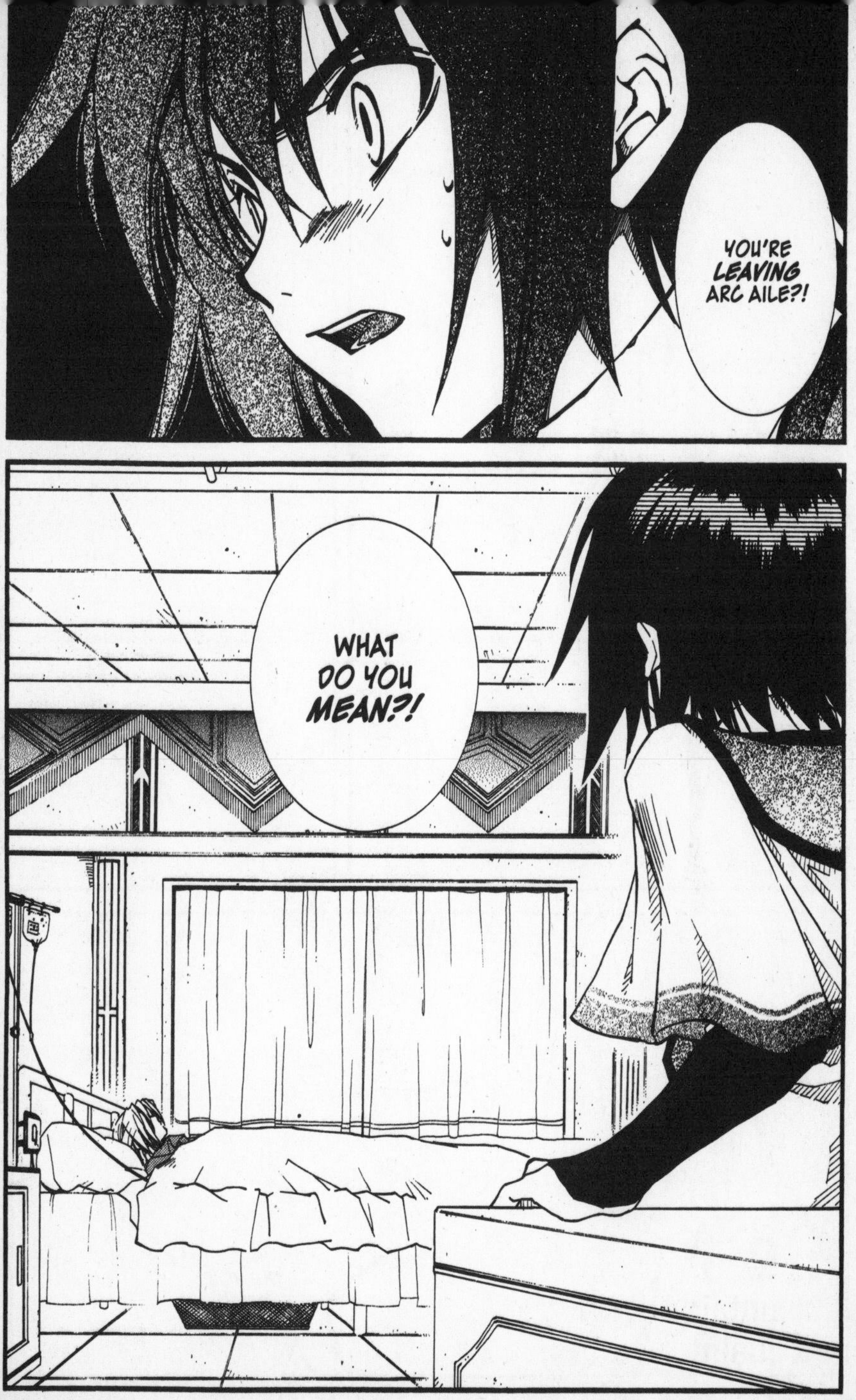
YOU'RE LEAVING ARC AILE?!
WHAT DO YOU MEAN?!

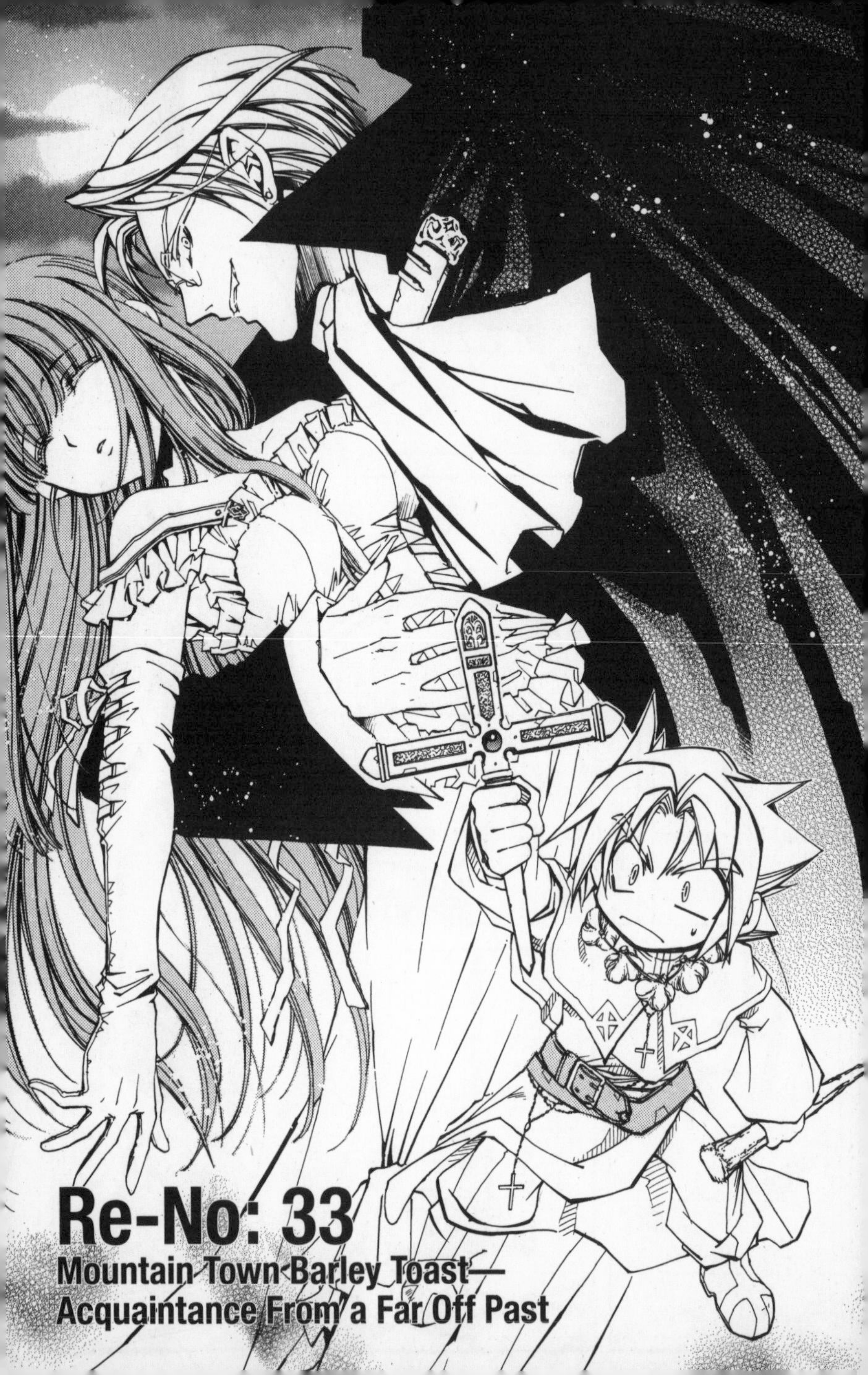
Re-No: 33
Mountain Town Barley Toast—
Acquaintance From a Far Off Past

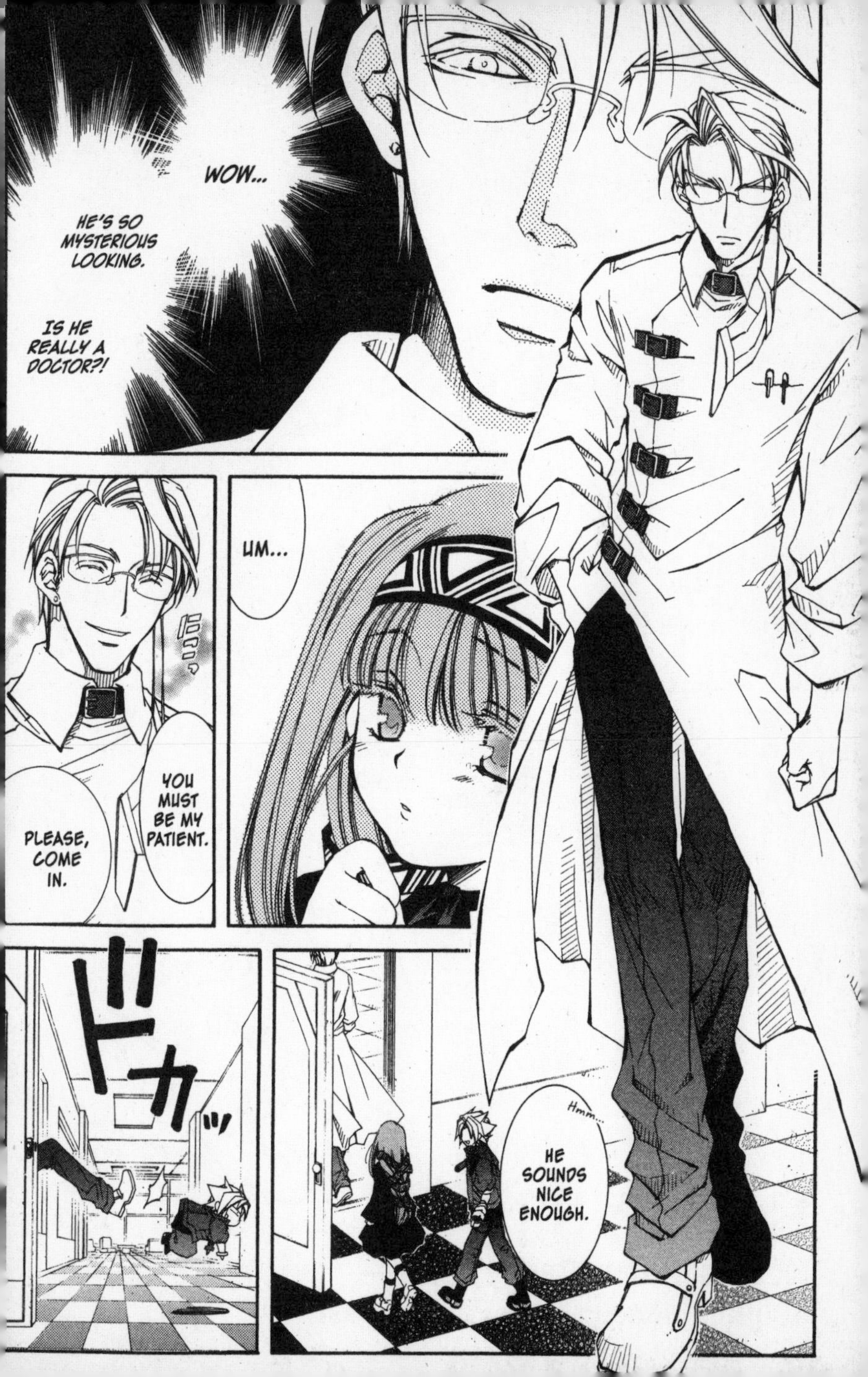
WOW...
HE'S SO MYSTERIOUS LOOKING.
IS HE REALLY A DOCTOR?!
UM...
YOU MUST BE MY PATIENT.
PLEASE, COME IN.
にこっ
Hmm...
HE SOUNDS NICE ENOUGH.
ドカッ

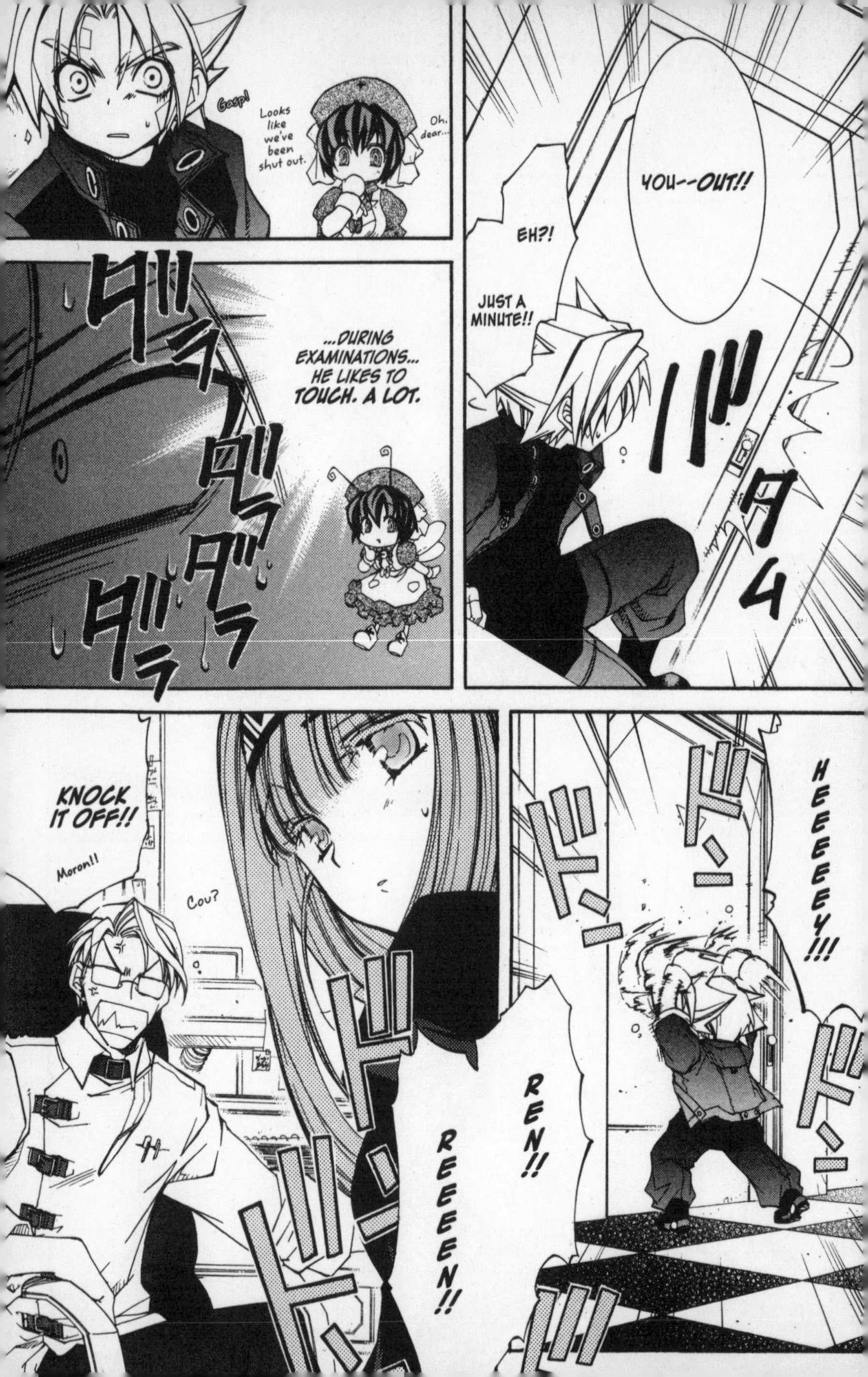
YOU--OUT!!
EH?!
JUST A MINUTE!!
Gasp!
Looks like we've been shut out.
Oh, dear...
...DURING EXAMINATIONS... HE LIKES TO TOUCH. A LOT.
HEEEEEY!!!
KNOCK IT OFF!!
Moron!!
Cou?
REN!!
REEEEEN!!

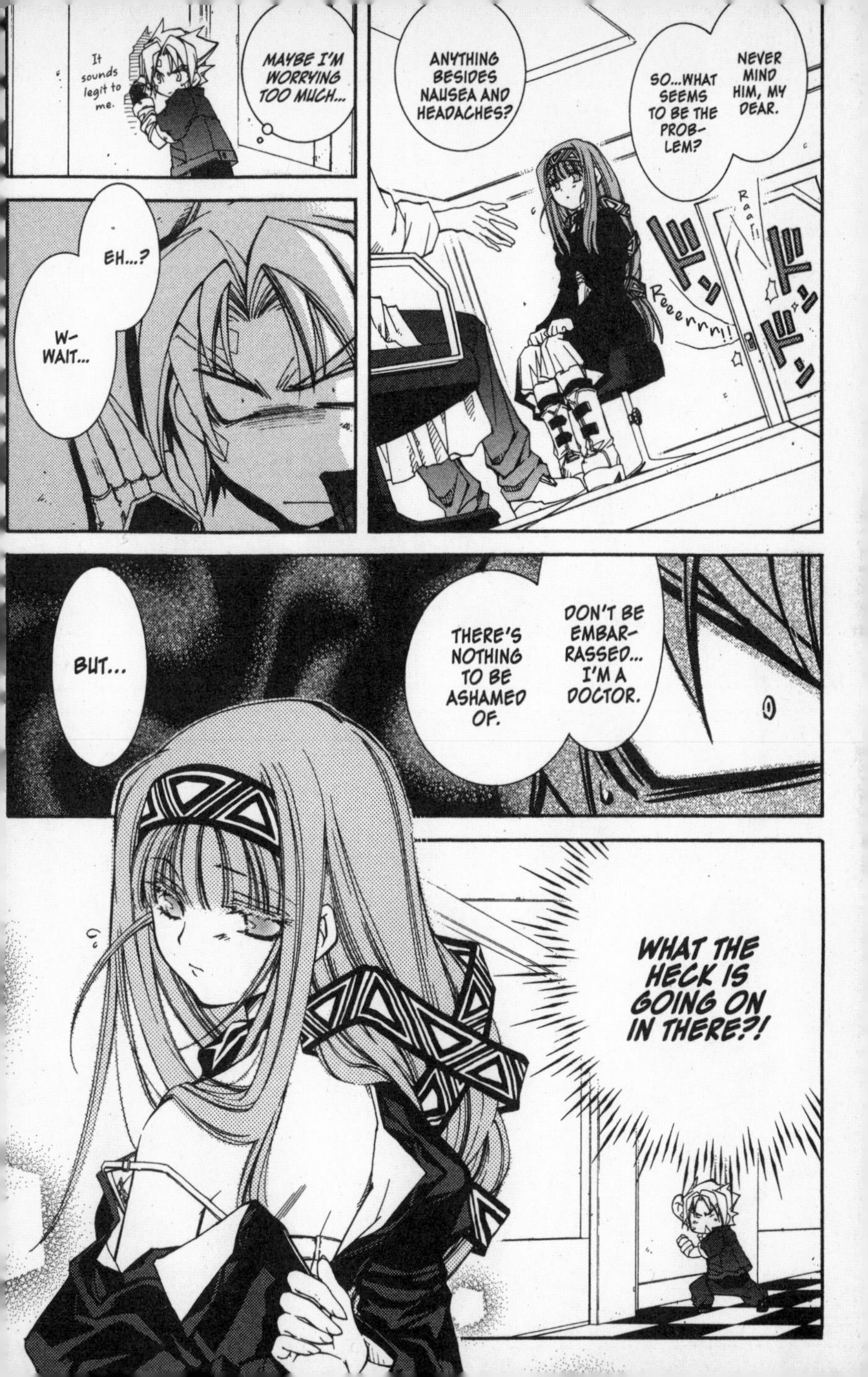
NEVER MIND HIM, MY DEAR.
SO...WHAT SEEMS TO BE THE PROB-LEM?
Raa!!
Reeeerrrr!!
ANYTHING BESIDES NAUSEA AND HEADACHES?
MAYBE I'M WORRYING TOO MUCH...
It sounds legit to me.
EH...?
W-WAIT...
DON'T BE EMBAR-RASSED... I'M A DOCTOR.
THERE'S NOTHING TO BE ASHAMED OF.
BUT...
WHAT THE HECK IS GOING ON IN THERE?!

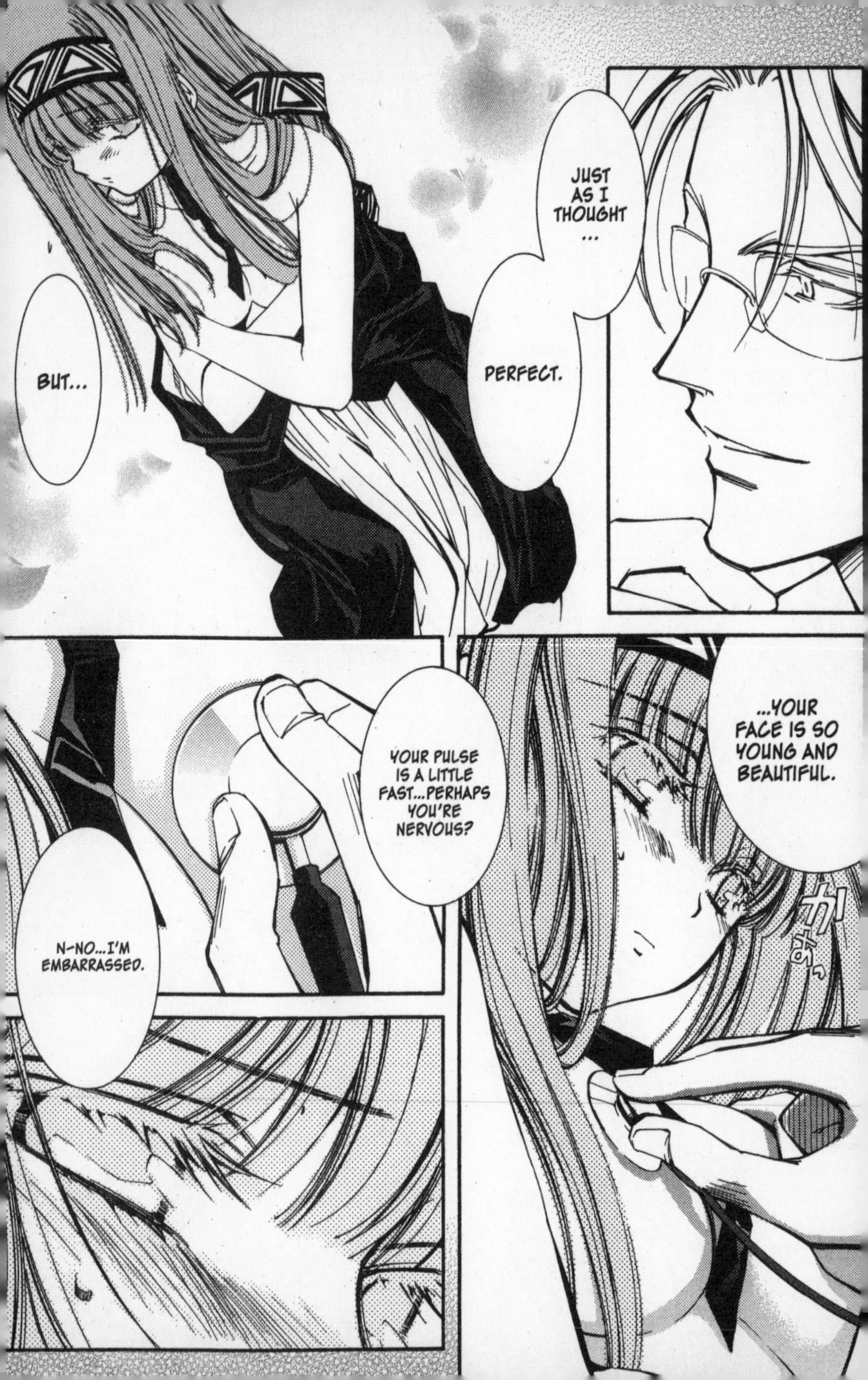
JUST AS I THOUGHT ...
PERFECT.
BUT...
...YOUR FACE IS SO YOUNG AND BEAUTIFUL.
YOUR PULSE IS A LITTLE FAST...PERHAPS YOU'RE NERVOUS?
N-NO...I'M EMBARRASSED.

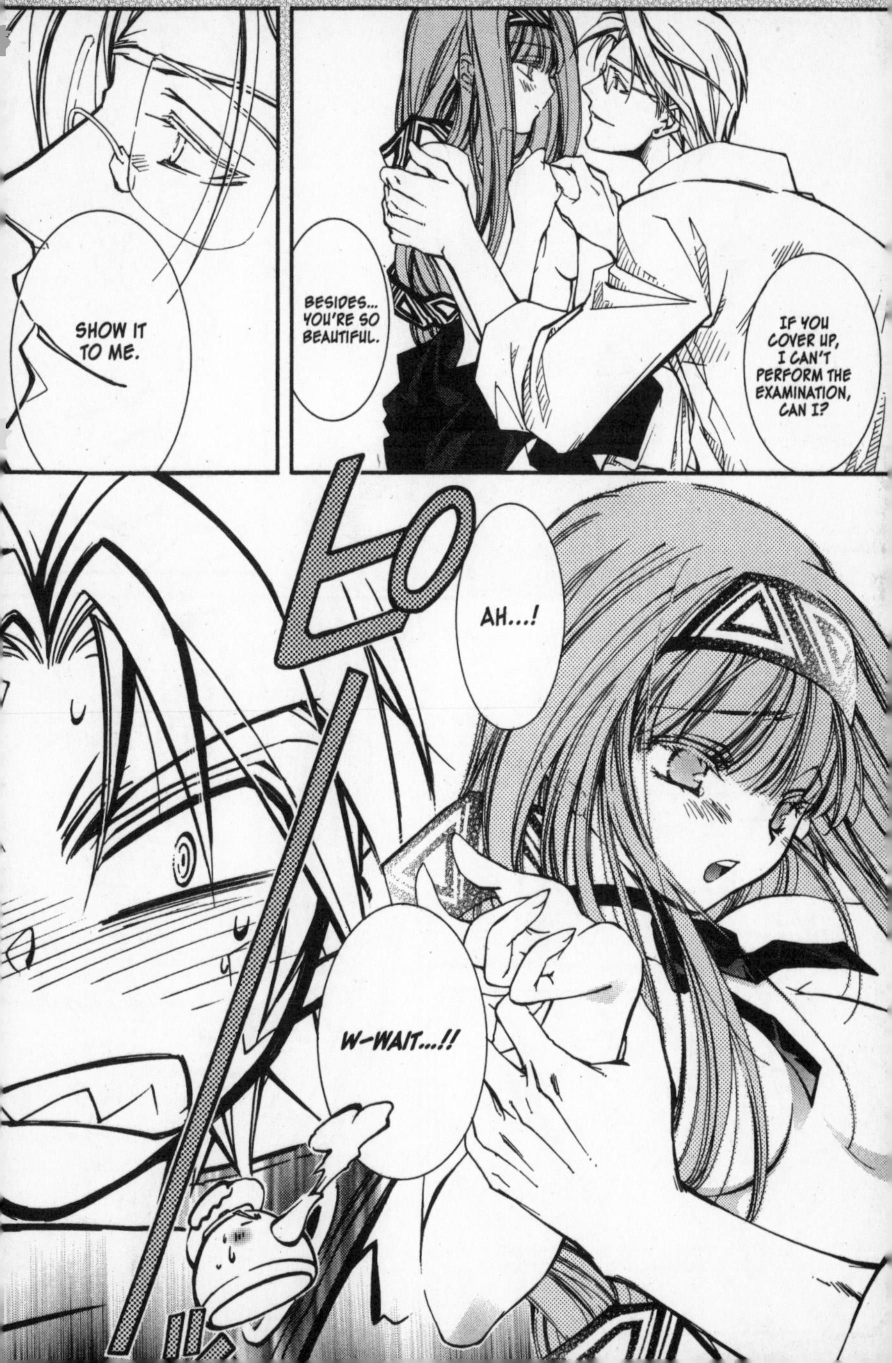
IF YOU COVER UP, I CAN'T PERFORM THE EXAMINATION, CAN I?
BESIDES... YOU'RE SO BEAUTIFUL.
SHOW IT TO ME.
AH...!
W-WAIT...!!

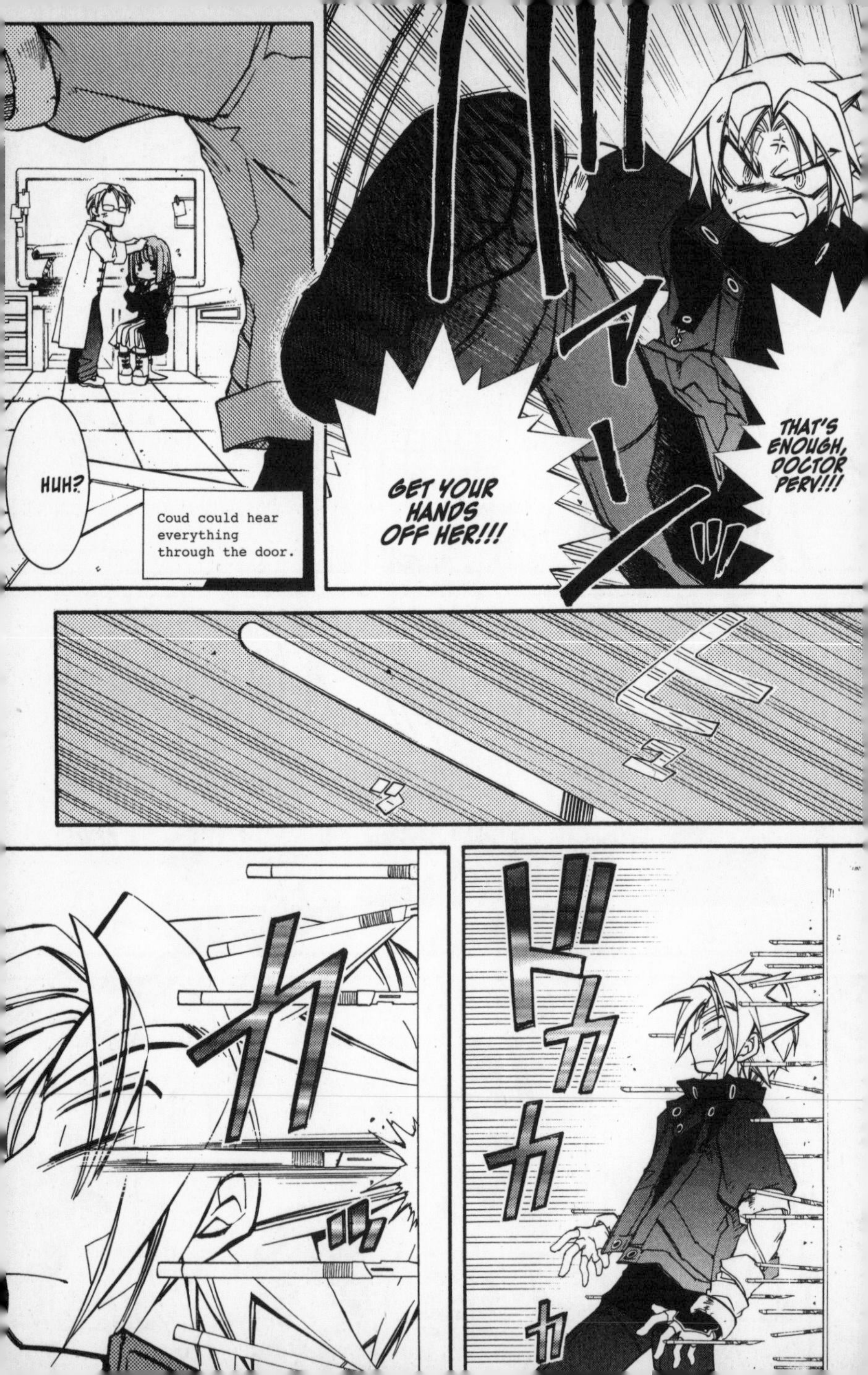
THAT'S ENOUGH, DOCTOR PERV!!!
GET YOUR HANDS OFF HER!!!
Coud could hear everything through the door.
HUH?

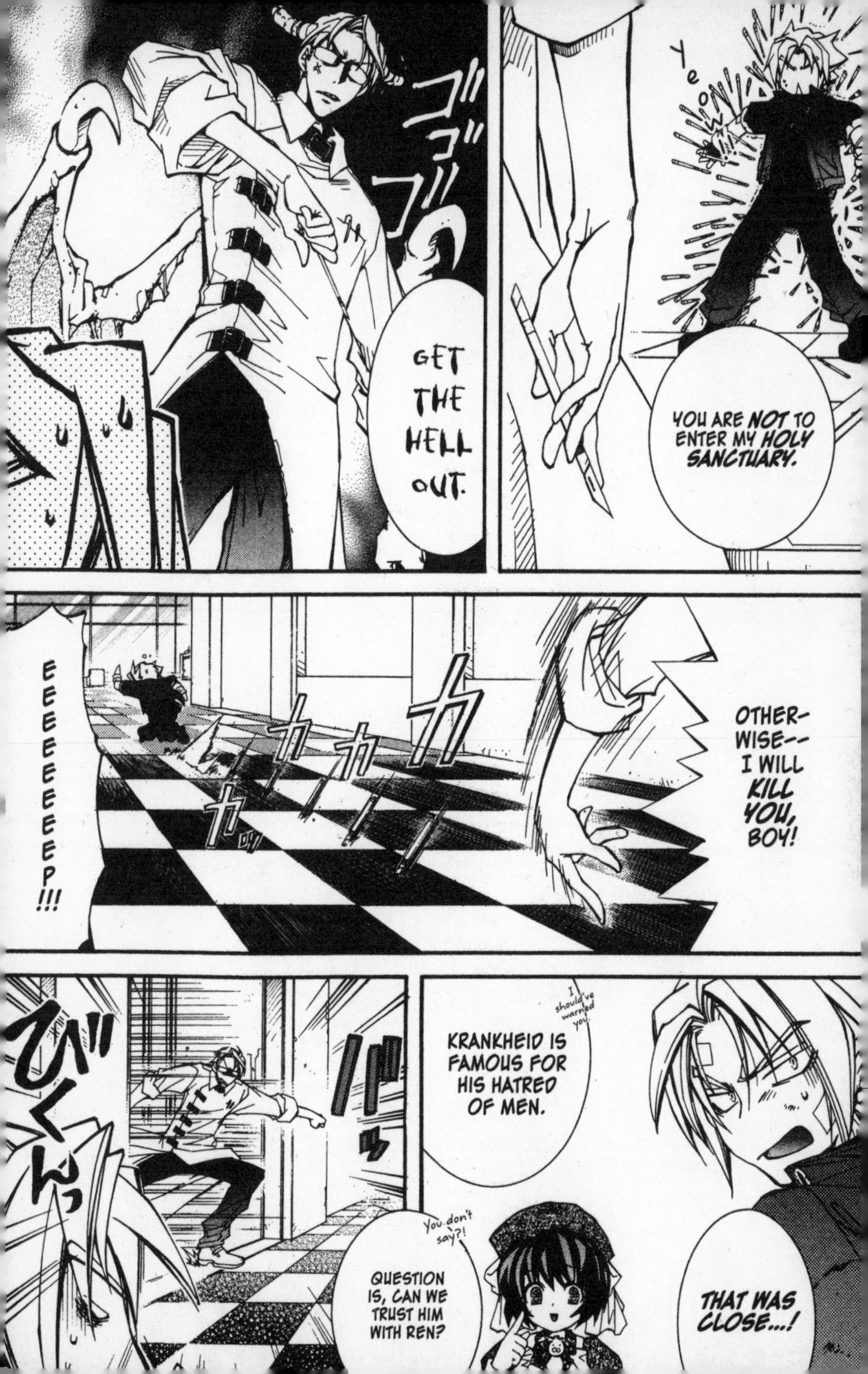
Yeow
YOU ARE NOT TO ENTER MY HOLY SANCTUARY.
ゴゴゴ
GET THE HELL OUT.
OTHER-WISE-- I WILL KILL YOU, BOY!
カカカカ
EEEEEEEEEEP!!!
KRANKHEID IS FAMOUS FOR HIS HATRED OF MEN.
I should've warned you.
THAT WAS CLOSE...!
You don't say?!
QUESTION IS, CAN WE TRUST HIM WITH REN?

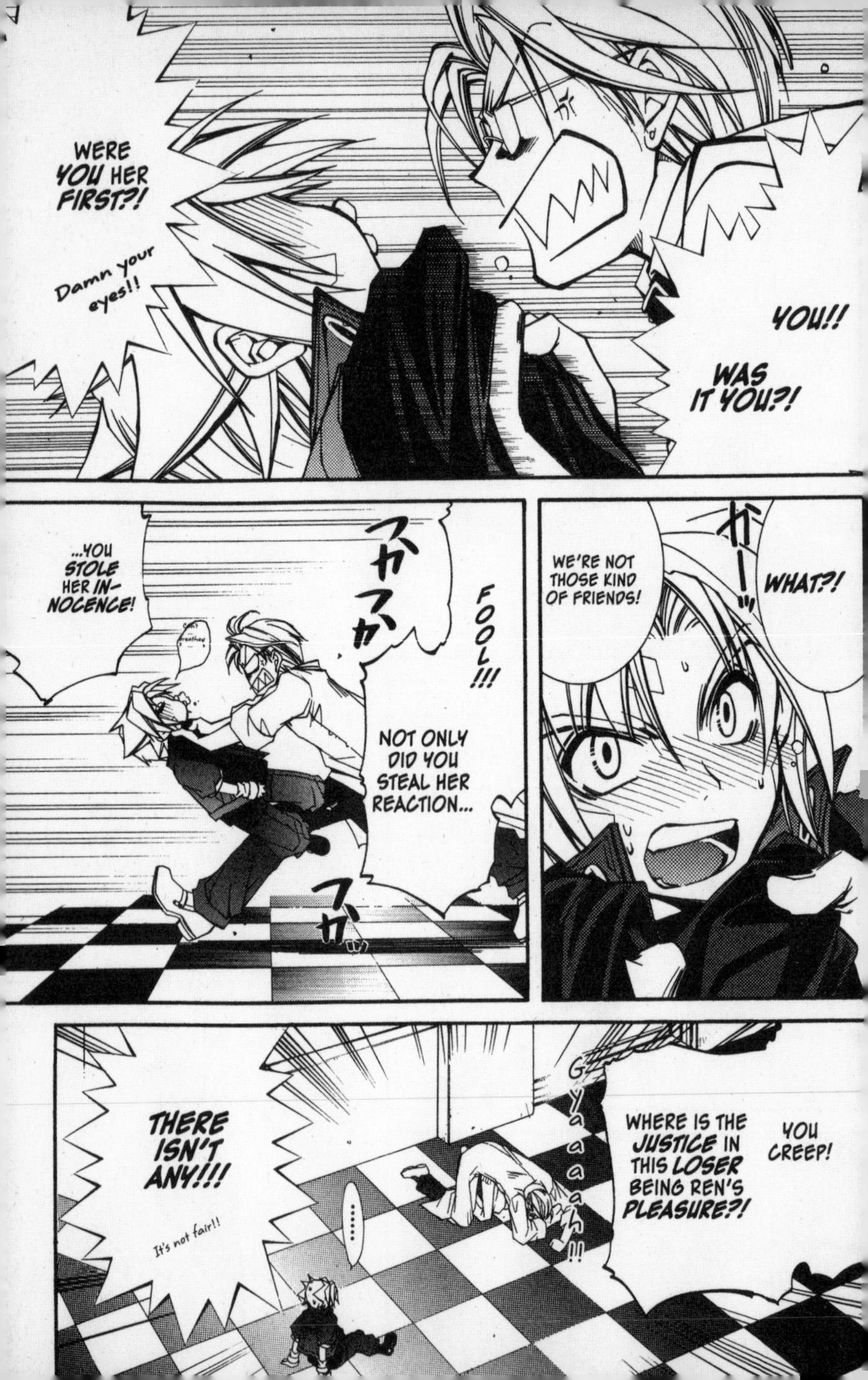
YOU!!
WAS IT YOU?!
WERE YOU HER FIRST?!
Damn your eyes!!
WHAT?!
WE'RE NOT THOSE KIND OF FRIENDS!
FOOL!!!
NOT ONLY DID YOU STEAL HER REACTION...
...YOU STOLE HER INNOCENCE!
YOU CREEP!
WHERE IS THE JUSTICE IN THIS LOSER BEING REN'S PLEASURE?!
Gyaaaaah!!
......
THERE ISN'T ANY!!!
It's not fair!!

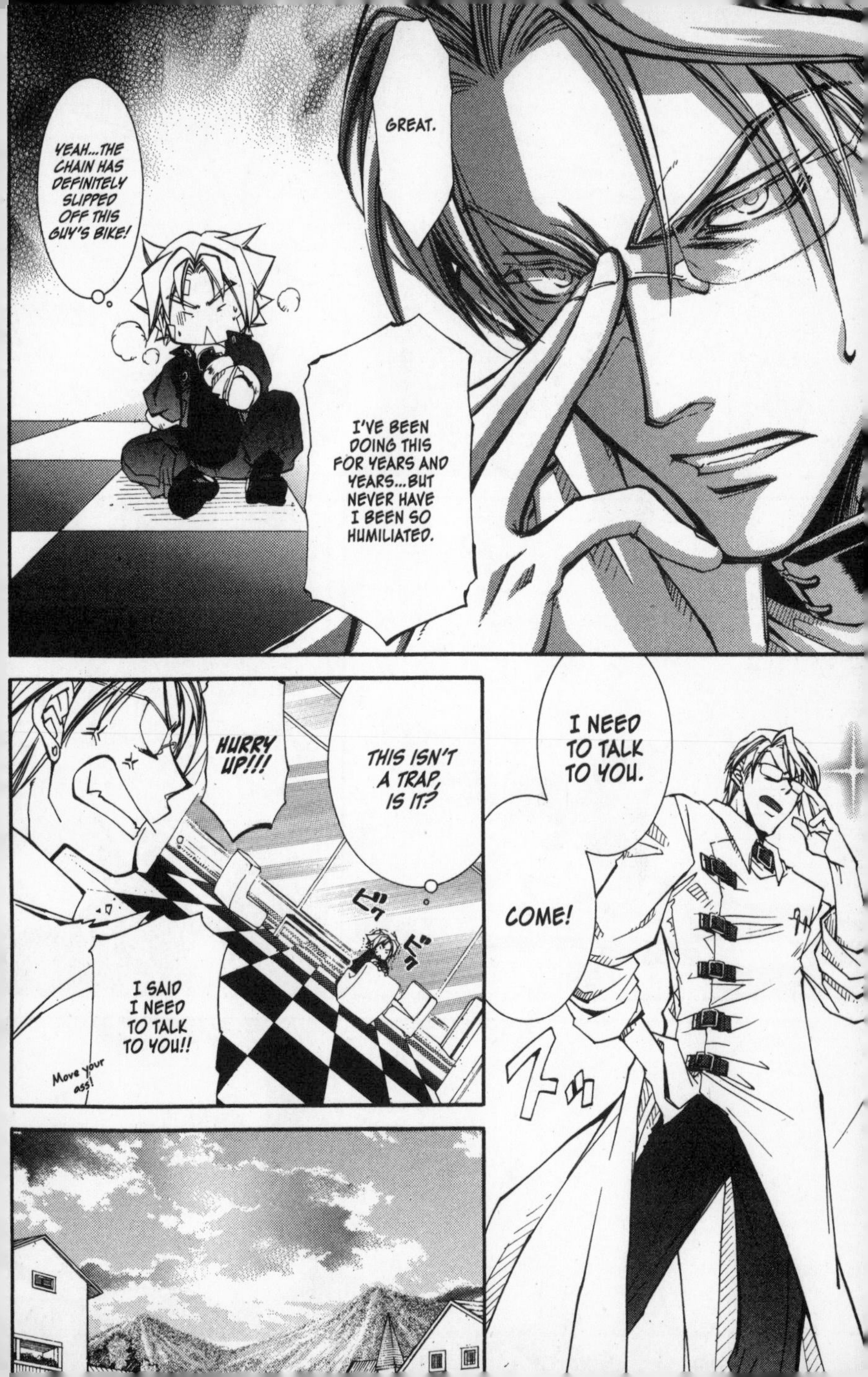
GREAT.
I'VE BEEN DOING THIS FOR YEARS AND YEARS...BUT NEVER HAVE I BEEN SO HUMILIATED.
YEAH...THE CHAIN HAS DEFINITELY SLIPPED OFF THIS GUY'S BIKE!
I NEED TO TALK TO YOU.
COME!
THIS ISN'T A TRAP, IS IT?
HURRY UP!!!
I SAID I NEED TO TALK TO YOU!!
Move your ass!

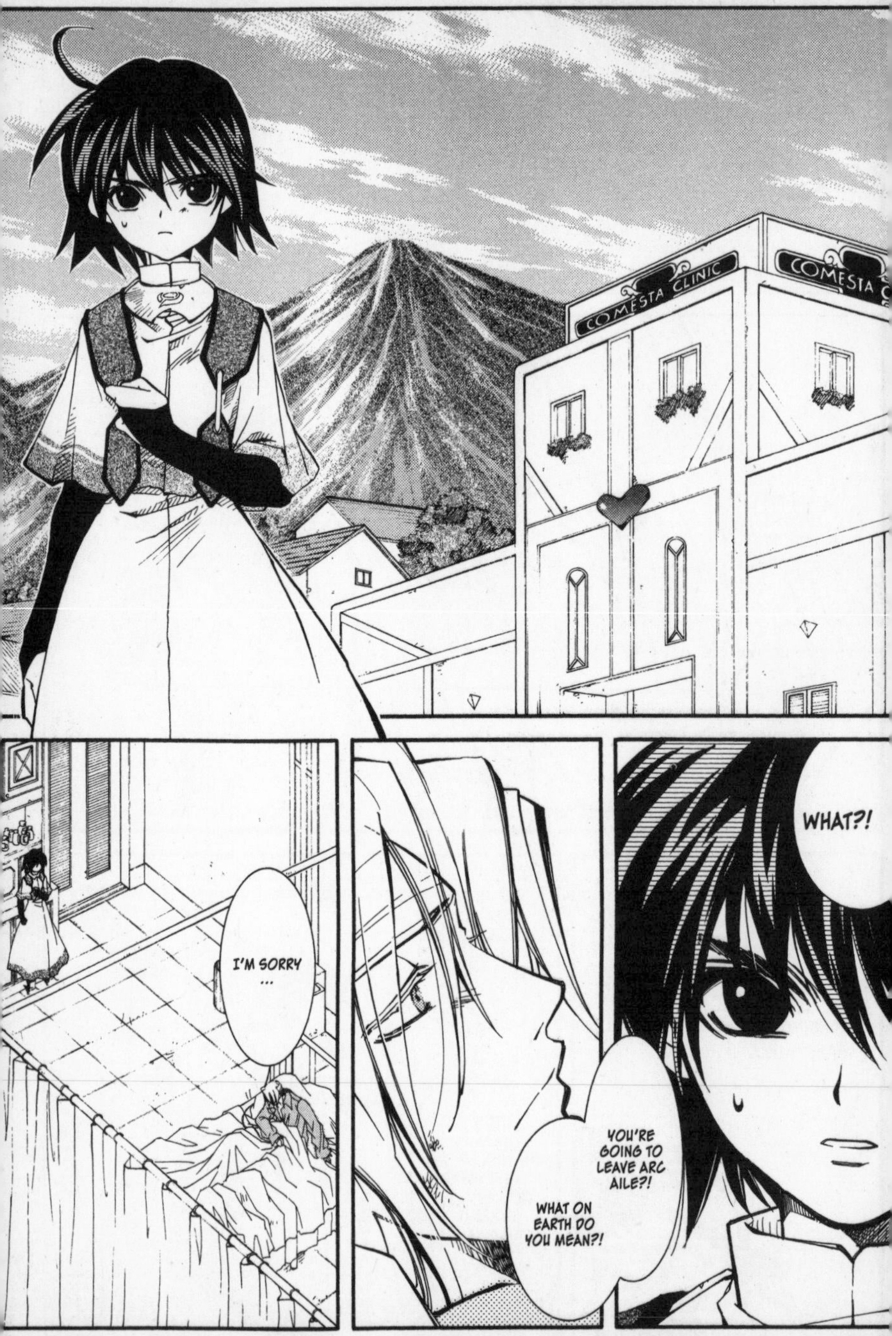
COMESTA CLINIC
COMESTA C
WHAT?!
YOU'RE GOING TO LEAVE ARC AILE?!
WHAT ON EARTH DO YOU MEAN?!
I'M SORRY ...

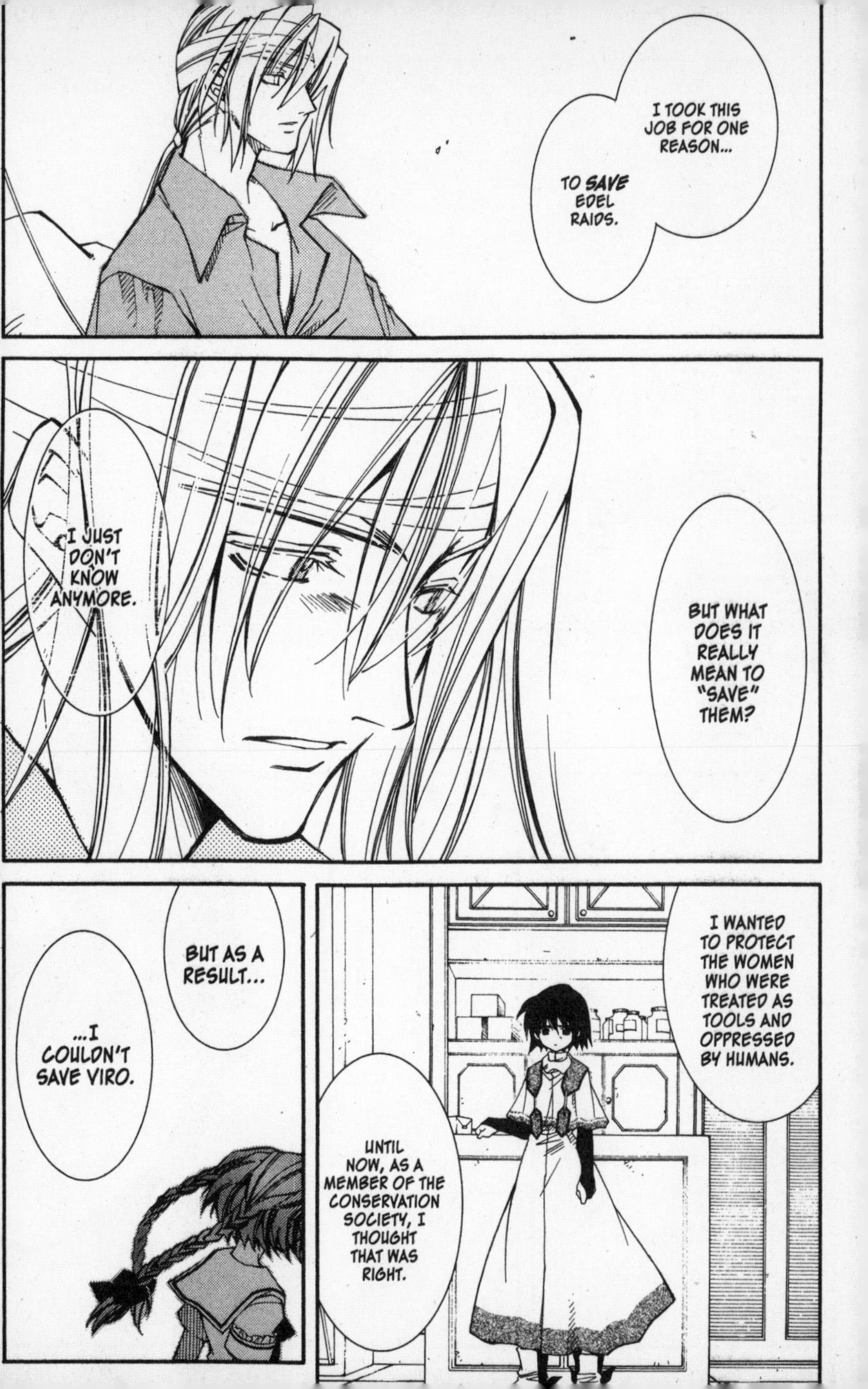
I TOOK THIS JOB FOR ONE REASON...
TO SAVE EDEL RAIDS.
BUT WHAT DOES IT REALLY MEAN TO "SAVE" THEM?
I JUST DON'T KNOW ANYMORE.
I WANTED TO PROTECT THE WOMEN WHO WERE TREATED AS TOOLS AND OPPRESSED BY HUMANS.
UNTIL NOW, AS A MEMBER OF THE CONSERVATION SOCIETY, I THOUGHT THAT WAS RIGHT.
BUT AS A RESULT...
...I COULDN'T SAVE VIRO.

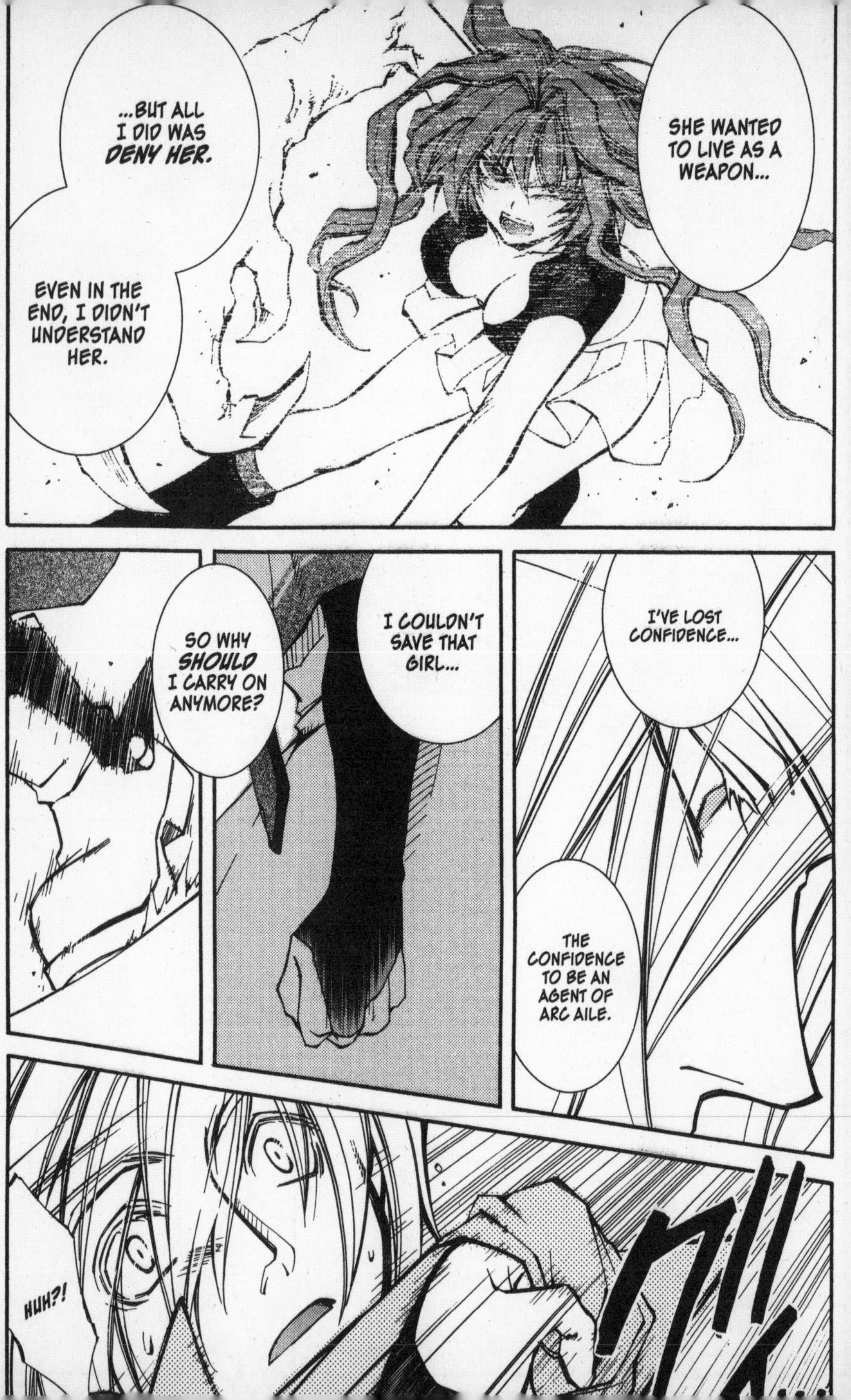
SHE WANTED TO LIVE AS A WEAPON...
...BUT ALL I DID WAS DENY HER.
EVEN IN THE END, I DIDN'T UNDERSTAND HER.
I'VE LOST CONFIDENCE...
THE CONFIDENCE TO BE AN AGENT OF ARC AILE.
I COULDN'T SAVE THAT GIRL...
SO WHY SHOULD I CARRY ON ANYMORE?
HUH?!

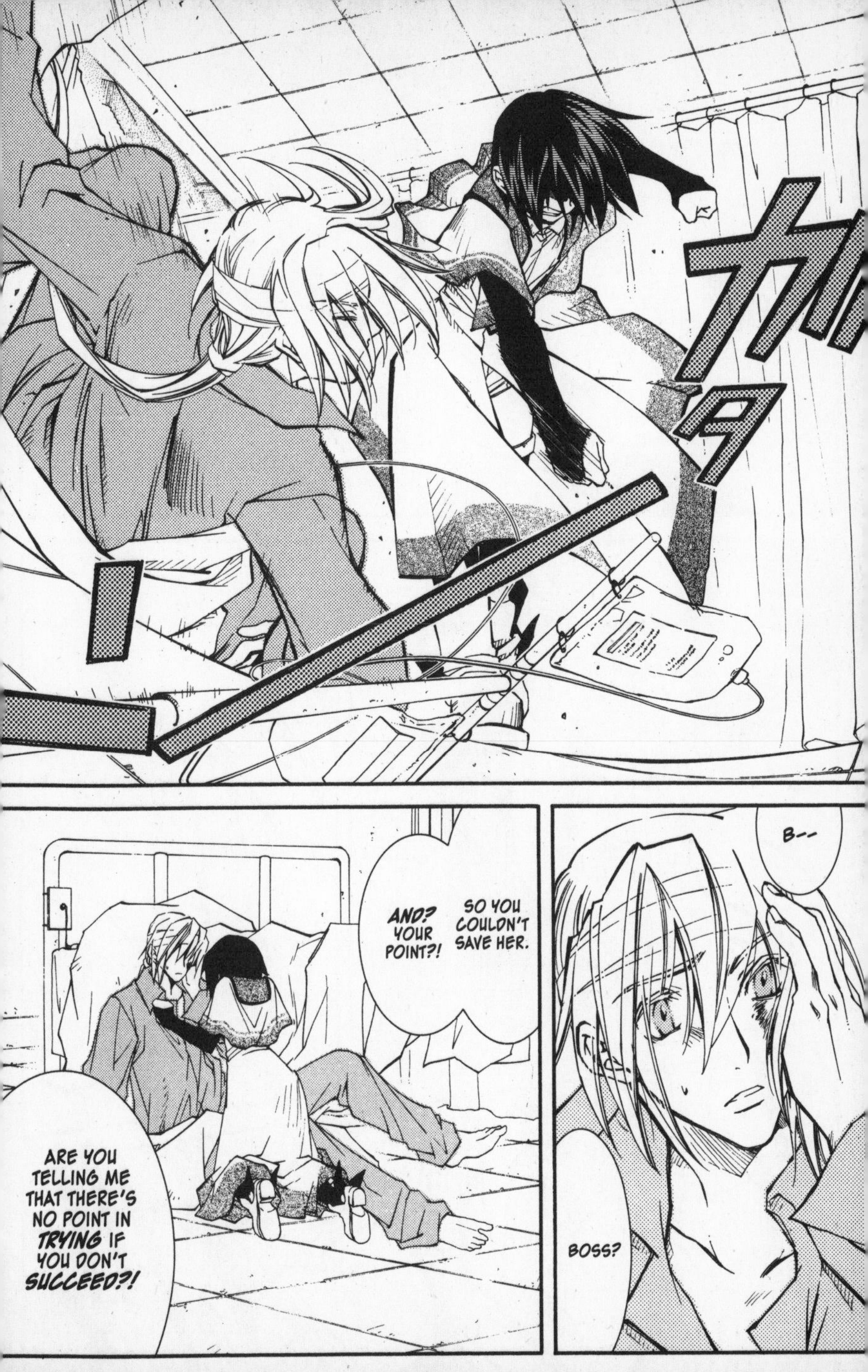
B--
BOSS?
SO YOU COULDN'T SAVE HER.
AND? YOUR POINT?!
ARE YOU TELLING ME THAT THERE'S NO POINT IN TRYING IF YOU DON'T SUCCEED?!

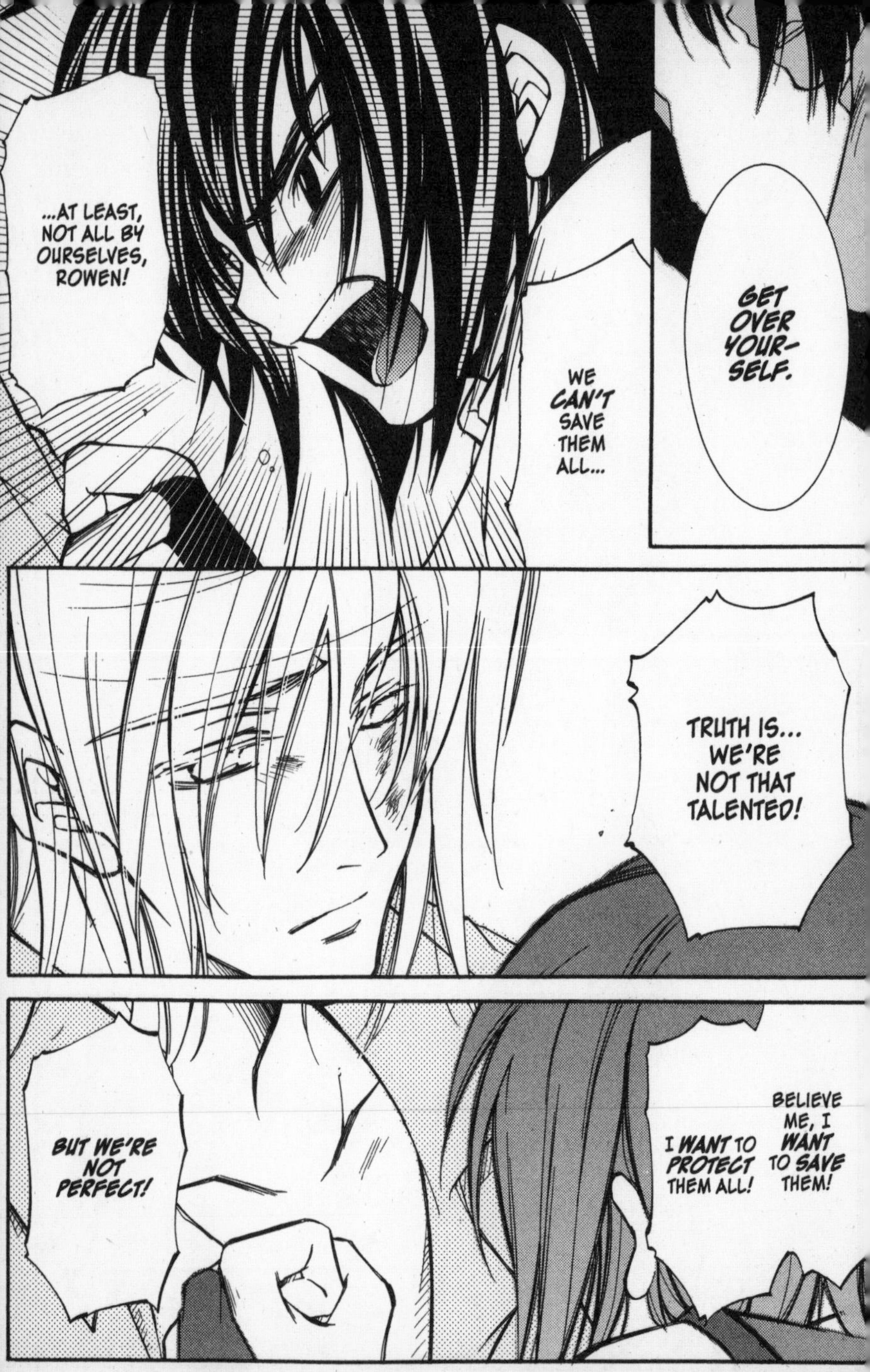
GET OVER YOURSELF.
WE CAN'T SAVE THEM ALL...
...AT LEAST, NOT ALL BY OURSELVES, ROWEN!
TRUTH IS... WE'RE NOT THAT TALENTED!
BELIEVE ME, I WANT TO SAVE THEM!
I WANT TO PROTECT THEM ALL!
BUT WE'RE NOT PERFECT!

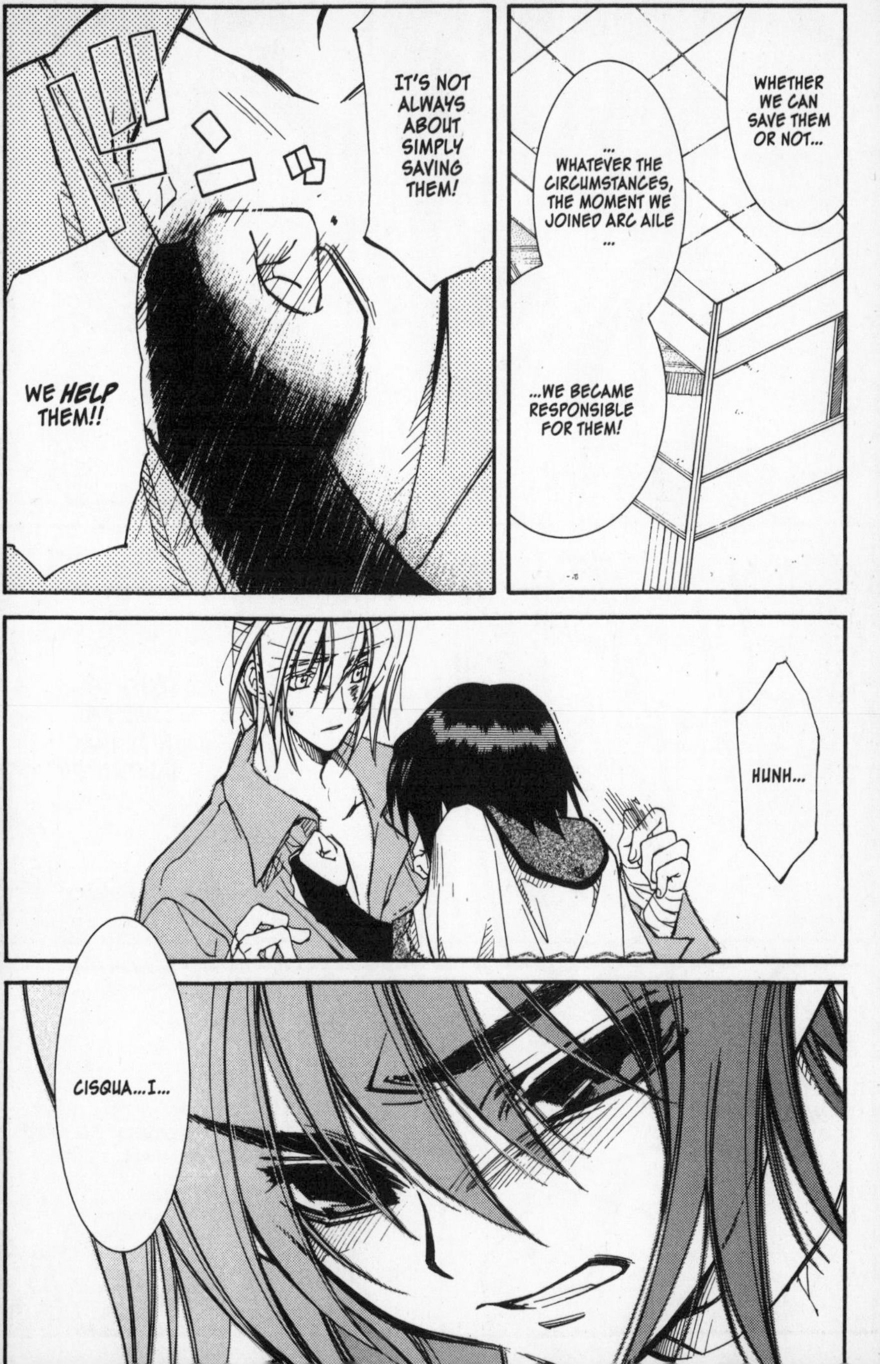
WHETHER WE CAN SAVE THEM OR NOT...
... WHATEVER THE CIRCUMSTANCES, THE MOMENT WE JOINED ARC AILE ...
...WE BECAME RESPONSIBLE FOR THEM!
IT'S NOT ALWAYS ABOUT SIMPLY SAVING THEM!
WE *HELP* THEM!!
HUNH...
CISQUA...I...

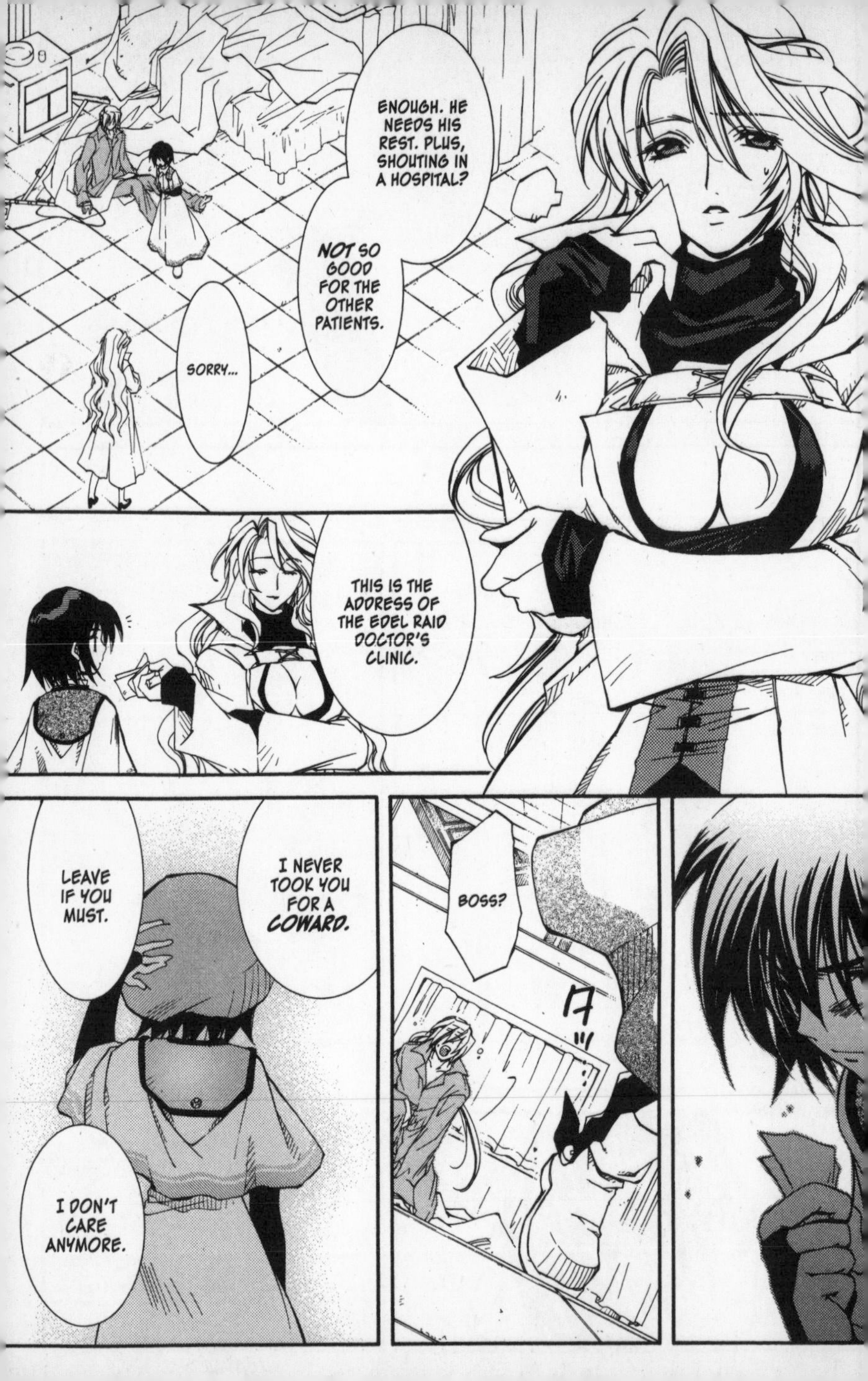
ENOUGH. HE NEEDS HIS REST. PLUS, SHOUTING IN A HOSPITAL?
NOT SO GOOD FOR THE OTHER PATIENTS.
SORRY...
THIS IS THE ADDRESS OF THE EDEL RAID DOCTOR'S CLINIC.
BOSS?
I NEVER TOOK YOU FOR A COWARD.
LEAVE IF YOU MUST.
I DON'T CARE ANYMORE.

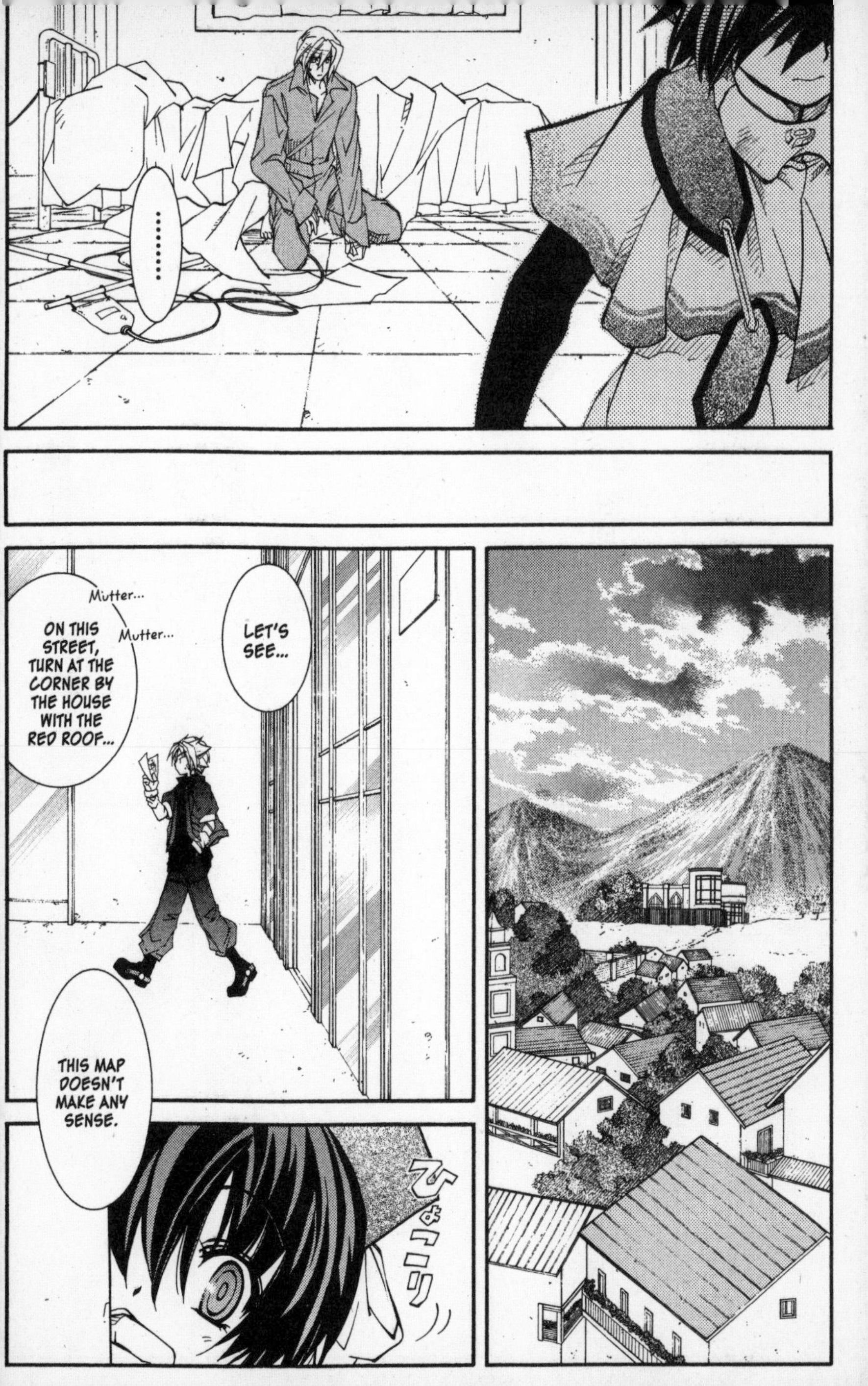
......
LET'S SEE...
Mutter... Mutter...
ON THIS STREET, TURN AT THE CORNER BY THE HOUSE WITH THE RED ROOF...
THIS MAP DOESN'T MAKE ANY SENSE.

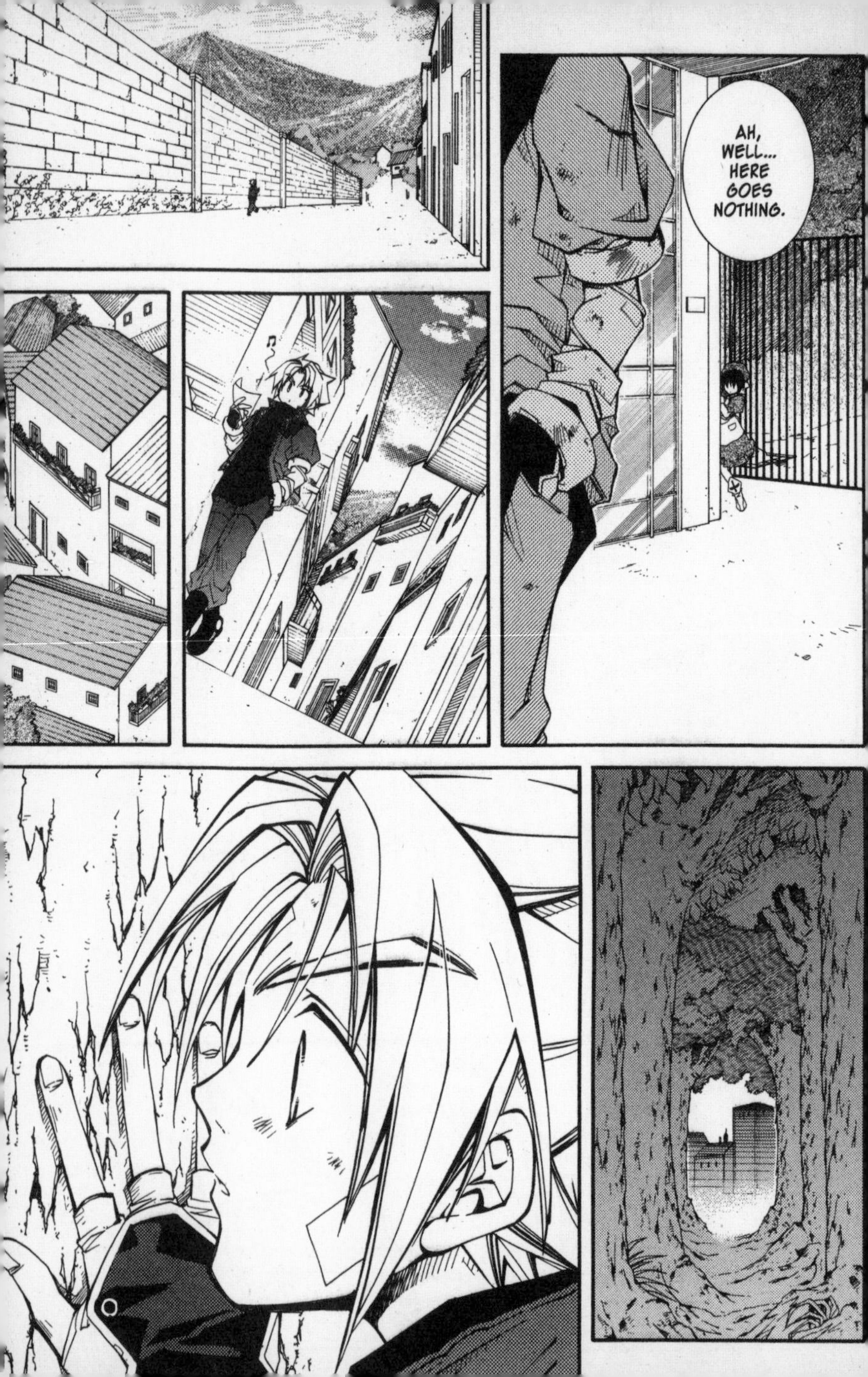
AH, WELL... HERE GOES NOTHING.

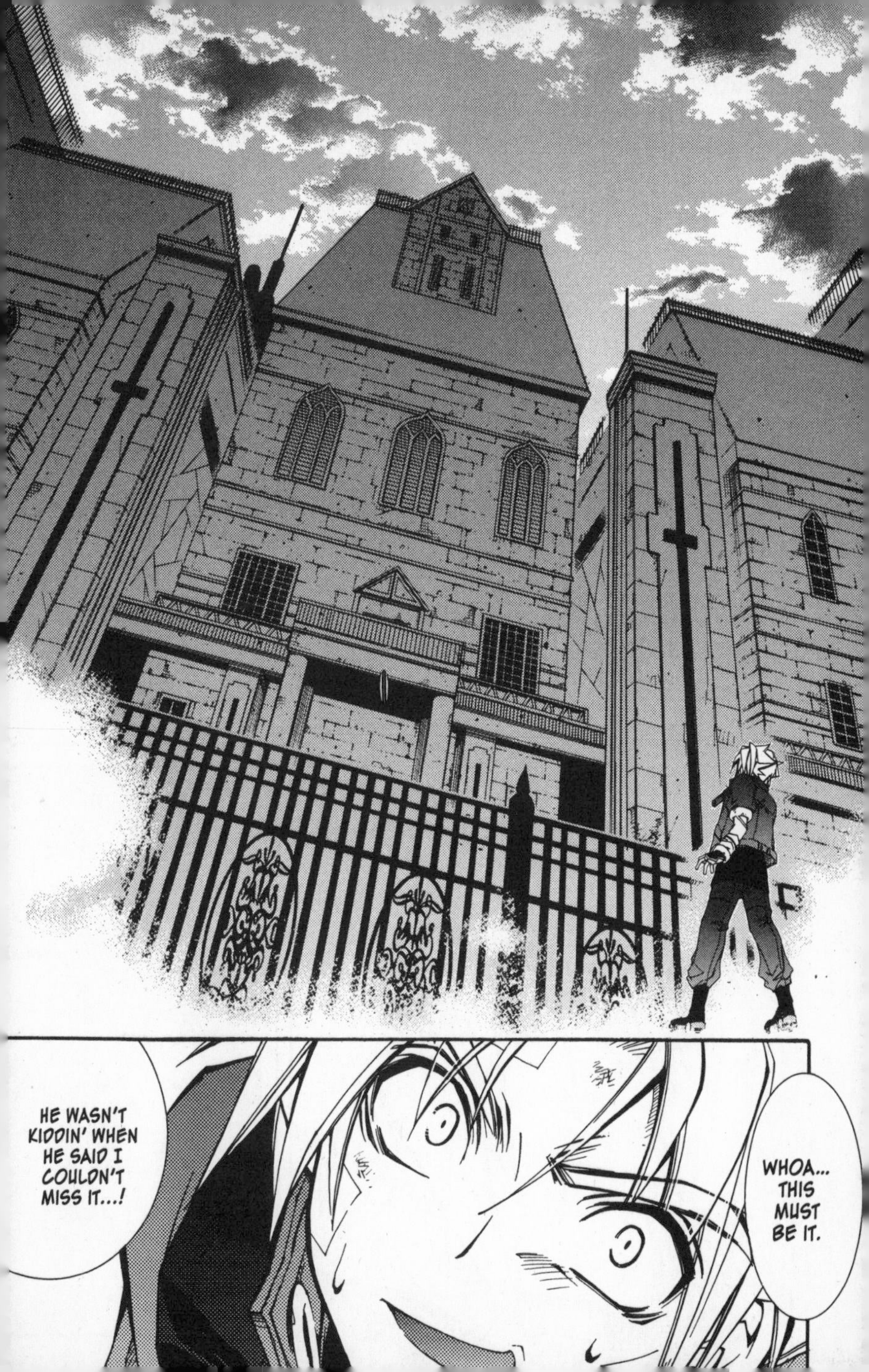
WHOA... THIS MUST BE IT.
HE WASN'T KIDDIN' WHEN HE SAID I COULDN'T MISS IT...!

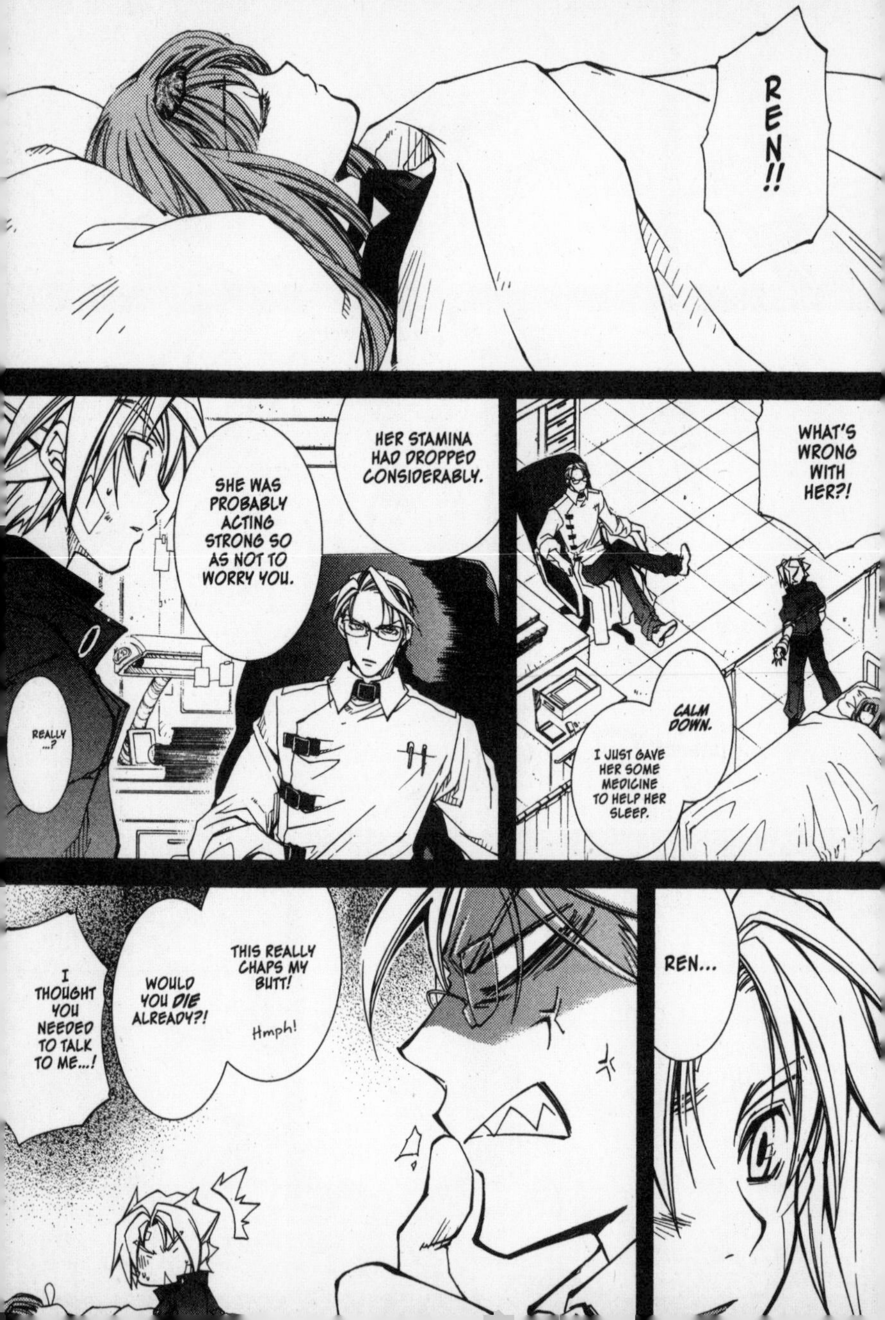
REN!!
WHAT'S WRONG WITH HER?!
CALM DOWN.
I JUST GAVE HER SOME MEDICINE TO HELP HER SLEEP.
HER STAMINA HAD DROPPED CONSIDERABLY.
SHE WAS PROBABLY ACTING STRONG SO AS NOT TO WORRY YOU.
REALLY ...?
REN...
THIS REALLY CHAPS MY BUTT!
Hmph!
WOULD YOU *DIE* ALREADY?!
I THOUGHT YOU NEEDED TO TALK TO ME...!

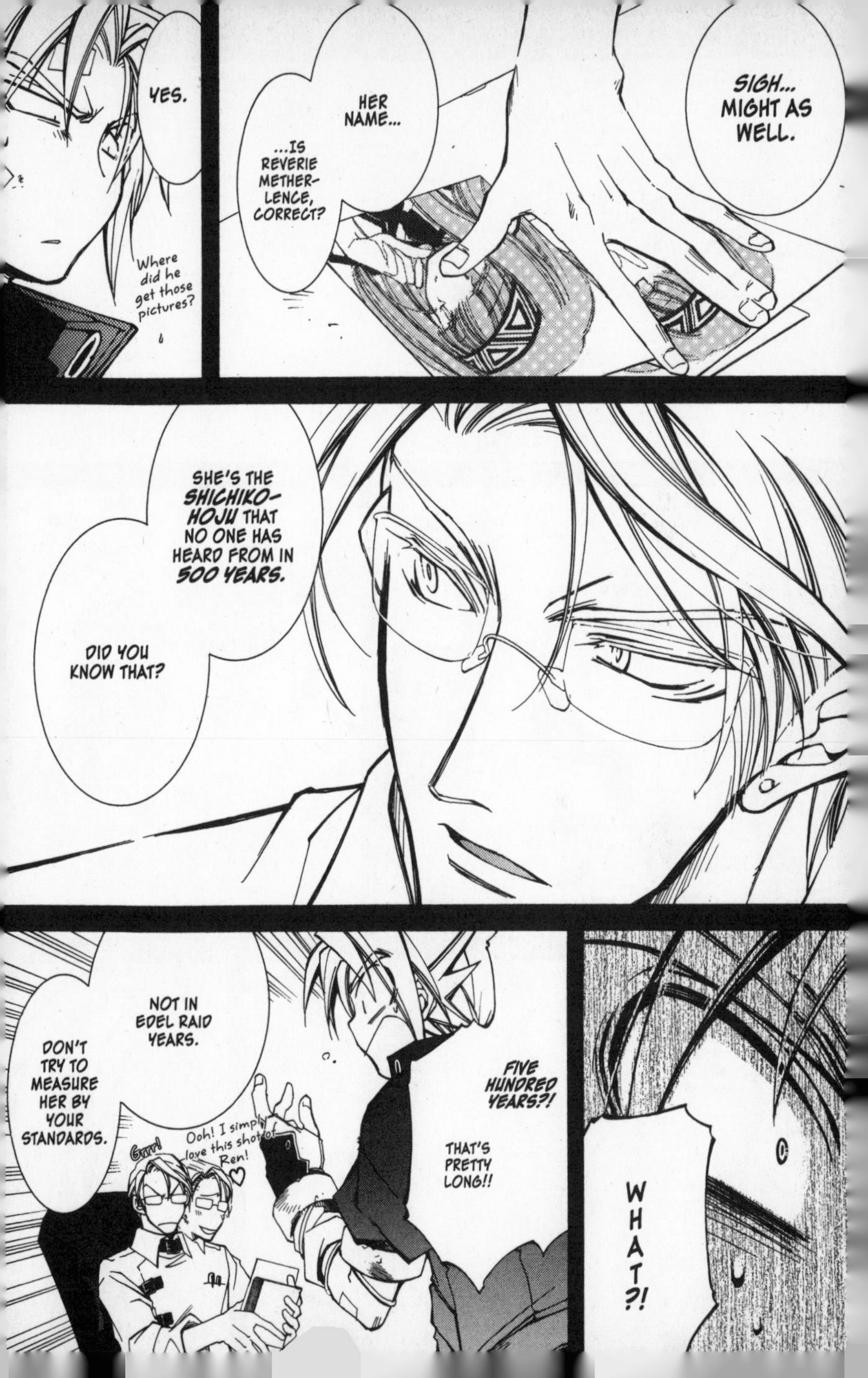
SIGH... MIGHT AS WELL.
HER NAME...
...IS REVERIE METHER-LENCE, CORRECT?
YES.
Where did he get those pictures?
SHE'S THE *SHICHIKO-HOJU* THAT NO ONE HAS HEARD FROM IN **500 YEARS.**
DID YOU KNOW THAT?
WHAT?!
FIVE HUNDRED YEARS?!
THAT'S PRETTY LONG!!
NOT IN EDEL RAID YEARS.
DON'T TRY TO MEASURE HER BY YOUR STANDARDS.
Grrr!
Ooh! I simply love this shot of Ren!

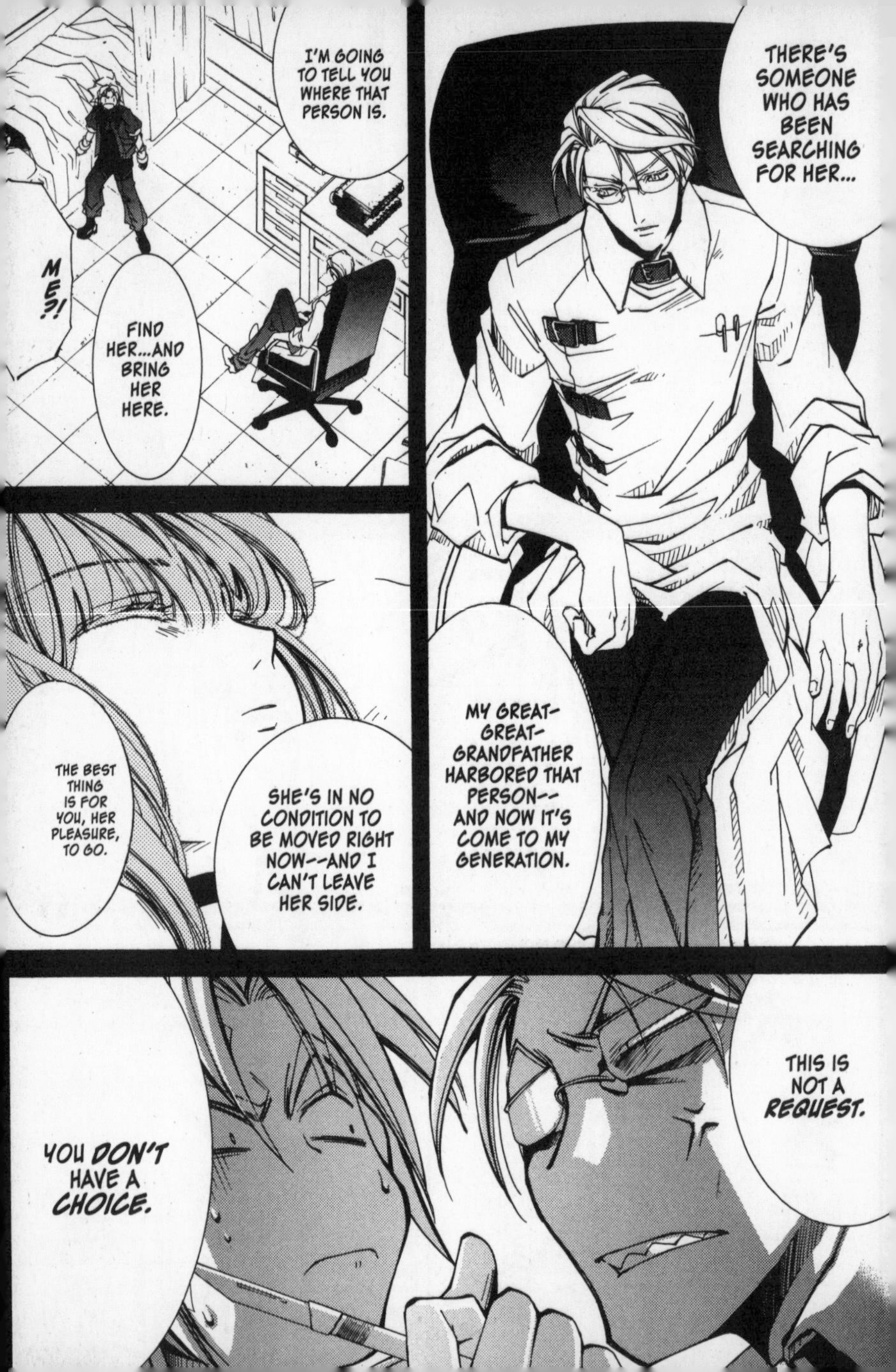
THERE'S SOMEONE WHO HAS BEEN SEARCHING FOR HER...
MY GREAT-GREAT-GRANDFATHER HARBORED THAT PERSON--AND NOW IT'S COME TO MY GENERATION.
I'M GOING TO TELL YOU WHERE THAT PERSON IS.
FIND HER...AND BRING HER HERE.
ME?!
SHE'S IN NO CONDITION TO BE MOVED RIGHT NOW--AND I CAN'T LEAVE HER SIDE.
THE BEST THING IS FOR YOU, HER PLEASURE, TO GO.
THIS IS NOT A *REQUEST.*
YOU *DON'T* HAVE A *CHOICE.*

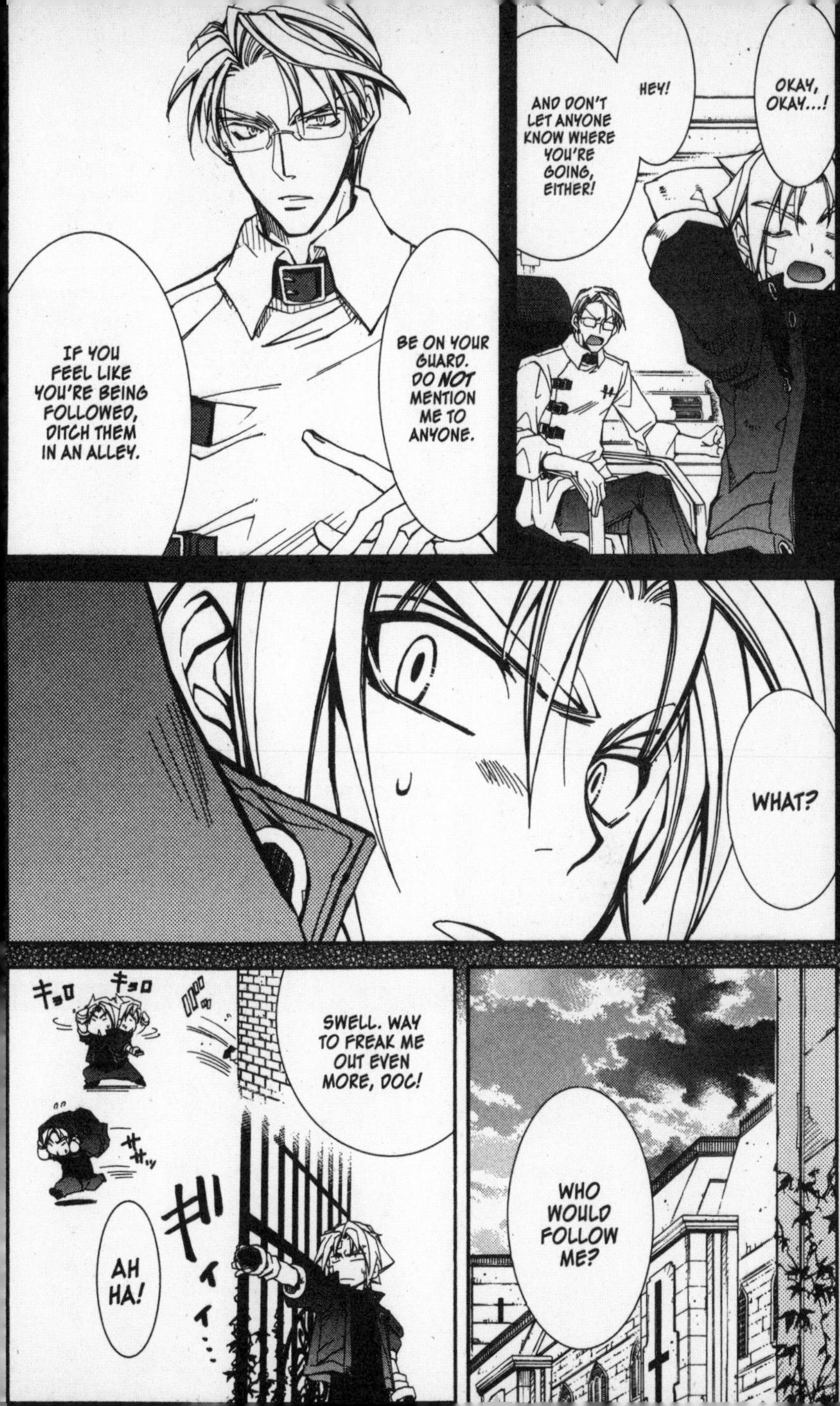
OKAY, OKAY...!
HEY!
AND DON'T LET ANYONE KNOW WHERE YOU'RE GOING, EITHER!
BE ON YOUR GUARD. DO NOT MENTION ME TO ANYONE.
IF YOU FEEL LIKE YOU'RE BEING FOLLOWED, DITCH THEM IN AN ALLEY.
WHAT?
WHO WOULD FOLLOW ME?
SWELL. WAY TO FREAK ME OUT EVEN MORE, DOC!
キョロ キョロ
AH HA!

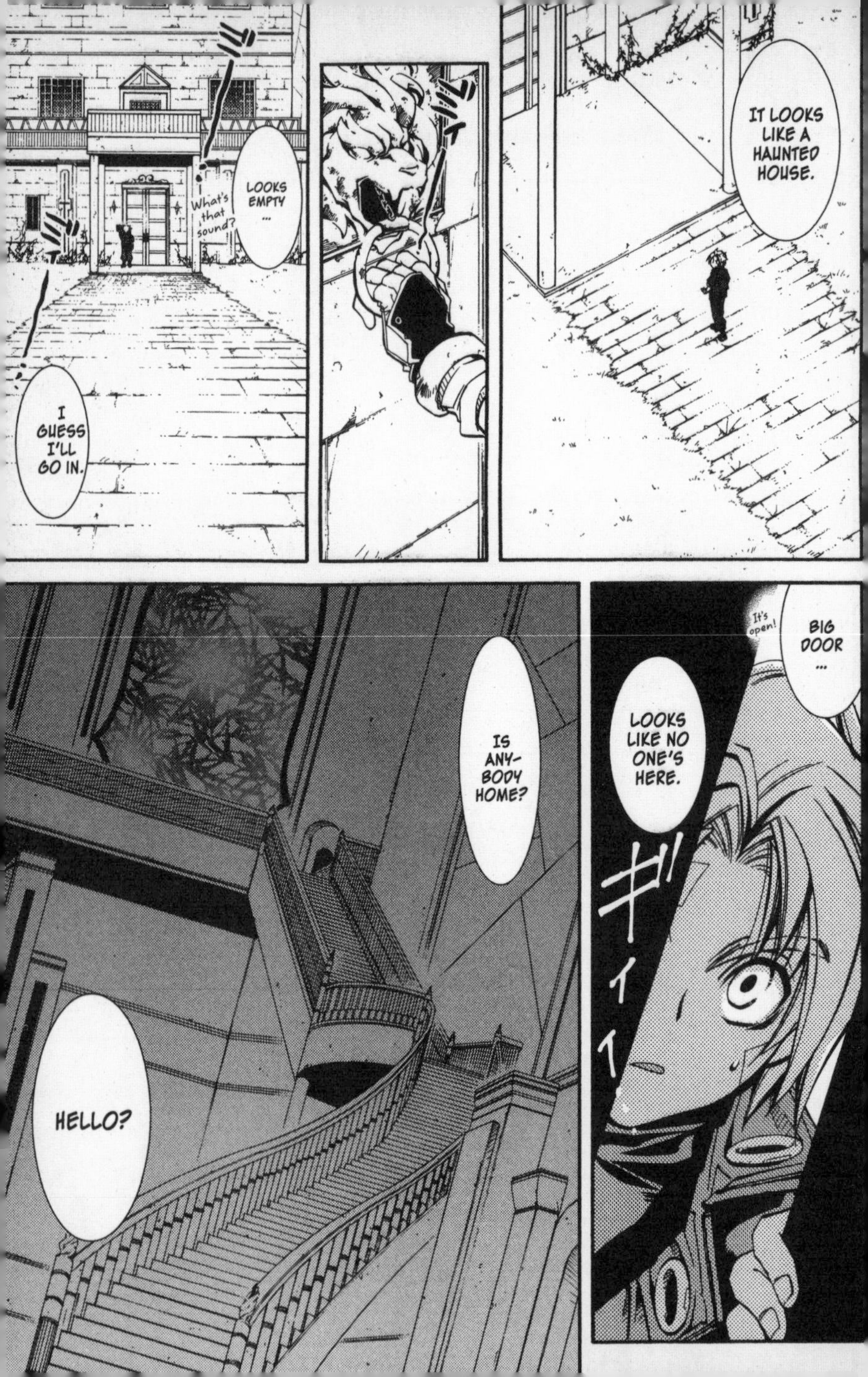
IT LOOKS LIKE A HAUNTED HOUSE.
LOOKS EMPTY ...
What's that sound?
I GUESS I'LL GO IN.
BIG DOOR ...
It's open!
LOOKS LIKE NO ONE'S HERE.
IS ANY-BODY HOME?
HELLO?

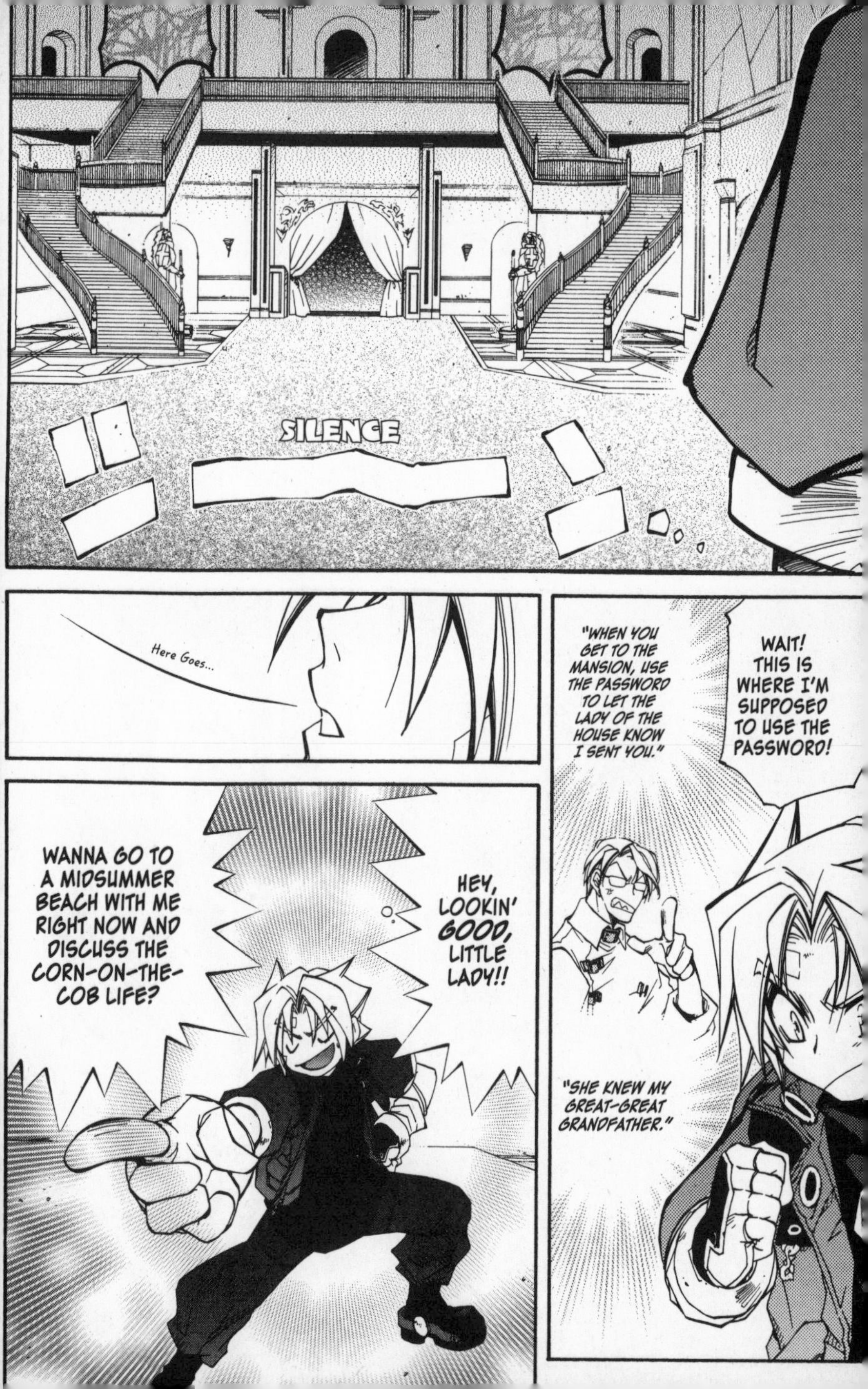
SILENCE
WAIT! THIS IS WHERE I'M SUPPOSED TO USE THE PASSWORD!
"WHEN YOU GET TO THE MANSION, USE THE PASSWORD TO LET THE LADY OF THE HOUSE KNOW I SENT YOU."
"SHE KNEW MY GREAT-GREAT GRANDFATHER."
Here Goes...
HEY, LOOKIN' GOOD, LITTLE LADY!!
WANNA GO TO A MIDSUMMER BEACH WITH ME RIGHT NOW AND DISCUSS THE CORN-ON-THE-COB LIFE?

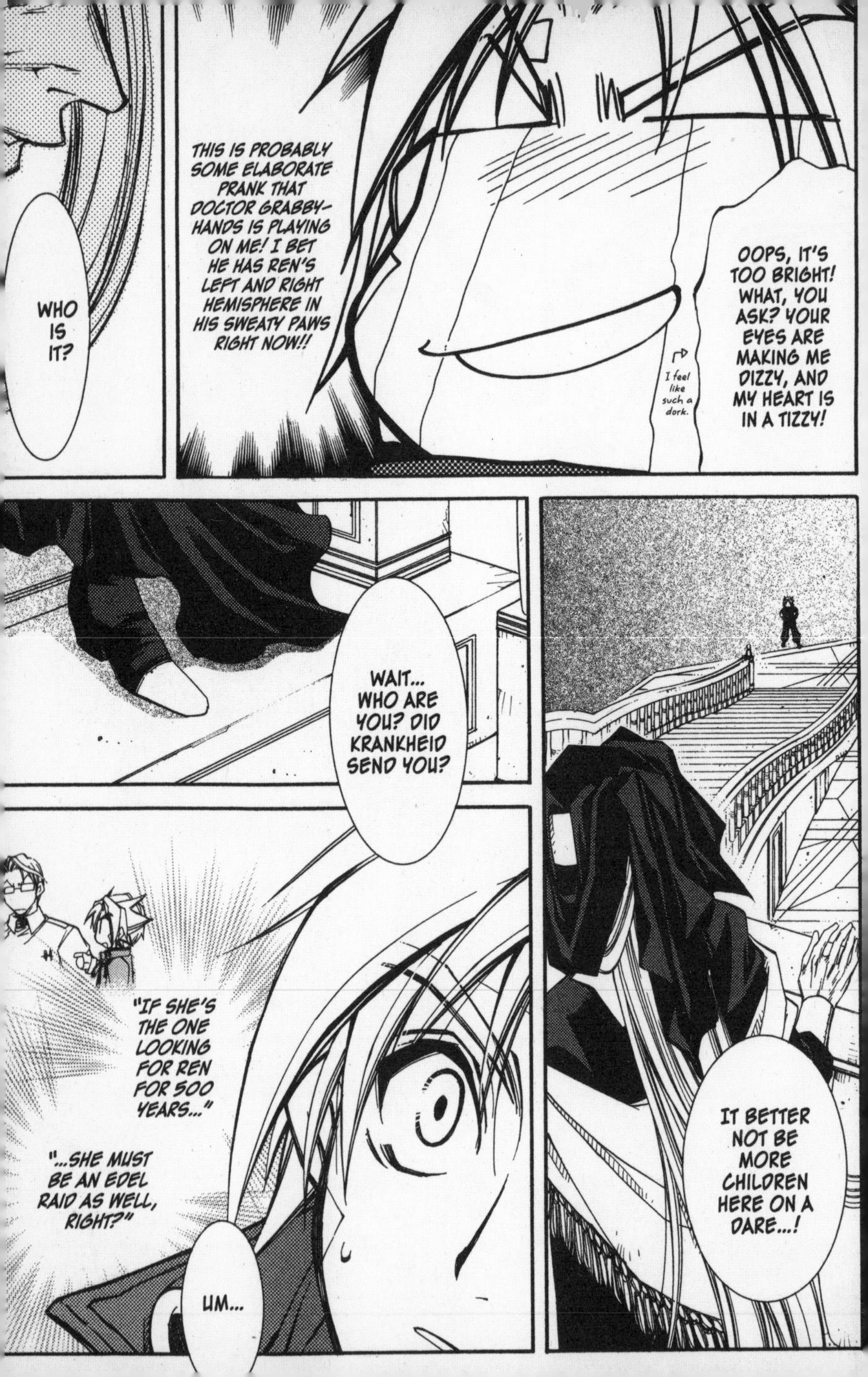
OOPS, IT'S TOO BRIGHT! WHAT, YOU ASK? YOUR EYES ARE MAKING ME DIZZY, AND MY HEART IS IN A TIZZY!
I feel like such a dork.
THIS IS PROBABLY SOME ELABORATE PRANK THAT DOCTOR GRABBY-HANDS IS PLAYING ON ME! I BET HE HAS REN'S LEFT AND RIGHT HEMISPHERE IN HIS SWEATY PAWS RIGHT NOW!!
WHO IS IT?
IT BETTER NOT BE MORE CHILDREN HERE ON A DARE...!
WAIT... WHO ARE YOU? DID KRANKHEID SEND YOU?
"IF SHE'S THE ONE LOOKING FOR REN FOR 500 YEARS..."
"...SHE MUST BE AN EDEL RAID AS WELL, RIGHT?"
UM...

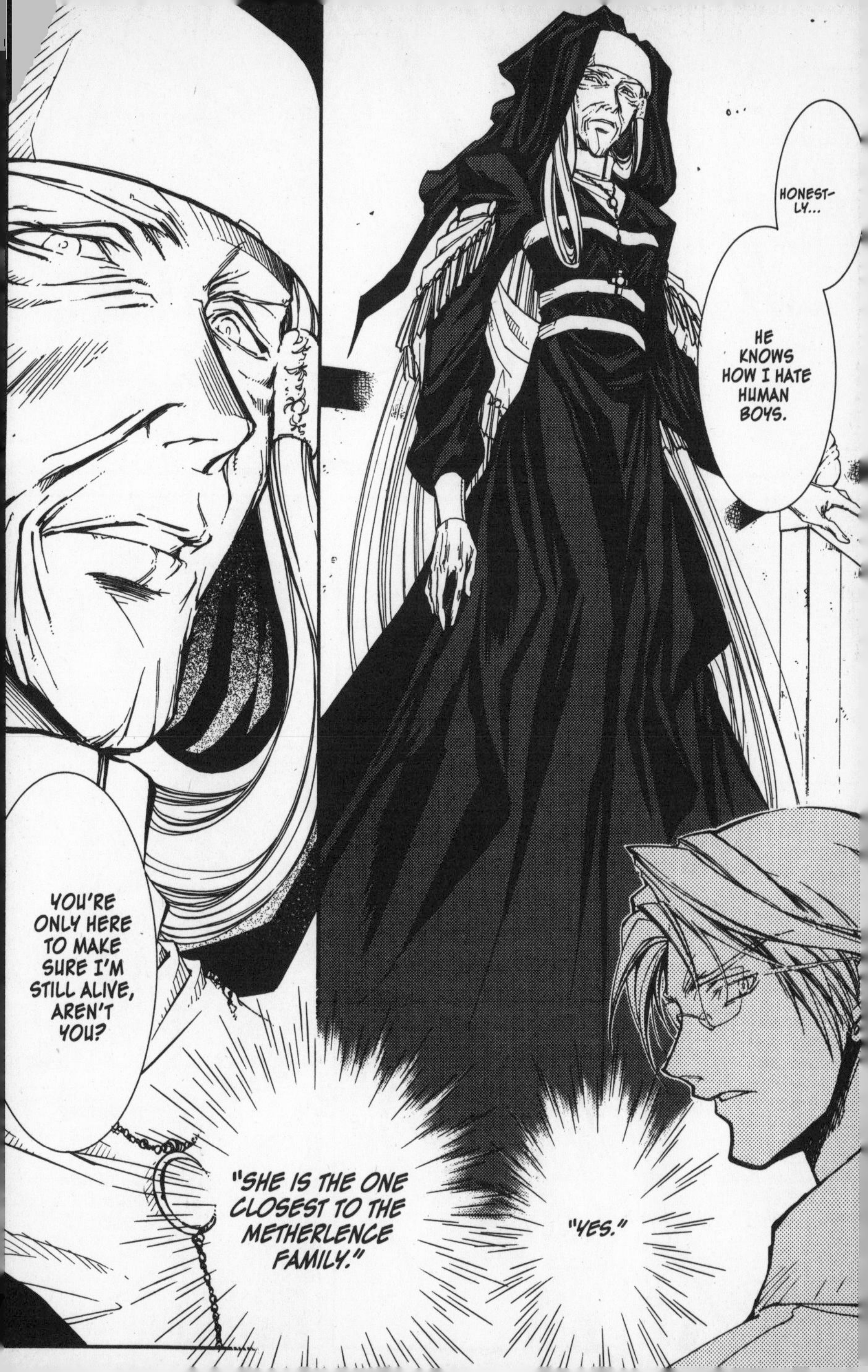
HONEST-LY...
HE KNOWS HOW I HATE HUMAN BOYS.
YOU'RE ONLY HERE TO MAKE SURE I'M STILL ALIVE, AREN'T YOU?
"SHE IS THE ONE CLOSEST TO THE METHERLENCE FAMILY."
"YES."

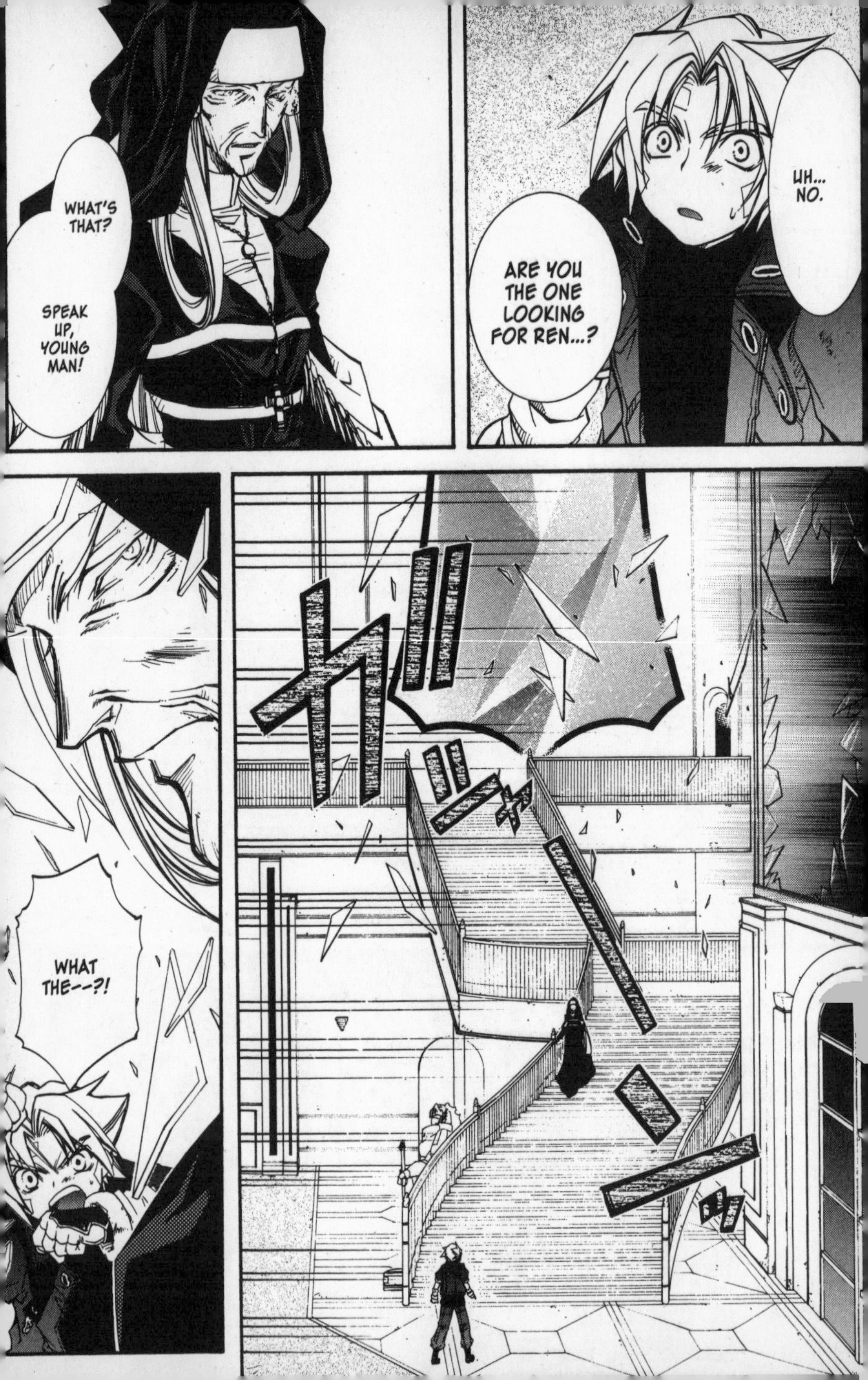
UH... NO.
ARE YOU THE ONE LOOKING FOR REN...?
WHAT'S THAT?
SPEAK UP, YOUNG MAN!
WHAT THE--?!

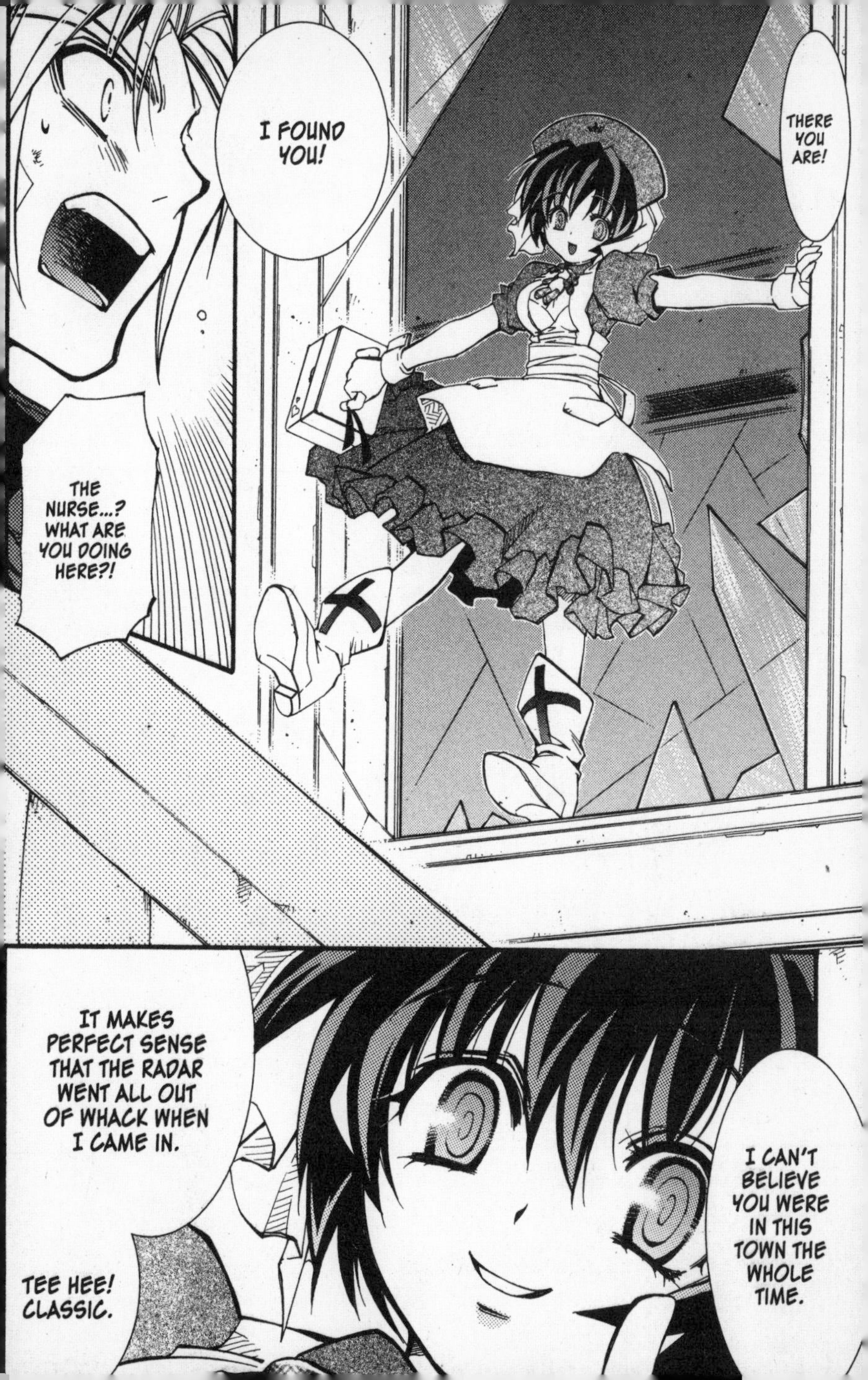
THERE YOU ARE!
I FOUND YOU!
THE NURSE...? WHAT ARE YOU DOING HERE?!
I CAN'T BELIEVE YOU WERE IN THIS TOWN THE WHOLE TIME.
IT MAKES PERFECT SENSE THAT THE RADAR WENT ALL OUT OF WHACK WHEN I CAME IN.
TEE HEE! CLASSIC.

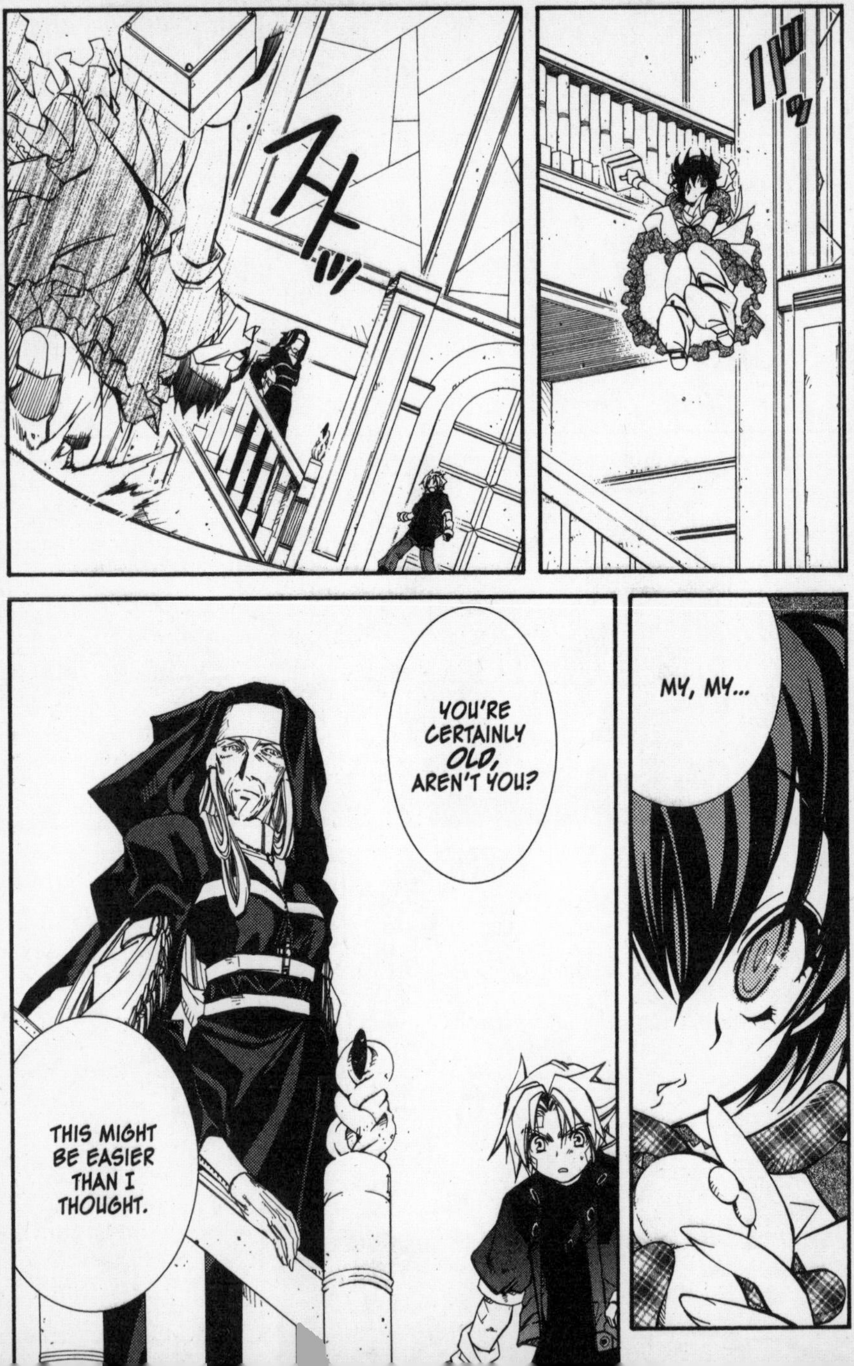
MY, MY...
YOU'RE CERTAINLY OLD, AREN'T YOU?
THIS MIGHT BE EASIER THAN I THOUGHT.

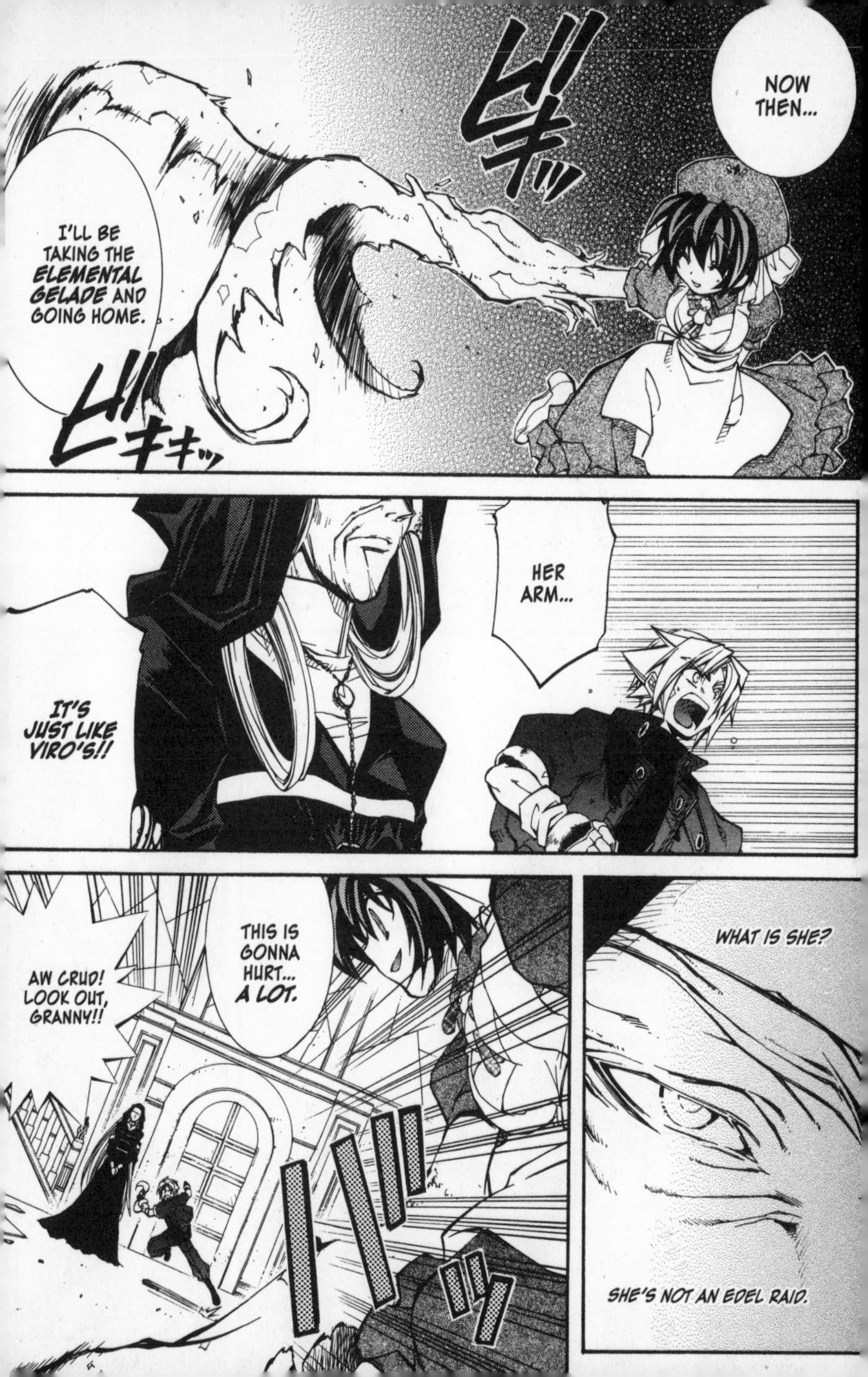
NOW THEN...
ビキッ
I'LL BE TAKING THE ELEMENTAL GELADE AND GOING HOME.
ビキキッ
HER ARM...
IT'S JUST LIKE VIRO'S!!
WHAT IS SHE?
SHE'S NOT AN EDEL RAID.
THIS IS GONNA HURT... A LOT.
AW CRUD! LOOK OUT, GRANNY!!

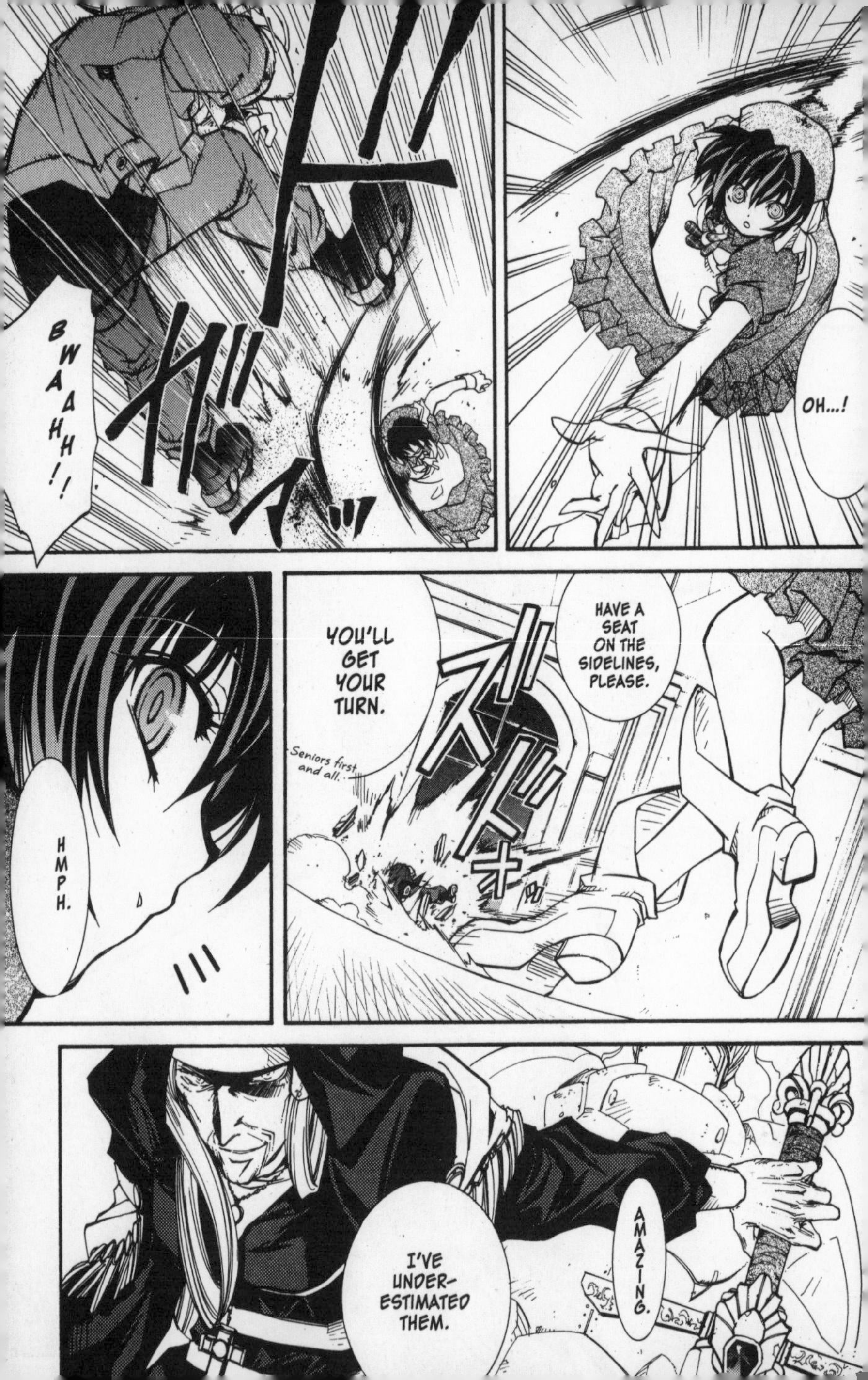
OH...!
BWAAHH!!
HAVE A SEAT ON THE SIDELINES, PLEASE.
YOU'LL GET YOUR TURN.
Seniors first and all.
HMPH.
AMAZING.
I'VE UNDER-ESTIMATED THEM.

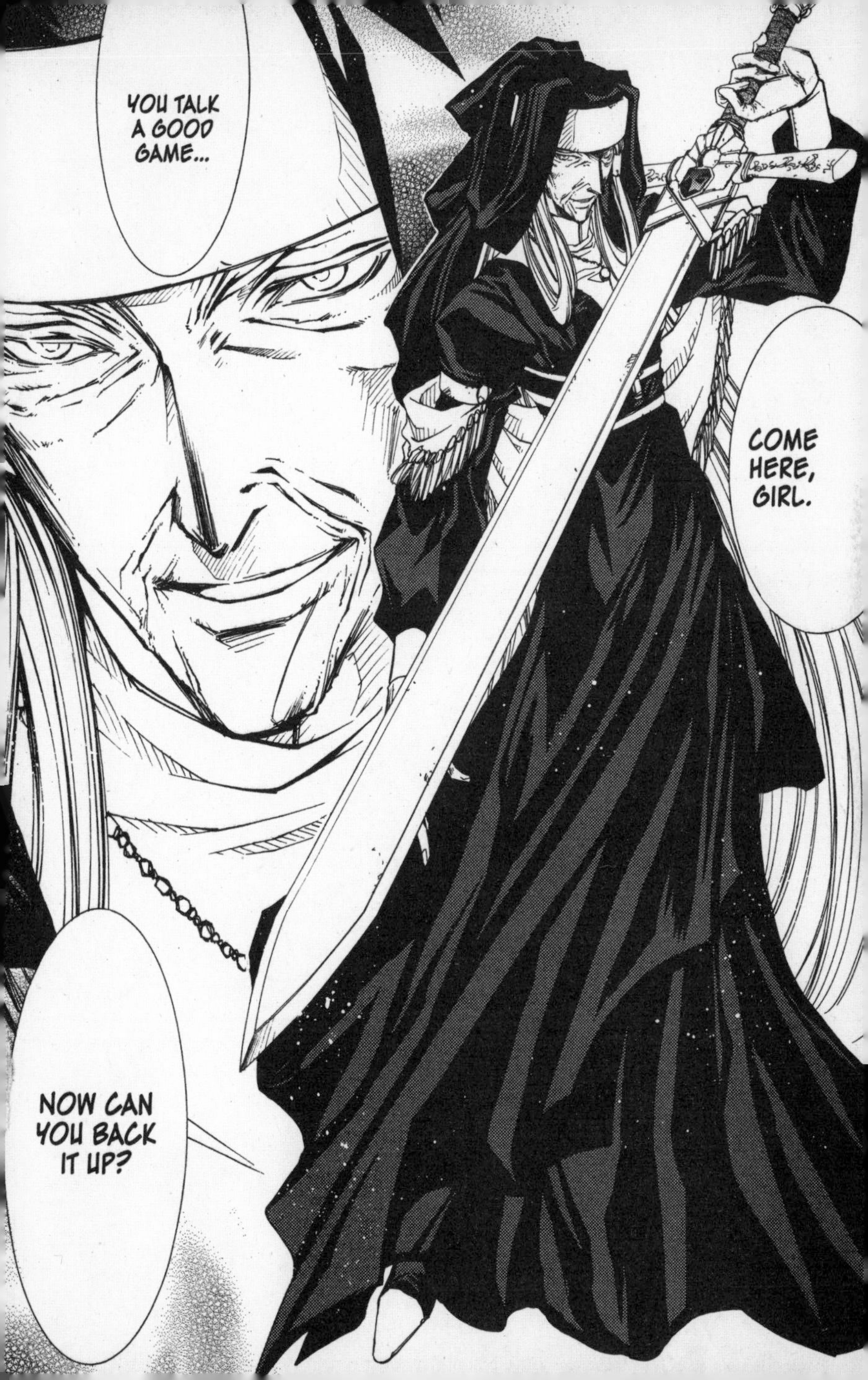
YOU TALK A GOOD GAME...
COME HERE, GIRL.
NOW CAN YOU BACK IT UP?

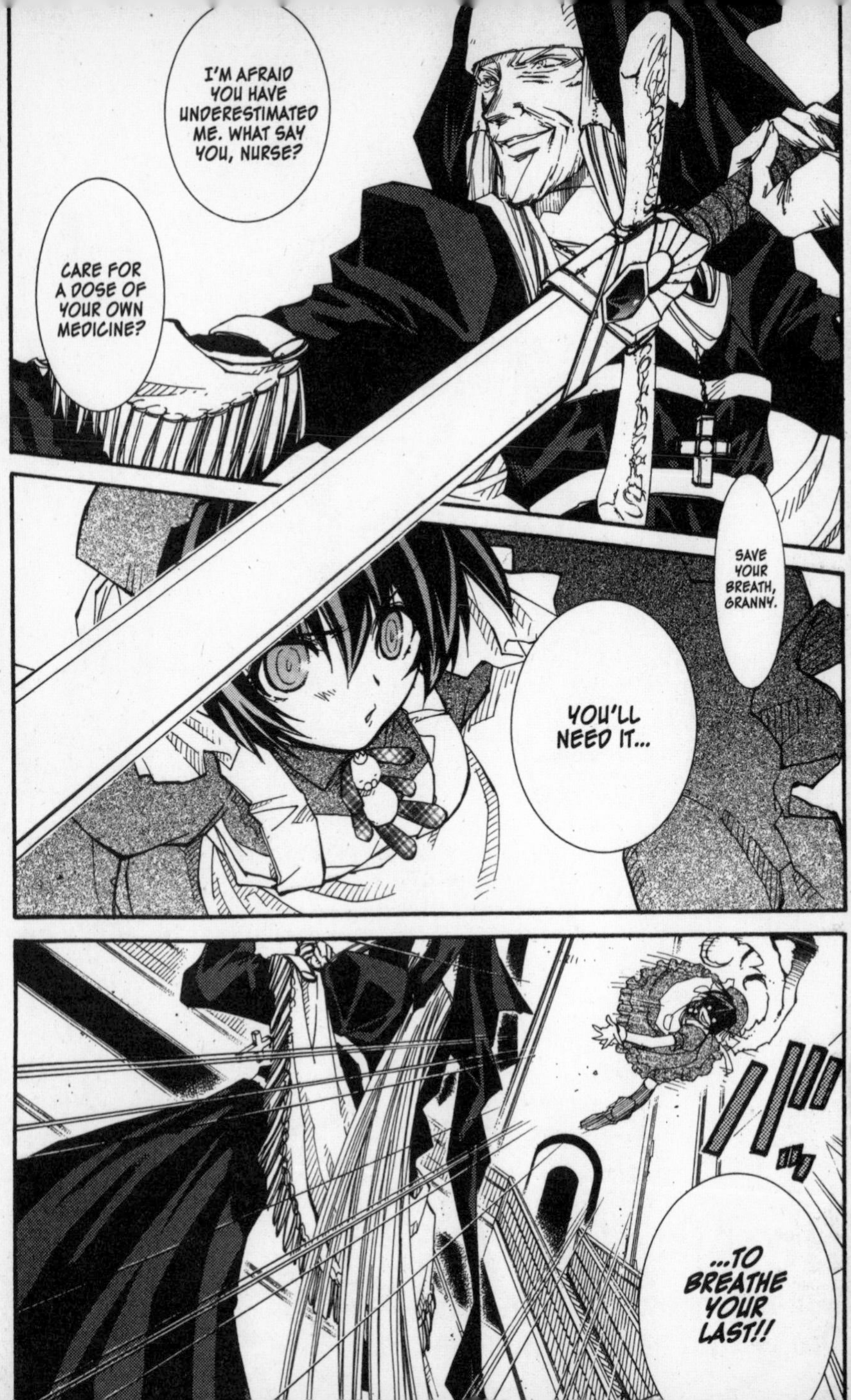
I'M AFRAID YOU HAVE UNDERESTIMATED ME. WHAT SAY YOU, NURSE?
CARE FOR A DOSE OF YOUR OWN MEDICINE?
SAVE YOUR BREATH, GRANNY.
YOU'LL NEED IT...
...TO BREATHE YOUR LAST!!

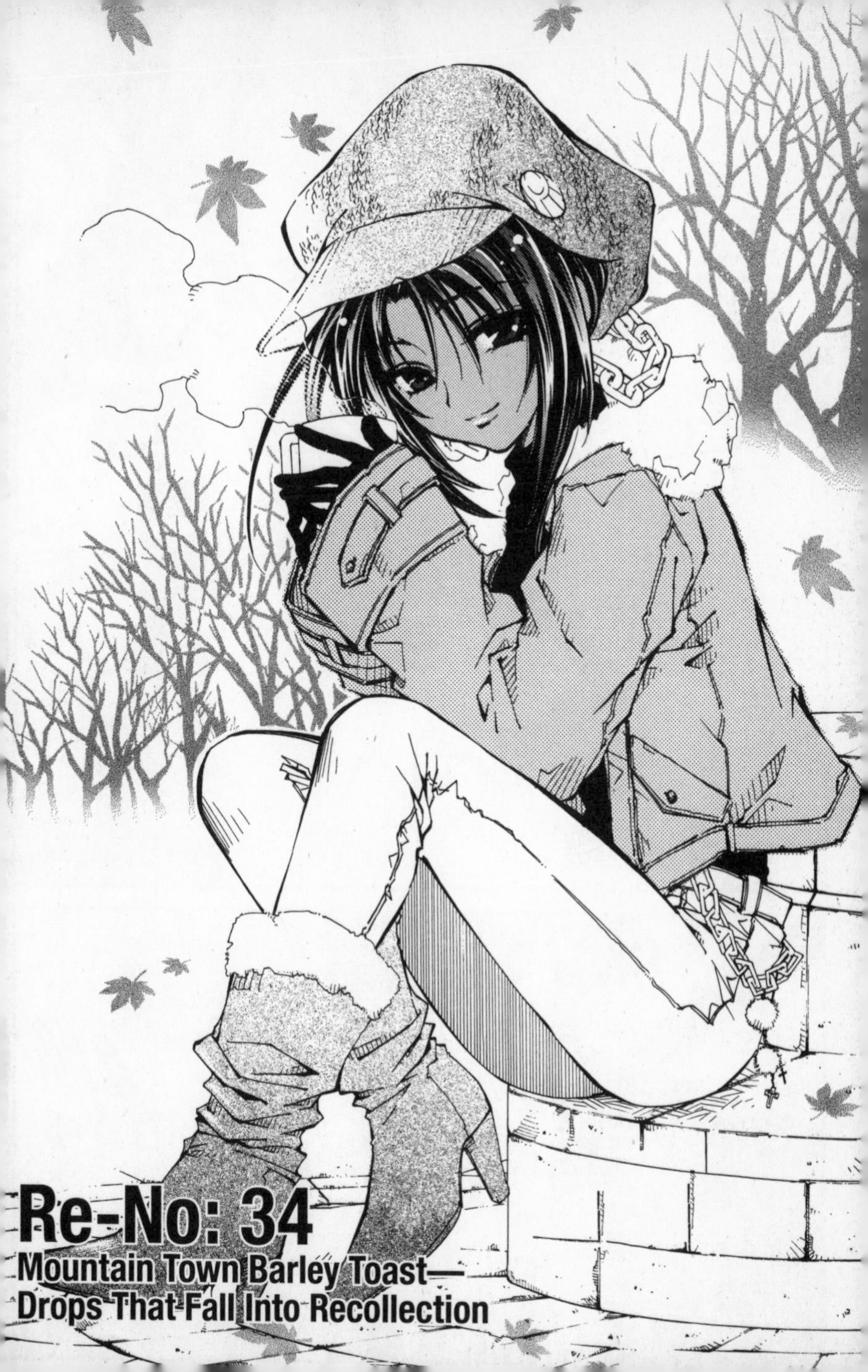

Re-No: 34
Mountain Town Barley Toast—Drops That Fall Into Recollection

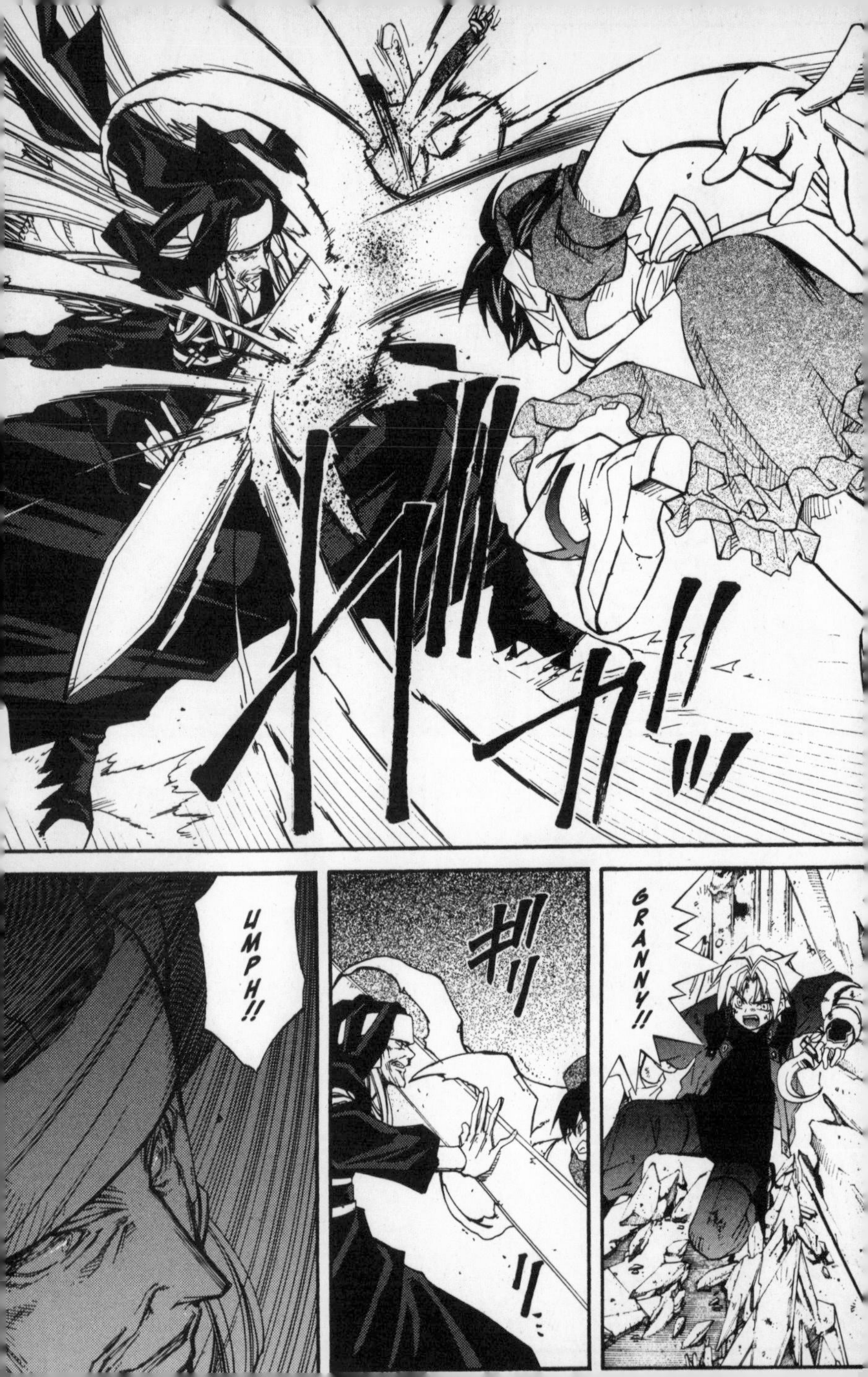
GRANNY!!
UMPH!!

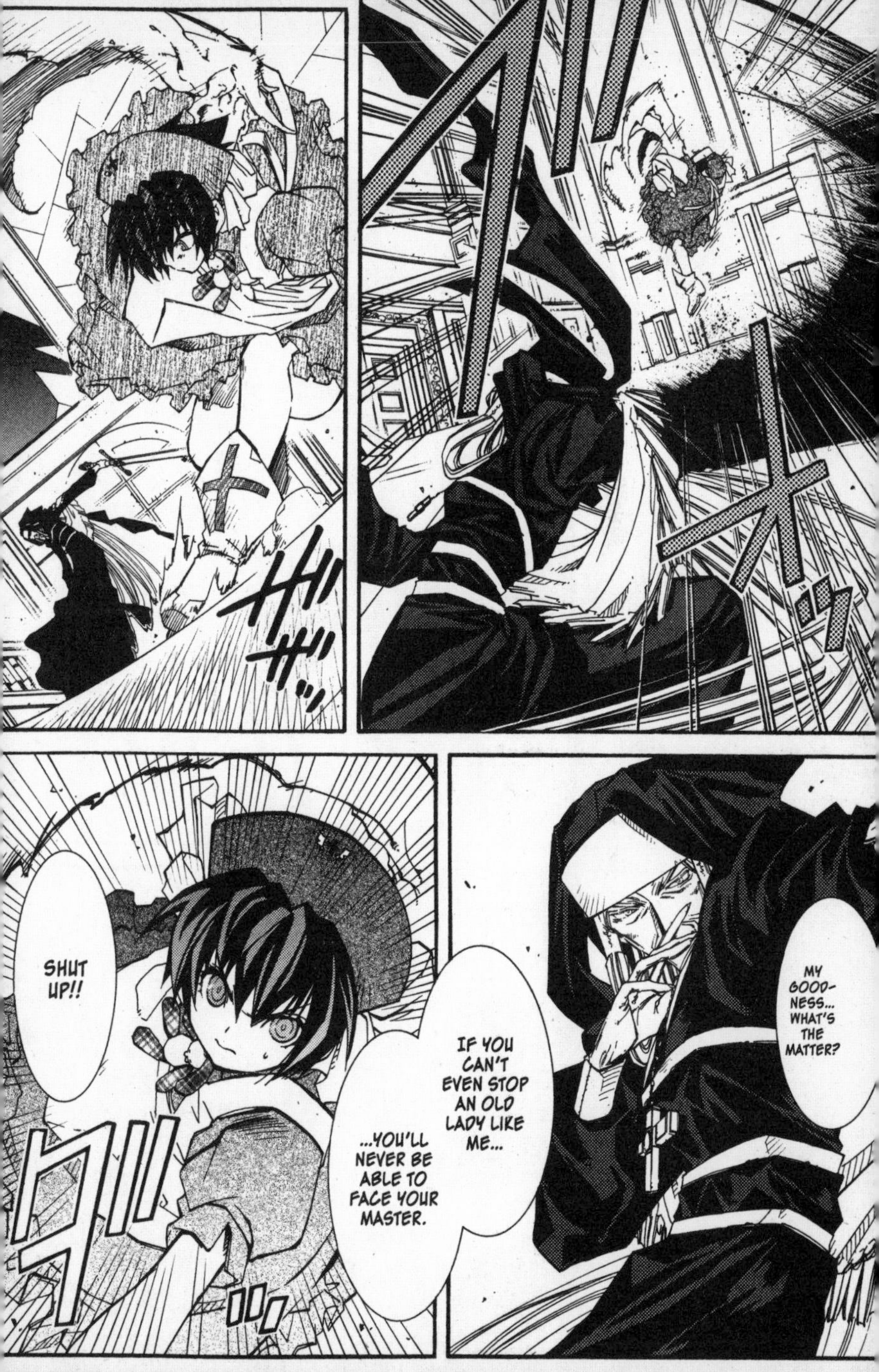
MY GOODNESS... WHAT'S THE MATTER?
IF YOU CAN'T EVEN STOP AN OLD LADY LIKE ME...
...YOU'LL NEVER BE ABLE TO FACE YOUR MASTER.
SHUT UP!!

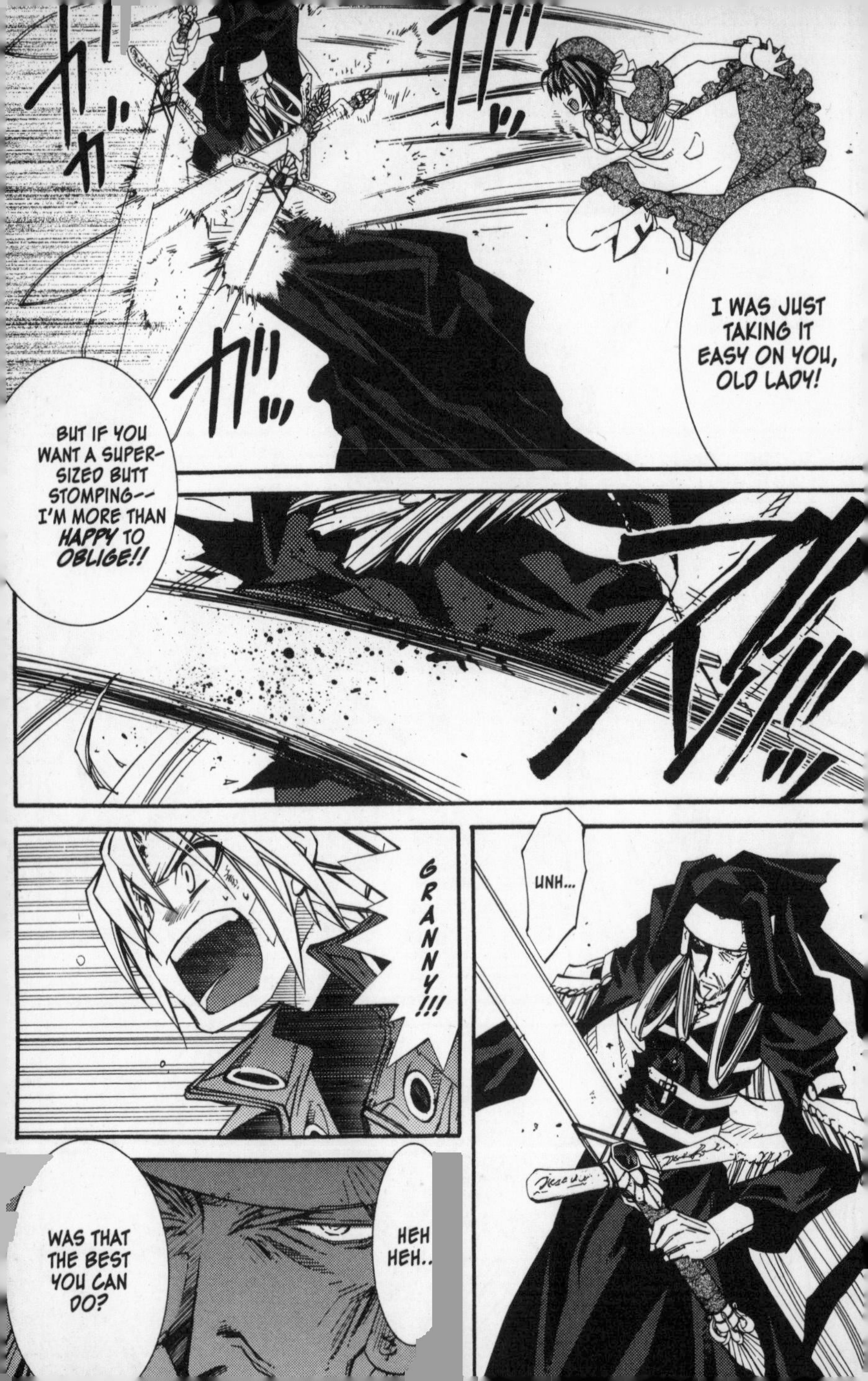
I WAS JUST TAKING IT EASY ON YOU, OLD LADY!
BUT IF YOU WANT A SUPER-SIZED BUTT STOMPING-- I'M MORE THAN HAPPY TO OBLIGE!!
UNH...
GRANNY!!!
HEH HEH...
WAS THAT THE BEST YOU CAN DO?

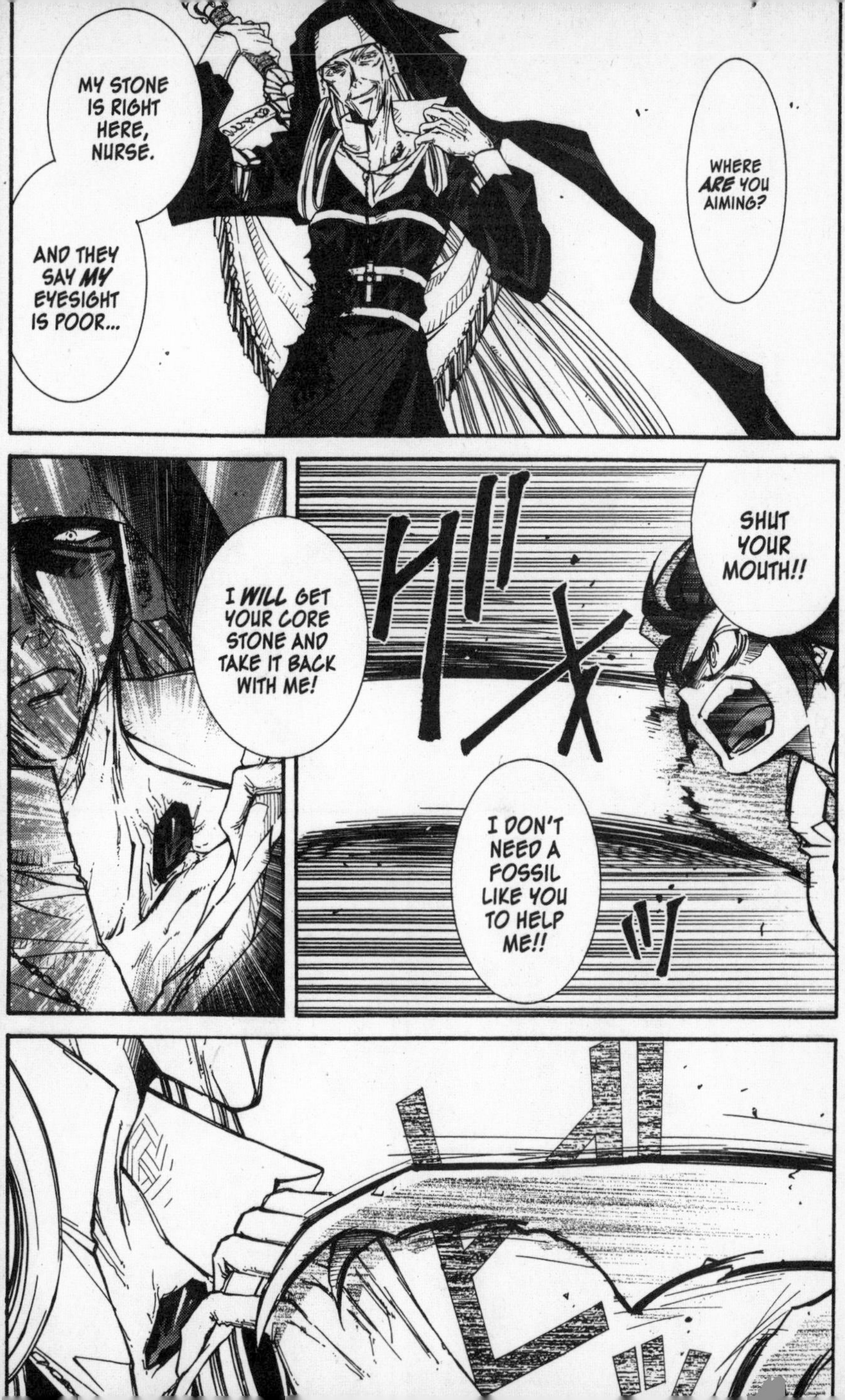
WHERE *ARE* YOU AIMING?
MY STONE IS RIGHT HERE, NURSE.
AND THEY SAY *MY* EYESIGHT IS POOR...
SHUT YOUR MOUTH!!
I DON'T NEED A FOSSIL LIKE YOU TO HELP ME!!
I *WILL* GET YOUR CORE STONE AND TAKE IT BACK WITH ME!

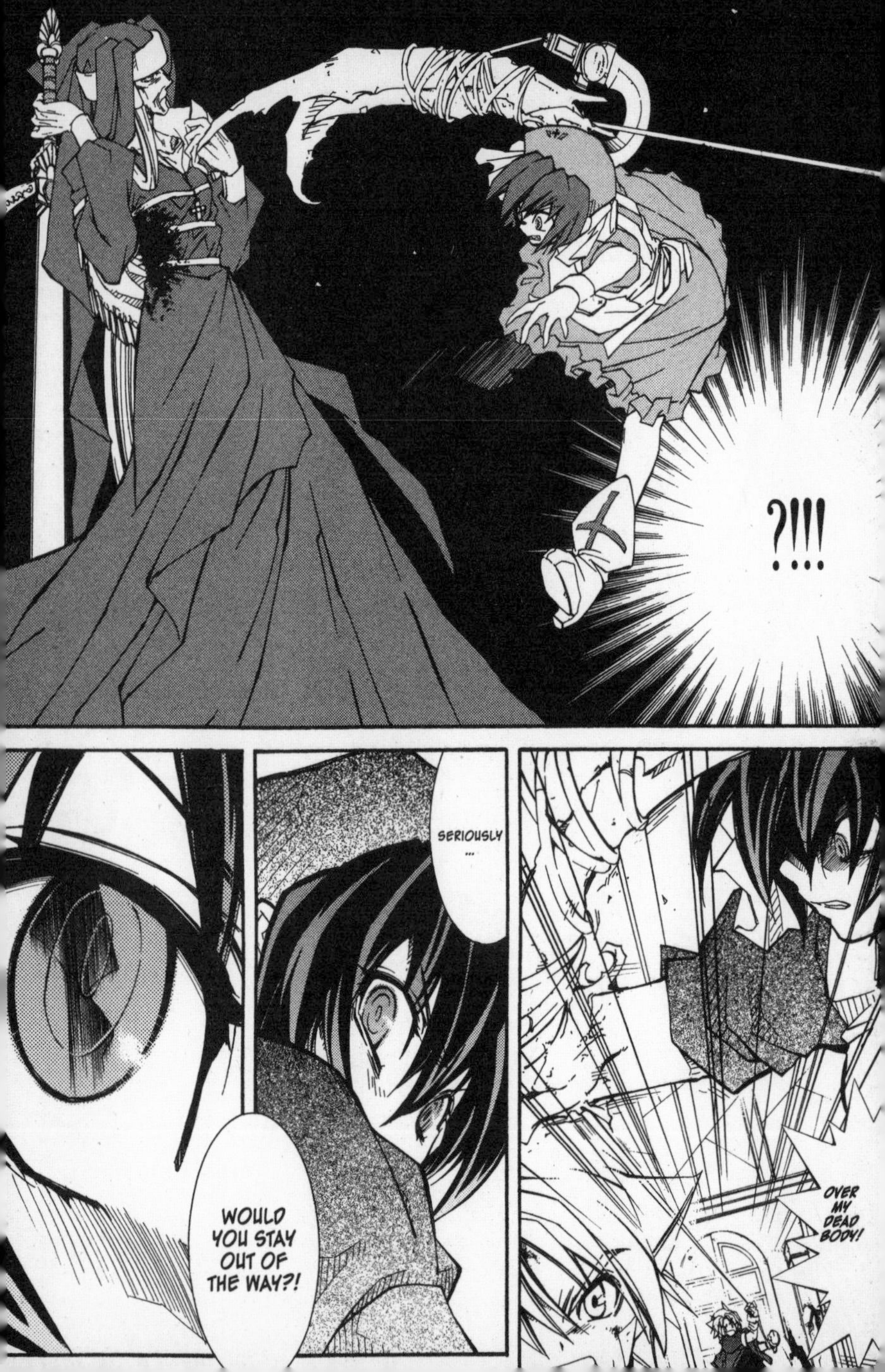
?!!!
OVER MY DEAD BODY!
SERIOUSLY...
WOULD YOU STAY OUT OF THE WAY?!

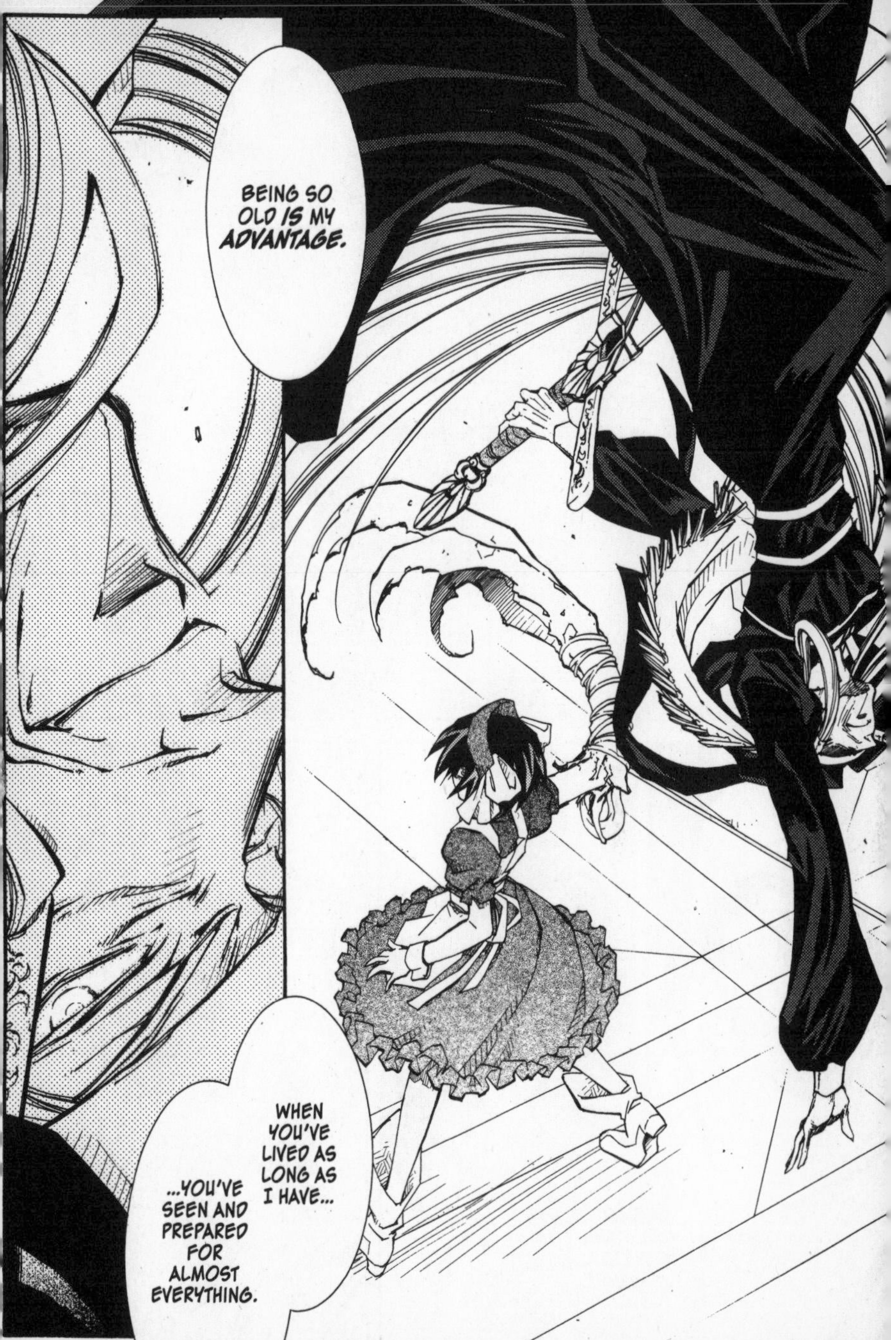
BEING SO OLD IS MY ADVANTAGE.
WHEN YOU'VE LIVED AS LONG AS I HAVE...
...YOU'VE SEEN AND PREPARED FOR ALMOST EVERYTHING.

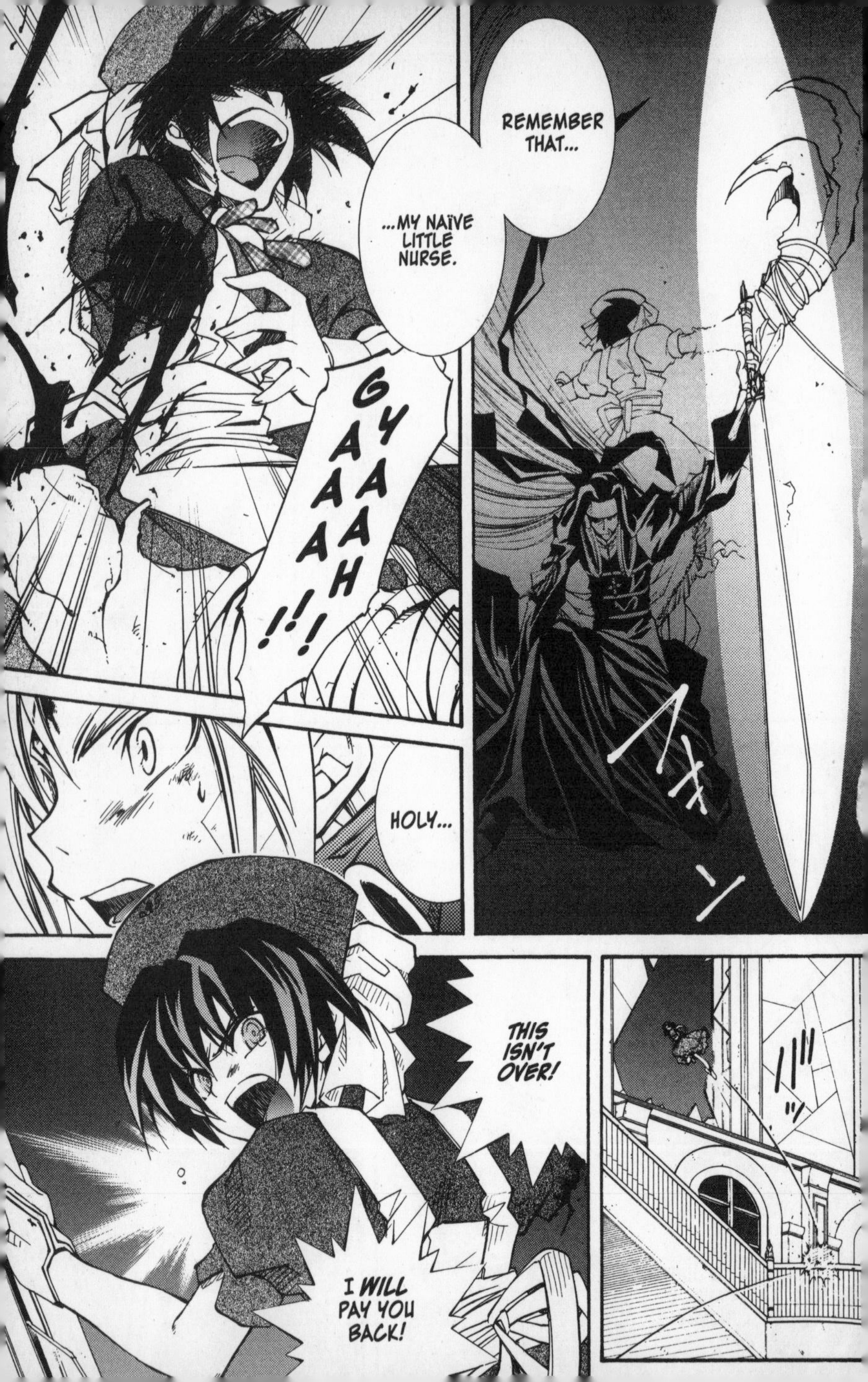
REMEMBER THAT...
...MY NAÏVE LITTLE NURSE.
GYAAAAAAH!!!
HOLY...
THIS ISN'T OVER!
I WILL PAY YOU BACK!

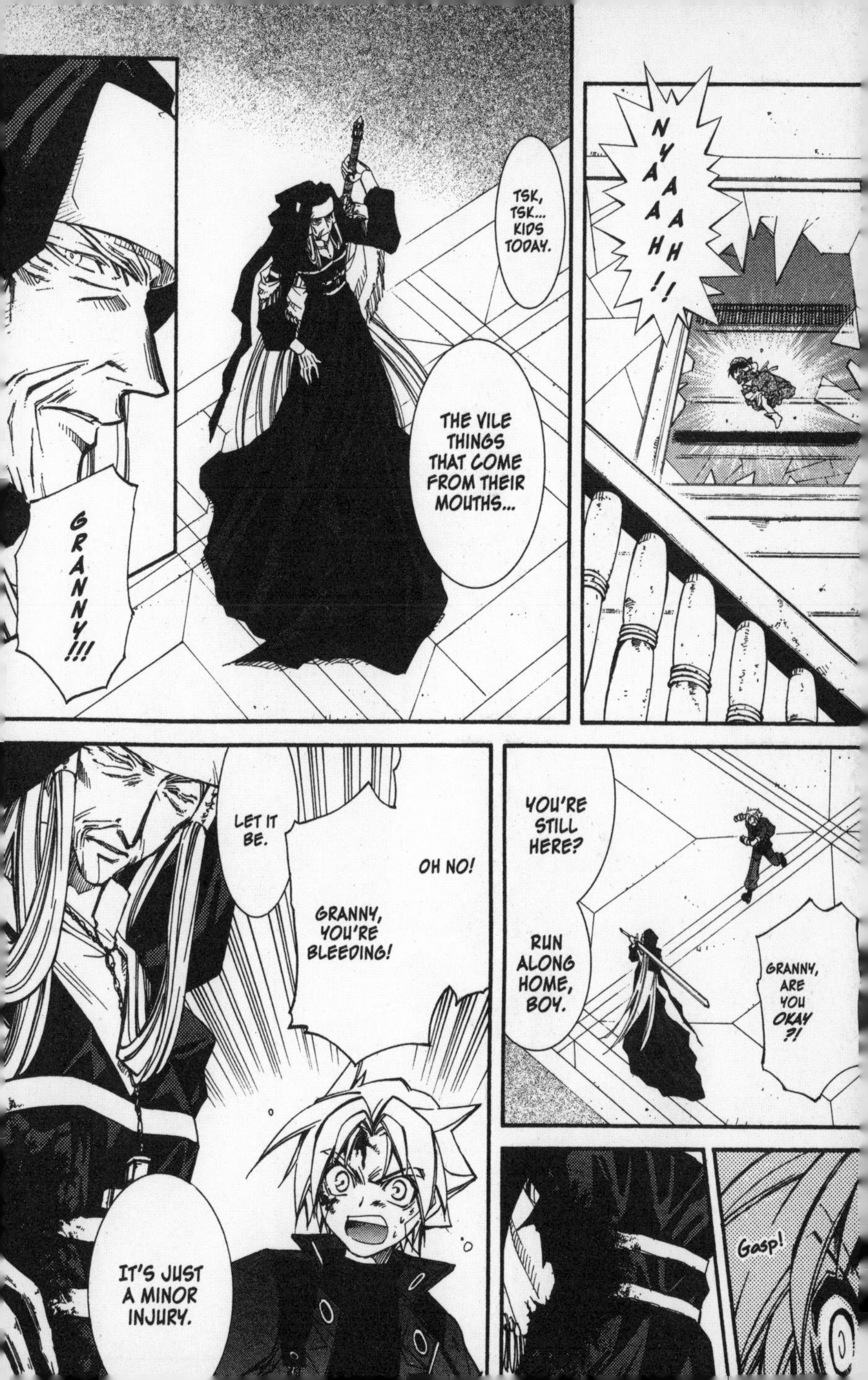
NYAAAAAH!!
TSK, TSK... KIDS TODAY.
THE VILE THINGS THAT COME FROM THEIR MOUTHS...
GRANNY!!!
GRANNY, ARE YOU OKAY?!
YOU'RE STILL HERE?
RUN ALONG HOME, BOY.
Gasp!
OH NO!
GRANNY, YOU'RE BLEEDING!
LET IT BE.
IT'S JUST A MINOR INJURY.

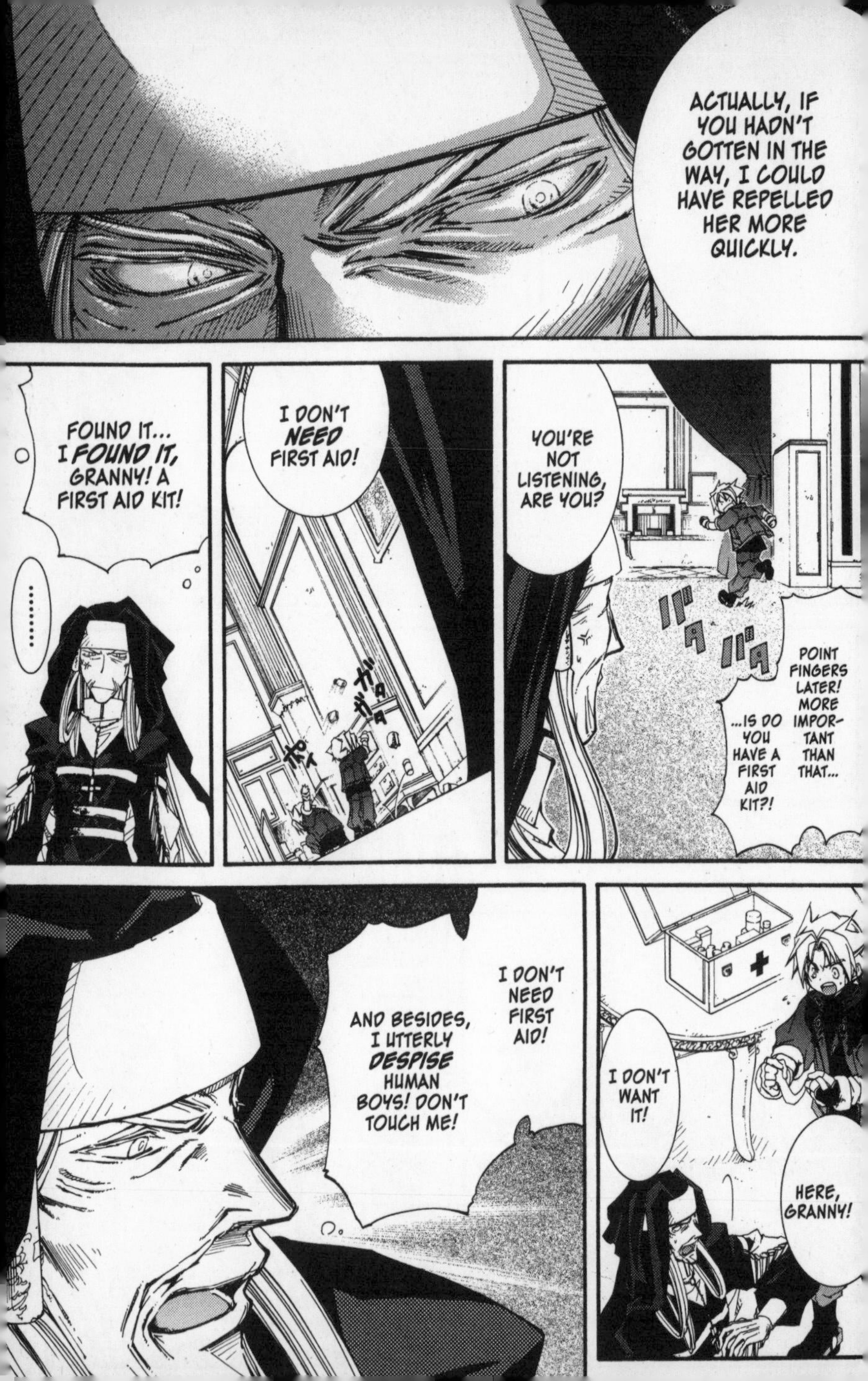
ACTUALLY, IF YOU HADN'T GOTTEN IN THE WAY, I COULD HAVE REPELLED HER MORE QUICKLY.
YOU'RE NOT LISTENING, ARE YOU?
バタ バタ
POINT FINGERS LATER! MORE IMPORTANT THAN THAT...
...IS DO YOU HAVE A FIRST AID KIT?!
I DON'T **NEED** FIRST AID!
ガタ ガタ
ポイ
FOUND IT... I ***FOUND IT,*** GRANNY! A FIRST AID KIT!
......
HERE, GRANNY!
I DON'T WANT IT!
I DON'T NEED FIRST AID!
AND BESIDES, I UTTERLY ***DESPISE*** HUMAN BOYS! DON'T TOUCH ME!

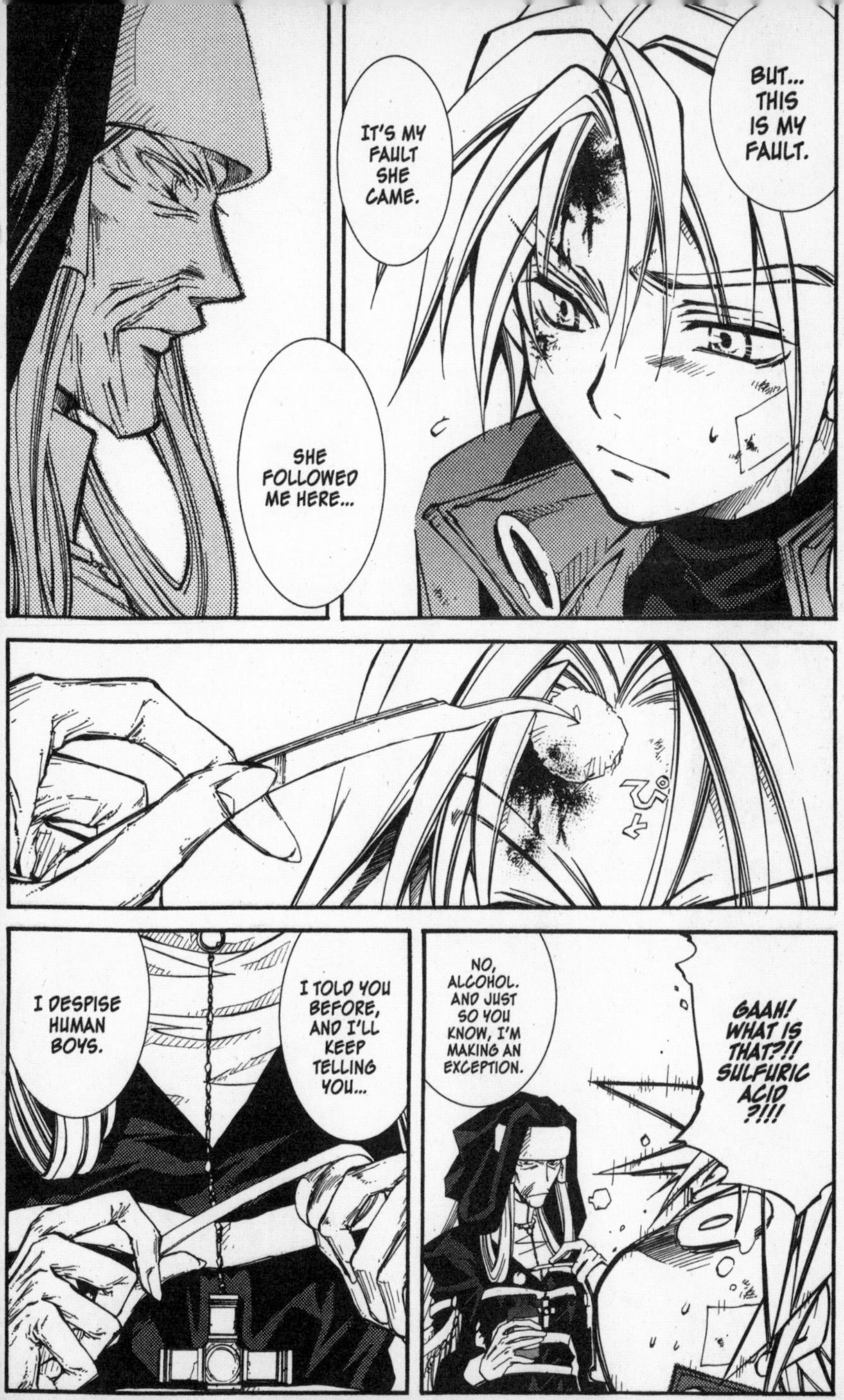
BUT... THIS IS MY FAULT.
IT'S MY FAULT SHE CAME.
SHE FOLLOWED ME HERE...
ぴと
GAAH! WHAT IS THAT?!! SULFURIC ACID?!!!
NO, ALCOHOL. AND JUST SO YOU KNOW, I'M MAKING AN EXCEPTION.
I TOLD YOU BEFORE, AND I'LL KEEP TELLING YOU...
I DESPISE HUMAN BOYS.

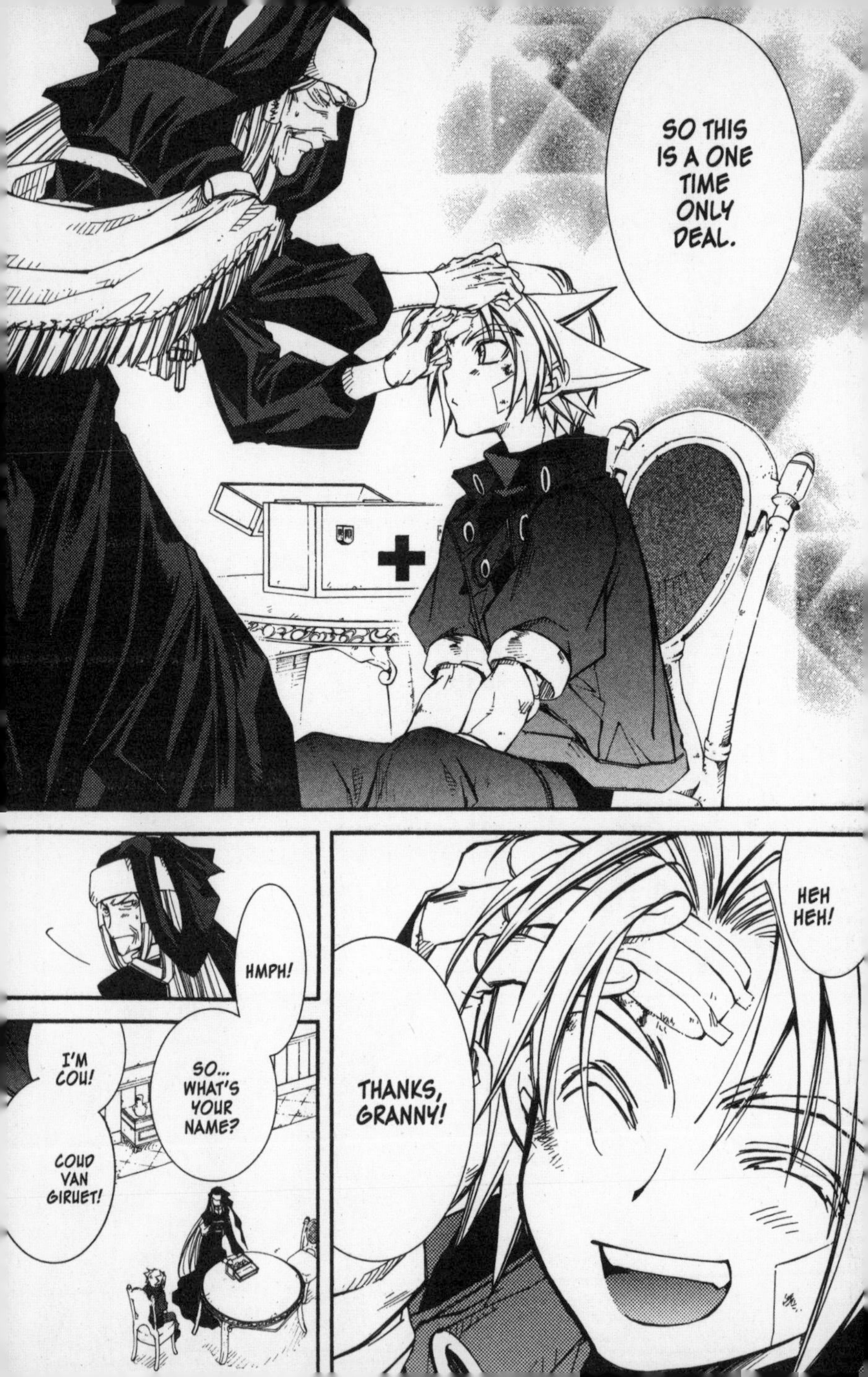
SO THIS IS A ONE TIME ONLY DEAL.
HEH HEH!
THANKS, GRANNY!
HMPH!
SO... WHAT'S YOUR NAME?
I'M COU!
COUD VAN GIRUET!

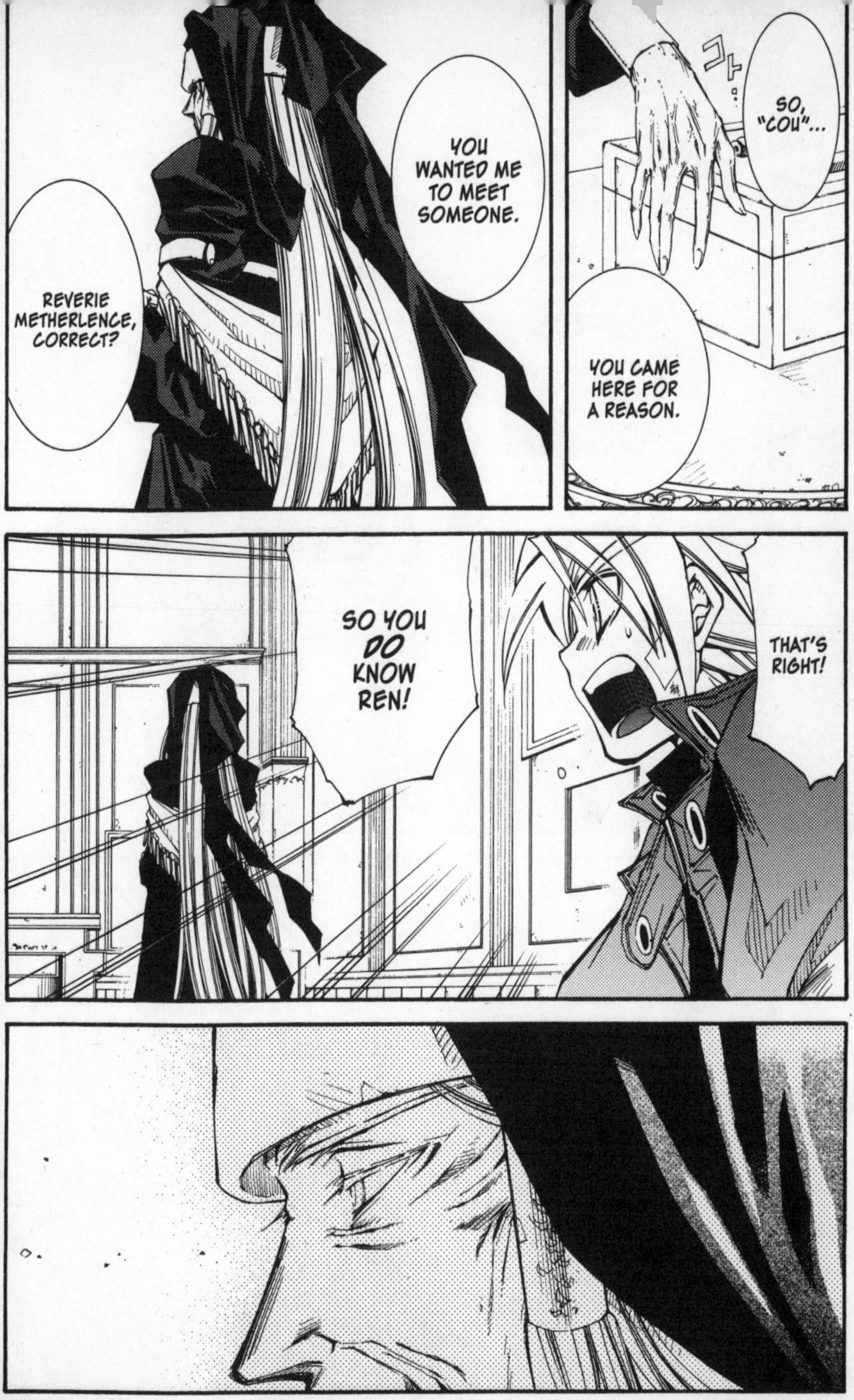
コト
SO, "COU"...
YOU CAME HERE FOR A REASON.
YOU WANTED ME TO MEET SOMEONE.
REVERIE METHERLENCE, CORRECT?
THAT'S RIGHT!
SO YOU *DO* KNOW REN!

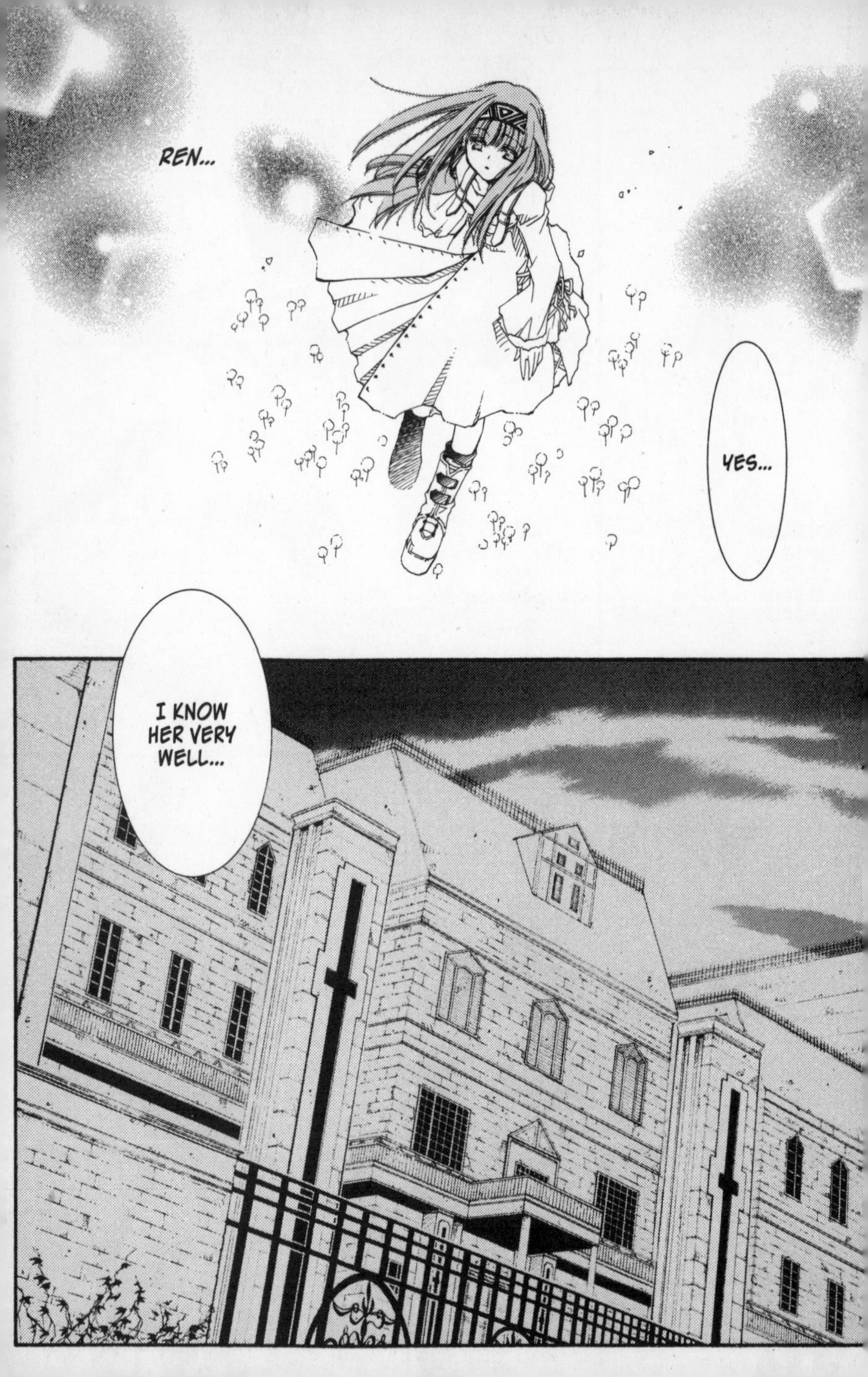
REN...
YES...
I KNOW HER VERY WELL...

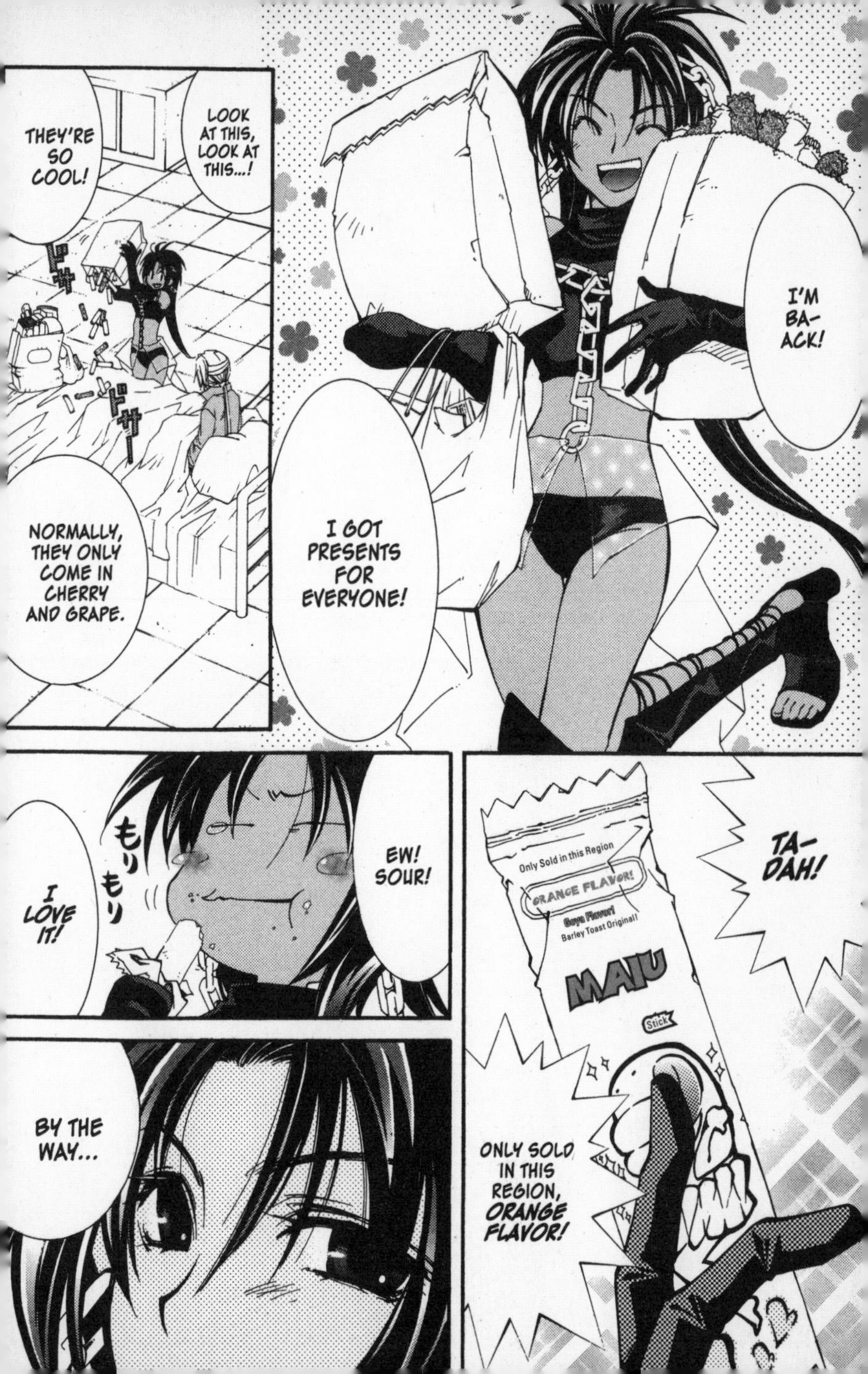
I'M BA-ACK!
I GOT PRESENTS FOR EVERYONE!
LOOK AT THIS, LOOK AT THIS...!
THEY'RE SO COOL!
NORMALLY, THEY ONLY COME IN CHERRY AND GRAPE.
TA-DAH!
Only Sold in this Region
ORANGE FLAVOR!
Goya Flavor!
Barley Toast Original!
MAIU
Stick
ONLY SOLD IN THIS REGION, ORANGE FLAVOR!
EW! SOUR!
もり もり
I LOVE IT!
BY THE WAY...

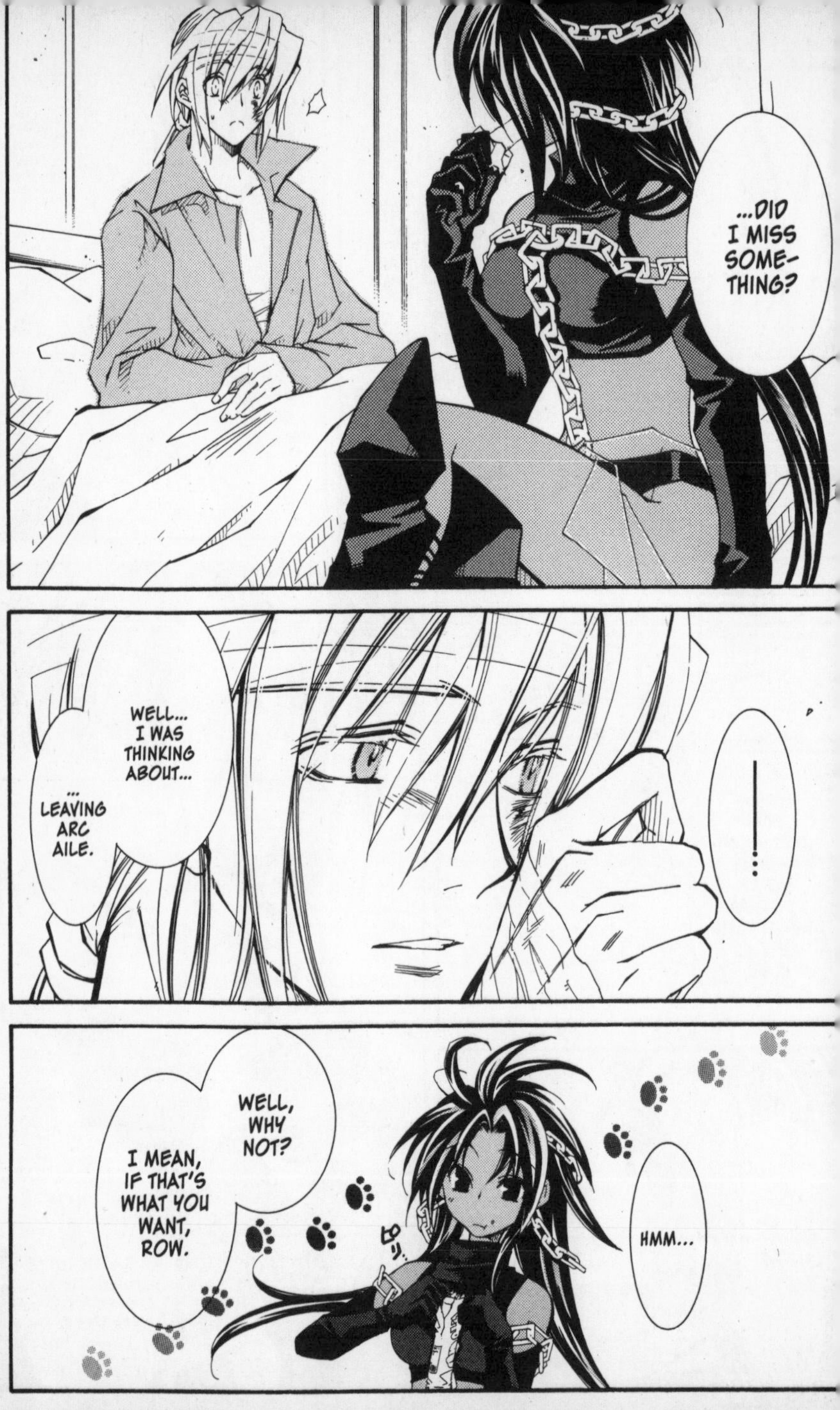
...DID I MISS SOMETHING?
!...
WELL... I WAS THINKING ABOUT...
... LEAVING ARC AILE.
HMM...
WELL, WHY NOT?
I MEAN, IF THAT'S WHAT YOU WANT, ROW.

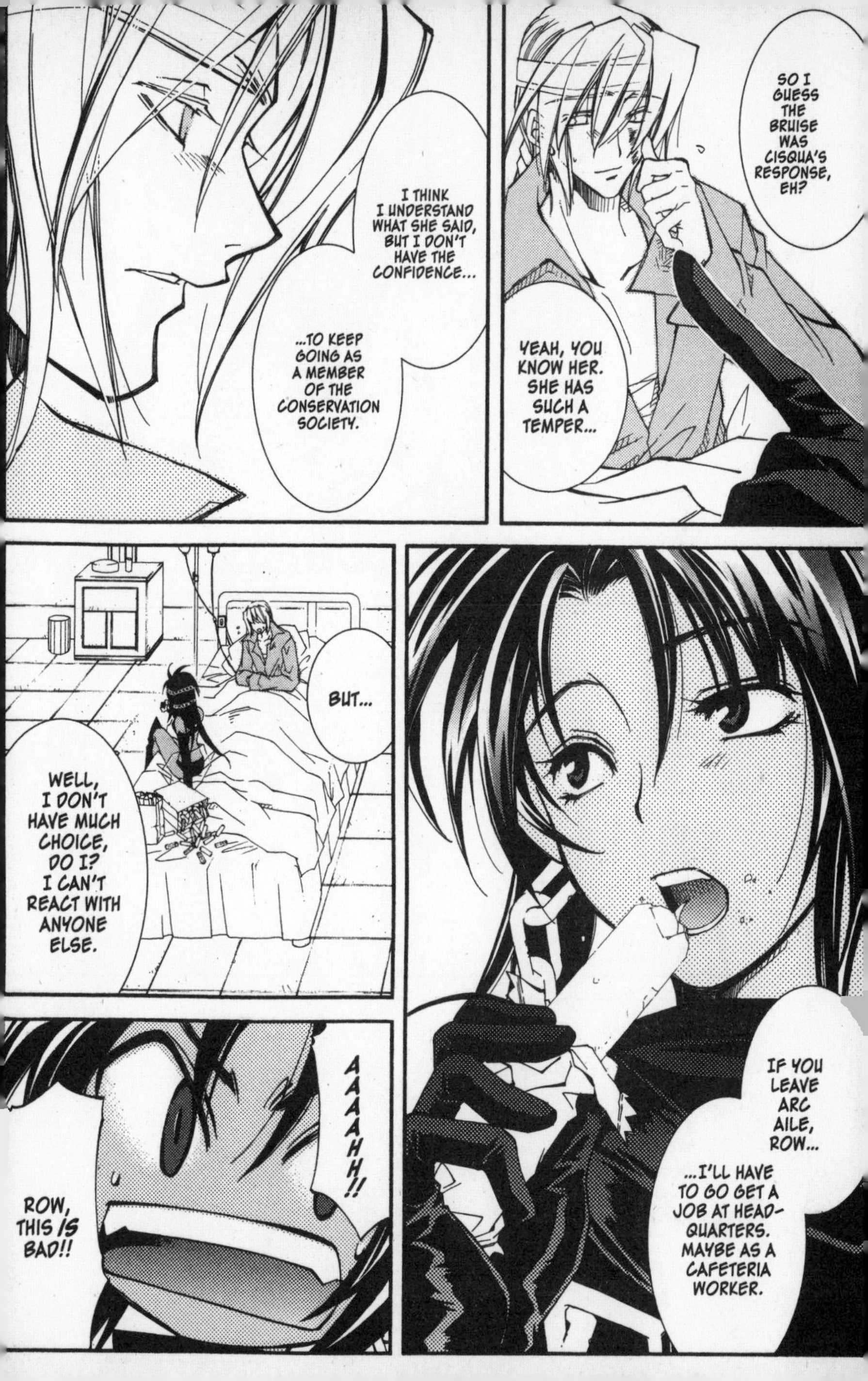
SO I GUESS THE BRUISE WAS CISQUA'S RESPONSE, EH?
YEAH, YOU KNOW HER. SHE HAS SUCH A TEMPER...
I THINK I UNDERSTAND WHAT SHE SAID, BUT I DON'T HAVE THE CONFIDENCE...
...TO KEEP GOING AS A MEMBER OF THE CONSERVATION SOCIETY.
IF YOU LEAVE ARC AILE, ROW...
...I'LL HAVE TO GO GET A JOB AT HEAD-QUARTERS. MAYBE AS A CAFETERIA WORKER.
BUT...
WELL, I DON'T HAVE MUCH CHOICE, DO I? I CAN'T REACT WITH ANYONE ELSE.
AAAAHH!!
ROW, THIS *IS* BAD!!

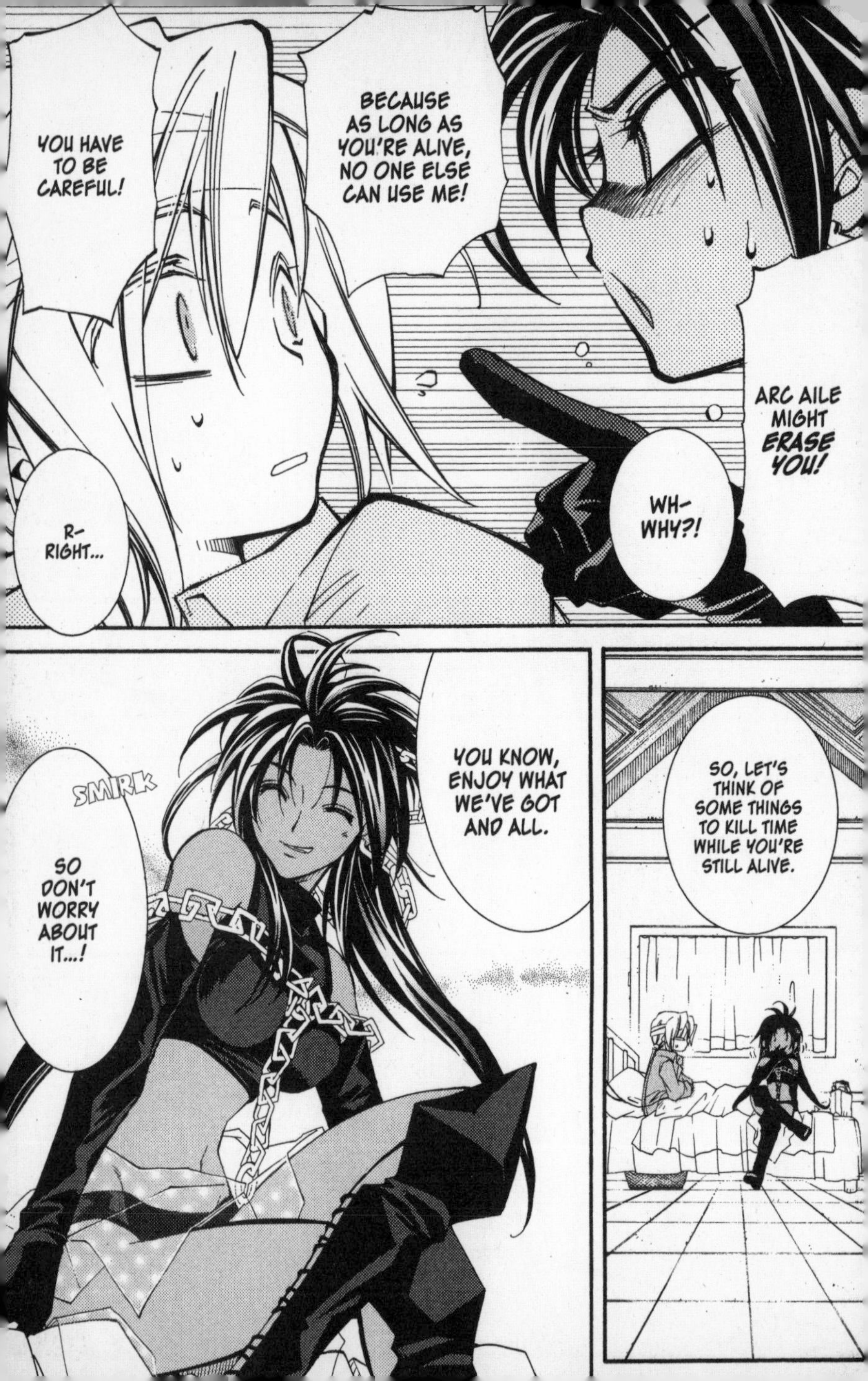
ARC AILE MIGHT ERASE YOU!
WH- WHY?!
BECAUSE AS LONG AS YOU'RE ALIVE, NO ONE ELSE CAN USE ME!
YOU HAVE TO BE CAREFUL!
R- RIGHT...
SO, LET'S THINK OF SOME THINGS TO KILL TIME WHILE YOU'RE STILL ALIVE.
YOU KNOW, ENJOY WHAT WE'VE GOT AND ALL.
SMIRK
SO DON'T WORRY ABOUT IT...!

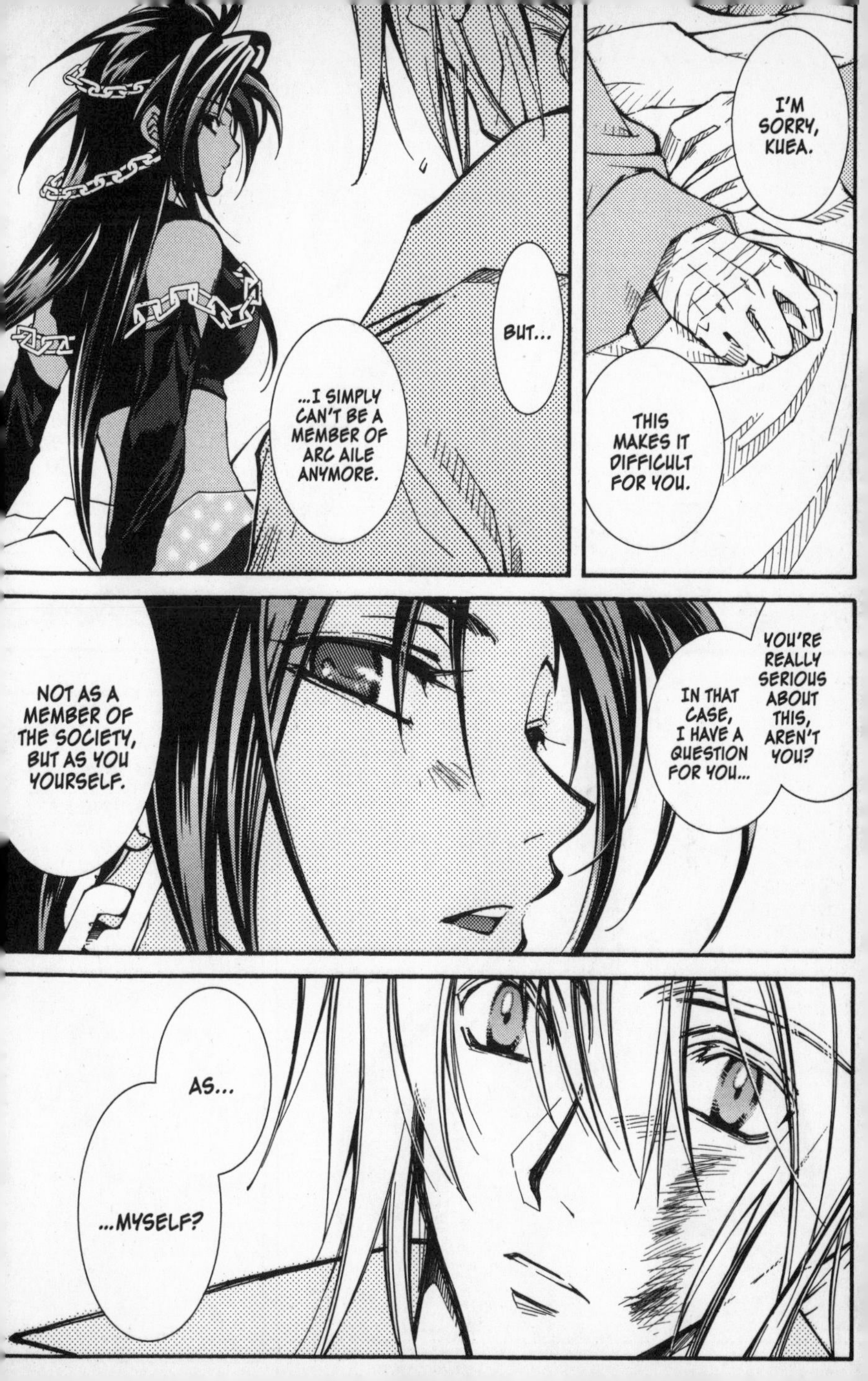
I'M SORRY, KUEA.
THIS MAKES IT DIFFICULT FOR YOU.
BUT...
...I SIMPLY CAN'T BE A MEMBER OF ARC AILE ANYMORE.
YOU'RE REALLY SERIOUS ABOUT THIS, AREN'T YOU?
IN THAT CASE, I HAVE A QUESTION FOR YOU...
NOT AS A MEMBER OF THE SOCIETY, BUT AS YOU YOURSELF.
AS...
...MYSELF?

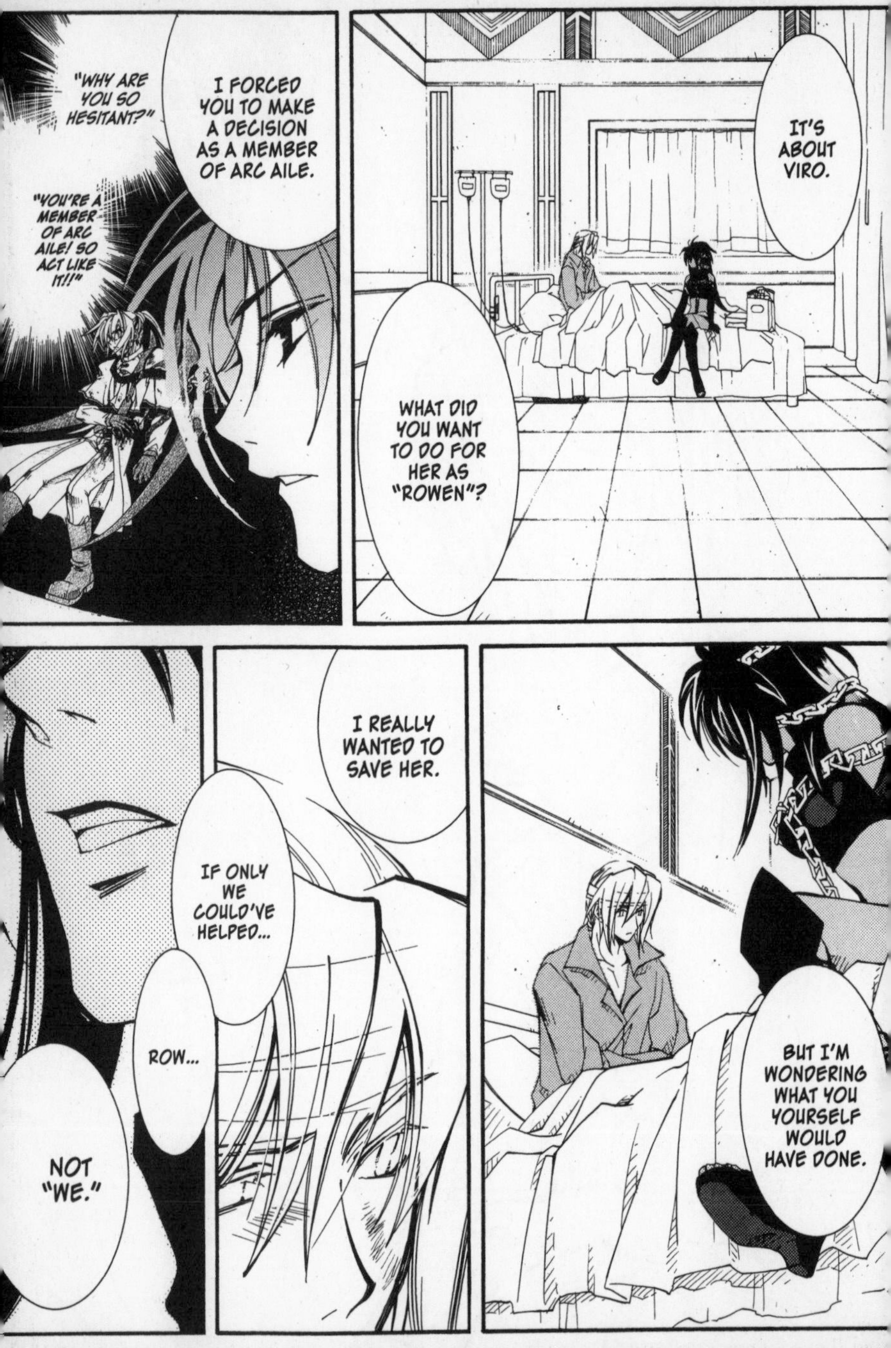
IT'S ABOUT VIRO.
WHAT DID YOU WANT TO DO FOR HER AS "ROWEN"?
I FORCED YOU TO MAKE A DECISION AS A MEMBER OF ARC AILE.
"WHY ARE YOU SO HESITANT?"
"YOU'RE A MEMBER OF ARC AILE! SO ACT LIKE IT!!"
BUT I'M WONDERING WHAT YOU YOURSELF WOULD HAVE DONE.
I REALLY WANTED TO SAVE HER.
IF ONLY WE COULD'VE HELPED...
ROW...
NOT "WE."

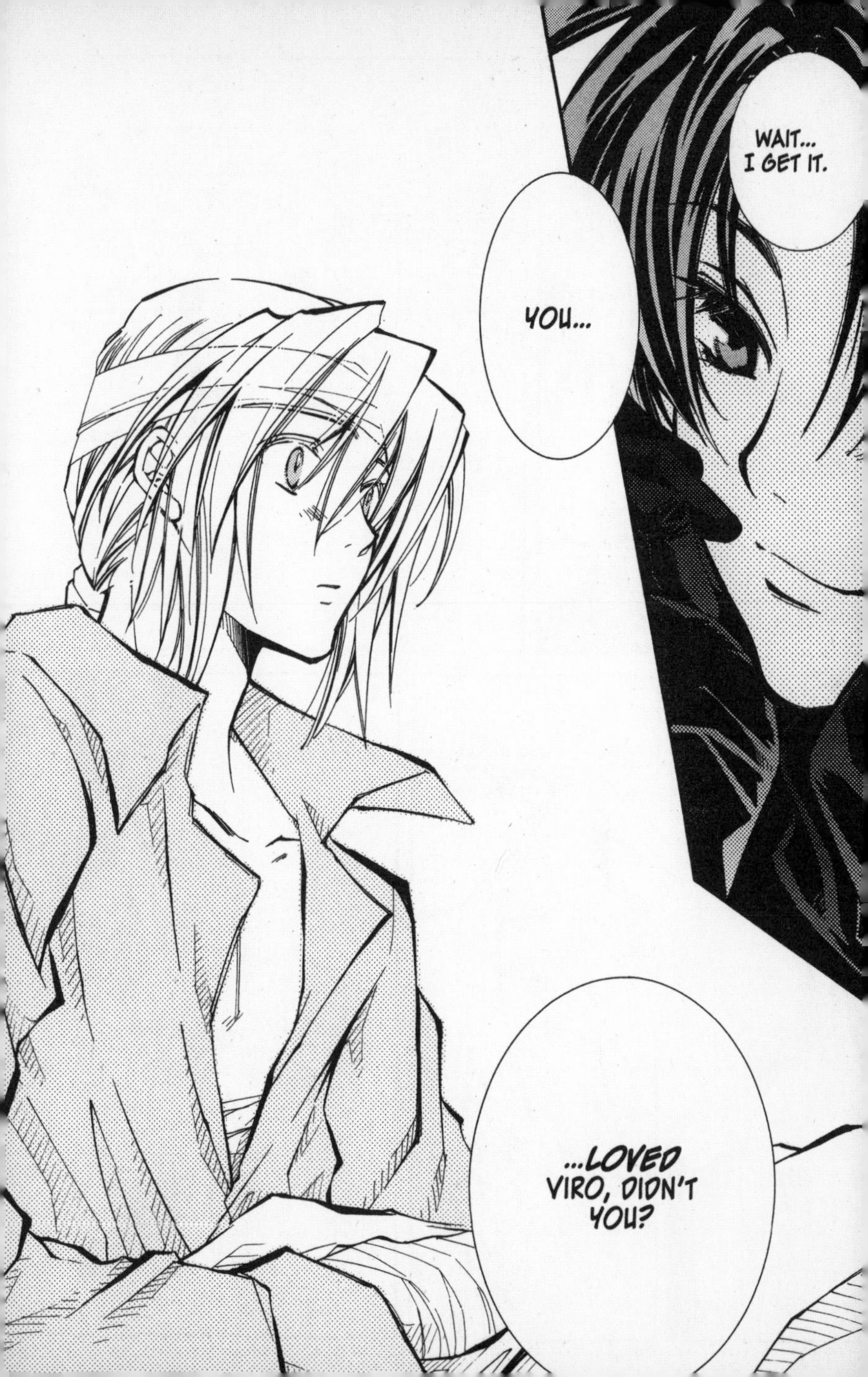
WAIT... I GET IT.
YOU...
...LOVED VIRO, DIDN'T YOU?

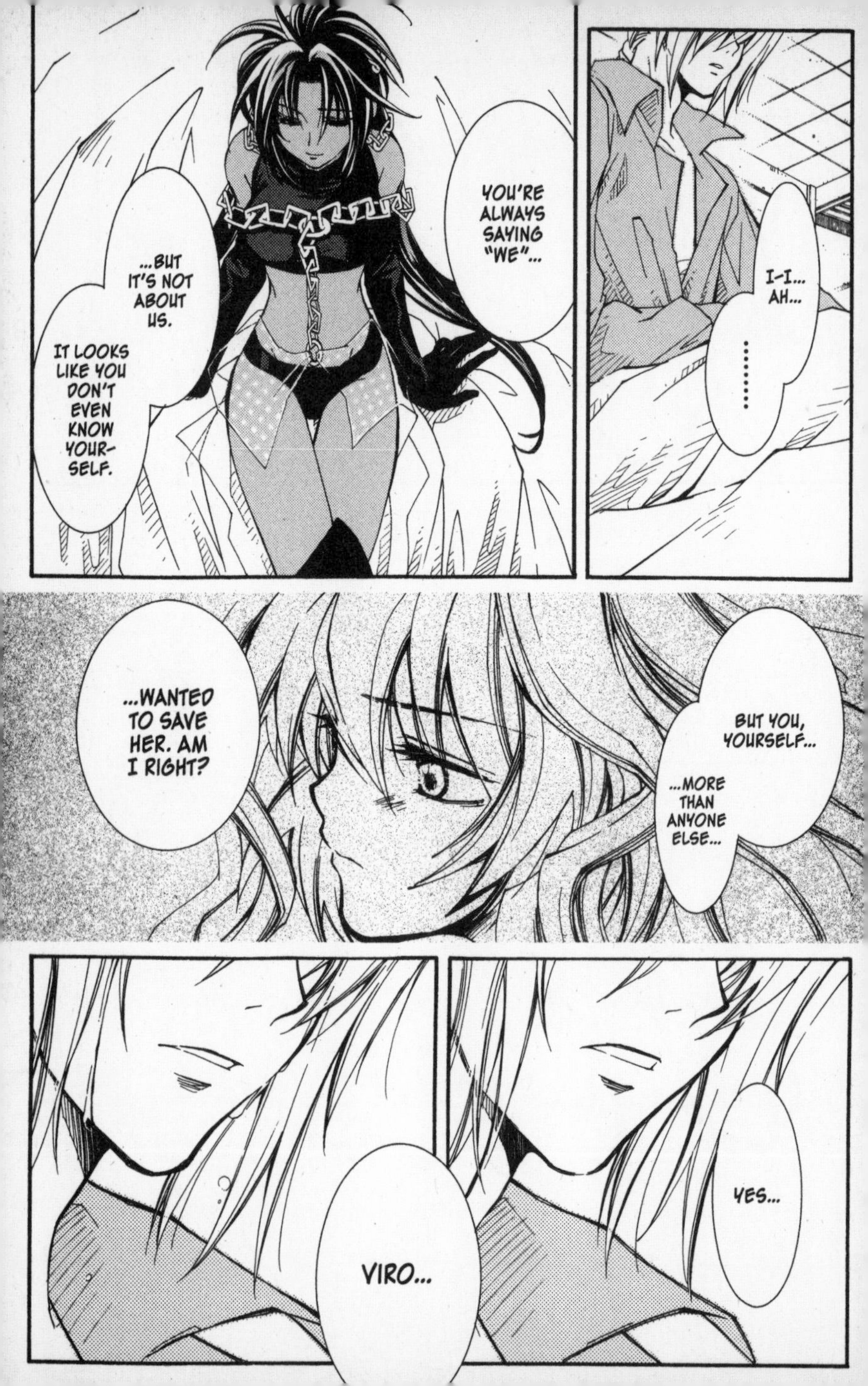
I-I... AH...
......
YOU'RE ALWAYS SAYING "WE"...
...BUT IT'S NOT ABOUT US.
IT LOOKS LIKE YOU DON'T EVEN KNOW YOURSELF.
BUT YOU, YOURSELF...
...MORE THAN ANYONE ELSE...
...WANTED TO SAVE HER. AM I RIGHT?
YES...
VIRO...

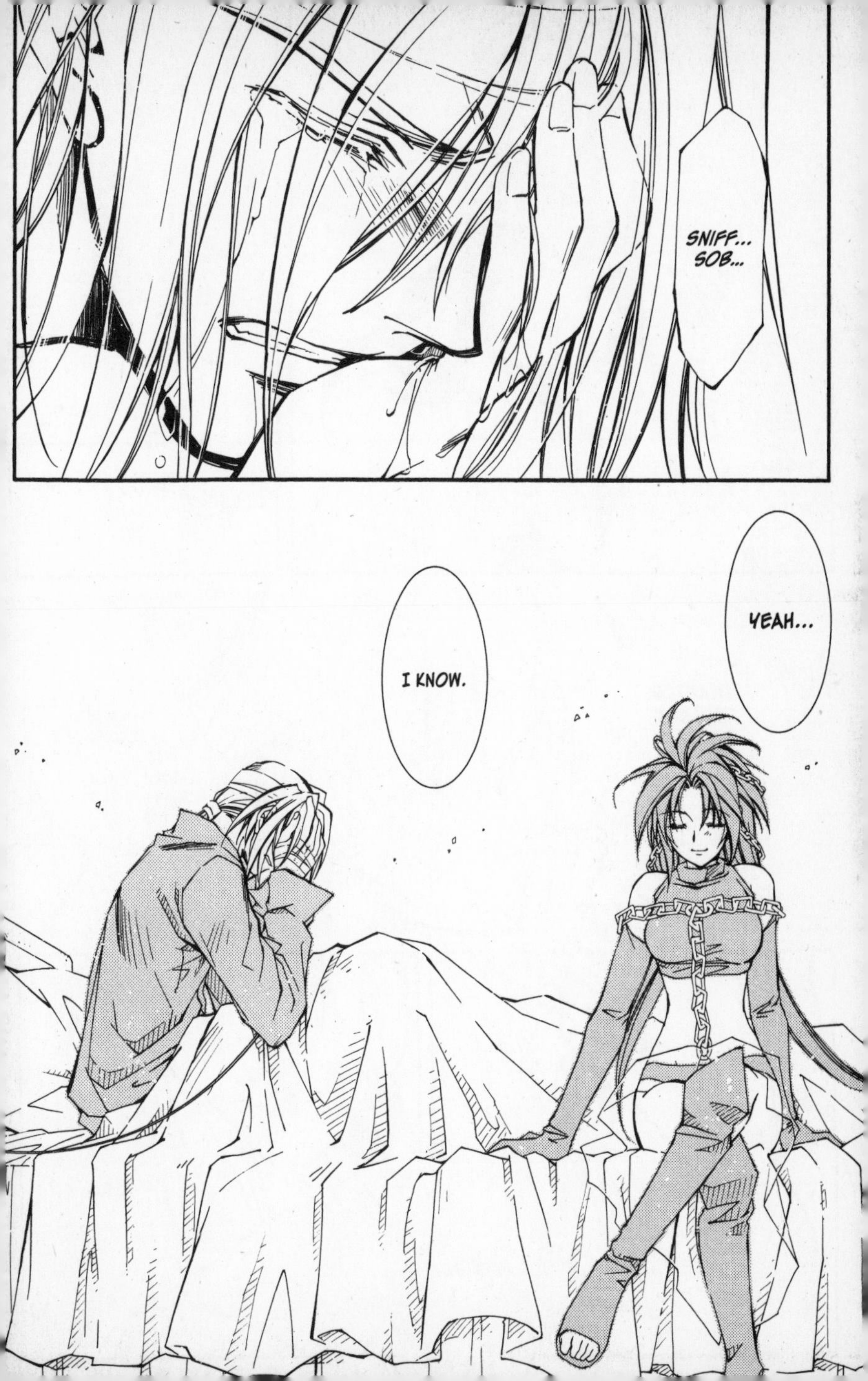
SNIFF... SOB...
YEAH...
I KNOW.

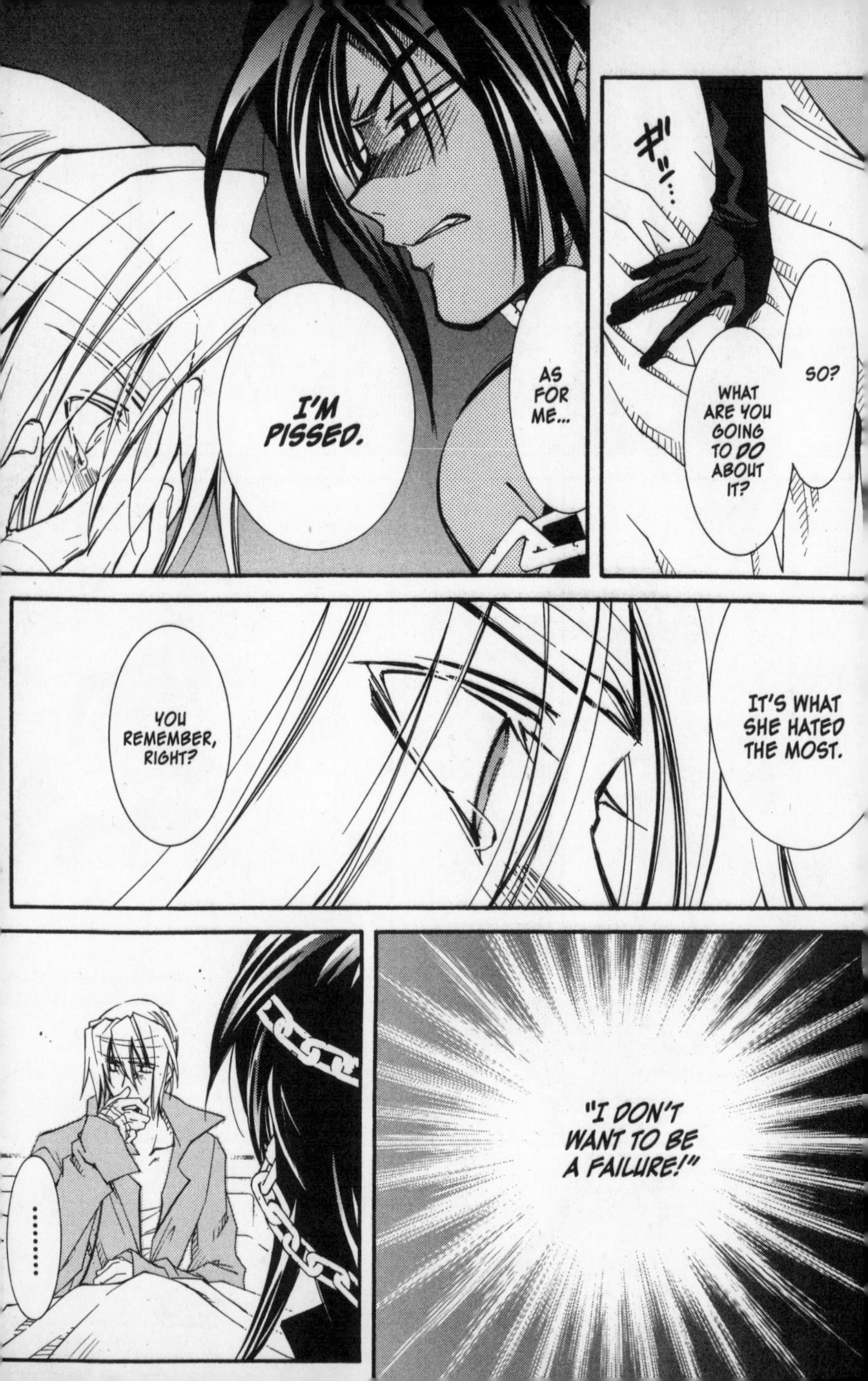

ギッ…
SO?
WHAT ARE YOU GOING TO DO ABOUT IT?
AS FOR ME...
I'M PISSED.
IT'S WHAT SHE HATED THE MOST.
YOU REMEMBER, RIGHT?
"I DON'T WANT TO BE A FAILURE!"
....

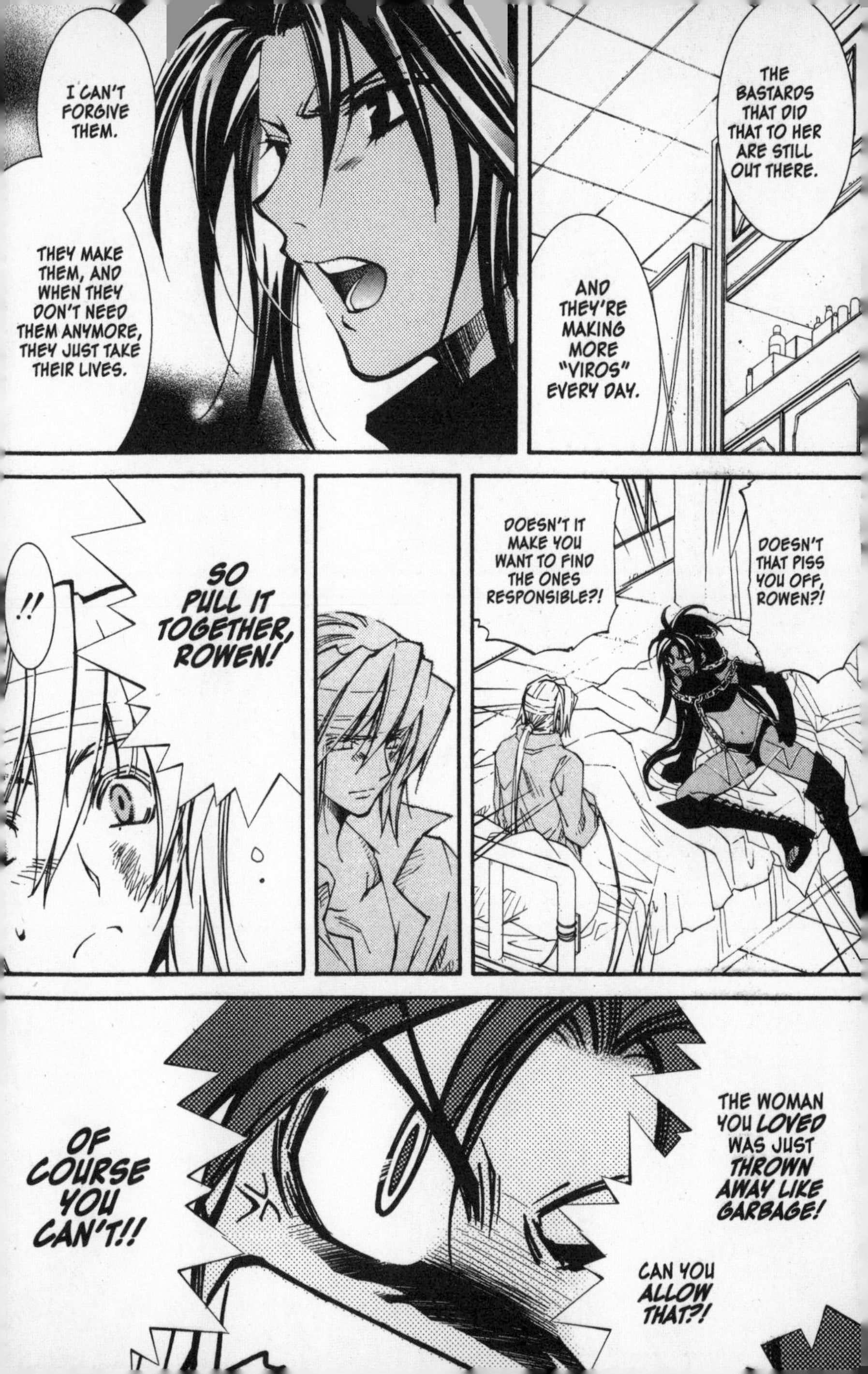
THE BASTARDS THAT DID THAT TO HER ARE STILL OUT THERE.
AND THEY'RE MAKING MORE "VIROS" EVERY DAY.
I CAN'T FORGIVE THEM.
THEY MAKE THEM, AND WHEN THEY DON'T NEED THEM ANYMORE, THEY JUST TAKE THEIR LIVES.
DOESN'T THAT PISS YOU OFF, ROWEN?!
DOESN'T IT MAKE YOU WANT TO FIND THE ONES RESPONSIBLE?!
SO PULL IT TOGETHER, ROWEN!
!!
THE WOMAN YOU LOVED WAS JUST THROWN AWAY LIKE GARBAGE!
CAN YOU ALLOW THAT?!
OF COURSE YOU CAN'T!!

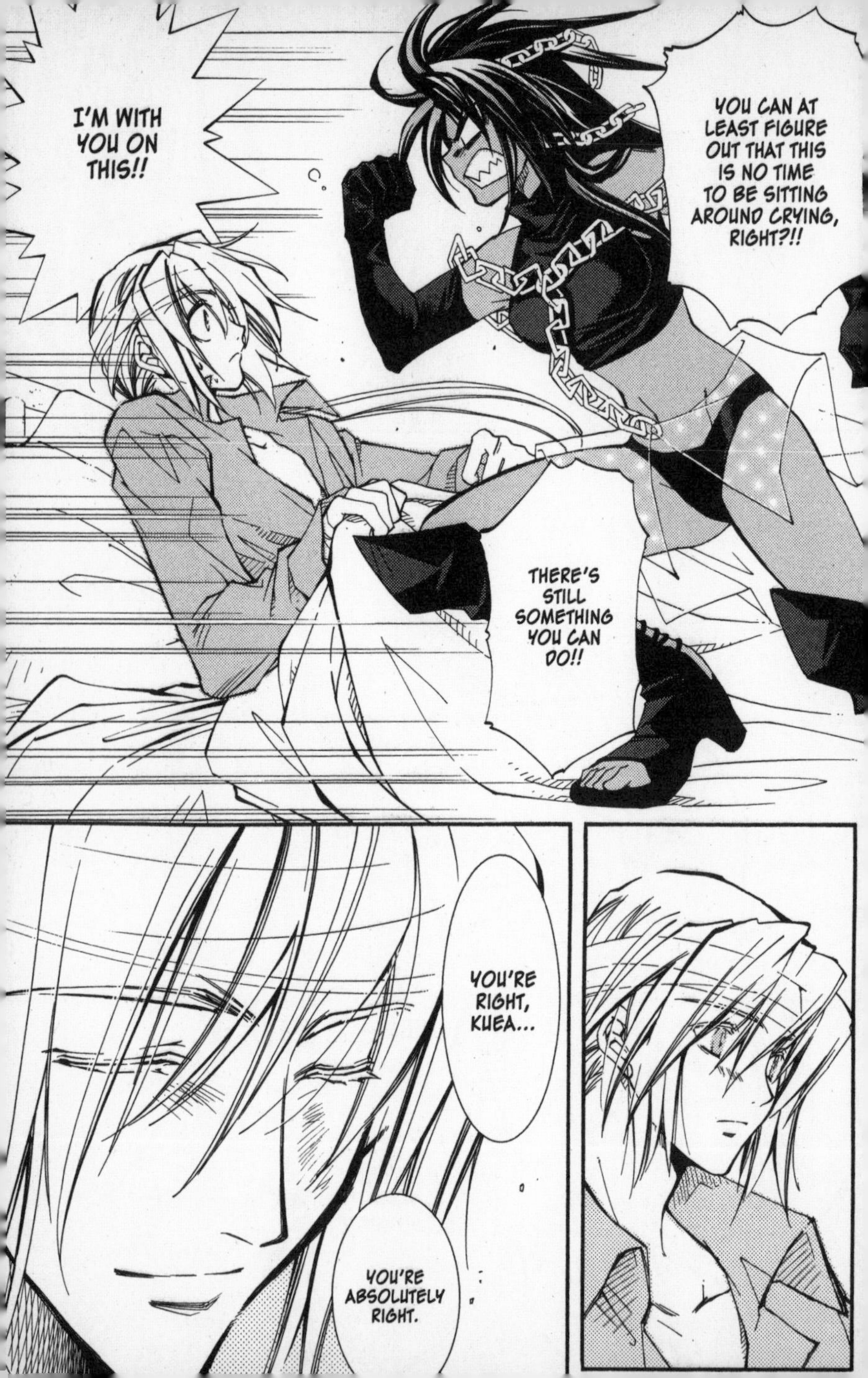
YOU CAN AT LEAST FIGURE OUT THAT THIS IS NO TIME TO BE SITTING AROUND CRYING, RIGHT?!!
I'M WITH YOU ON THIS!!
THERE'S STILL SOMETHING YOU CAN DO!!
YOU'RE RIGHT, KUEA...
YOU'RE ABSOLUTELY RIGHT.

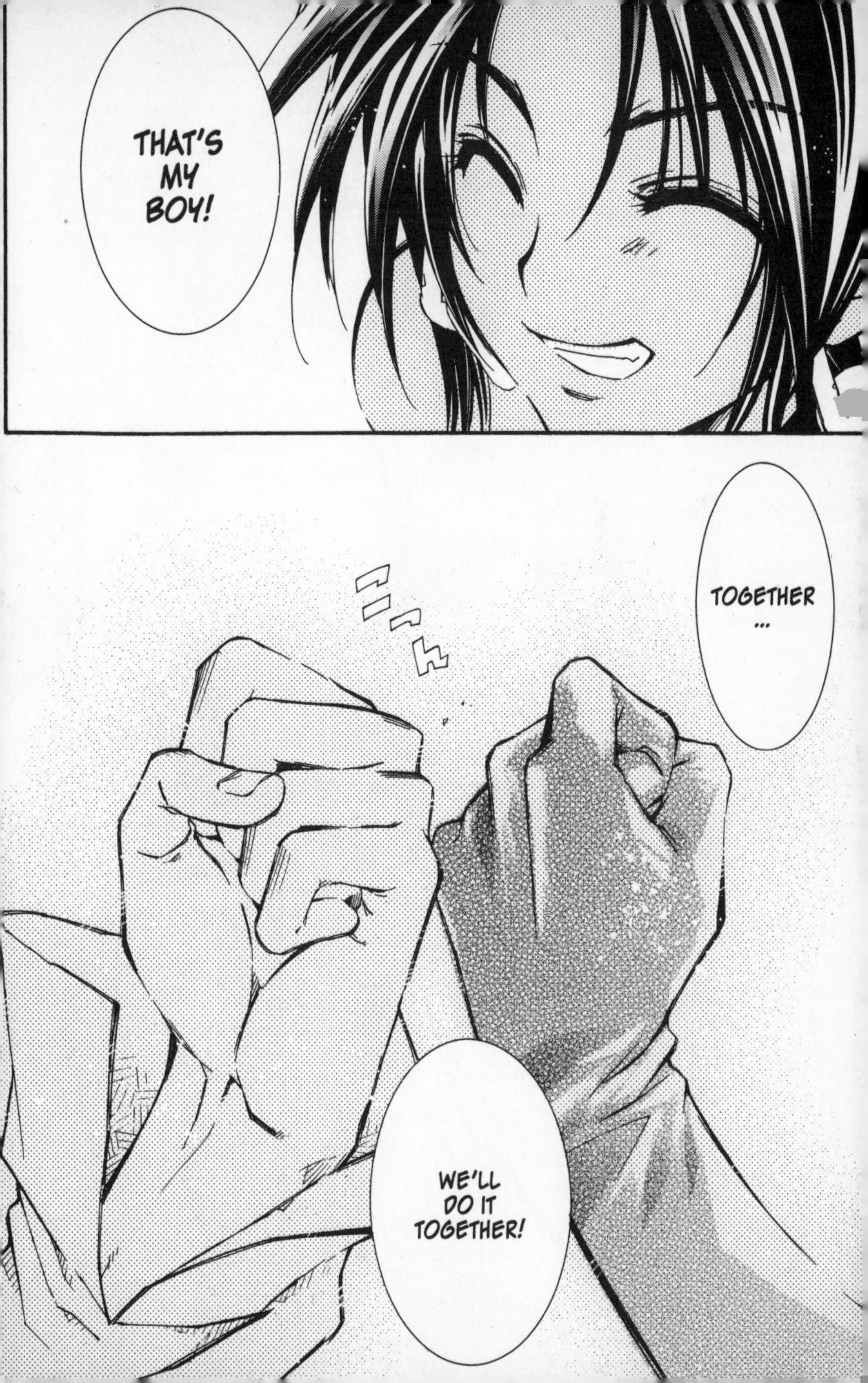
THAT'S MY BOY!
TOGETHER...
WE'LL DO IT TOGETHER!

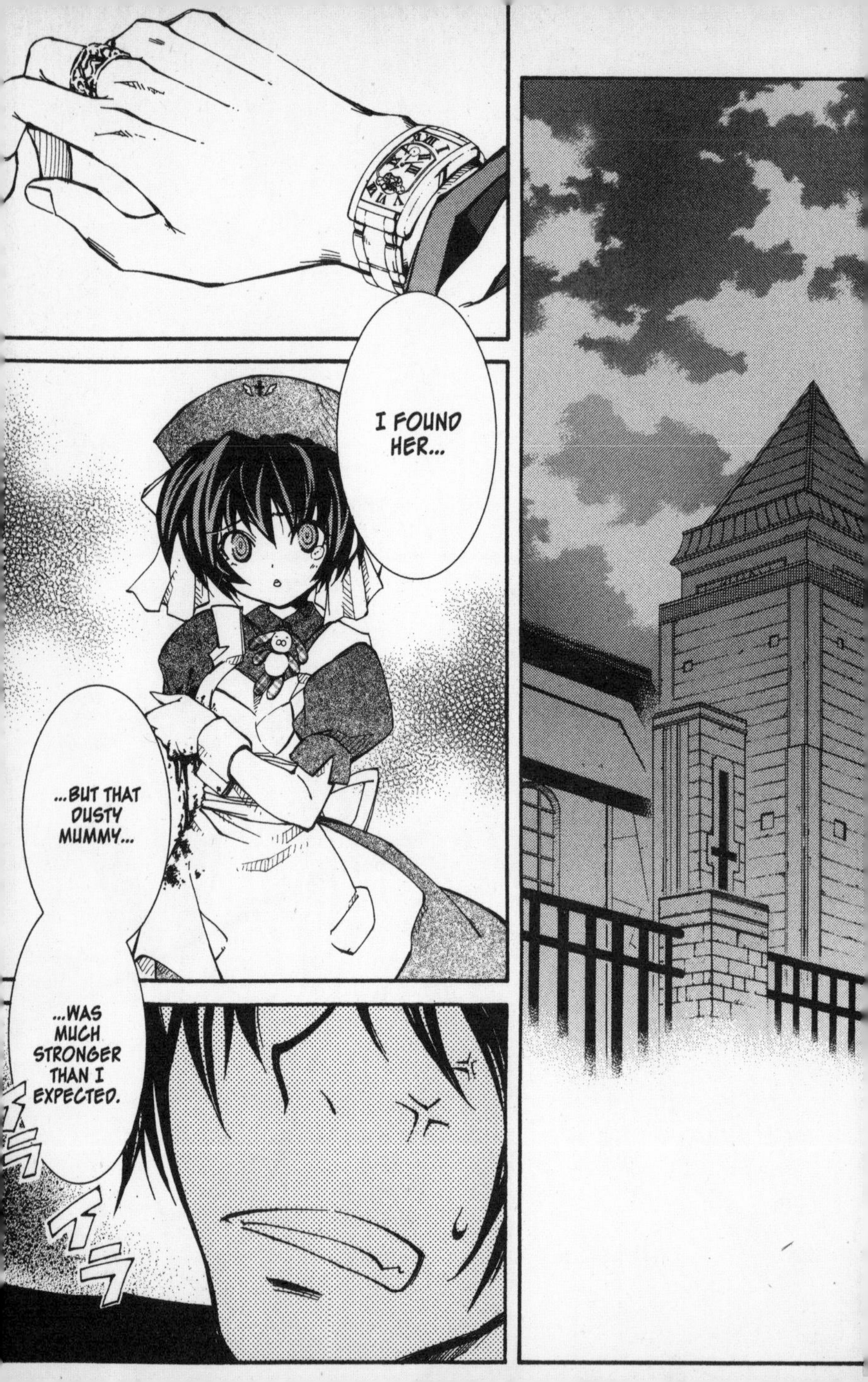
I FOUND HER...
...BUT THAT DUSTY MUMMY...
...WAS MUCH STRONGER THAN I EXPECTED.

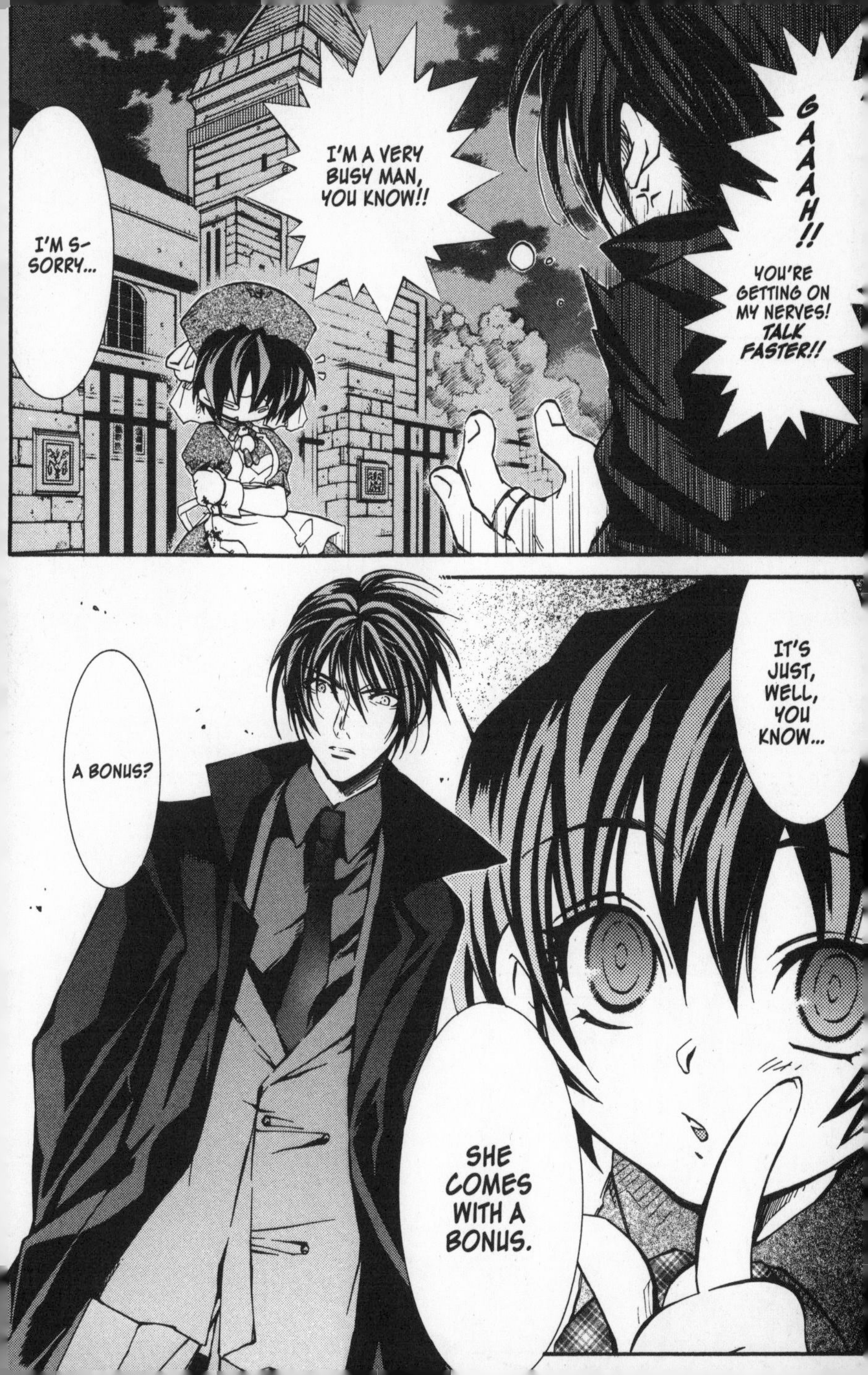
GAAAH!!
YOU'RE GETTING ON MY NERVES! TALK FASTER!!
I'M A VERY BUSY MAN, YOU KNOW!!
I'M S-SORRY...
IT'S JUST, WELL, YOU KNOW...
A BONUS?
SHE COMES WITH A BONUS.

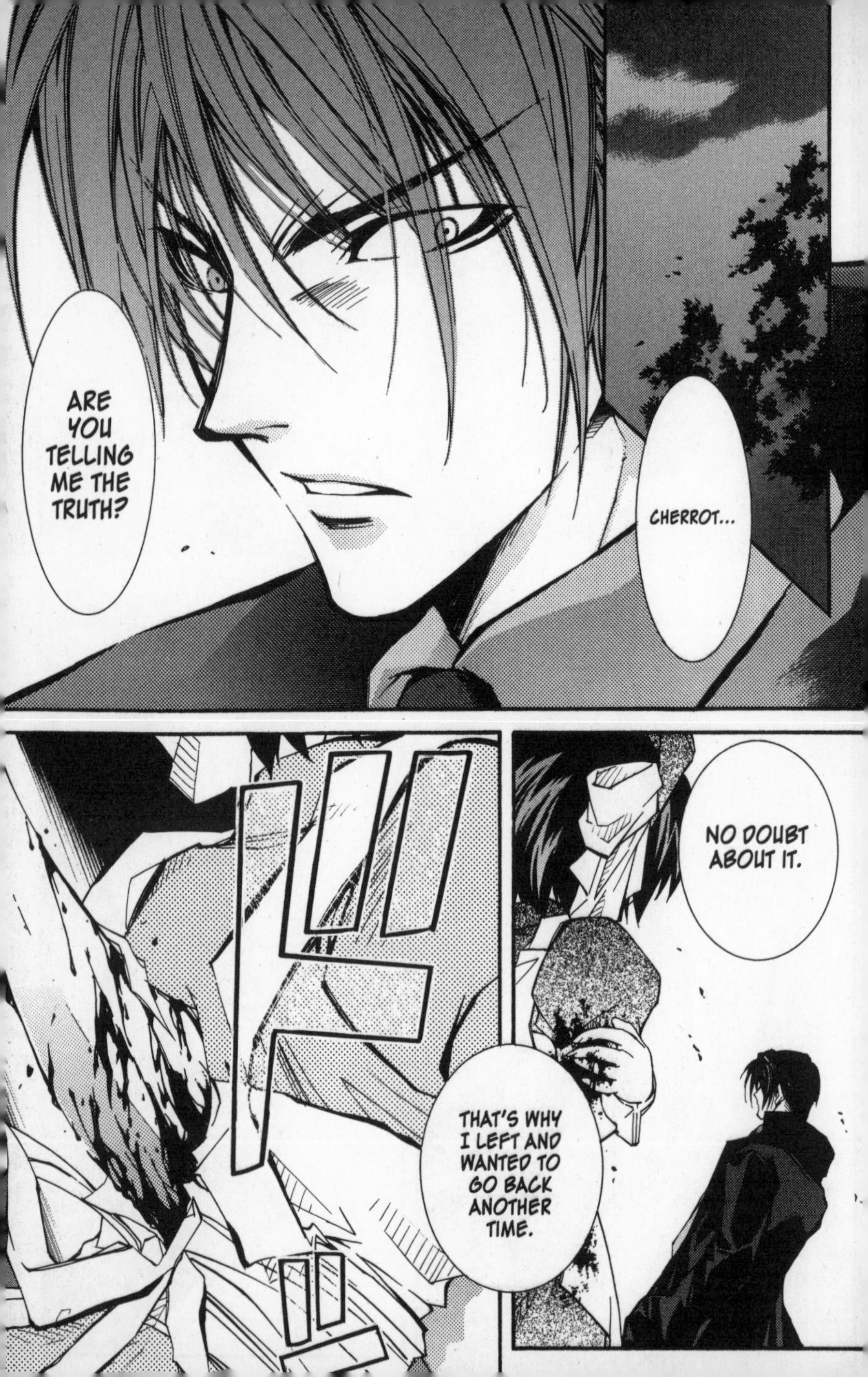
CHERROT...
ARE YOU TELLING ME THE TRUTH?
NO DOUBT ABOUT IT.
THAT'S WHY I LEFT AND WANTED TO GO BACK ANOTHER TIME.

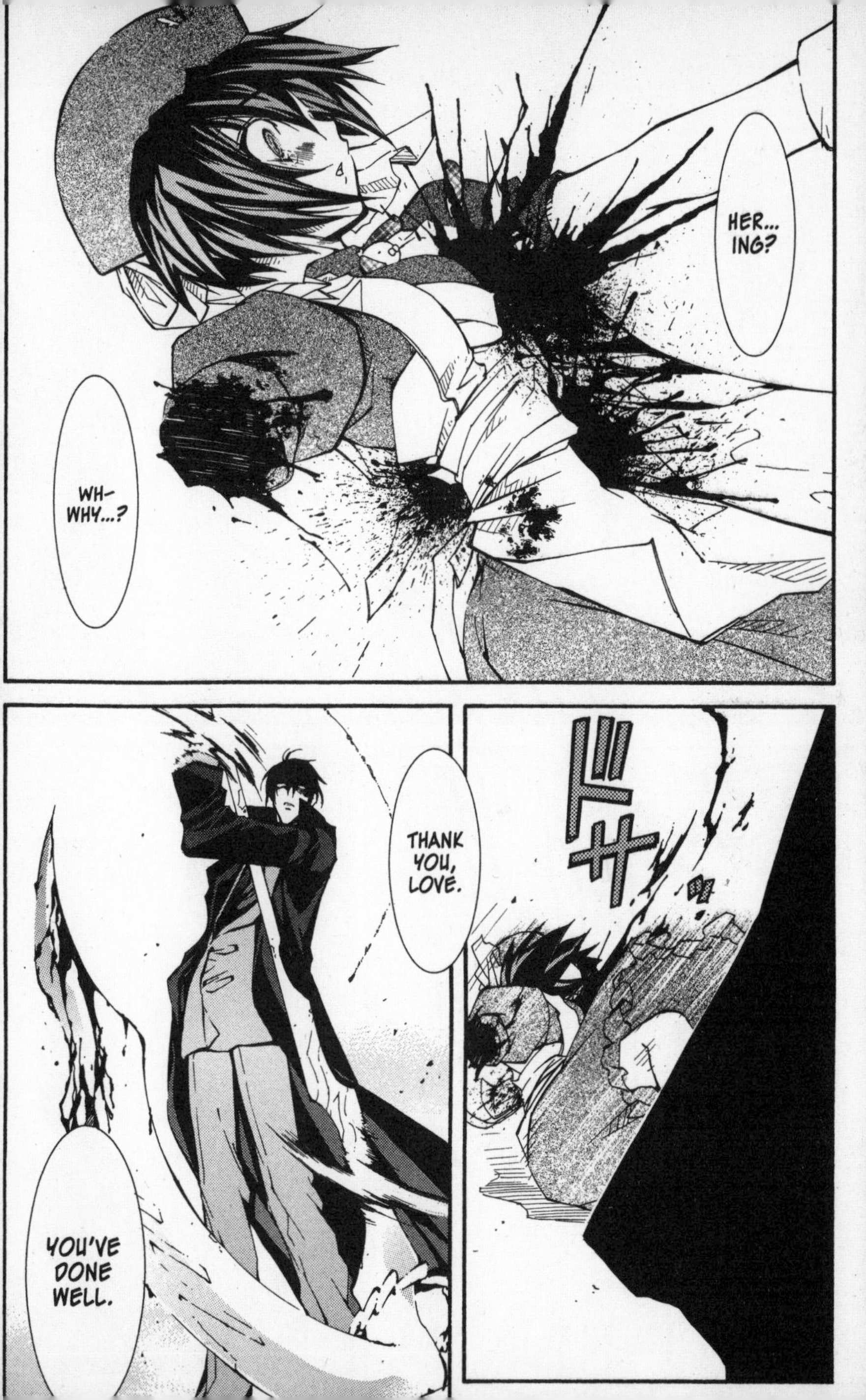
HER... ING?
WH- WHY...?
ドッ
THANK YOU, LOVE.
YOU'VE DONE WELL.

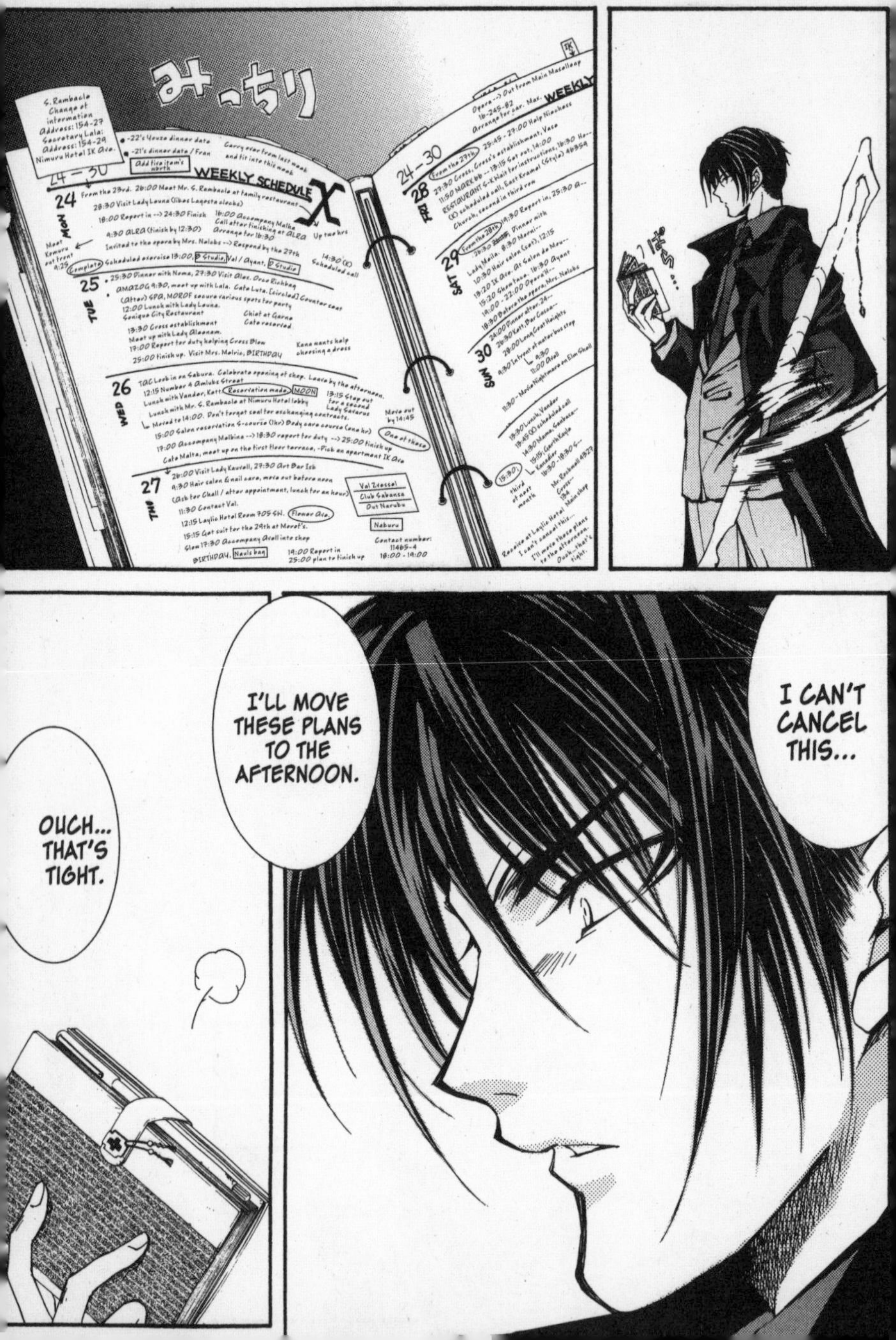

ぱら…
みっちり
S. Rambaclo Change of information Address: 154-27 Secretary Lala: Address: 154-29 Nimuru Hotel IK Ave.
WEEKLY SCHEDULE
24 MON
25 TUE
26 WED
27 THU
WEEKLY
28 FRI
29 SAT
30 SUN
I can't cancel this... I'll move these plans to the afternoon. Ouch...that's tight.
I CAN'T CANCEL THIS...
I'LL MOVE THESE PLANS TO THE AFTERNOON.
OUCH... THAT'S TIGHT.

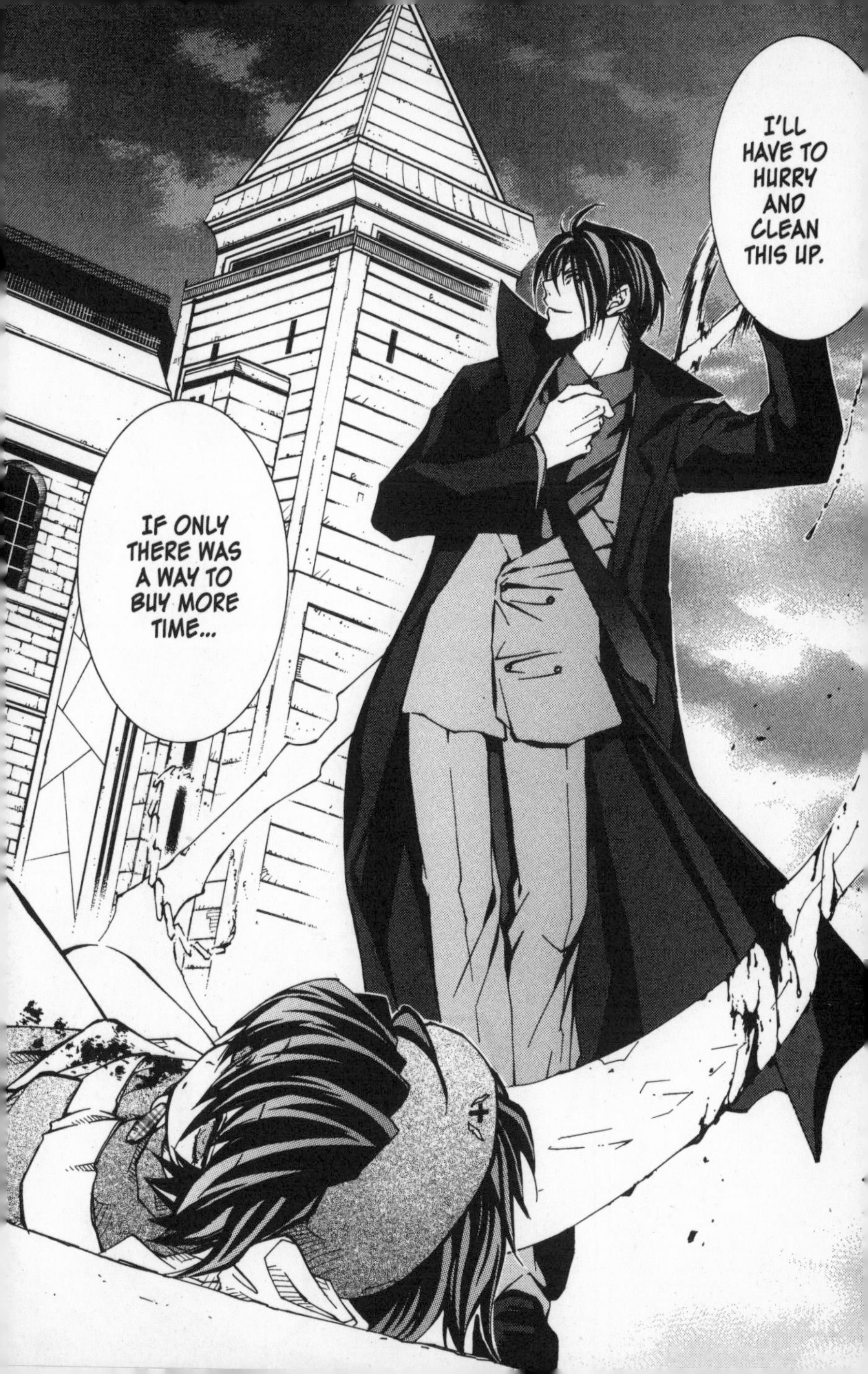
I'LL HAVE TO HURRY AND CLEAN THIS UP.
IF ONLY THERE WAS A WAY TO BUY MORE TIME...

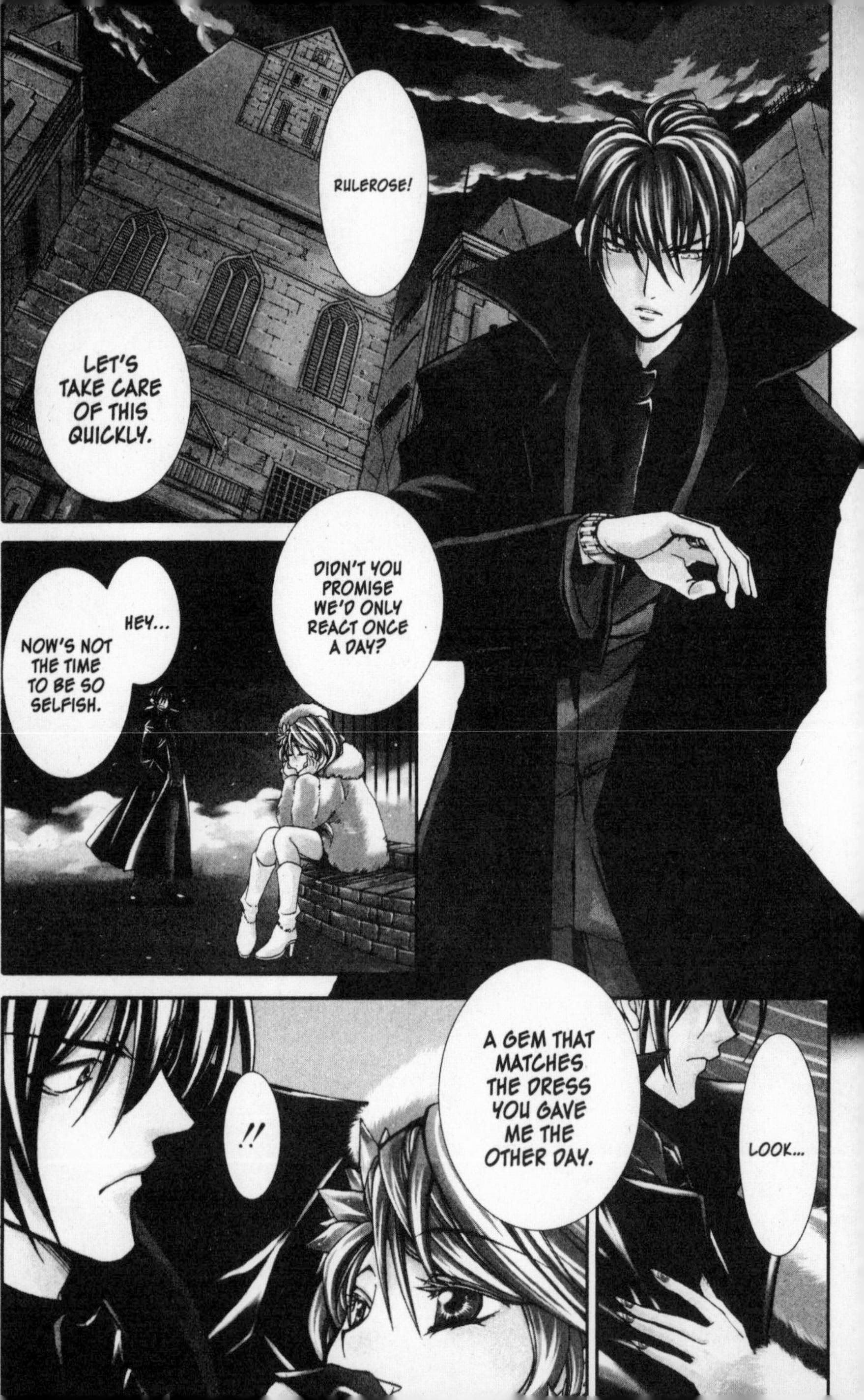

RULEROSE!
LET'S TAKE CARE OF THIS QUICKLY.
DIDN'T YOU PROMISE WE'D ONLY REACT ONCE A DAY?
HEY...
NOW'S NOT THE TIME TO BE SO SELFISH.
LOOK...
A GEM THAT MATCHES THE DRESS YOU GAVE ME THE OTHER DAY.
!!

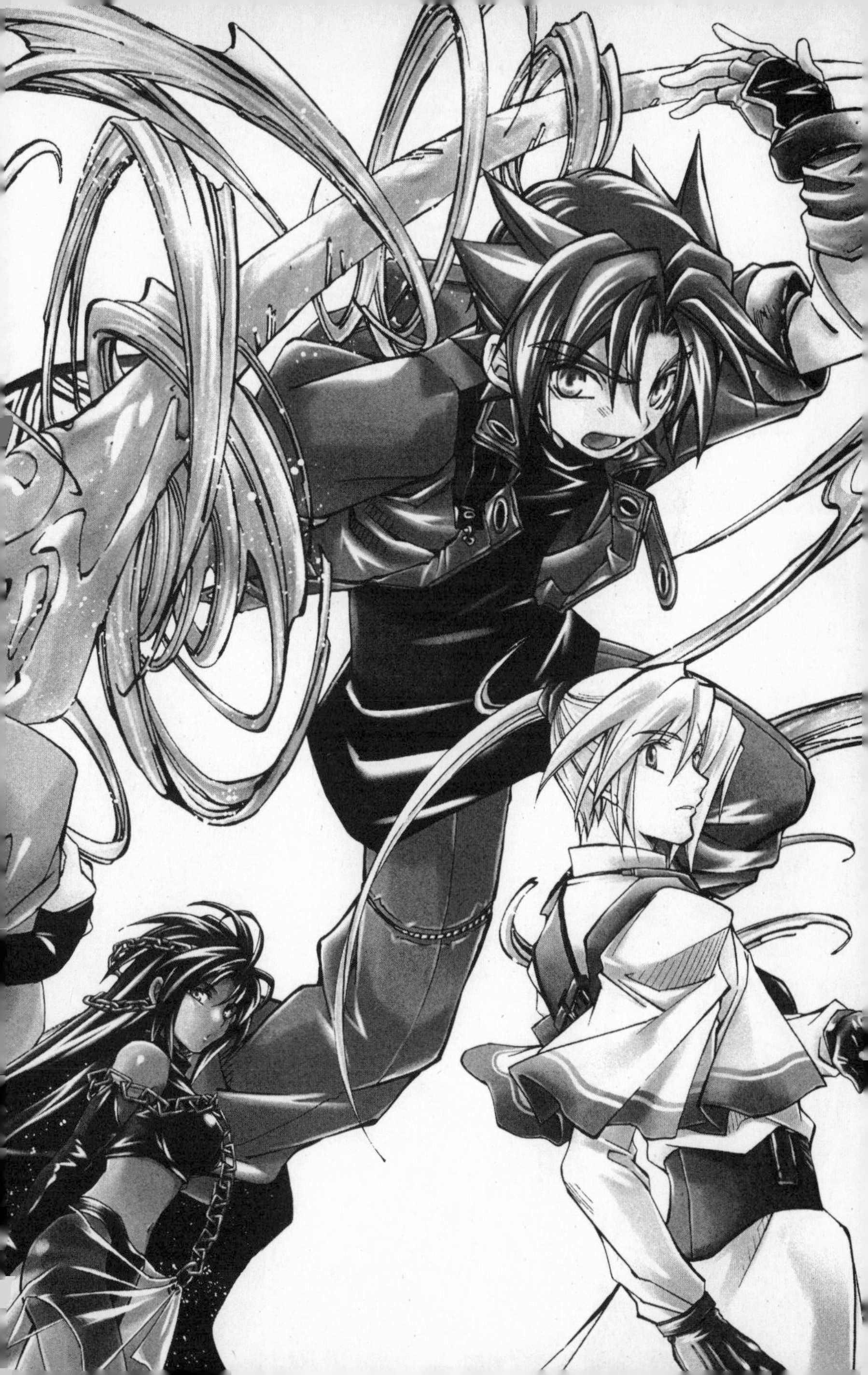

Re-No: 35
Mountain Town Barley Toast—Unending Night

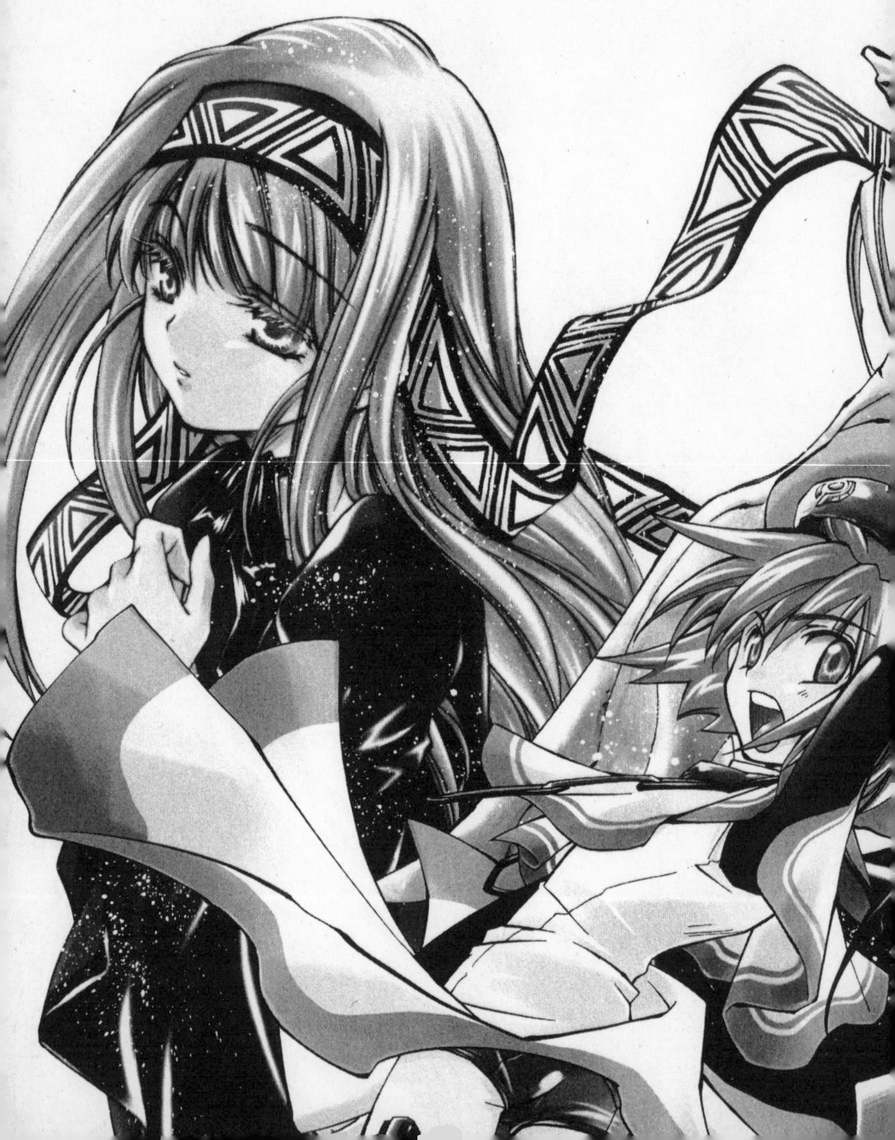

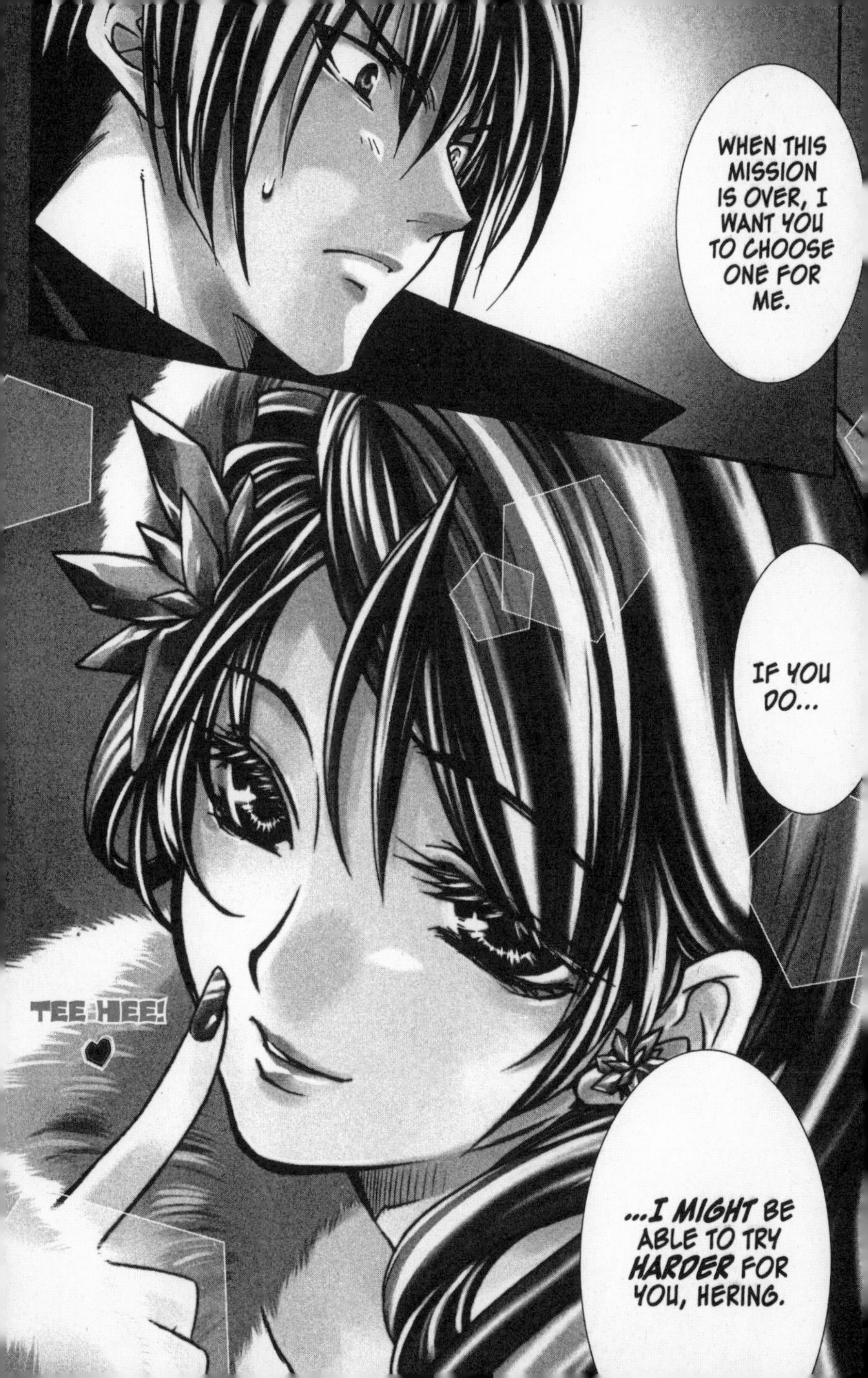

WHEN THIS MISSION IS OVER, I WANT YOU TO CHOOSE ONE FOR ME.
IF YOU DO...
...I MIGHT BE ABLE TO TRY HARDER FOR YOU, HERING.
TEE-HEE!

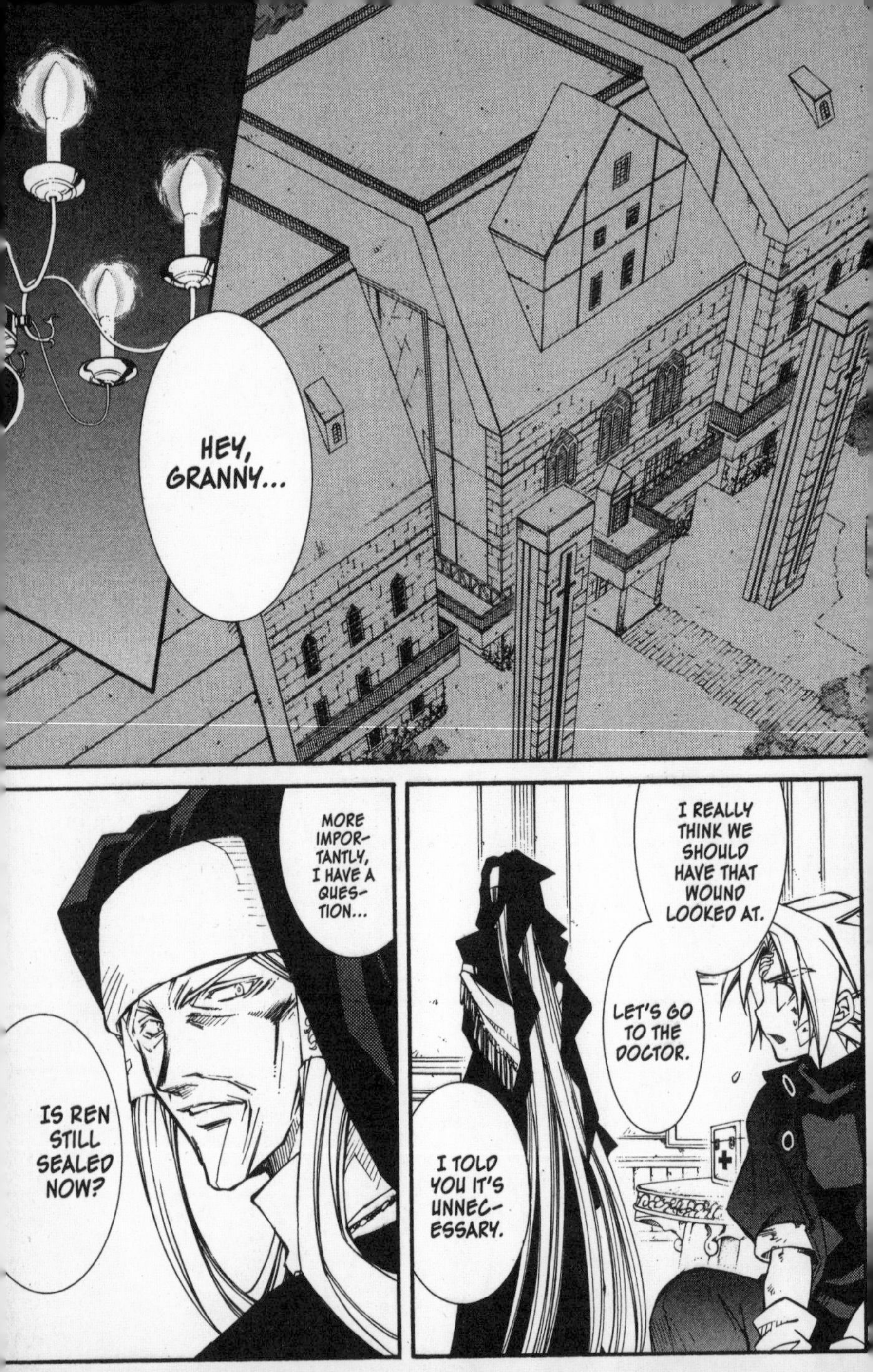
HEY, GRANNY...
I REALLY THINK WE SHOULD HAVE THAT WOUND LOOKED AT.
LET'S GO TO THE DOCTOR.
I TOLD YOU IT'S UNNEC-ESSARY.
MORE IMPOR-TANTLY, I HAVE A QUES-TION...
IS REN STILL SEALED NOW?

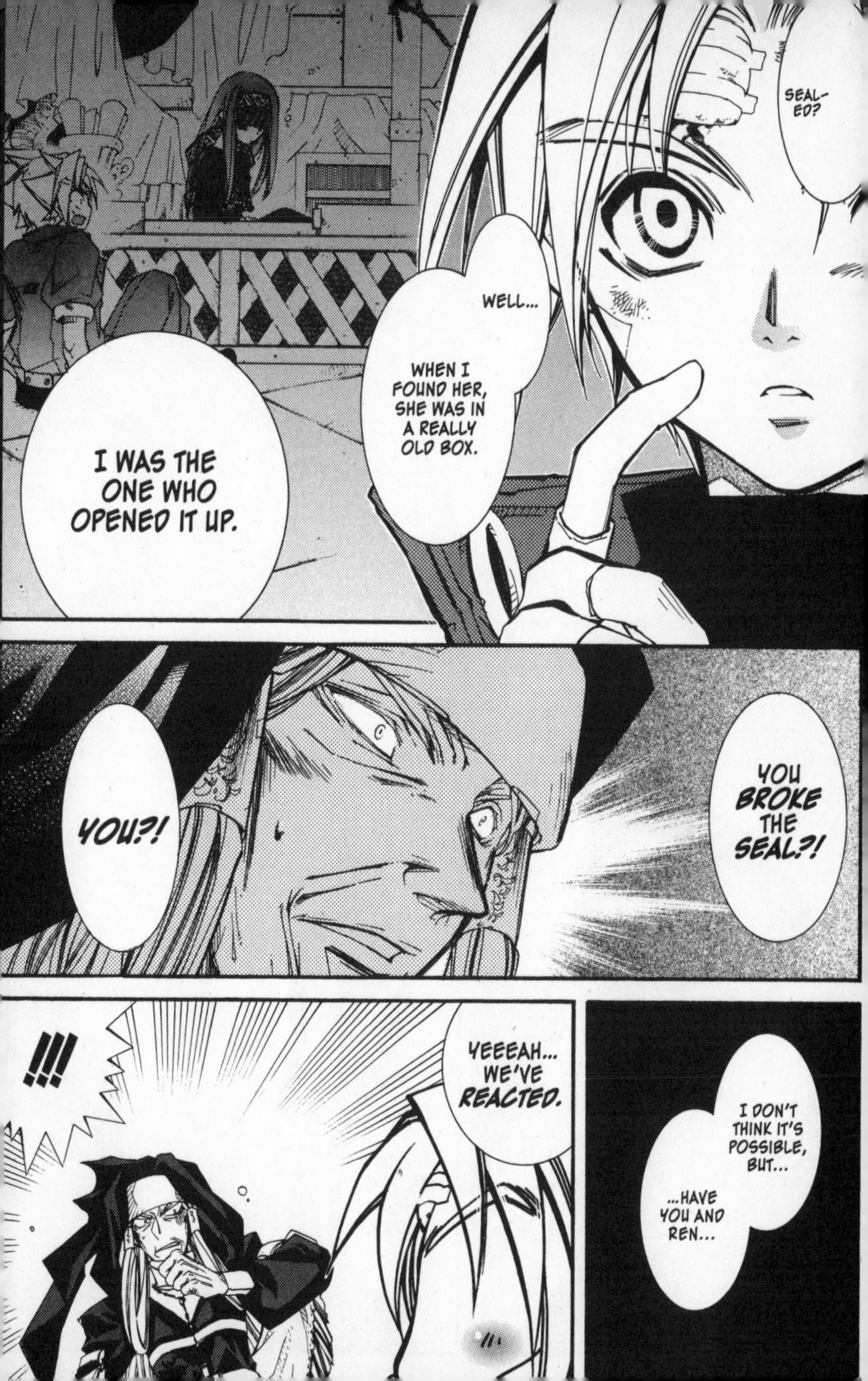
SEAL-ED?
WELL...
WHEN I FOUND HER, SHE WAS IN A REALLY OLD BOX.
I WAS THE ONE WHO OPENED IT UP.
YOU BROKE THE SEAL?!
YOU?!
I DON'T THINK IT'S POSSIBLE, BUT...
...HAVE YOU AND REN...
YEEEAH... WE'VE REACTED.
!!!

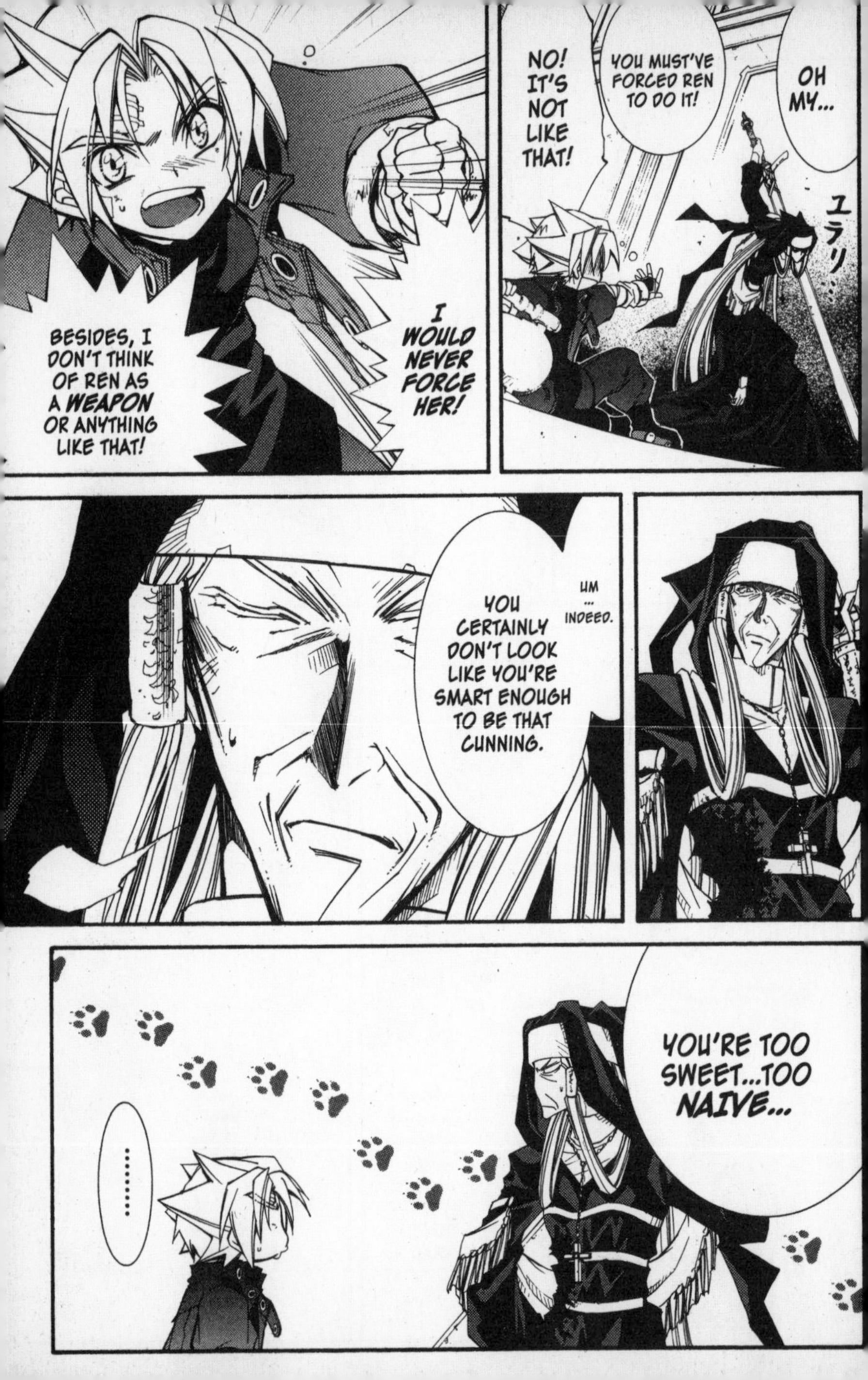
OH MY...
YOU MUST'VE FORCED REN TO DO IT!
NO! IT'S NOT LIKE THAT!
ユラリ…
I WOULD NEVER FORCE HER!
BESIDES, I DON'T THINK OF REN AS A WEAPON OR ANYTHING LIKE THAT!
UM ... INDEED.
YOU CERTAINLY DON'T LOOK LIKE YOU'RE SMART ENOUGH TO BE THAT CUNNING.
YOU'RE TOO SWEET...TOO NAIVE...
....

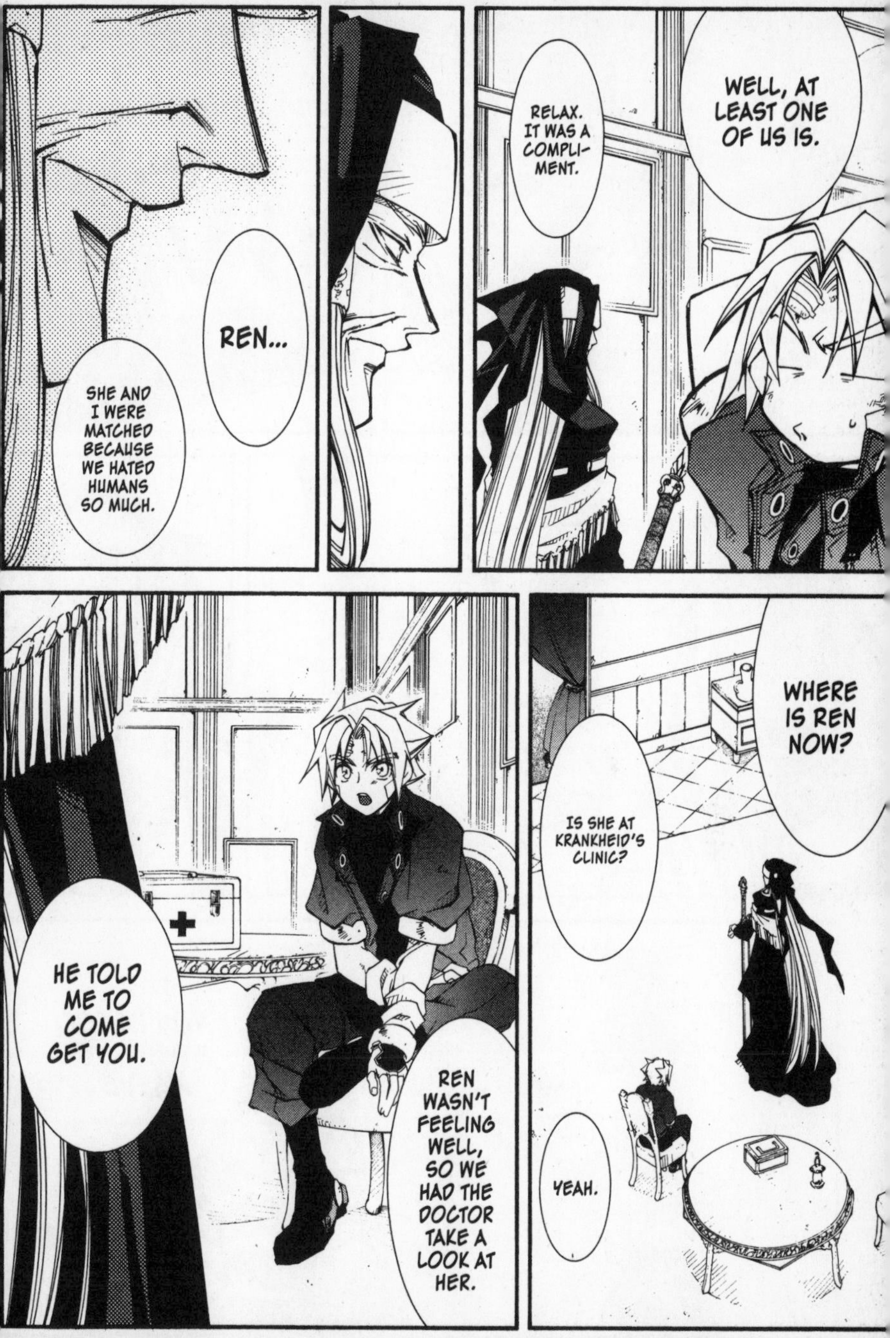
WELL, AT LEAST ONE OF US IS.
RELAX. IT WAS A COMPLIMENT.
REN...
SHE AND I WERE MATCHED BECAUSE WE HATED HUMANS SO MUCH.
WHERE IS REN NOW?
IS SHE AT KRANKHEID'S CLINIC?
YEAH.
REN WASN'T FEELING WELL, SO WE HAD THE DOCTOR TAKE A LOOK AT HER.
HE TOLD ME TO COME GET YOU.

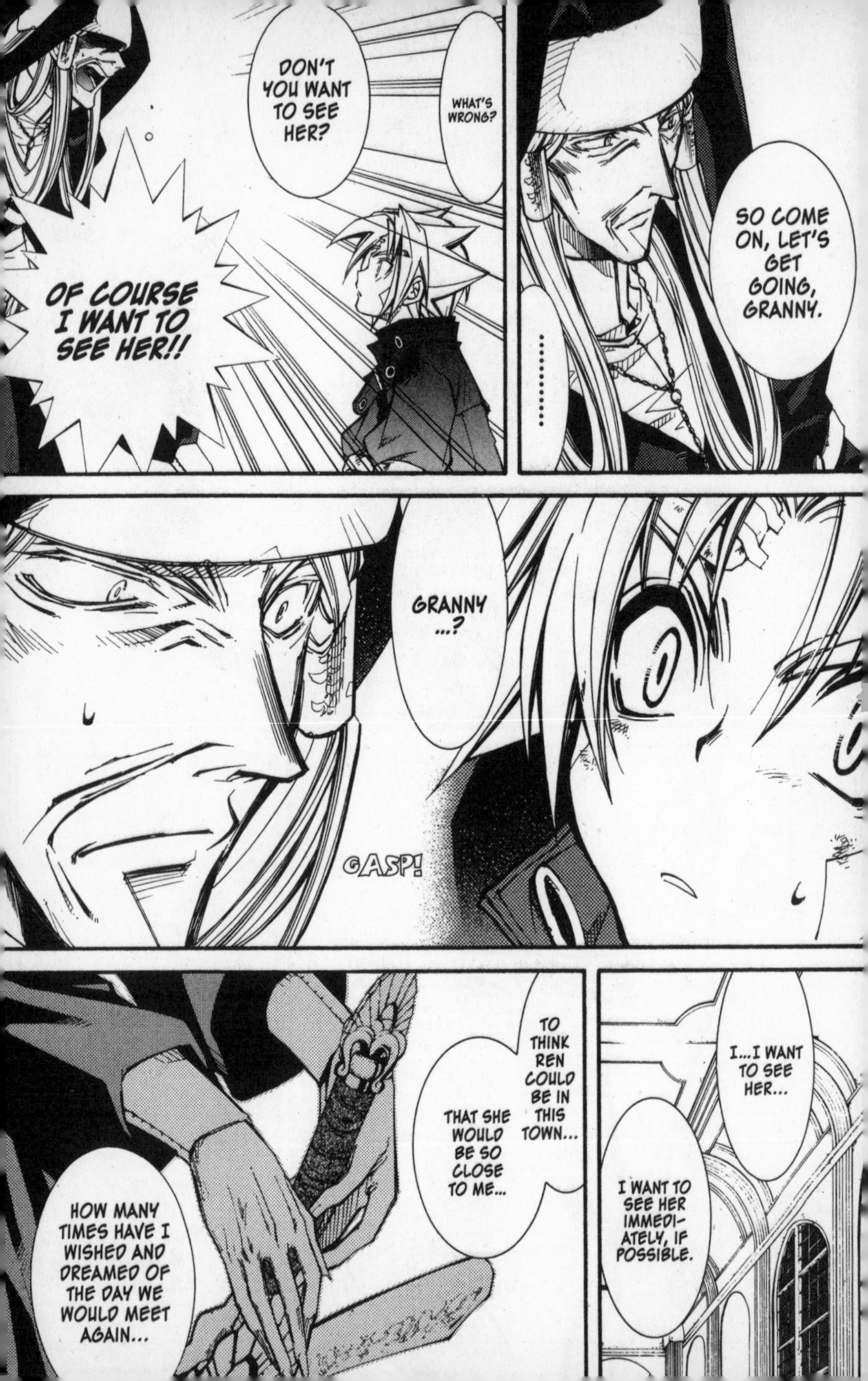
SO COME ON, LET'S GET GOING, GRANNY.
......
WHAT'S WRONG?
DON'T YOU WANT TO SEE HER?
OF COURSE I WANT TO SEE HER!!
GRANNY ...?
GASP!
I...I WANT TO SEE HER...
I WANT TO SEE HER IMMEDI-ATELY, IF POSSIBLE.
TO THINK REN COULD BE IN THIS TOWN...
THAT SHE WOULD BE SO CLOSE TO ME...
HOW MANY TIMES HAVE I WISHED AND DREAMED OF THE DAY WE WOULD MEET AGAIN...

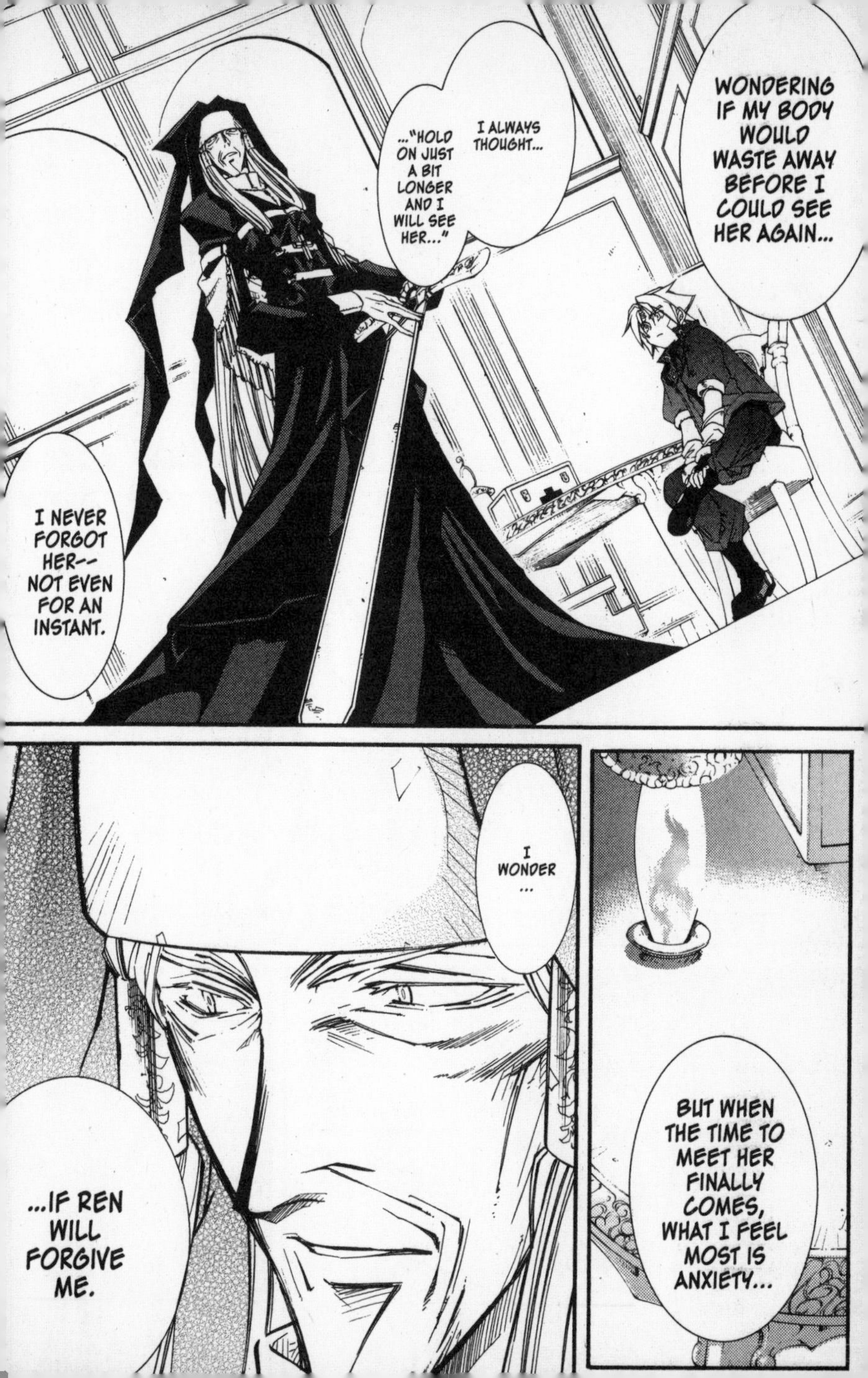
WONDERING IF MY BODY WOULD WASTE AWAY BEFORE I COULD SEE HER AGAIN...
I ALWAYS THOUGHT...
..."HOLD ON JUST A BIT LONGER AND I WILL SEE HER..."
I NEVER FORGOT HER-- NOT EVEN FOR AN INSTANT.
BUT WHEN THE TIME TO MEET HER FINALLY COMES, WHAT I FEEL MOST IS ANXIETY...
I WONDER...
...IF REN WILL FORGIVE ME.

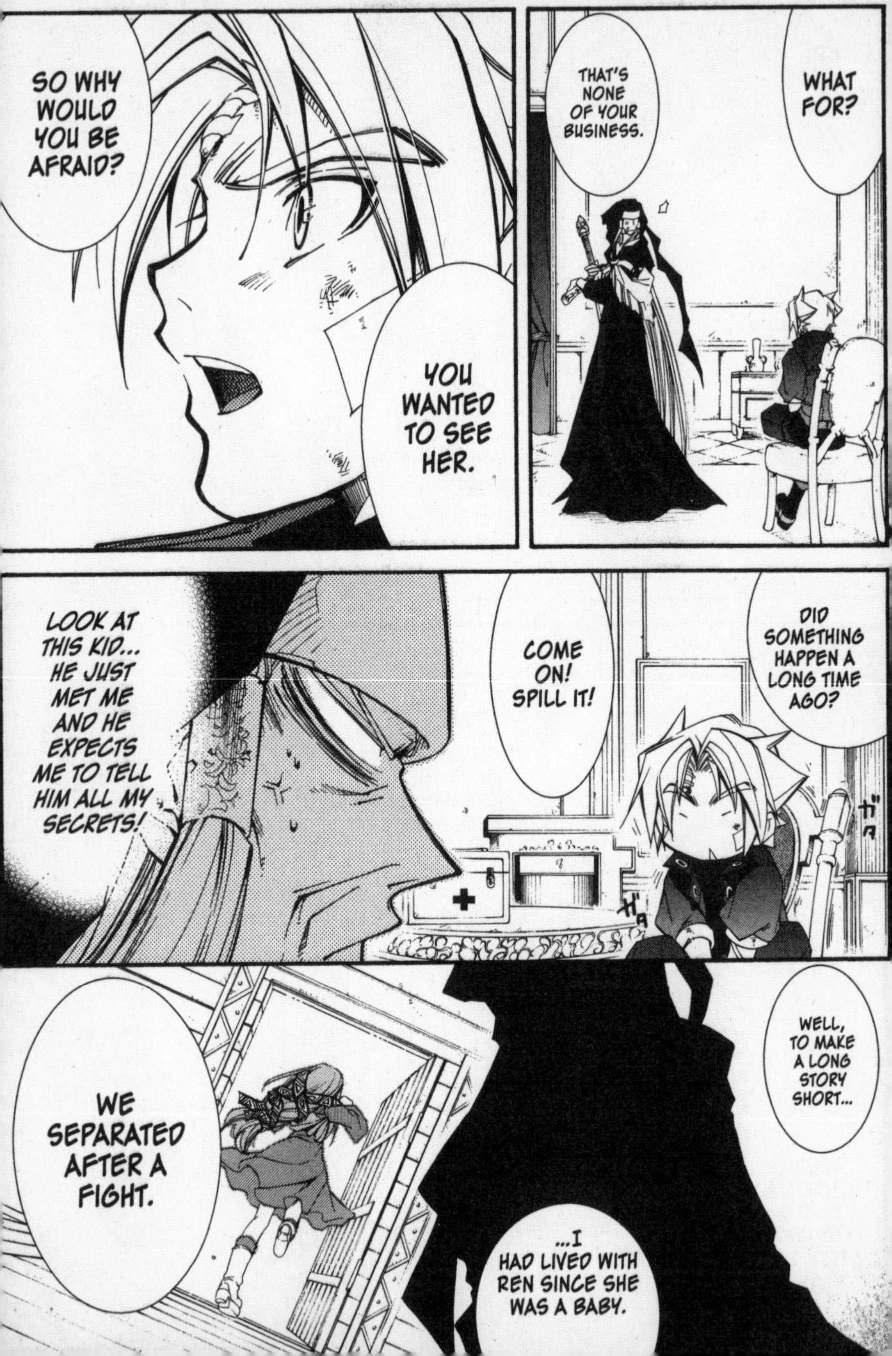
WHAT FOR?
THAT'S NONE OF YOUR BUSINESS.
YOU WANTED TO SEE HER.
SO WHY WOULD YOU BE AFRAID?
DID SOMETHING HAPPEN A LONG TIME AGO?
ガタ
COME ON! SPILL IT!
LOOK AT THIS KID... HE JUST MET ME AND HE EXPECTS ME TO TELL HIM ALL MY SECRETS!
WELL, TO MAKE A LONG STORY SHORT...
...I HAD LIVED WITH REN SINCE SHE WAS A BABY.
WE SEPARATED AFTER A FIGHT.

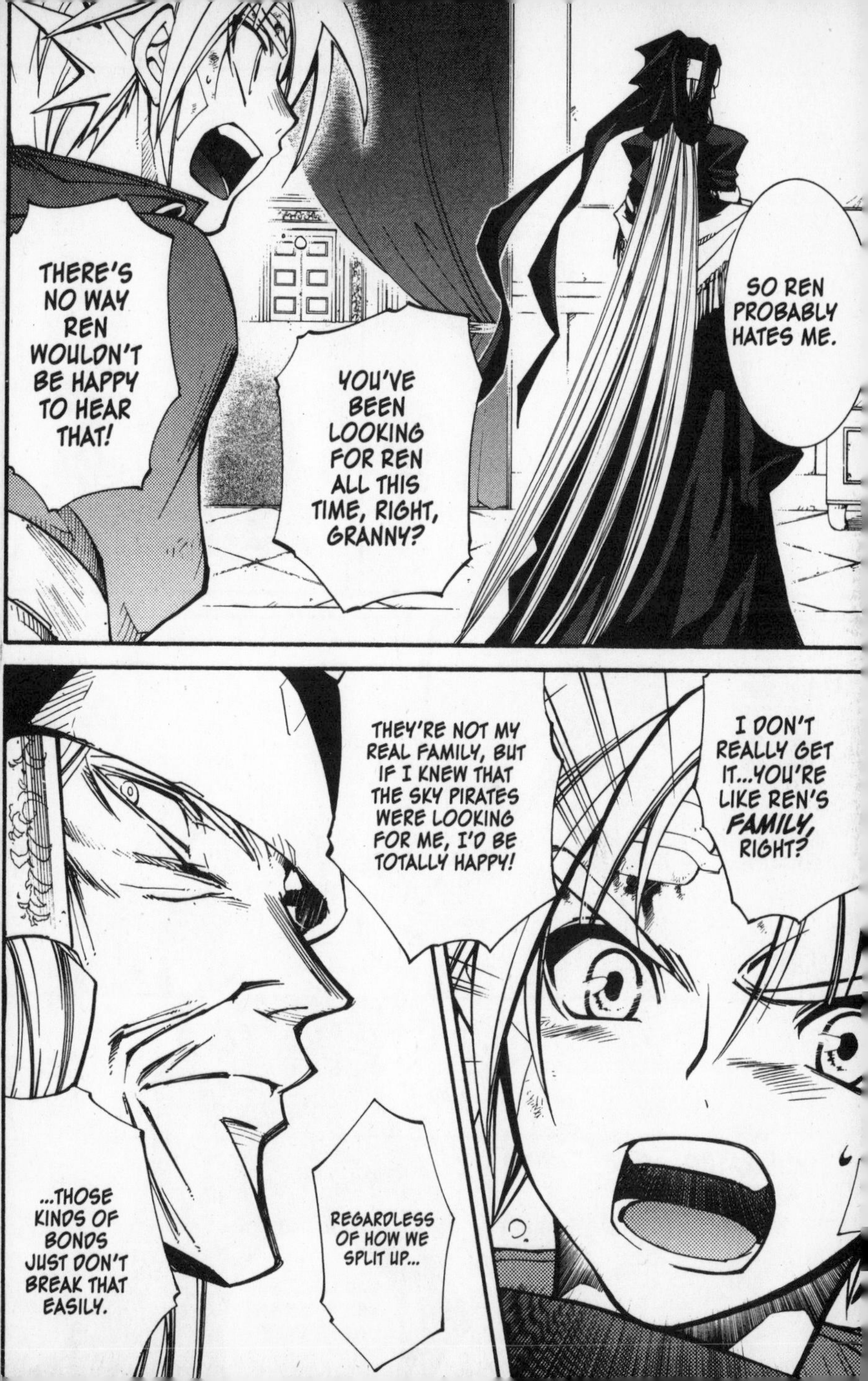
SO REN PROBABLY HATES ME.
YOU'VE BEEN LOOKING FOR REN ALL THIS TIME, RIGHT, GRANNY?
THERE'S NO WAY REN WOULDN'T BE HAPPY TO HEAR THAT!
I DON'T REALLY GET IT...YOU'RE LIKE REN'S *FAMILY,* RIGHT?
THEY'RE NOT MY REAL FAMILY, BUT IF I KNEW THAT THE SKY PIRATES WERE LOOKING FOR ME, I'D BE TOTALLY HAPPY!
REGARDLESS OF HOW WE SPLIT UP...
...THOSE KINDS OF BONDS JUST DON'T BREAK THAT EASILY.

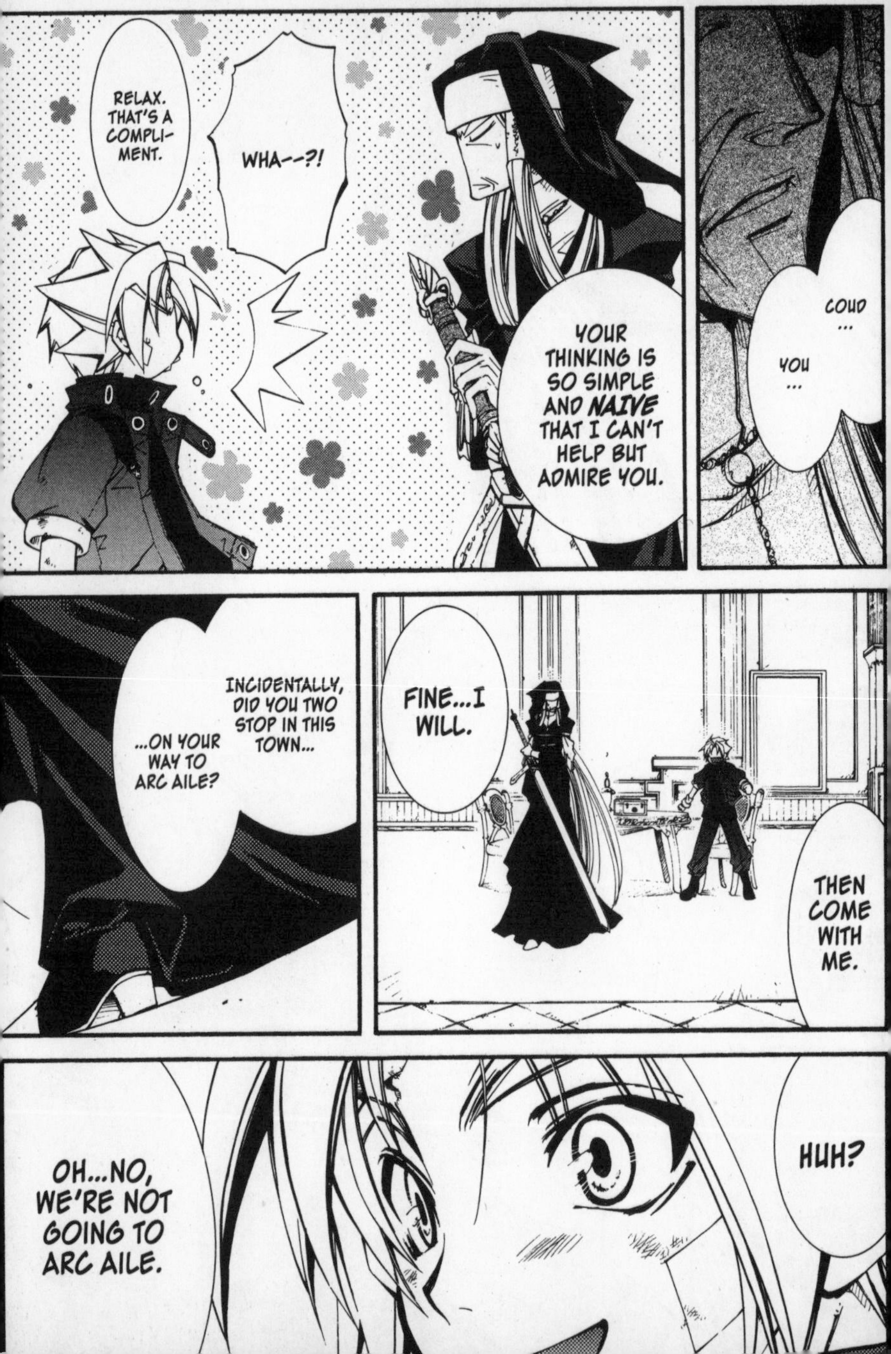
COUD ...
YOU ...
YOUR THINKING IS SO SIMPLE AND ***NAIVE*** THAT I CAN'T HELP BUT ADMIRE YOU.
WHA--?!
RELAX. THAT'S A COMPLIMENT.
THEN COME WITH ME.
FINE...I WILL.
INCIDENTALLY, DID YOU TWO STOP IN THIS TOWN...
...ON YOUR WAY TO ARC AILE?
HUH?
OH...NO, WE'RE NOT GOING TO ARC AILE.

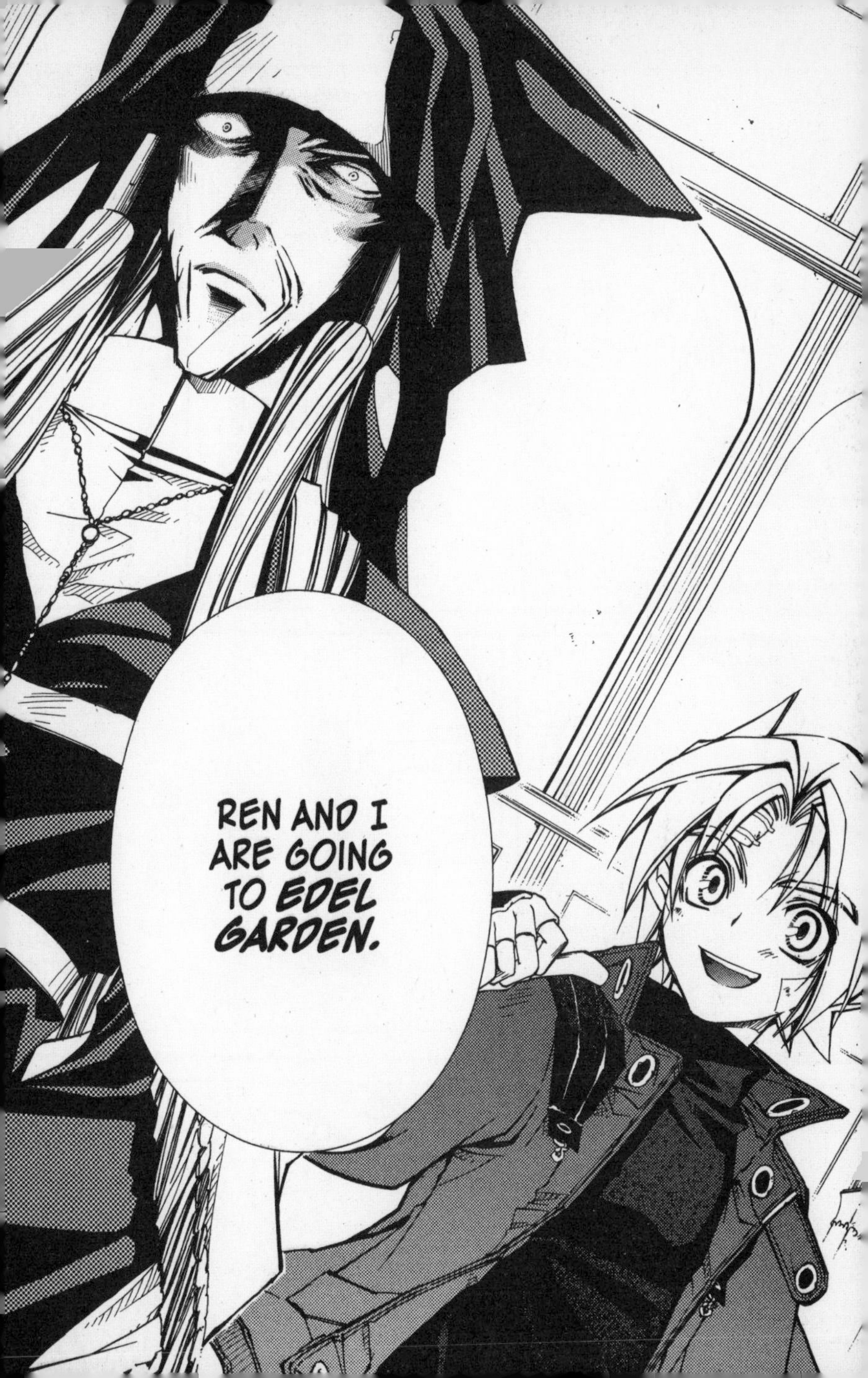
REN AND I ARE GOING TO EDEL GARDEN.

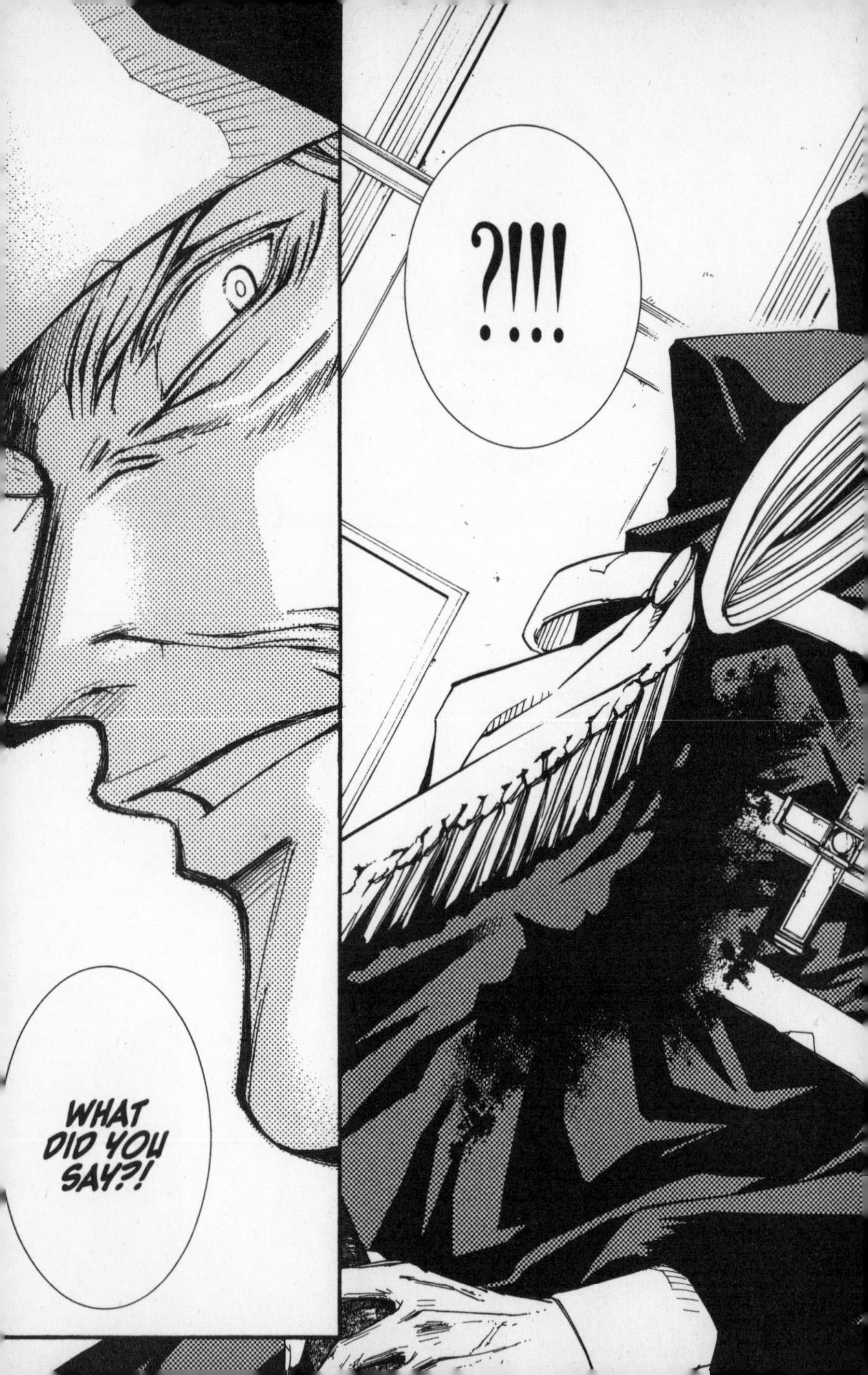
?!!!
WHAT DID YOU SAY?!

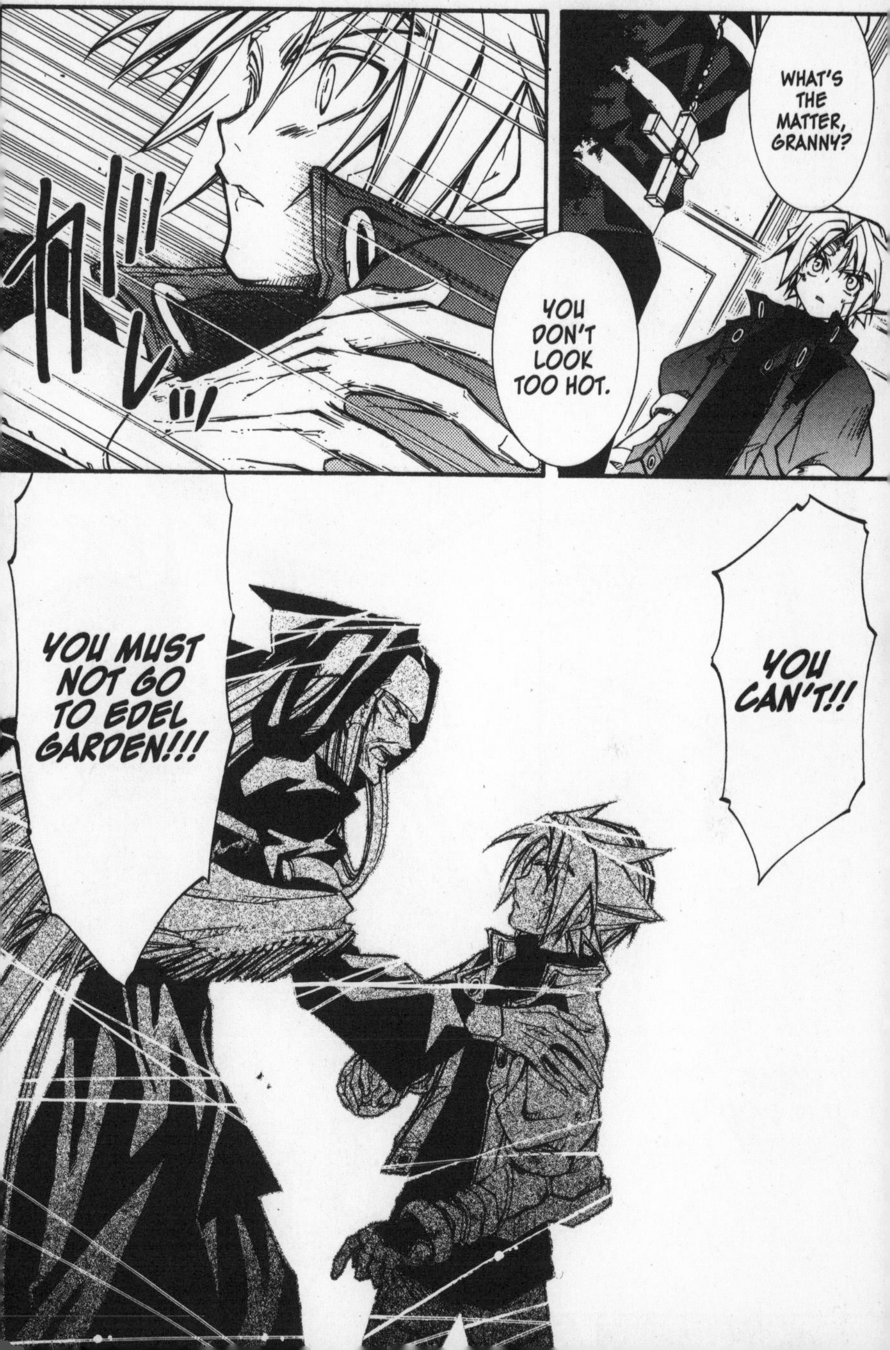
WHAT'S THE MATTER, GRANNY?
YOU DON'T LOOK TOO HOT.
YOU CAN'T!!
YOU MUST NOT GO TO EDEL GARDEN!!!

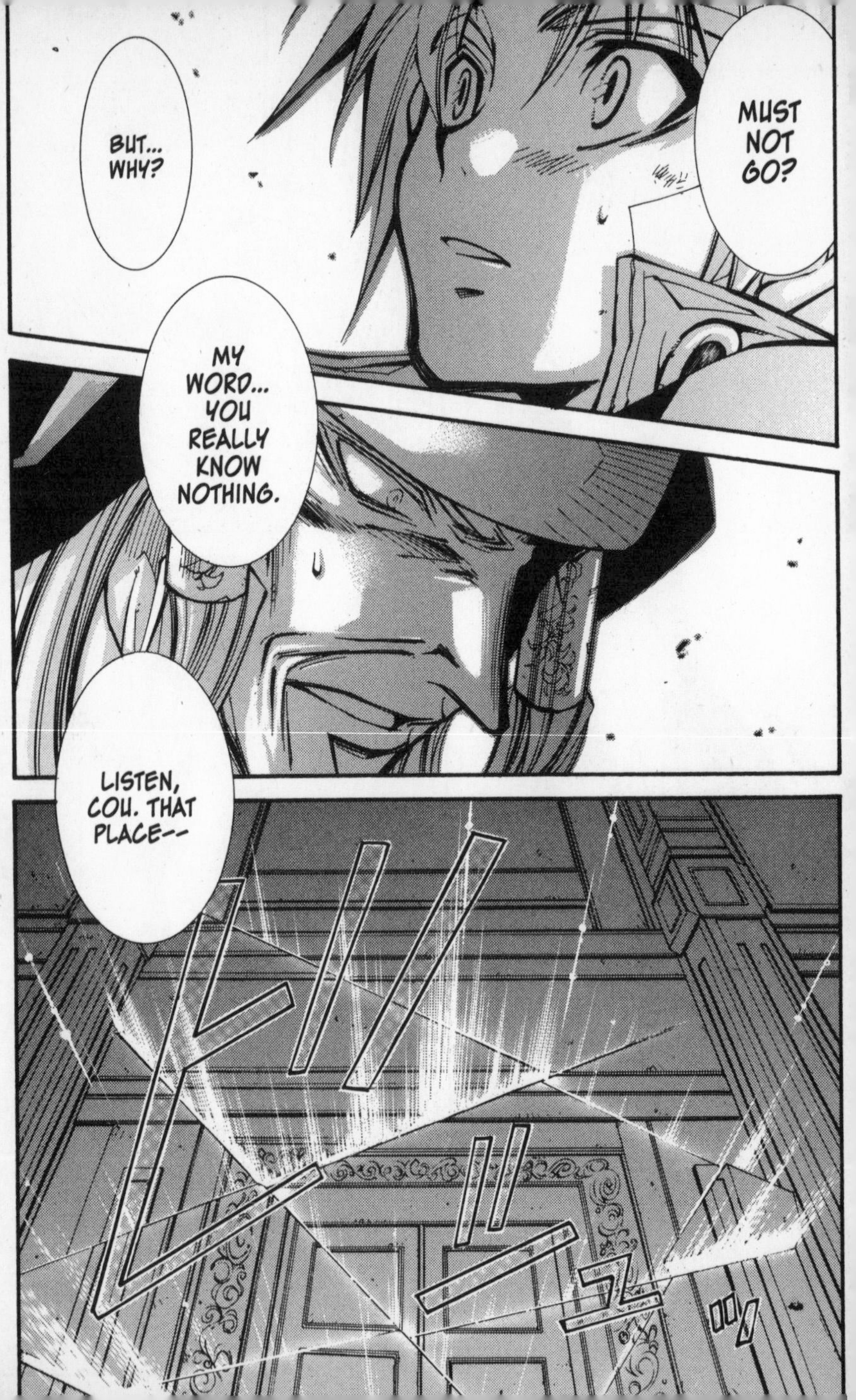
MUST NOT GO?
BUT... WHY?
MY WORD... YOU REALLY KNOW NOTHING.
LISTEN, COU. THAT PLACE--

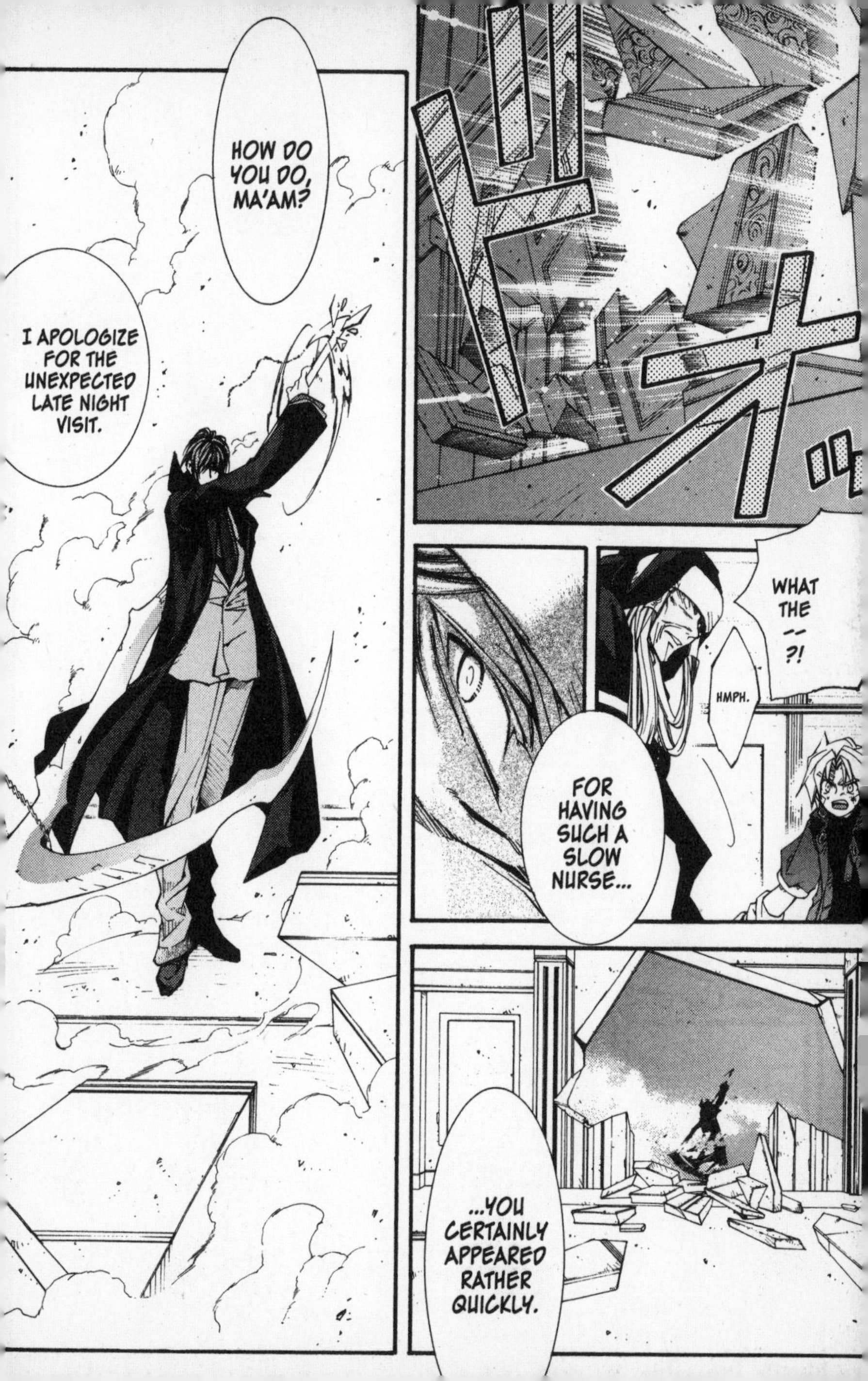
WHAT THE --?!
HMPH.
FOR HAVING SUCH A SLOW NURSE...
...YOU CERTAINLY APPEARED RATHER QUICKLY.
HOW DO YOU DO, MA'AM?
I APOLOGIZE FOR THE UNEXPECTED LATE NIGHT VISIT.

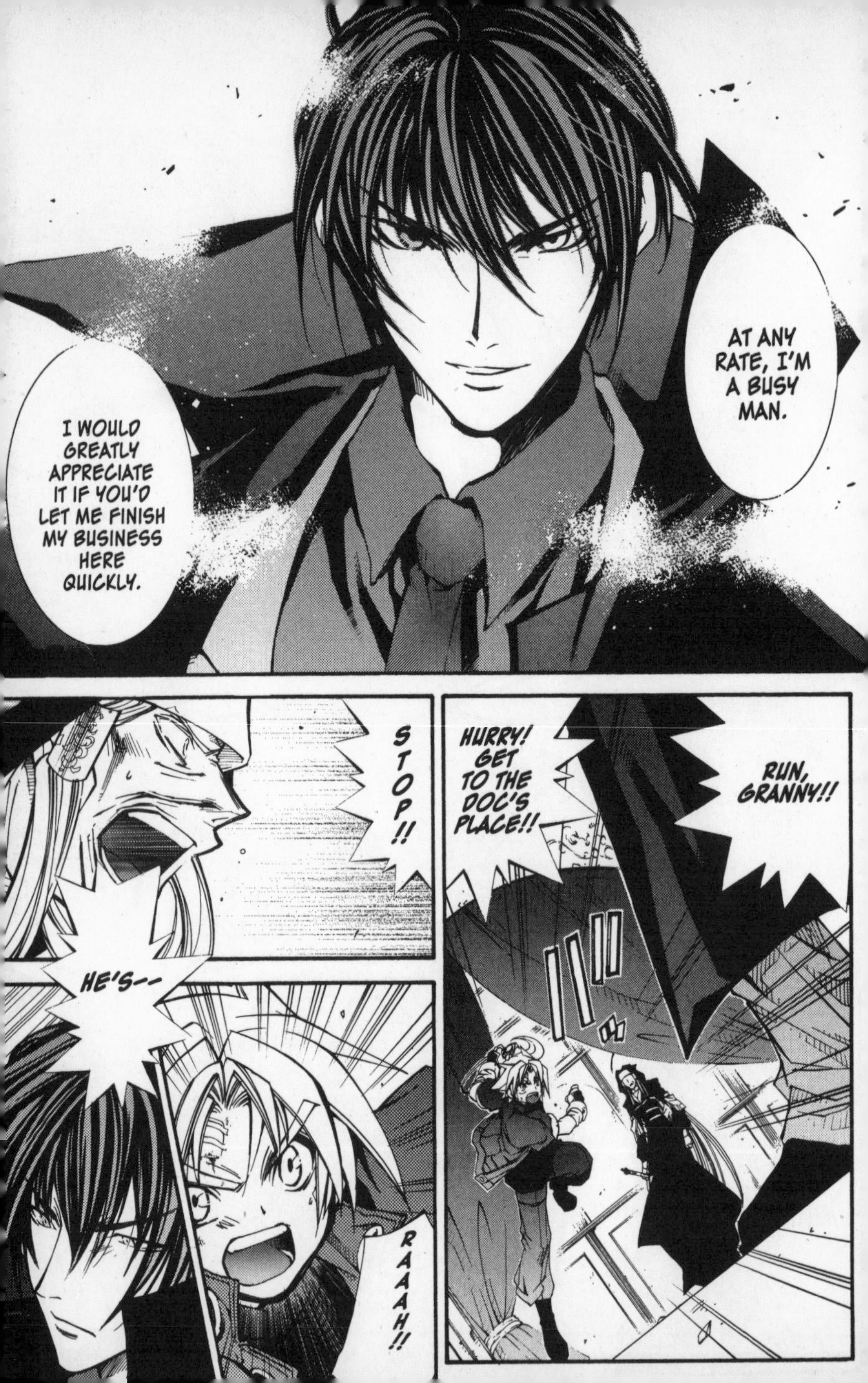
AT ANY RATE, I'M A BUSY MAN.
I WOULD GREATLY APPRECIATE IT IF YOU'D LET ME FINISH MY BUSINESS HERE QUICKLY.
RUN, GRANNY!!
HURRY! GET TO THE DOC'S PLACE!!
STOP!!
HE'S--
RAAAAH!!

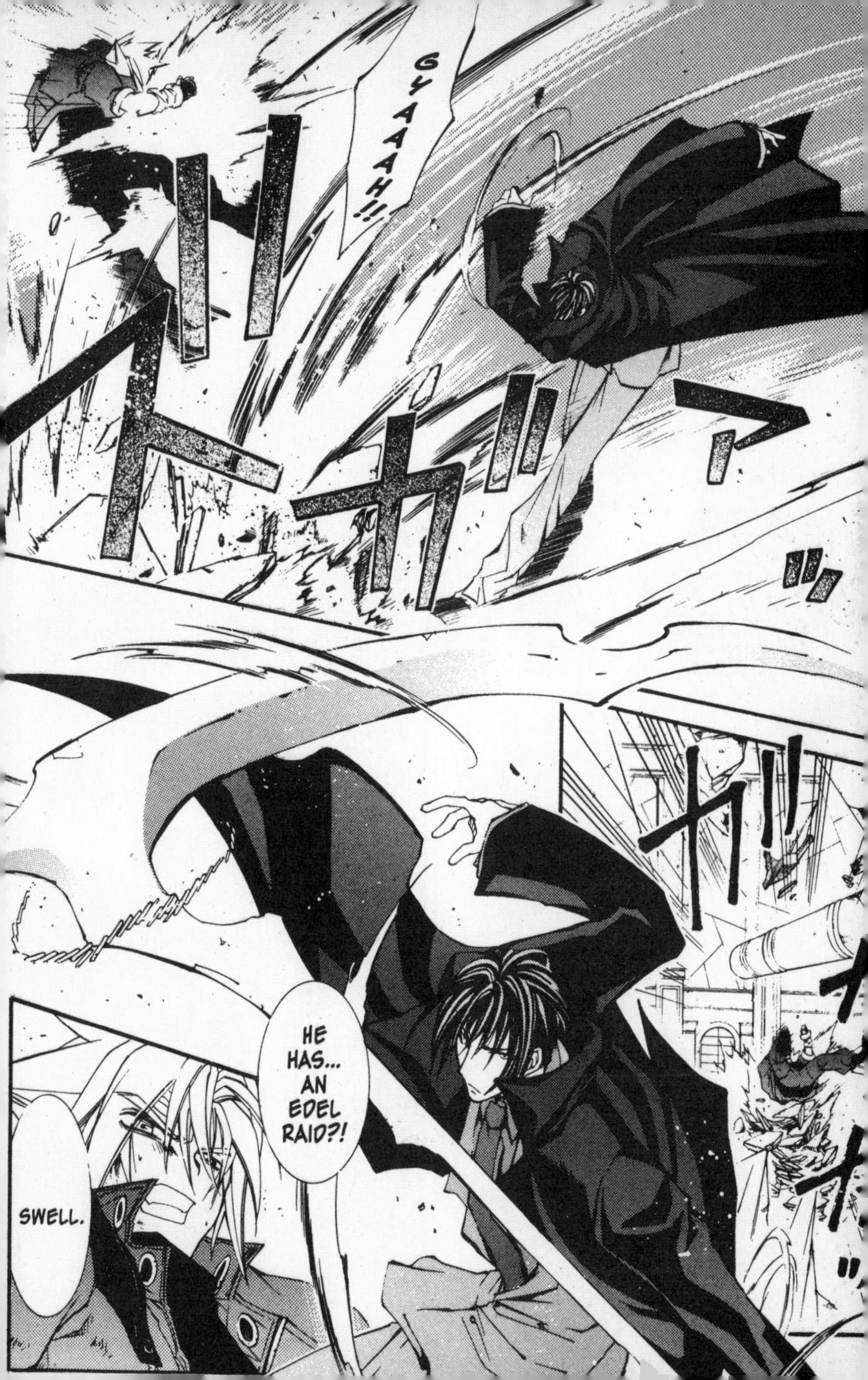
GYAAAAH!!
HE HAS... AN EDEL RAID?!
SWELL.

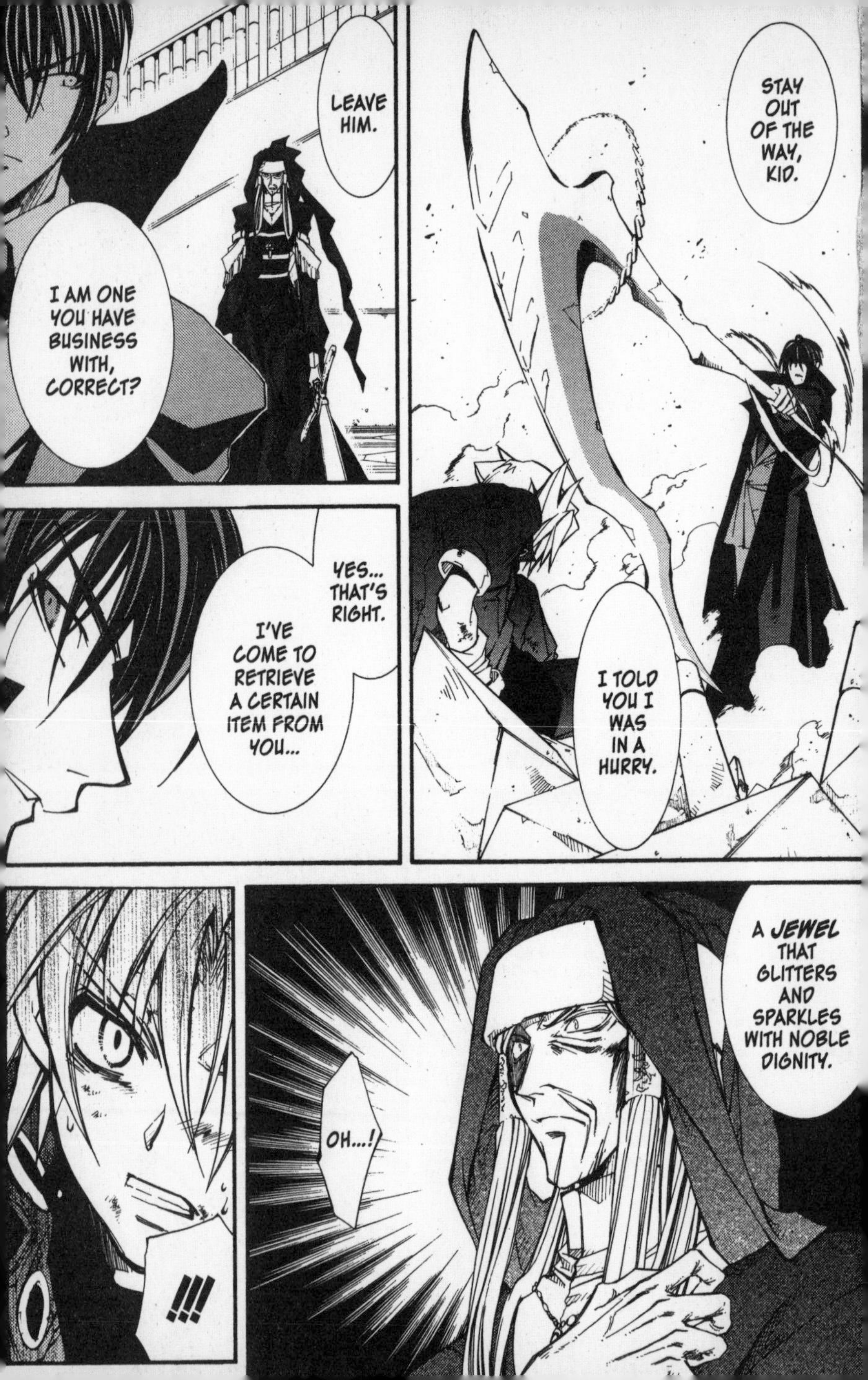
STAY OUT OF THE WAY, KID.
I TOLD YOU I WAS IN A HURRY.
LEAVE HIM.
I AM ONE YOU HAVE BUSINESS WITH, CORRECT?
YES... THAT'S RIGHT.
I'VE COME TO RETRIEVE A CERTAIN ITEM FROM YOU...
A *JEWEL* THAT GLITTERS AND SPARKLES WITH NOBLE DIGNITY.
OH...!
!!!

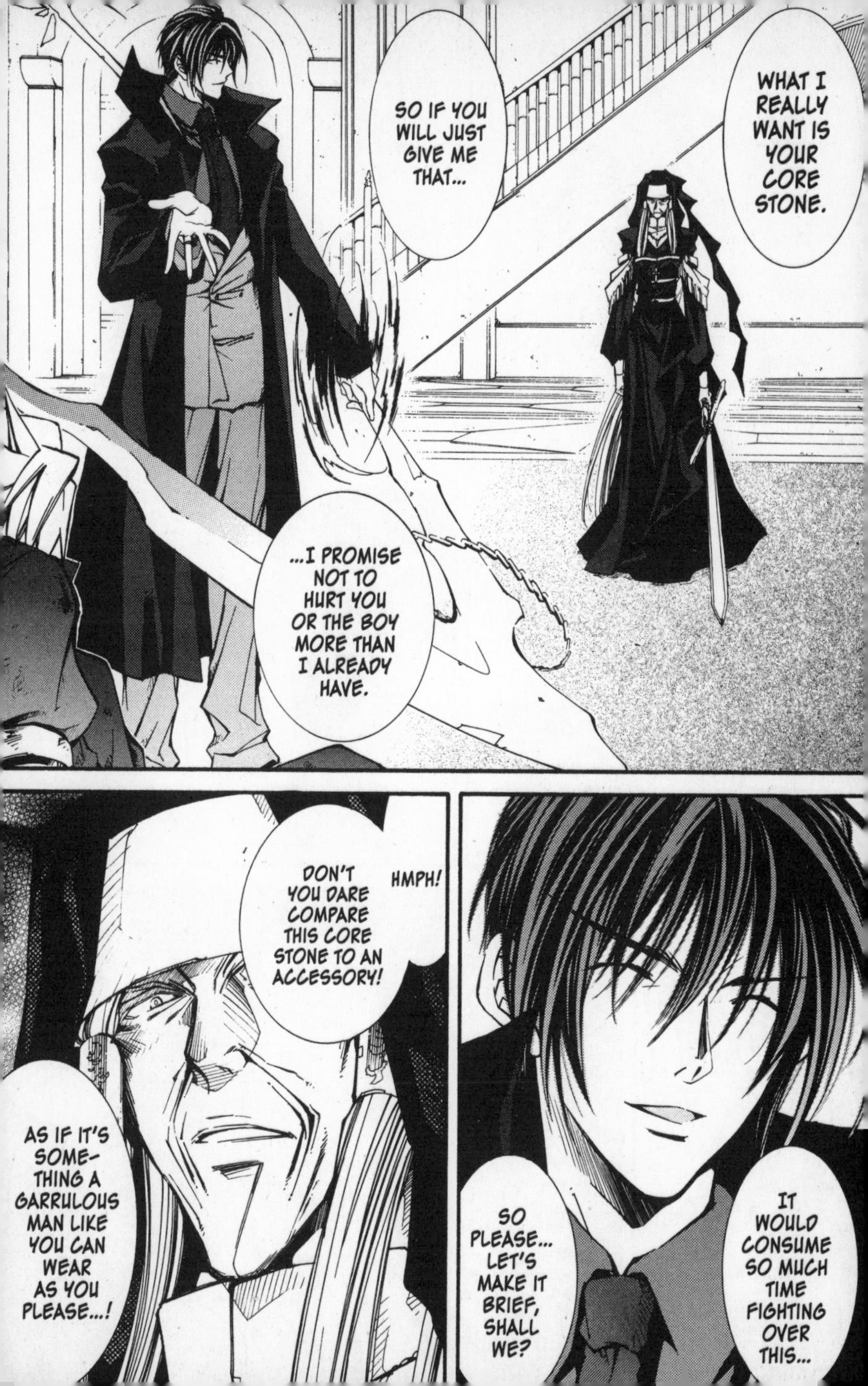
WHAT I REALLY WANT IS YOUR CORE STONE.
SO IF YOU WILL JUST GIVE ME THAT...
...I PROMISE NOT TO HURT YOU OR THE BOY MORE THAN I ALREADY HAVE.
IT WOULD CONSUME SO MUCH TIME FIGHTING OVER THIS...
SO PLEASE... LET'S MAKE IT BRIEF, SHALL WE?
HMPH!
DON'T YOU DARE COMPARE THIS CORE STONE TO AN ACCESSORY!
AS IF IT'S SOME-THING A GARRULOUS MAN LIKE YOU CAN WEAR AS YOU PLEASE...!

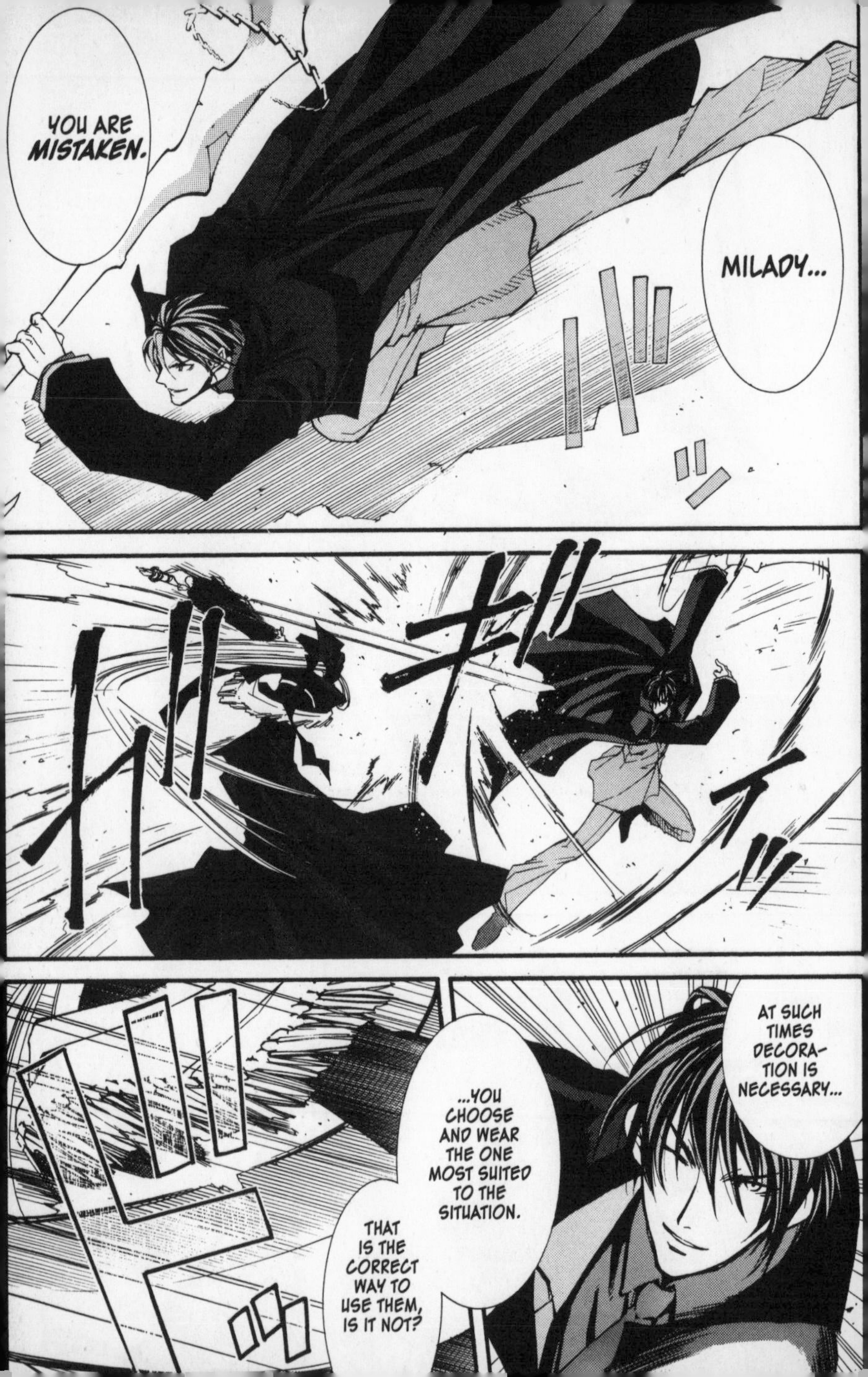
MILADY...
YOU ARE MISTAKEN.
AT SUCH TIMES DECORATION IS NECESSARY...
...YOU CHOOSE AND WEAR THE ONE MOST SUITED TO THE SITUATION.
THAT IS THE CORRECT WAY TO USE THEM, IS IT NOT?

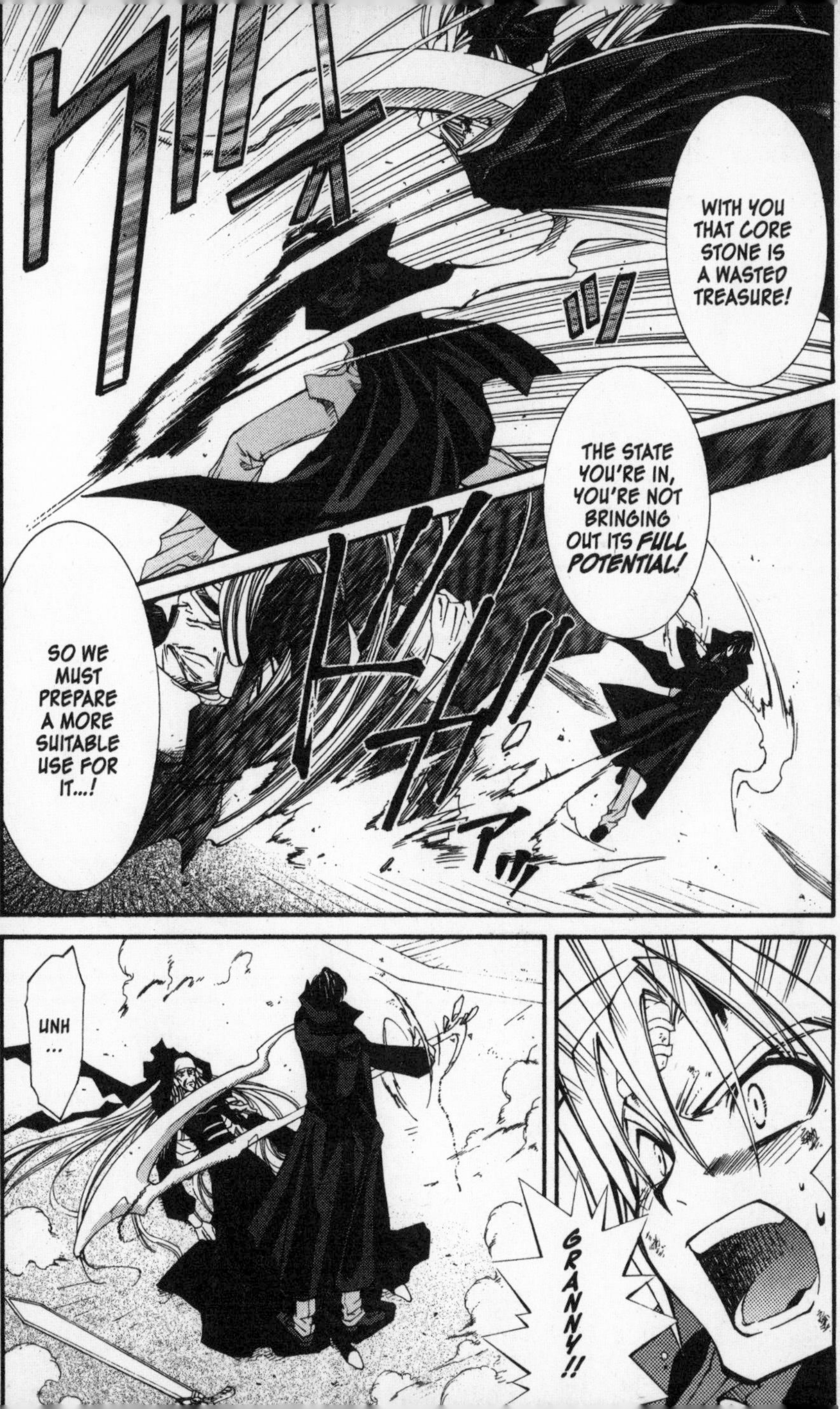
WITH YOU THAT CORE STONE IS A WASTED TREASURE!
THE STATE YOU'RE IN, YOU'RE NOT BRINGING OUT ITS FULL POTENTIAL!
SO WE MUST PREPARE A MORE SUITABLE USE FOR IT...!
GRANNY!!
UNH ...

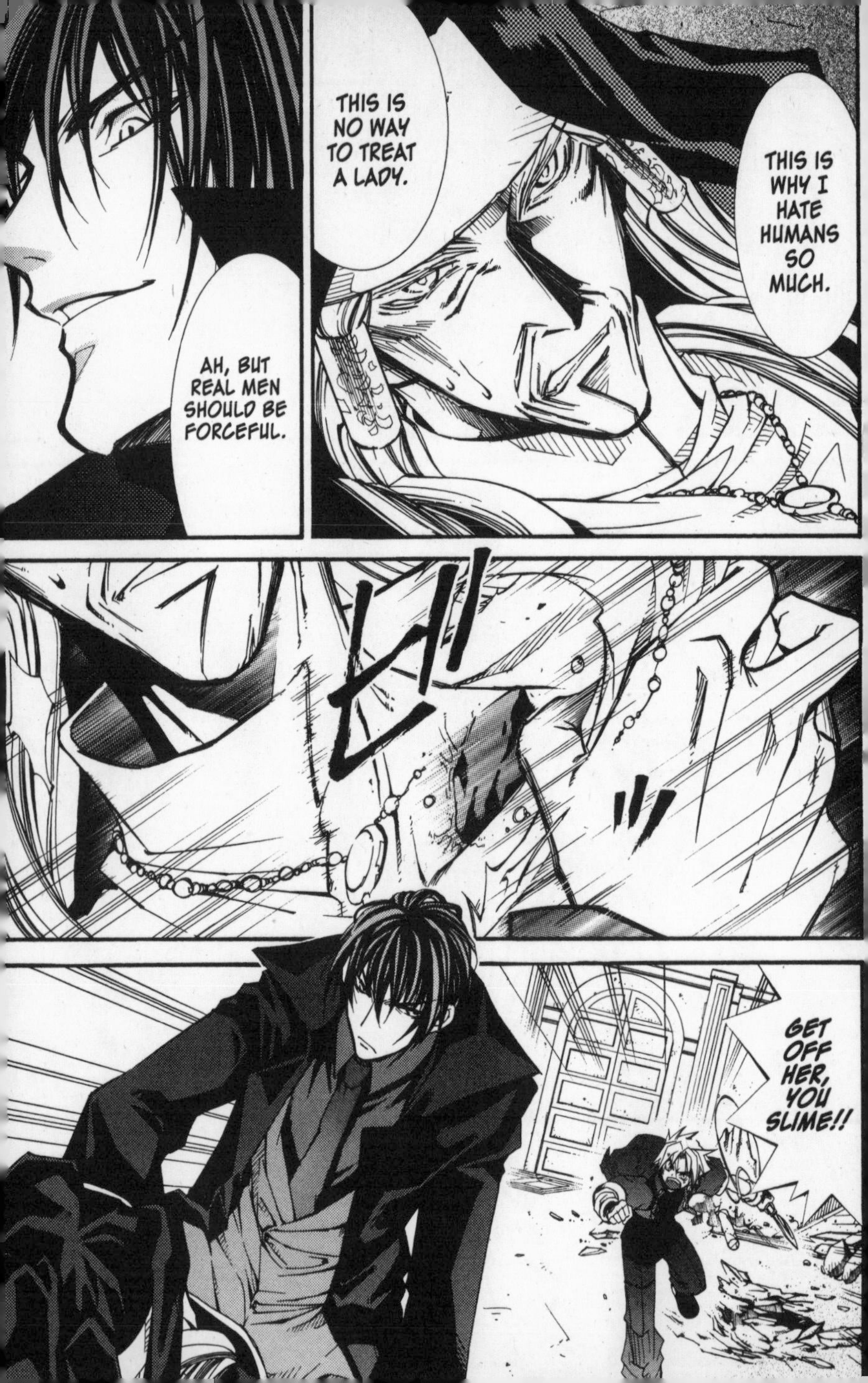
THIS IS NO WAY TO TREAT A LADY.
THIS IS WHY I HATE HUMANS SO MUCH.
AH, BUT REAL MEN SHOULD BE FORCEFUL.
GET OFF HER, YOU SLIME!!

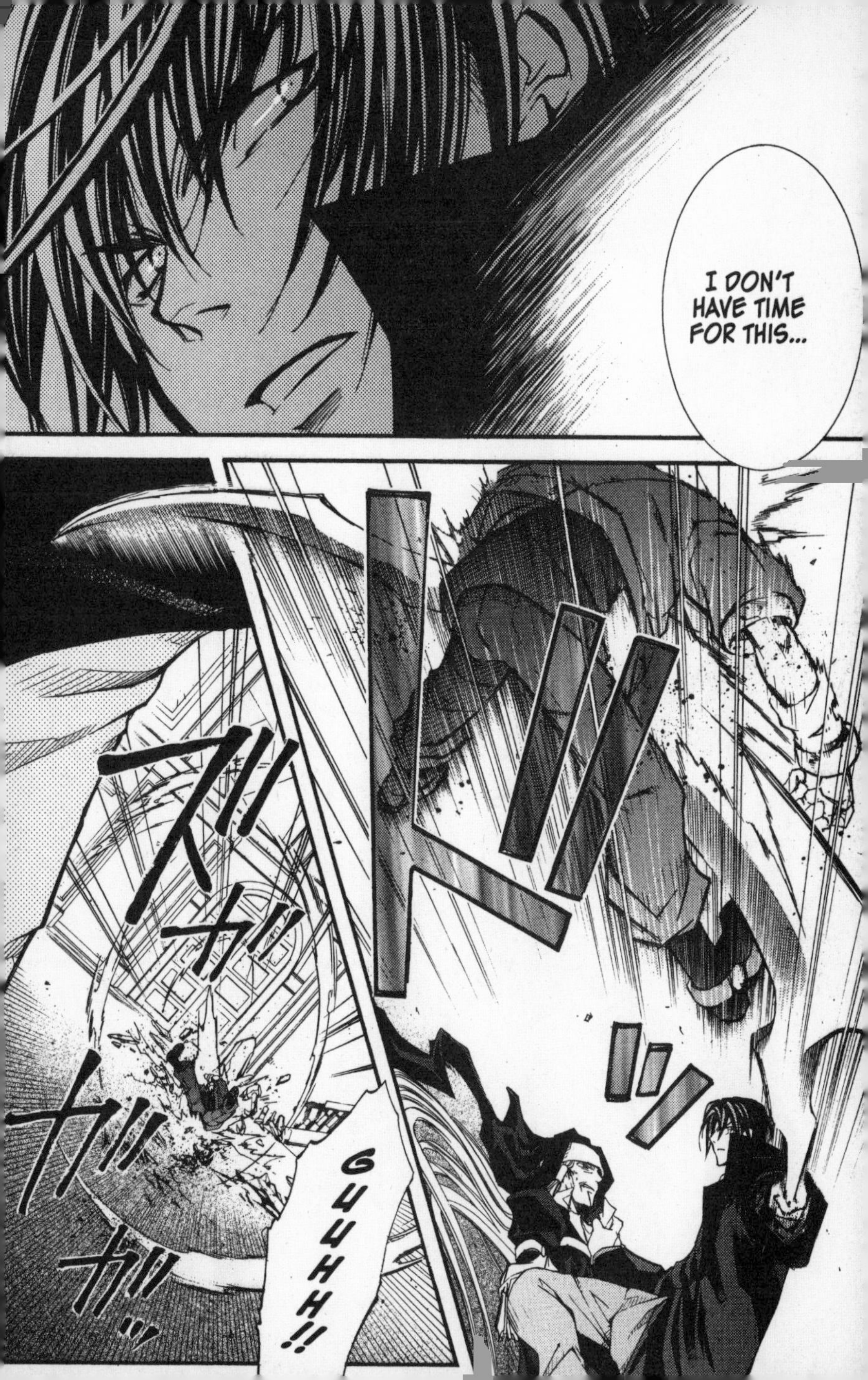
I DON'T HAVE TIME FOR THIS...
GUUHHH!!

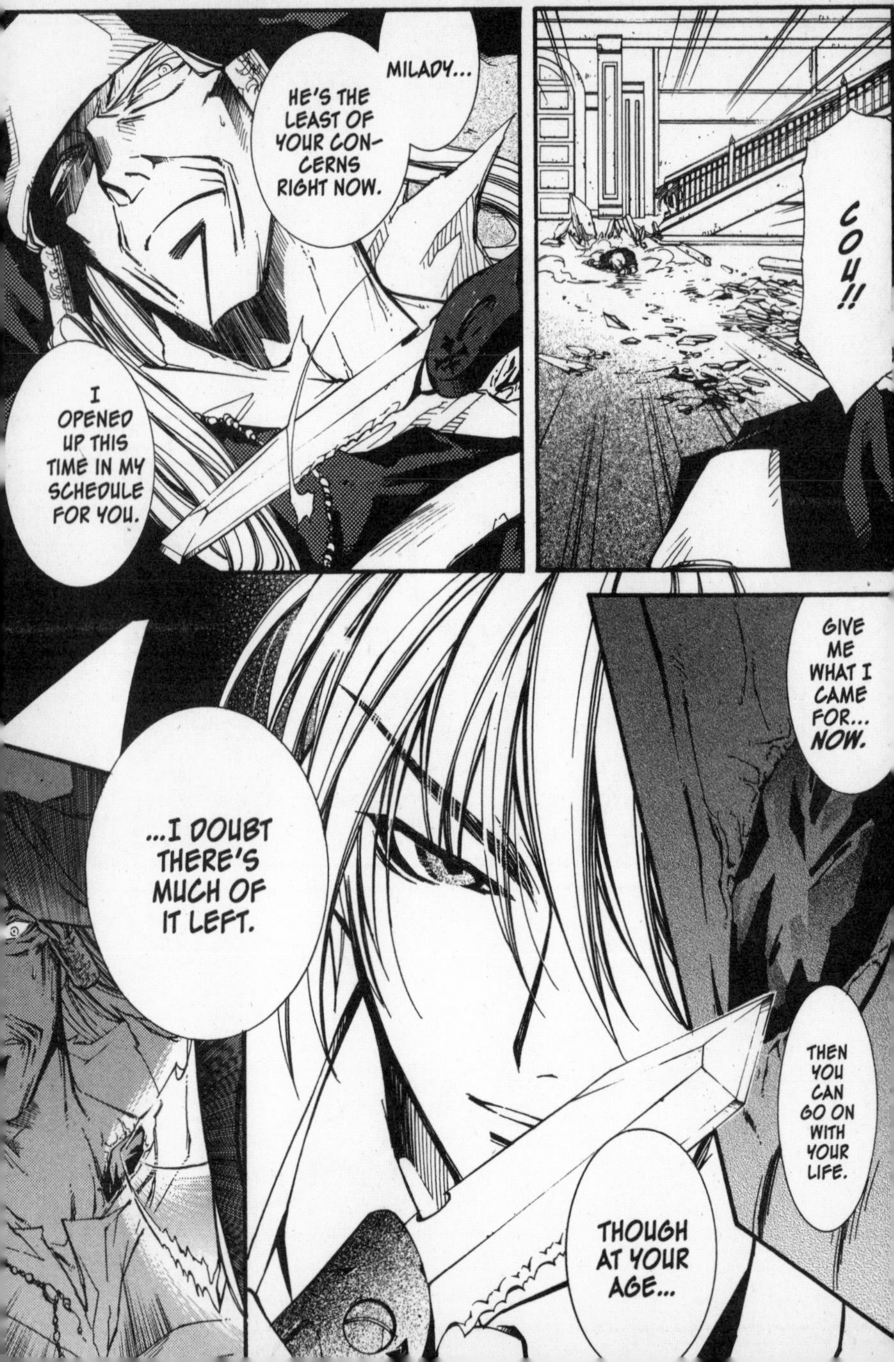
COU!!
MILADY...
HE'S THE LEAST OF YOUR CON-CERNS RIGHT NOW.
I OPENED UP THIS TIME IN MY SCHEDULE FOR YOU.
GIVE ME WHAT I CAME FOR... *NOW.*
THEN YOU CAN GO ON WITH YOUR LIFE.
THOUGH AT YOUR AGE...
...I DOUBT THERE'S MUCH OF IT LEFT.

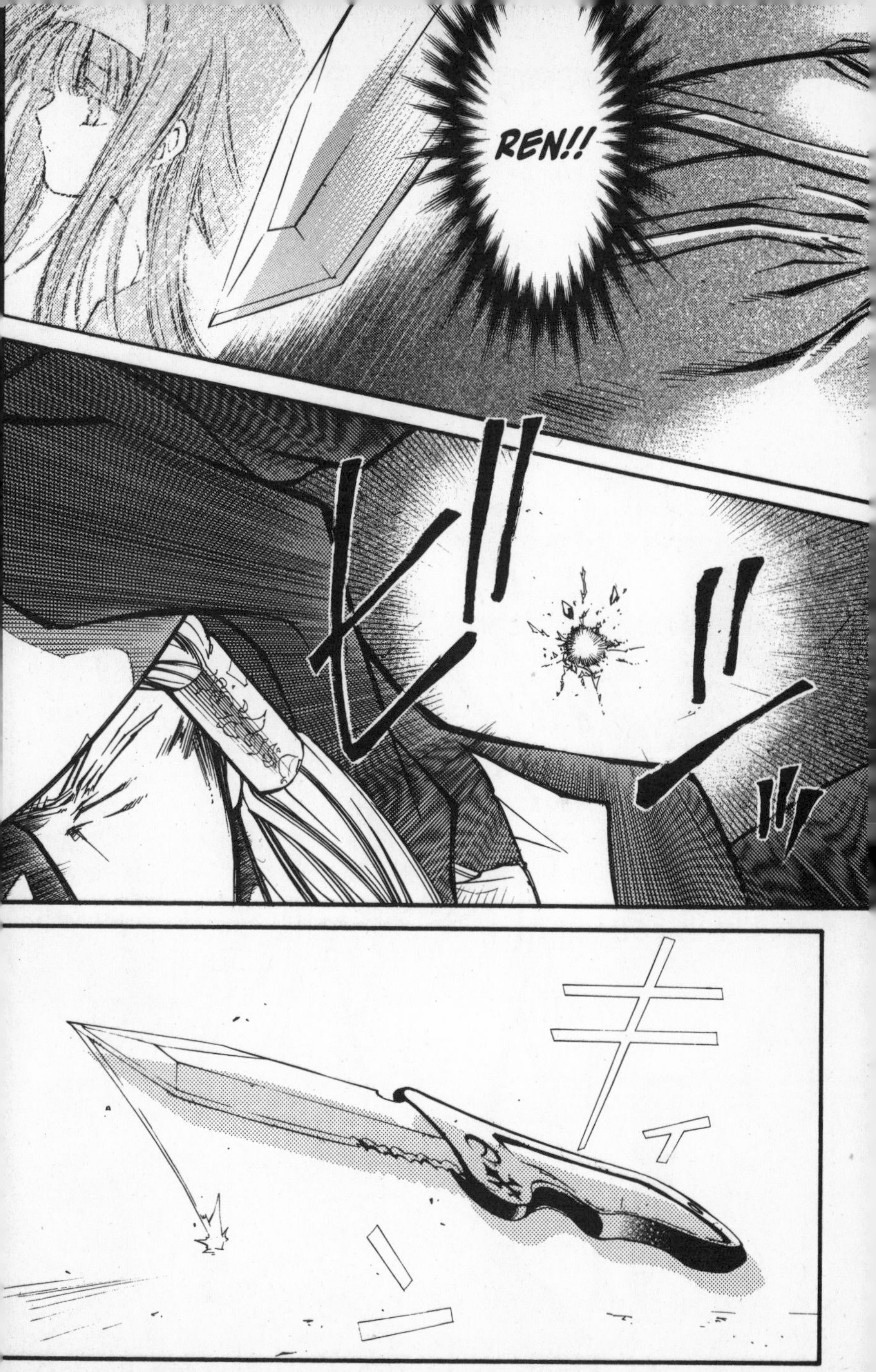
REN!!

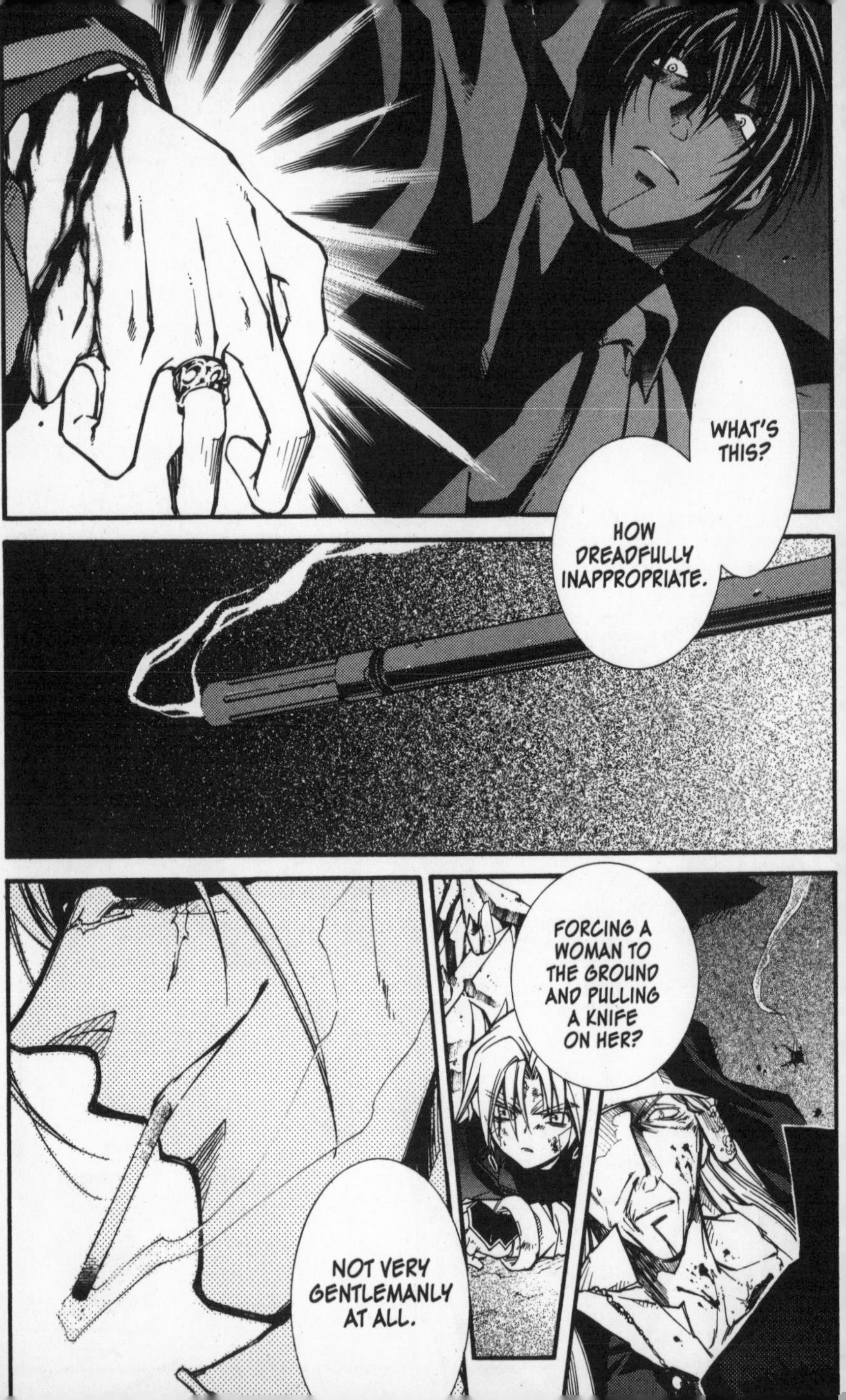
WHAT'S THIS?
HOW DREADFULLY INAPPROPRIATE.
FORCING A WOMAN TO THE GROUND AND PULLING A KNIFE ON HER?
NOT VERY GENTLEMANLY AT ALL.

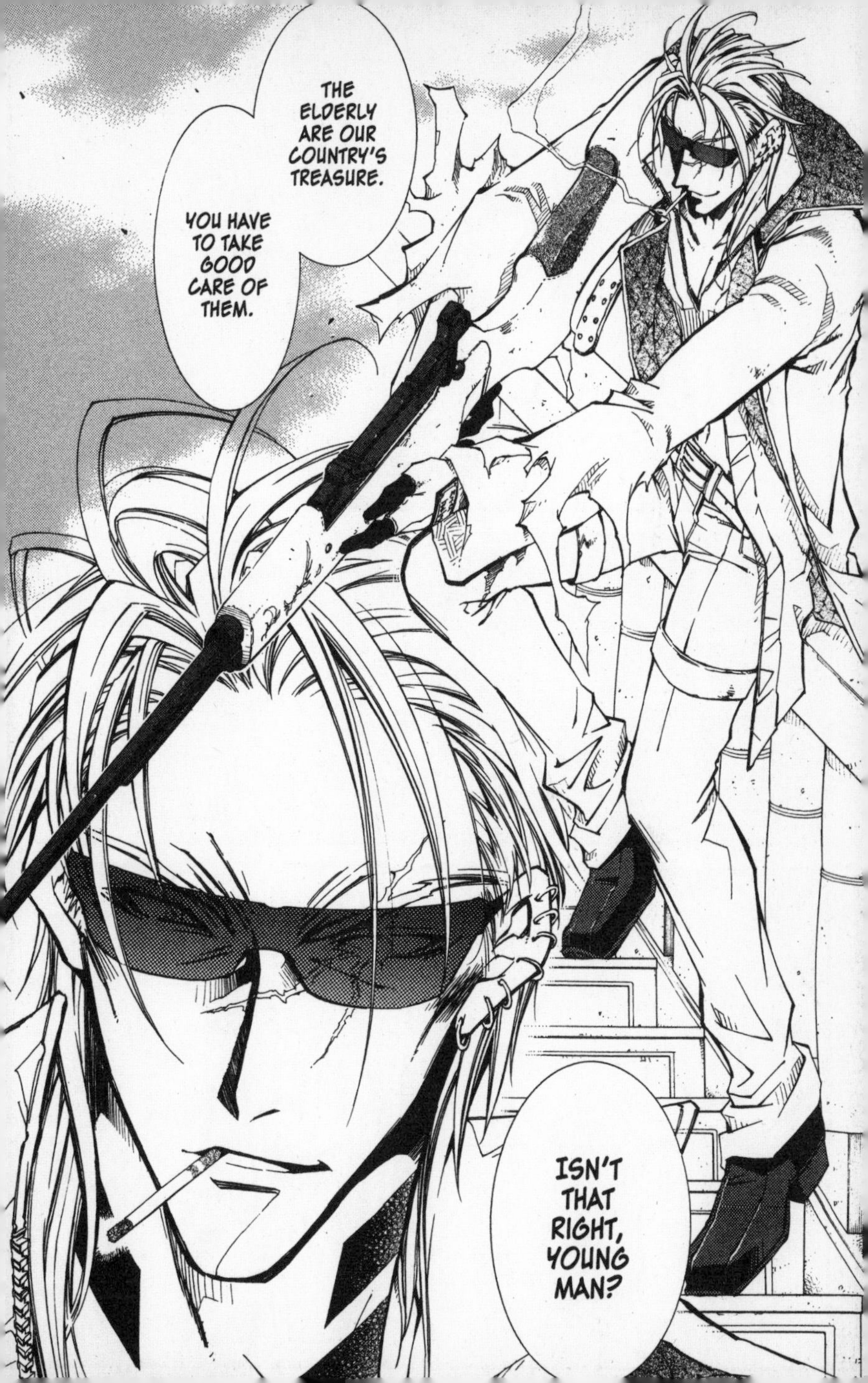
THE ELDERLY ARE OUR COUNTRY'S TREASURE.
YOU HAVE TO TAKE GOOD CARE OF THEM.
ISN'T THAT RIGHT, YOUNG MAN?

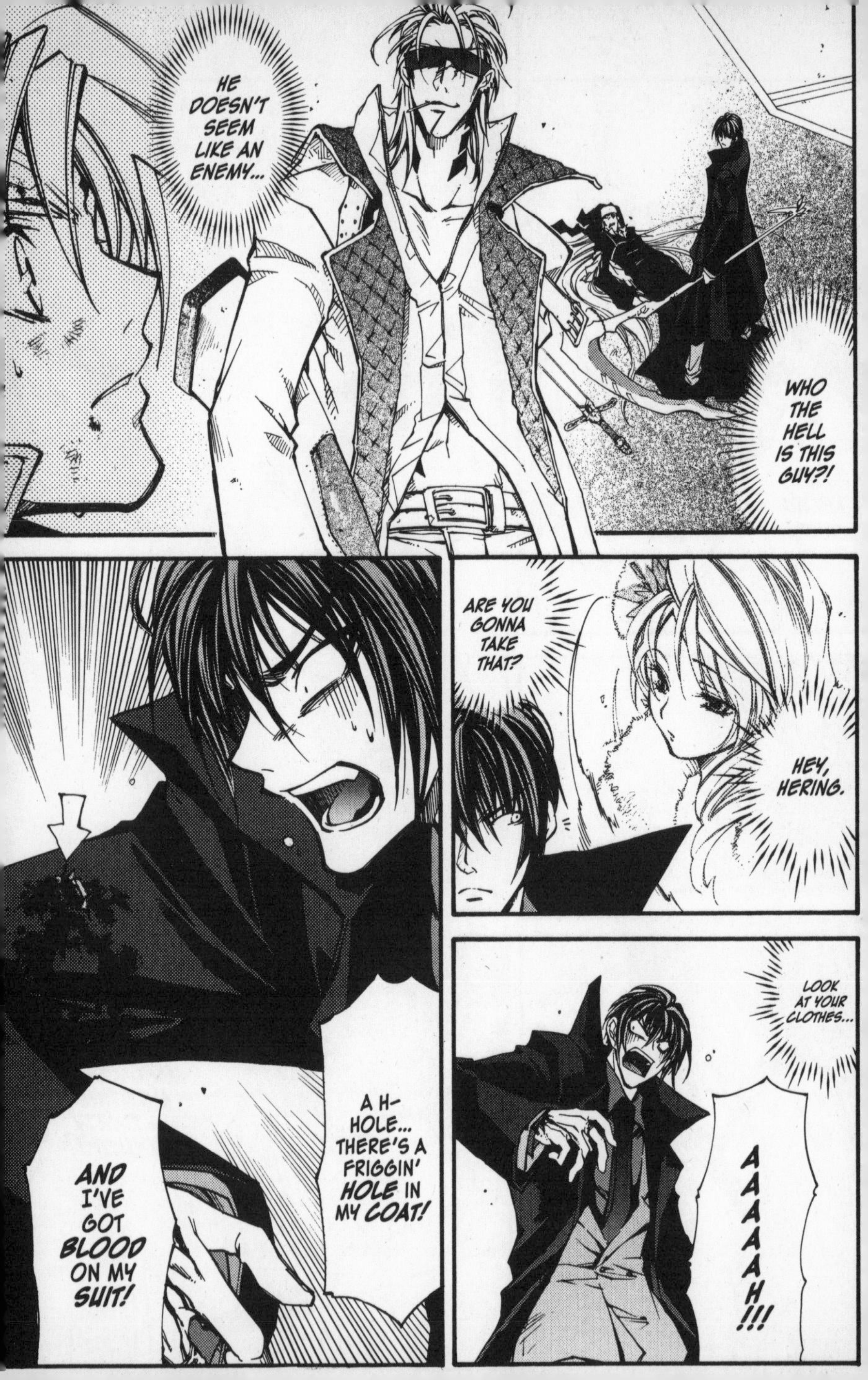

WHO THE HELL IS THIS GUY?!
HE DOESN'T SEEM LIKE AN ENEMY...
HEY, HERING.
ARE YOU GONNA TAKE THAT?
LOOK AT YOUR CLOTHES...
AAAAAAH!!!
A H-HOLE... THERE'S A FRIGGIN' HOLE IN MY COAT!
AND I'VE GOT BLOOD ON MY SUIT!

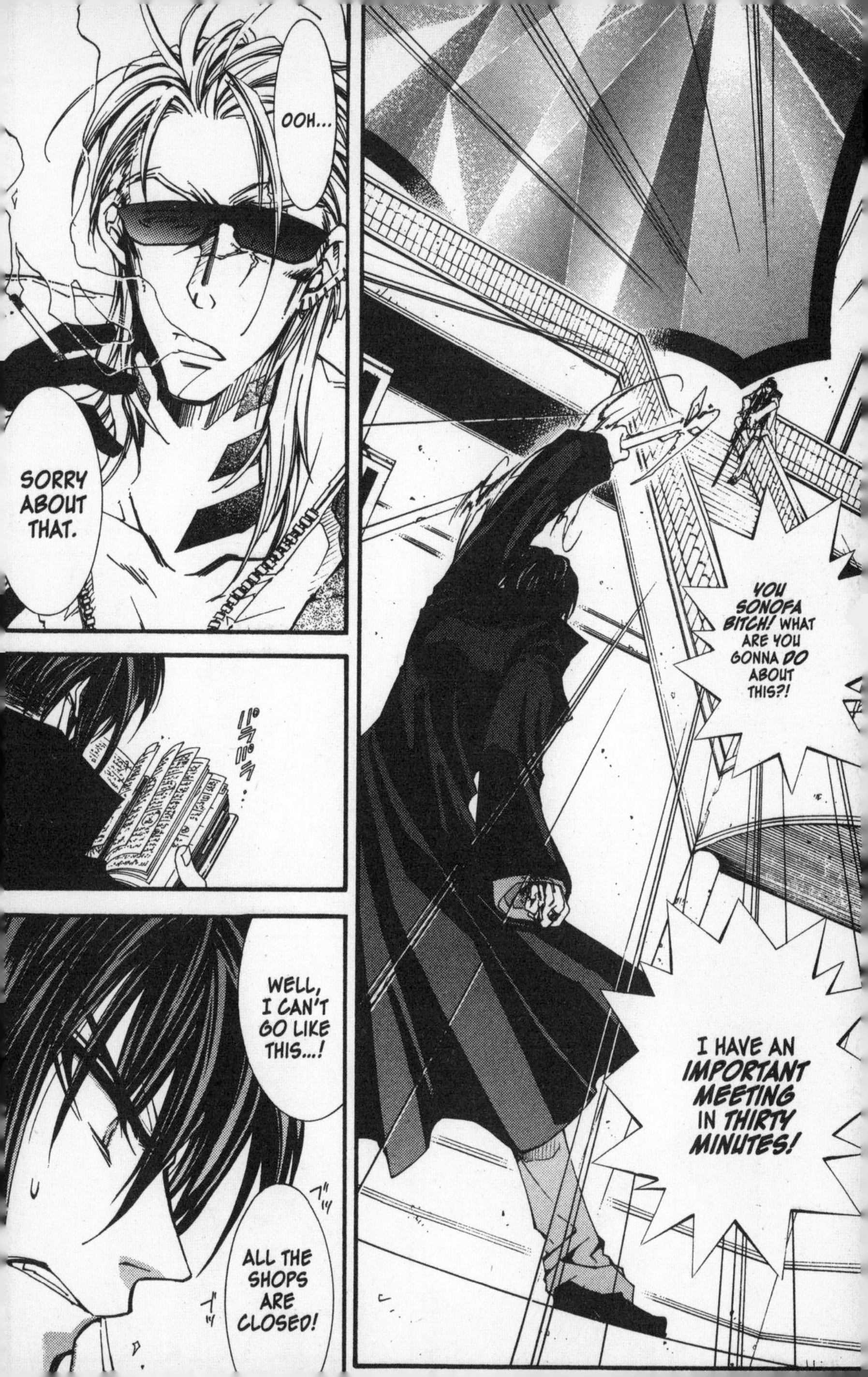
YOU SONOFA BITCH! WHAT ARE YOU GONNA DO ABOUT THIS?!
I HAVE AN IMPORTANT MEETING IN THIRTY MINUTES!
OOH...
SORRY ABOUT THAT.
WELL, I CAN'T GO LIKE THIS...!
ALL THE SHOPS ARE CLOSED!

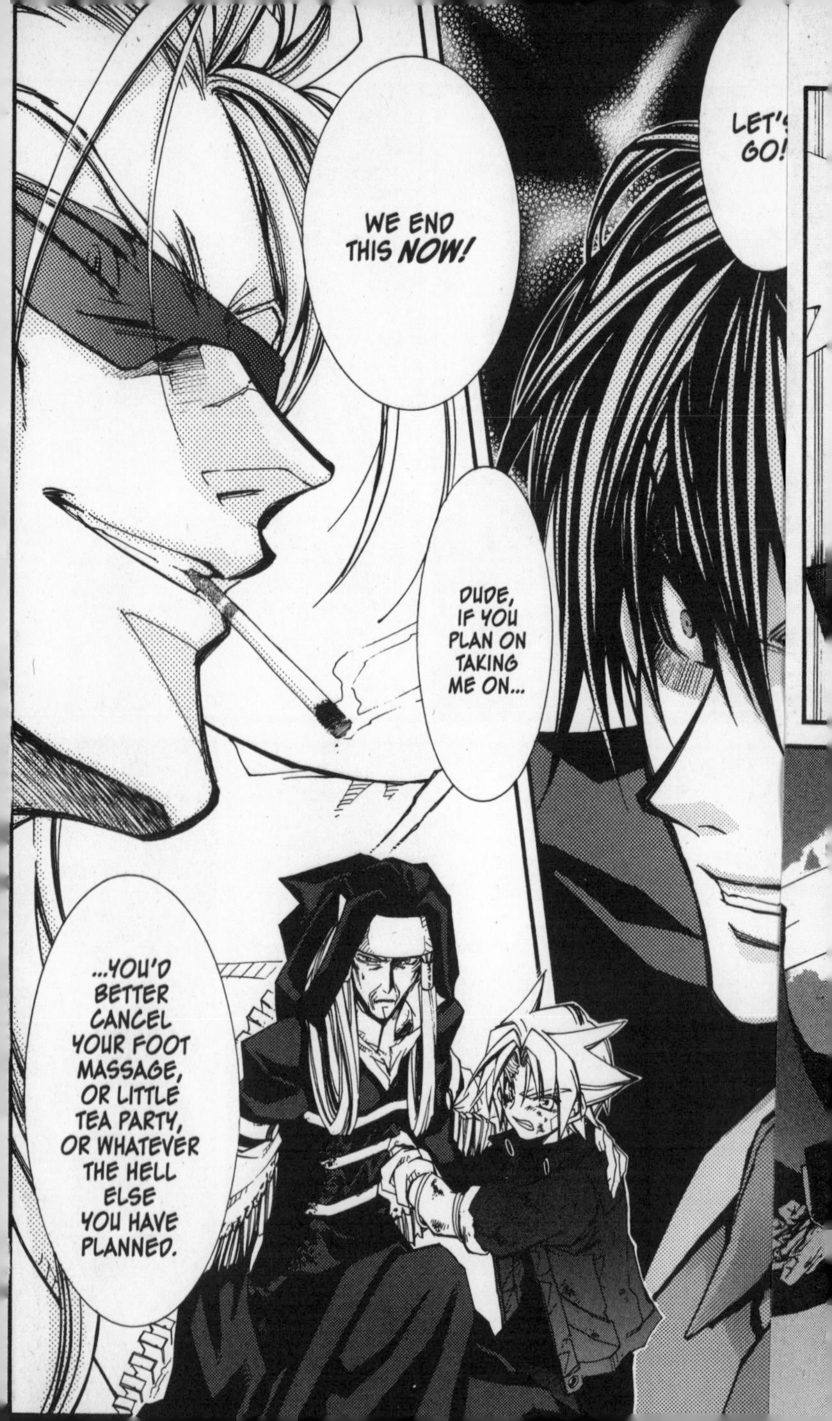
LET'S GO!
WE END THIS NOW!
DUDE, IF YOU PLAN ON TAKING ME ON...
...YOU'D BETTER CANCEL YOUR FOOT MASSAGE, OR LITTLE TEA PARTY, OR WHATEVER THE HELL ELSE YOU HAVE PLANNED.

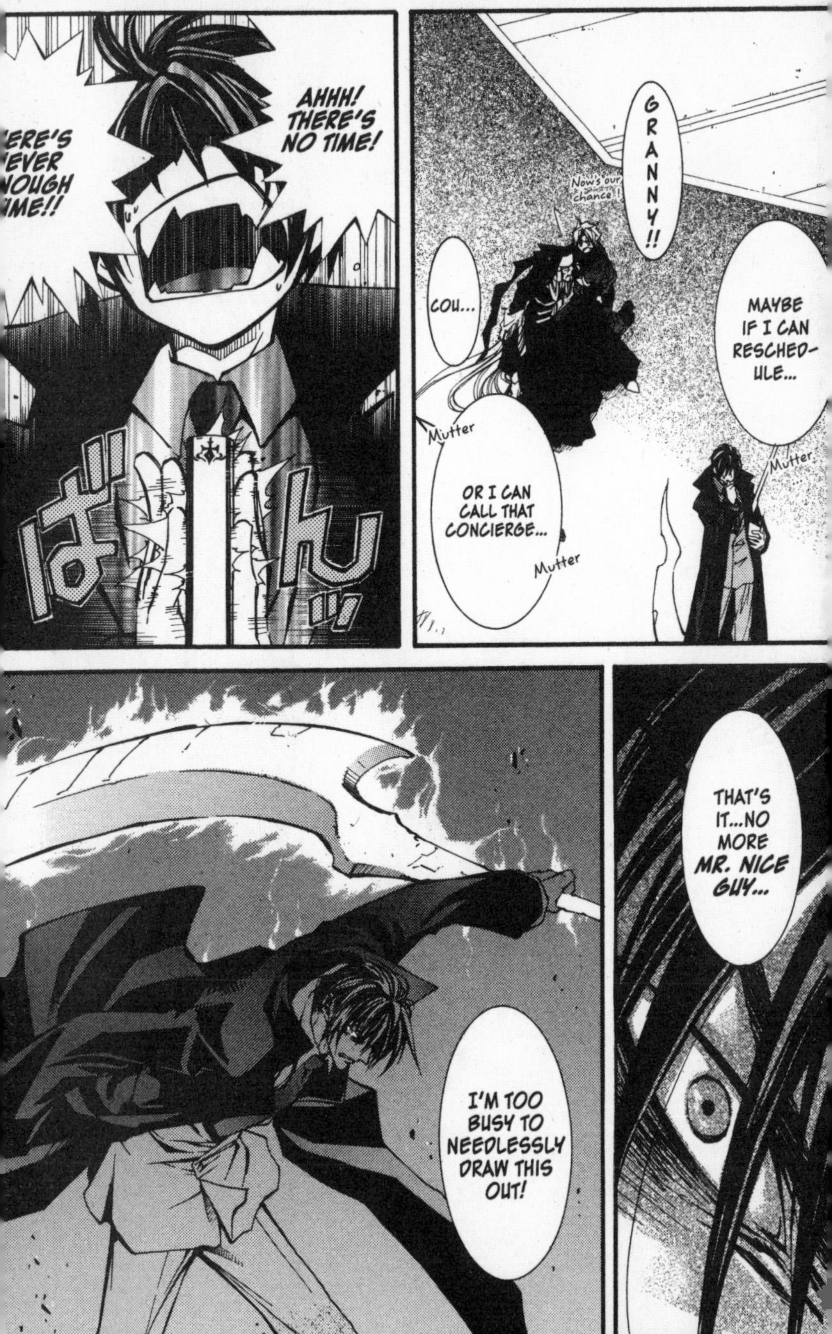
GRANNY!!
Now's our chance!
MAYBE IF I CAN RESCHED-ULE...
Mutter
COU...
Mutter
OR I CAN CALL THAT CONCIERGE...
Mutter
AHHH! THERE'S NO TIME!
ERE'S EVER NOUGH IME!!
ばーん
THAT'S IT...NO MORE MR. NICE GUY...
I'M TOO BUSY TO NEEDLESSLY DRAW THIS OUT!

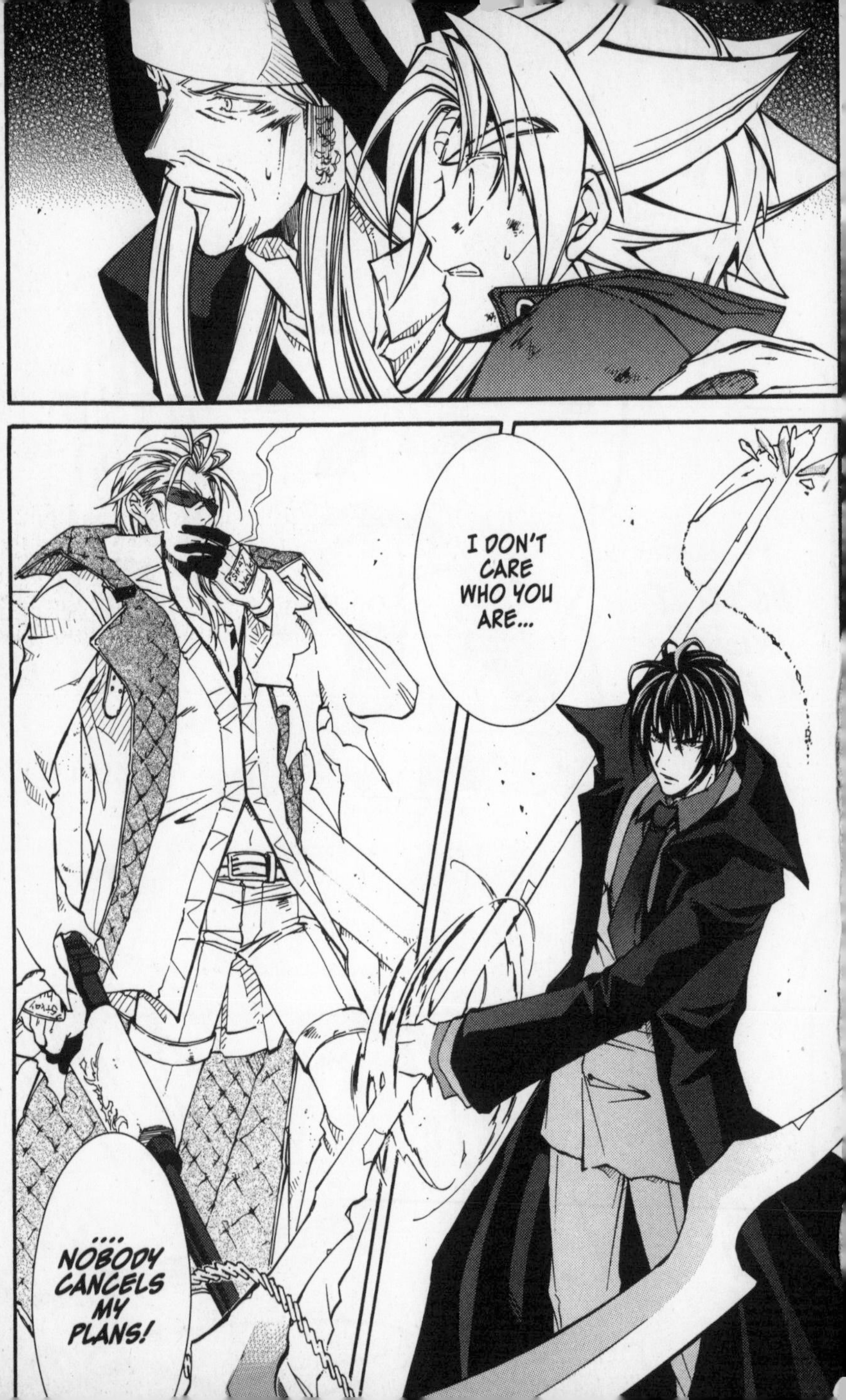
I DON'T CARE WHO YOU ARE...
.... NOBODY CANCELS MY PLANS!

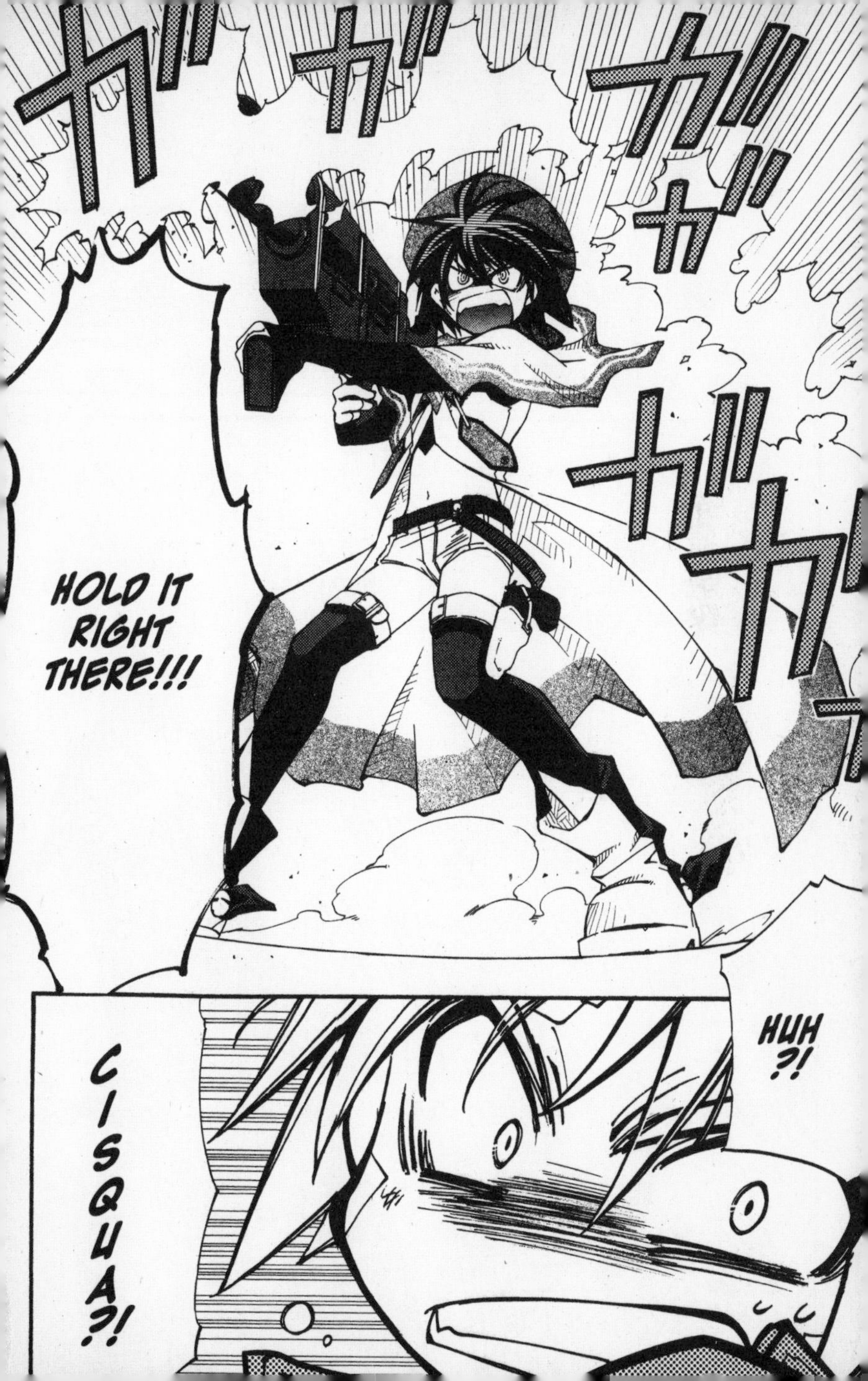
ガガガガガガ
HOLD IT RIGHT THERE!!!
HUH ?!
CISQUA?!

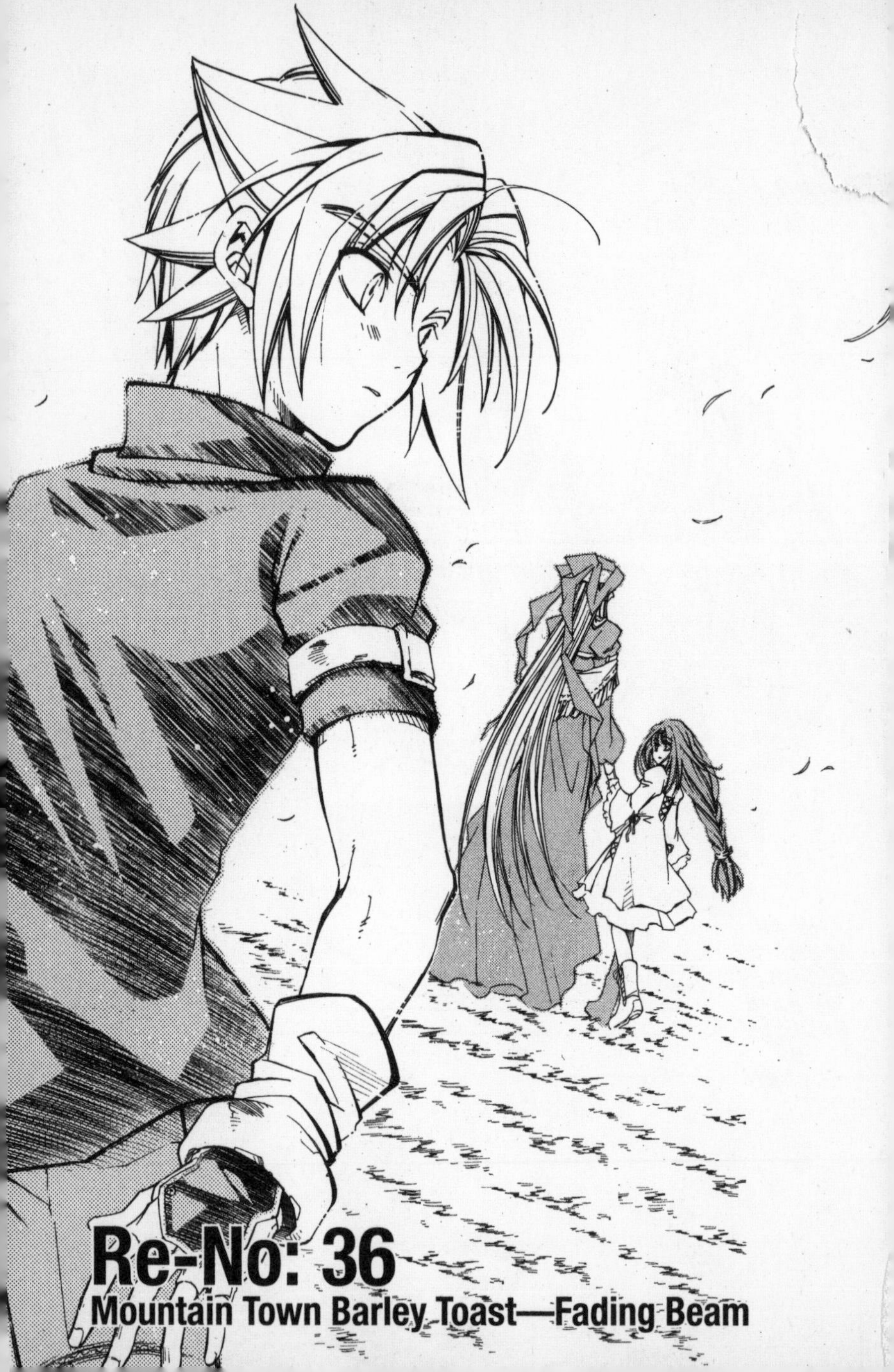
Re-No: 36
Mountain Town Barley Toast—Fading Beam

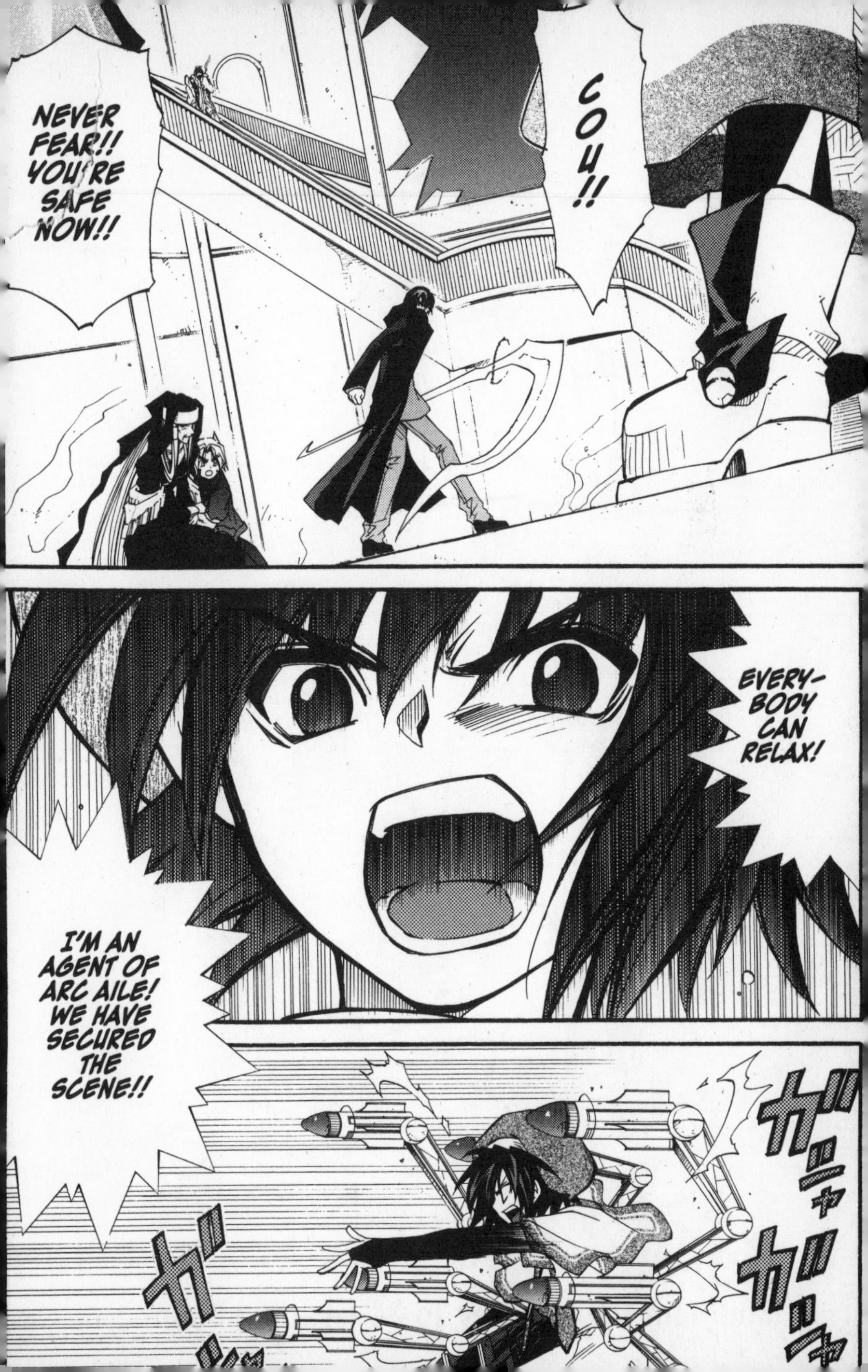
COU!!
NEVER FEAR!! YOU'RE SAFE NOW!!
EVERY-BODY CAN RELAX!
I'M AN AGENT OF ARC AILE! WE HAVE SECURED THE SCENE!!

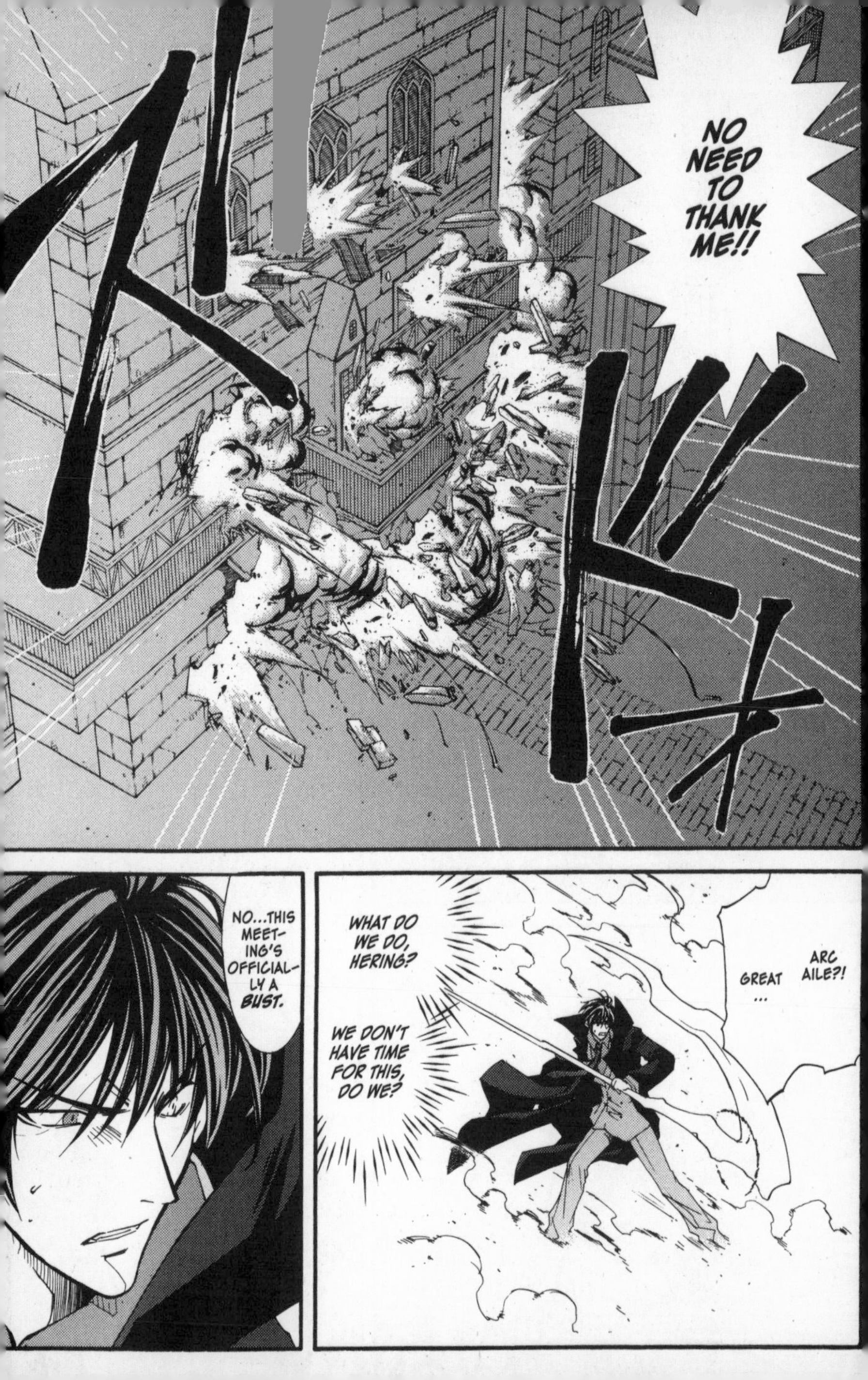
NO NEED TO THANK ME!!
ARC AILE?!
GREAT ...
WHAT DO WE DO, HERING?
WE DON'T HAVE TIME FOR THIS, DO WE?
NO...THIS MEET-ING'S OFFICIAL-LY A BUST.

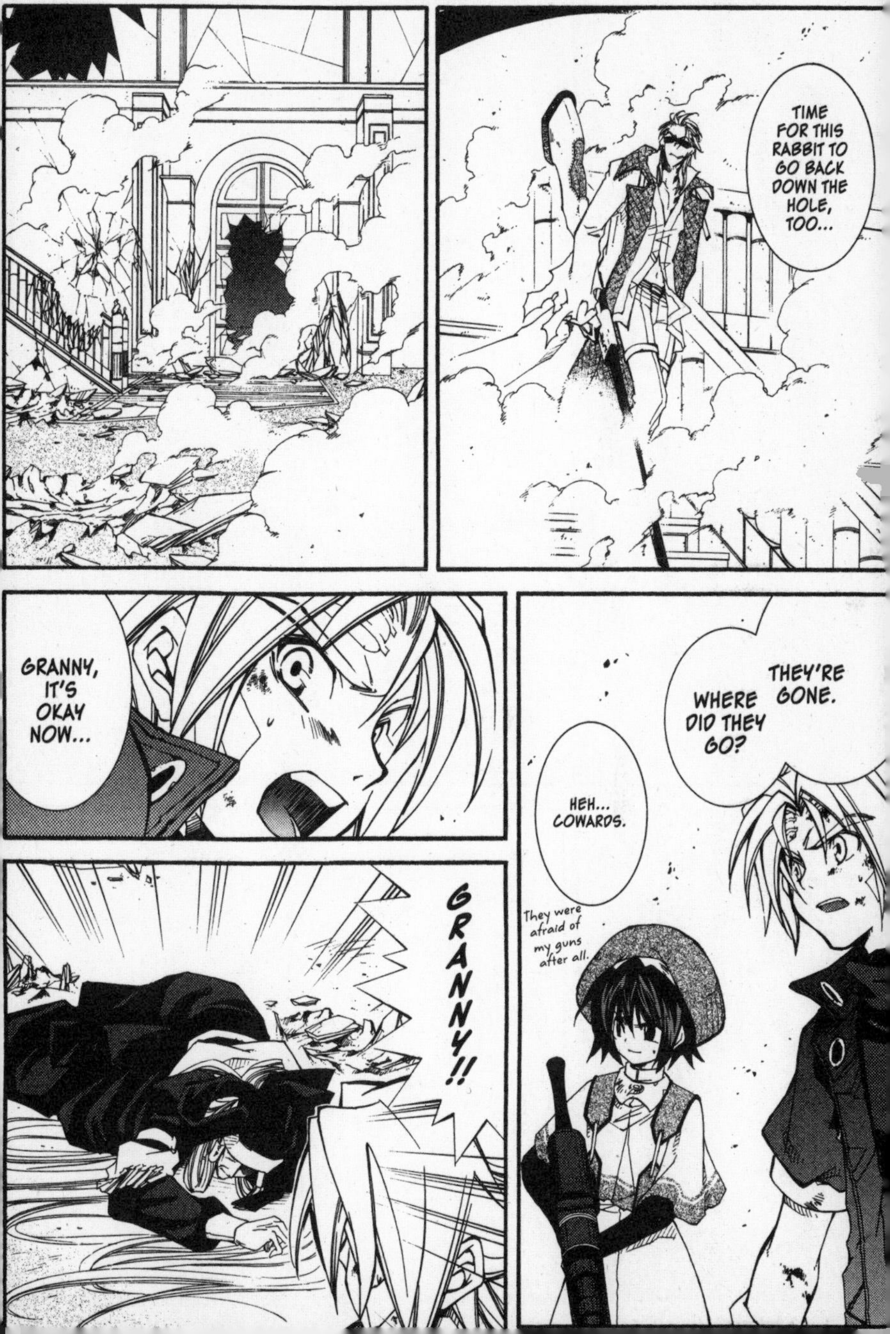
TIME FOR THIS RABBIT TO GO BACK DOWN THE HOLE, TOO...
THEY'RE GONE.
WHERE DID THEY GO?
HEH... COWARDS.
They were afraid of my guns after all.
GRANNY, IT'S OKAY NOW...
GRANNY!!

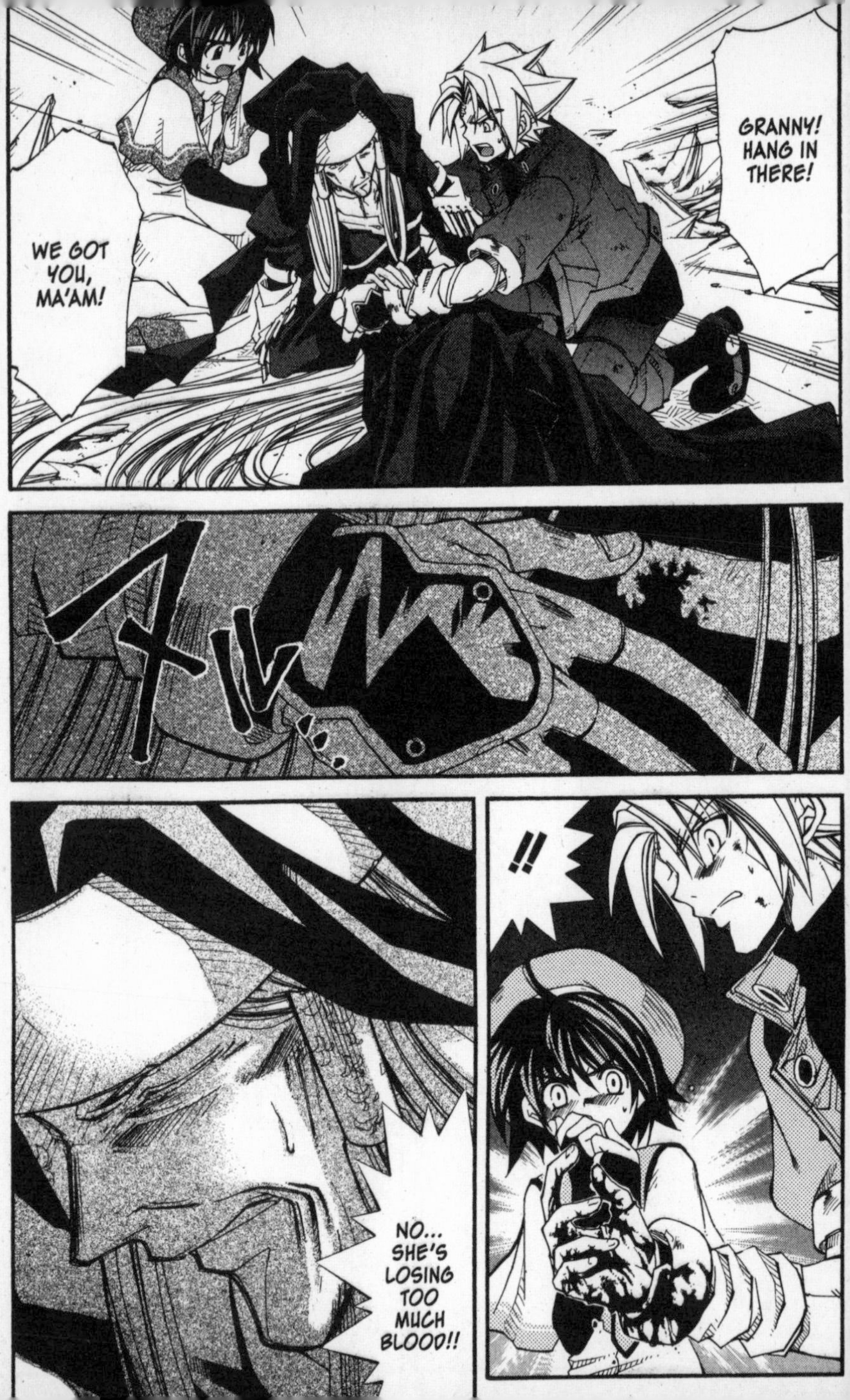
GRANNY! HANG IN THERE!
WE GOT YOU, MA'AM!
!!
NO... SHE'S LOSING TOO MUCH BLOOD!!

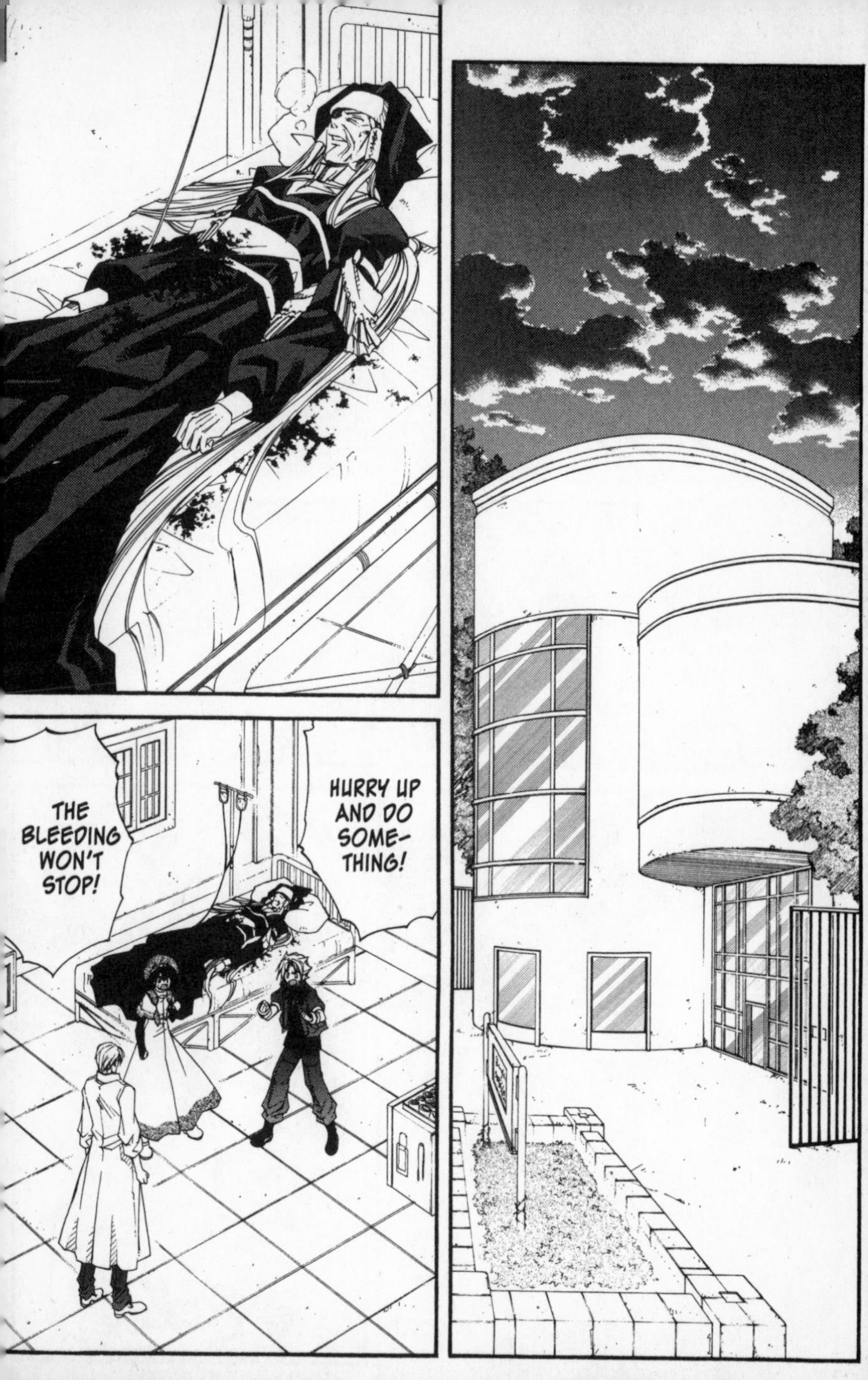
HURRY UP AND DO SOME-THING!
THE BLEEDING WON'T STOP!

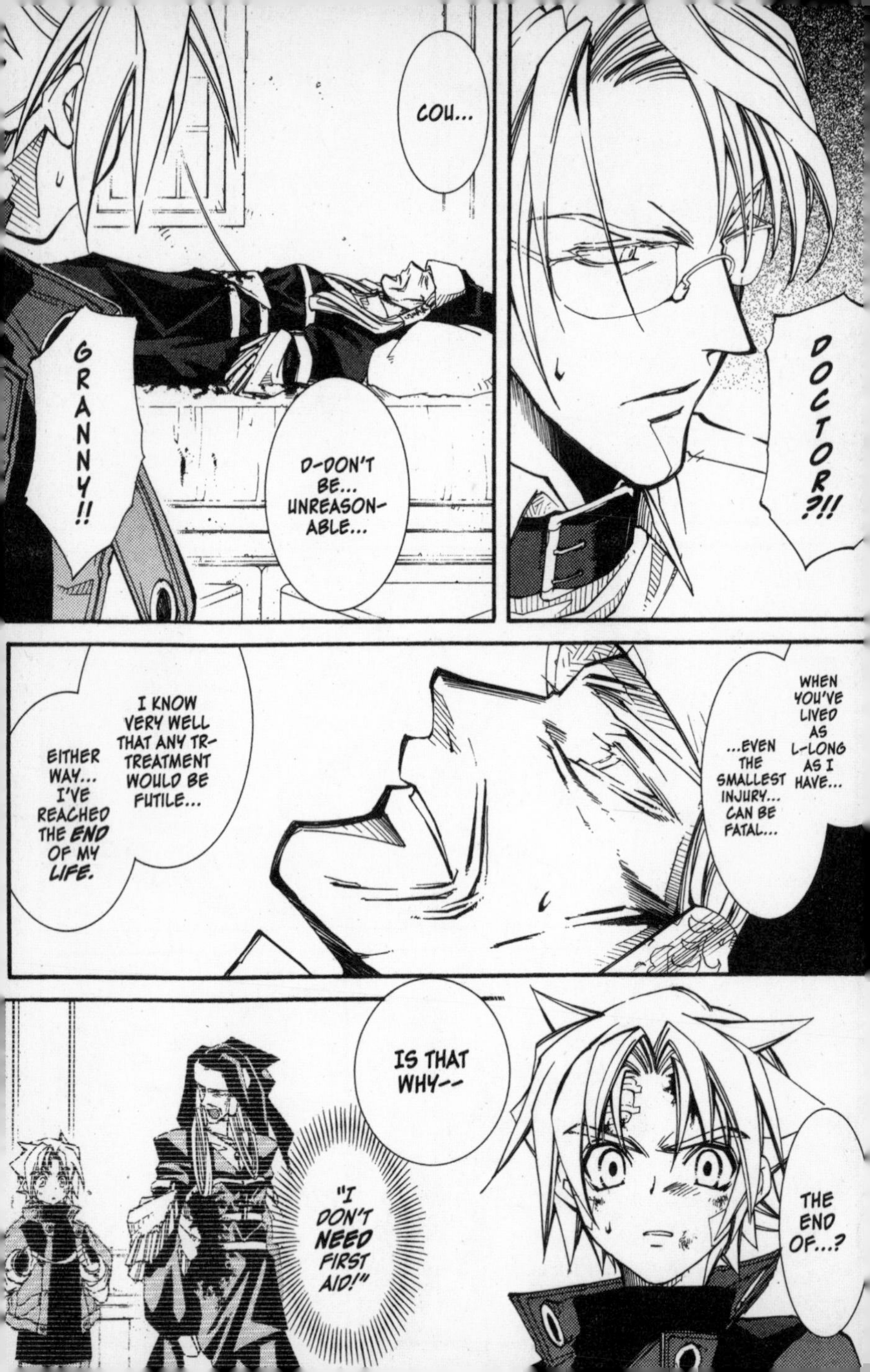
DOCTOR?!!
COU...
GRANNY!!
D-DON'T BE... UNREASONABLE...
WHEN YOU'VE LIVED AS L-LONG AS I HAVE...
...EVEN THE SMALLEST INJURY... CAN BE FATAL...
I KNOW VERY WELL THAT ANY TR-TREATMENT WOULD BE FUTILE...
EITHER WAY... I'VE REACHED THE END OF MY LIFE.
THE END OF...?
IS THAT WHY--
"I DON'T NEED FIRST AID!"

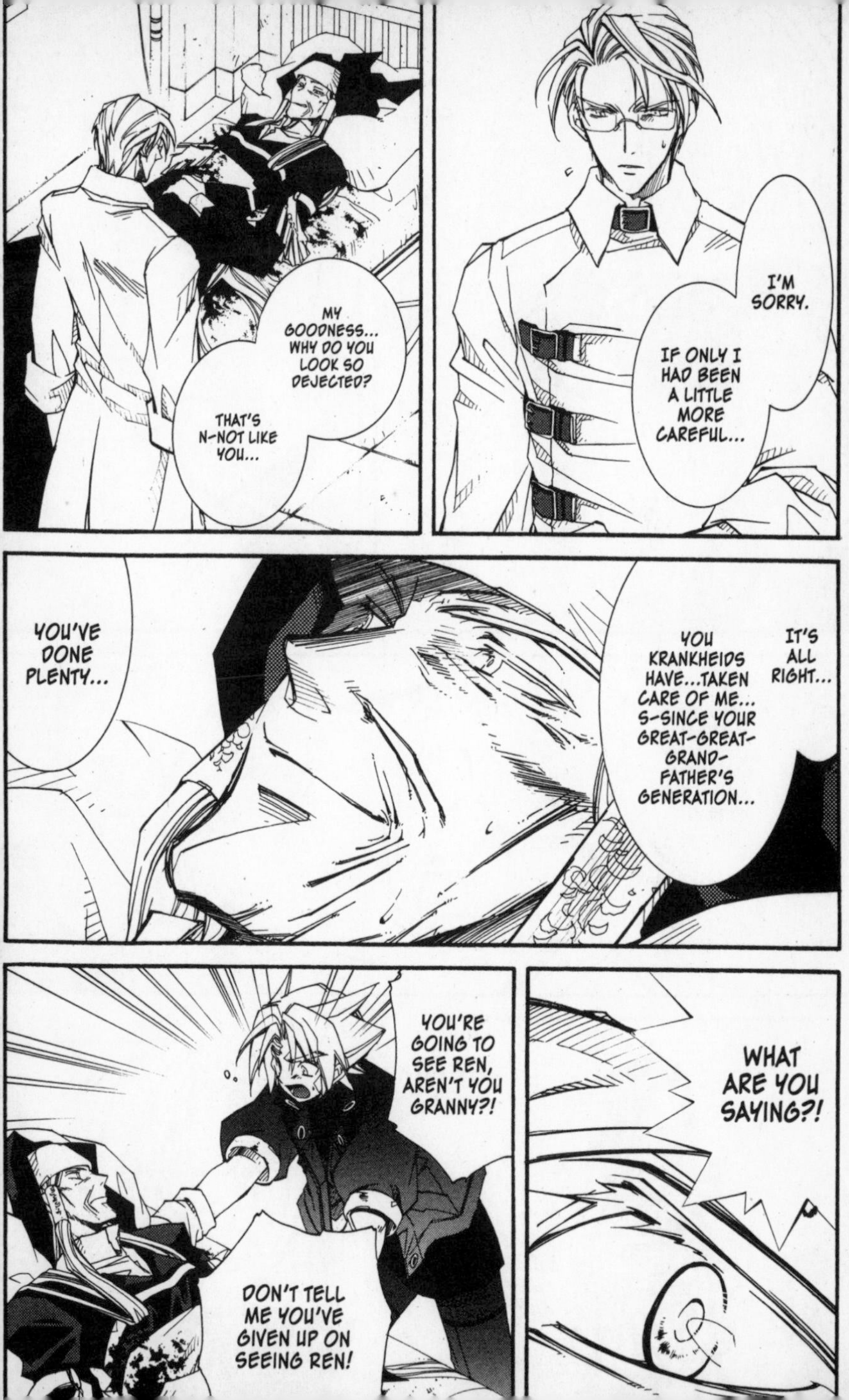
I'M SORRY.
IF ONLY I HAD BEEN A LITTLE MORE CAREFUL...
MY GOODNESS... WHY DO YOU LOOK SO DEJECTED?
THAT'S N-NOT LIKE YOU...
IT'S ALL RIGHT...
YOU KRANKHEIDS HAVE...TAKEN CARE OF ME... S-SINCE YOUR GREAT-GREAT-GRAND-FATHER'S GENERATION...
YOU'VE DONE PLENTY...
WHAT ARE YOU SAYING?!
YOU'RE GOING TO SEE REN, AREN'T YOU GRANNY?!
DON'T TELL ME YOU'VE GIVEN UP ON SEEING REN!

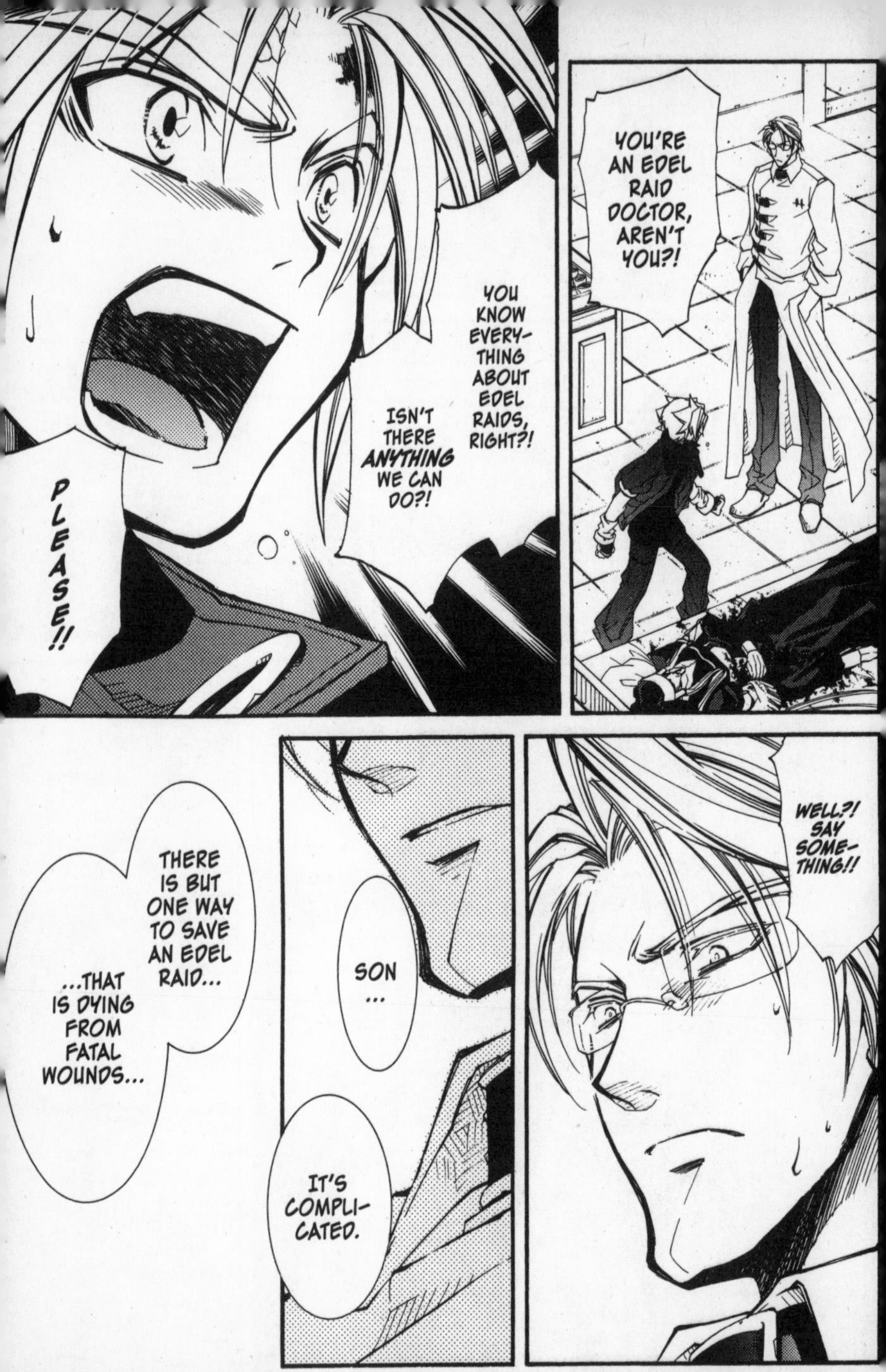
YOU'RE AN EDEL RAID DOCTOR, AREN'T YOU?!
YOU KNOW EVERY-THING ABOUT EDEL RAIDS, RIGHT?!
ISN'T THERE *ANYTHING* WE CAN DO?!
PLEASE!!
WELL?! SAY SOME-THING!!
SON...
IT'S COMPLI-CATED.
THERE IS BUT ONE WAY TO SAVE AN EDEL RAID...
...THAT IS DYING FROM FATAL WOUNDS...

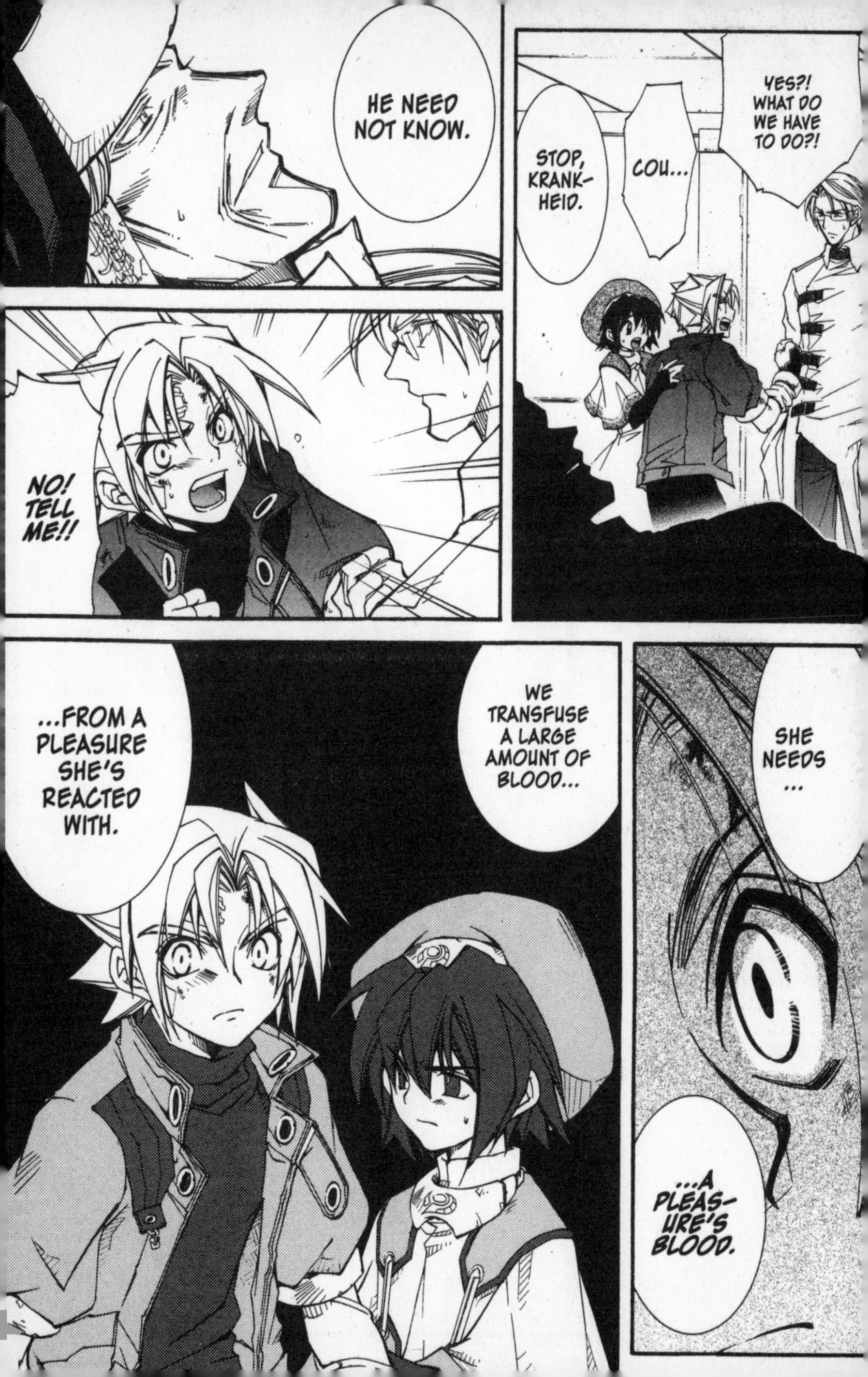
YES?! WHAT DO WE HAVE TO DO?!
COU...
STOP, KRANK-HEID.
HE NEED NOT KNOW.
NO! TELL ME!!
SHE NEEDS ...
...A PLEAS-URE'S BLOOD.
WE TRANSFUSE A LARGE AMOUNT OF BLOOD...
...FROM A PLEASURE SHE'S REACTED WITH.

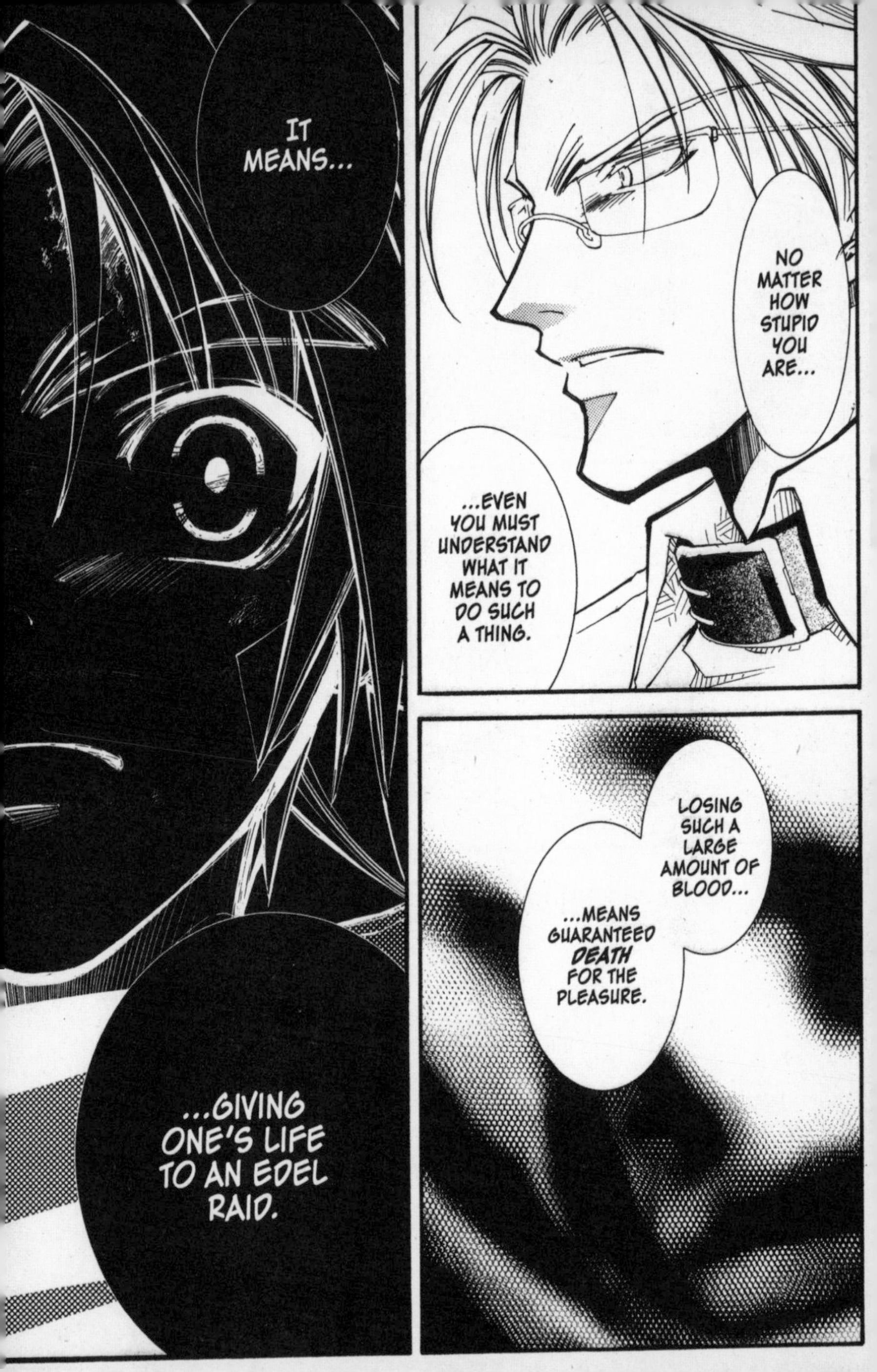
NO MATTER HOW STUPID YOU ARE...
...EVEN YOU MUST UNDERSTAND WHAT IT MEANS TO DO SUCH A THING.
LOSING SUCH A LARGE AMOUNT OF BLOOD...
...MEANS GUARANTEED **DEATH** FOR THE PLEASURE.
IT MEANS...
...GIVING ONE'S LIFE TO AN EDEL RAID.

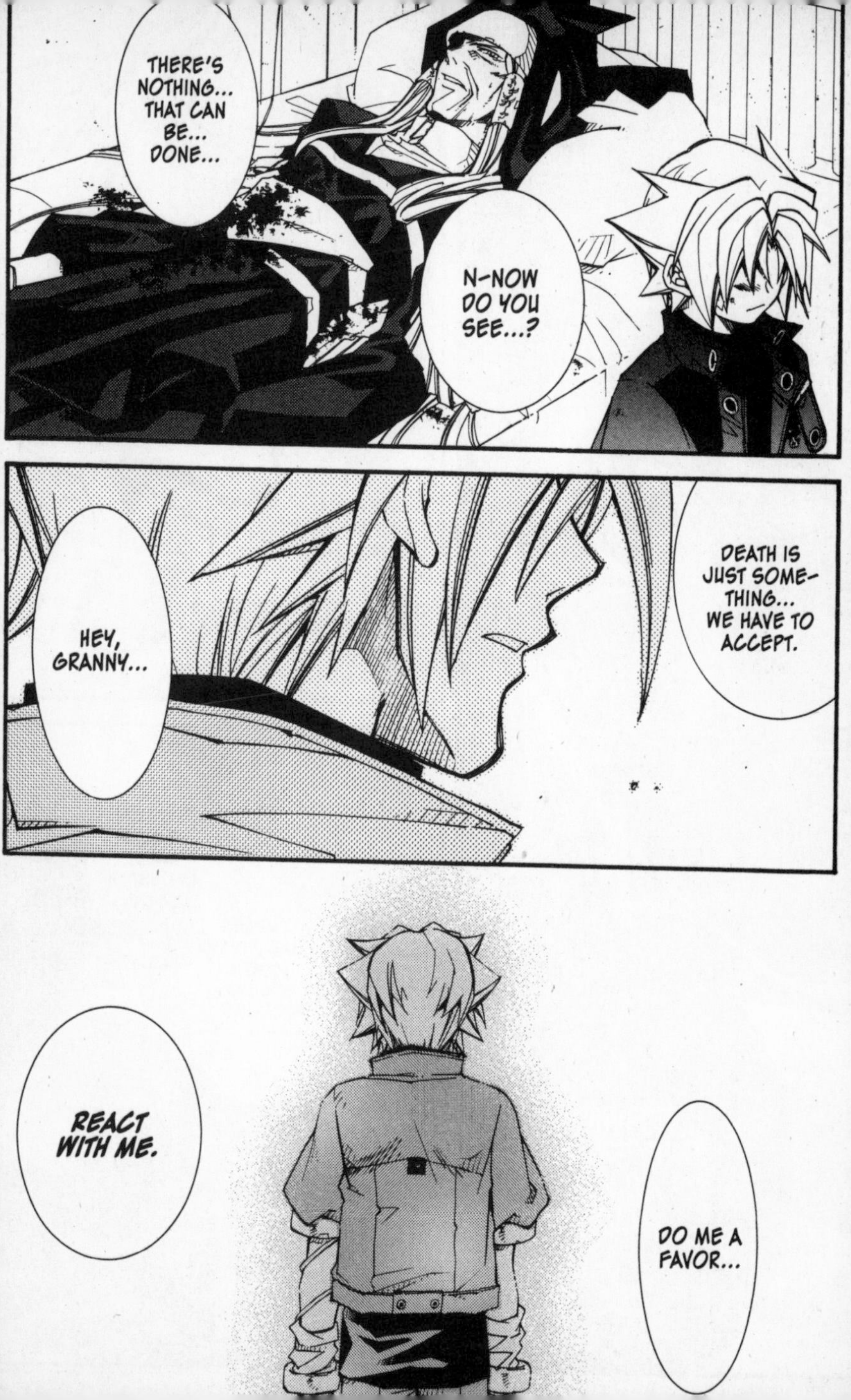
N-NOW DO YOU SEE...?
THERE'S NOTHING... THAT CAN BE... DONE...
DEATH IS JUST SOME-THING... WE HAVE TO ACCEPT.
HEY, GRANNY...
DO ME A FAVOR...
REACT WITH ME.

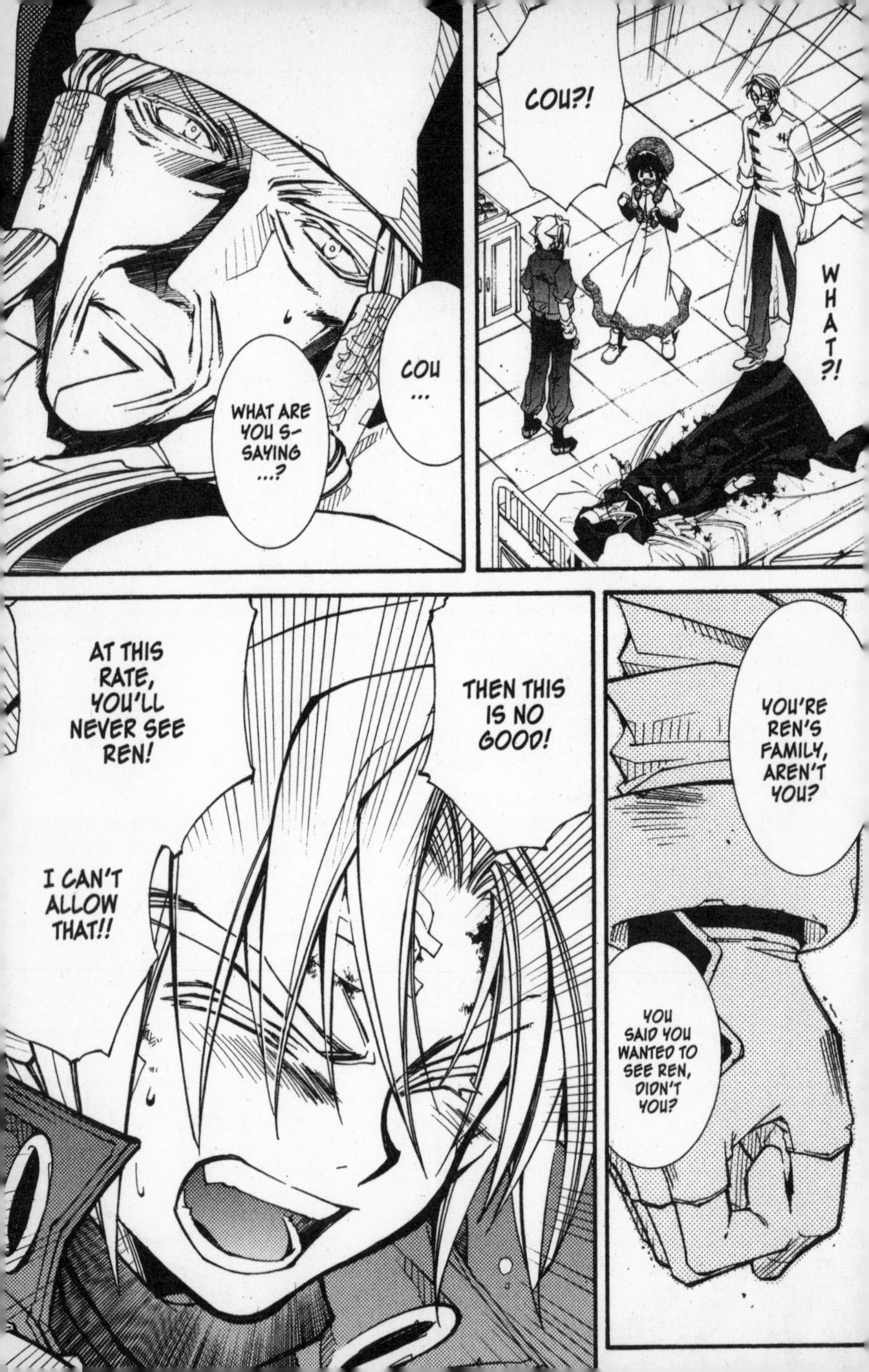
COU?!
WHAT?!
COU...
WHAT ARE YOU S-SAYING...?
YOU'RE REN'S FAMILY, AREN'T YOU?
YOU SAID YOU WANTED TO SEE REN, DIDN'T YOU?
THEN THIS IS NO GOOD!
AT THIS RATE, YOU'LL NEVER SEE REN!
I CAN'T ALLOW THAT!!

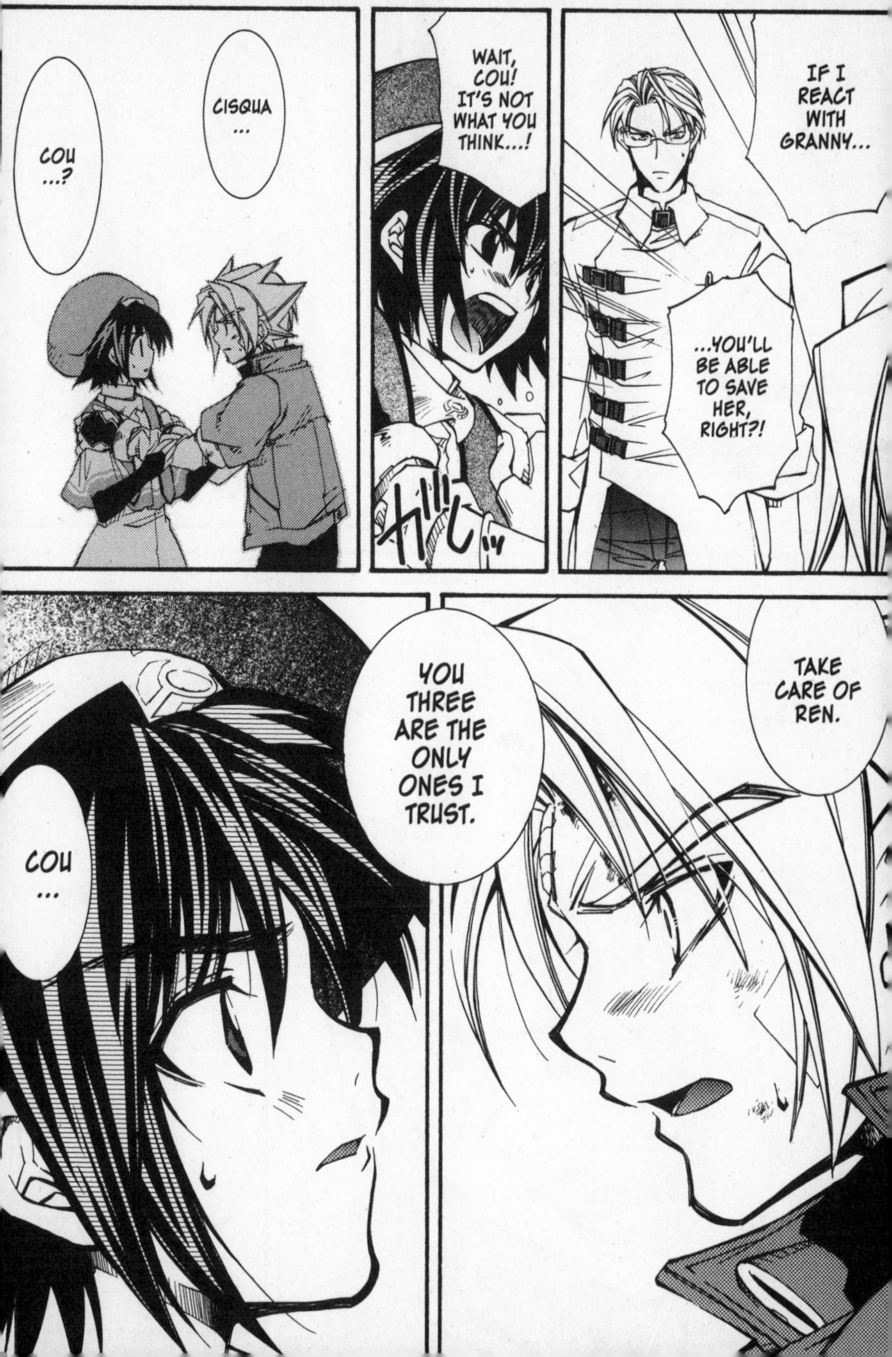
IF I REACT WITH GRANNY...
...YOU'LL BE ABLE TO SAVE HER, RIGHT?!
WAIT, COU! IT'S NOT WHAT YOU THINK...!
CISQUA ...
COU ...?
TAKE CARE OF REN.
YOU THREE ARE THE ONLY ONES I TRUST.
COU ...

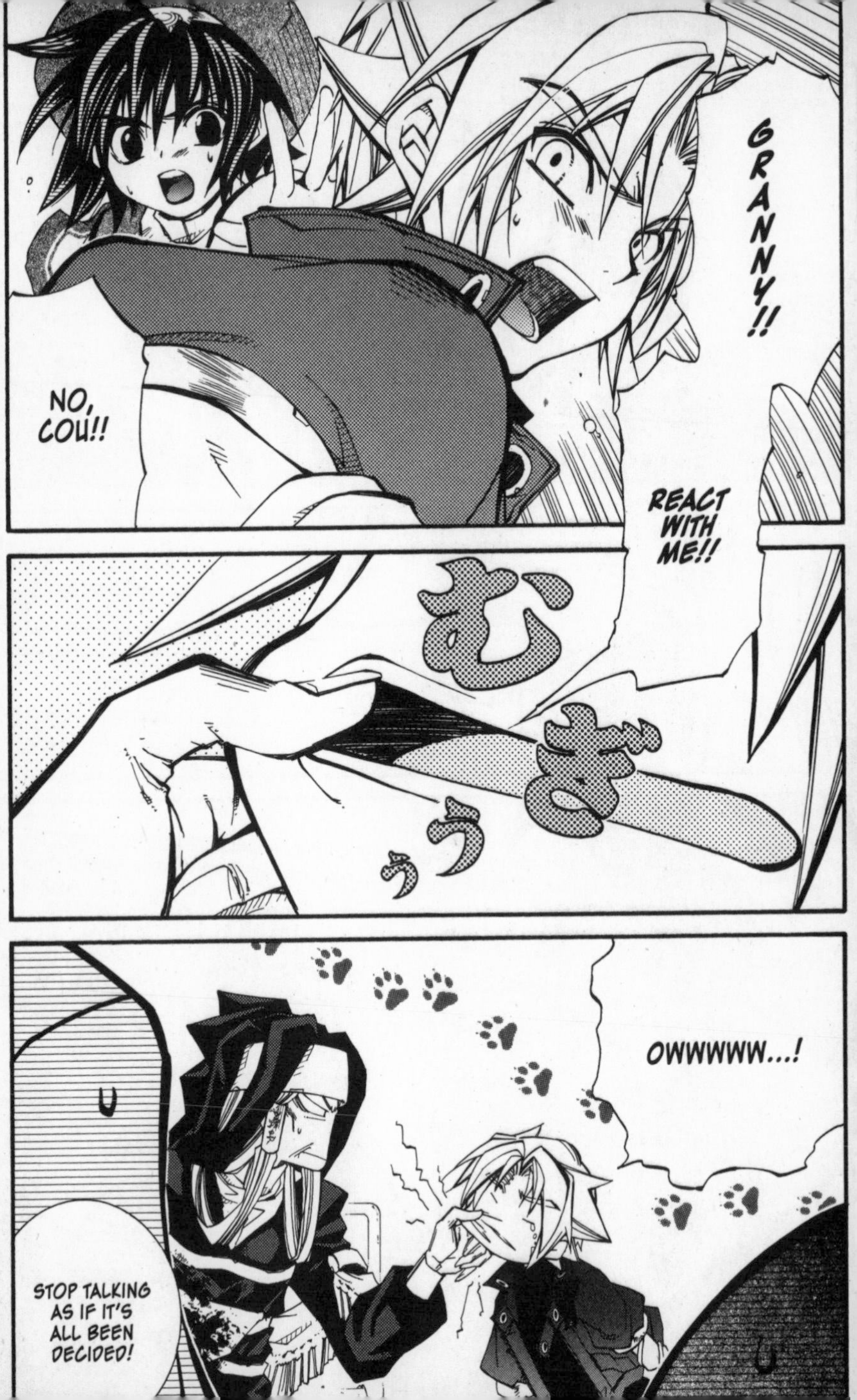
GRANNY!!
REACT WITH ME!!
NO, COU!!
むぎうぅ
OWWWWW...!
STOP TALKING AS IF IT'S ALL BEEN DECIDED!

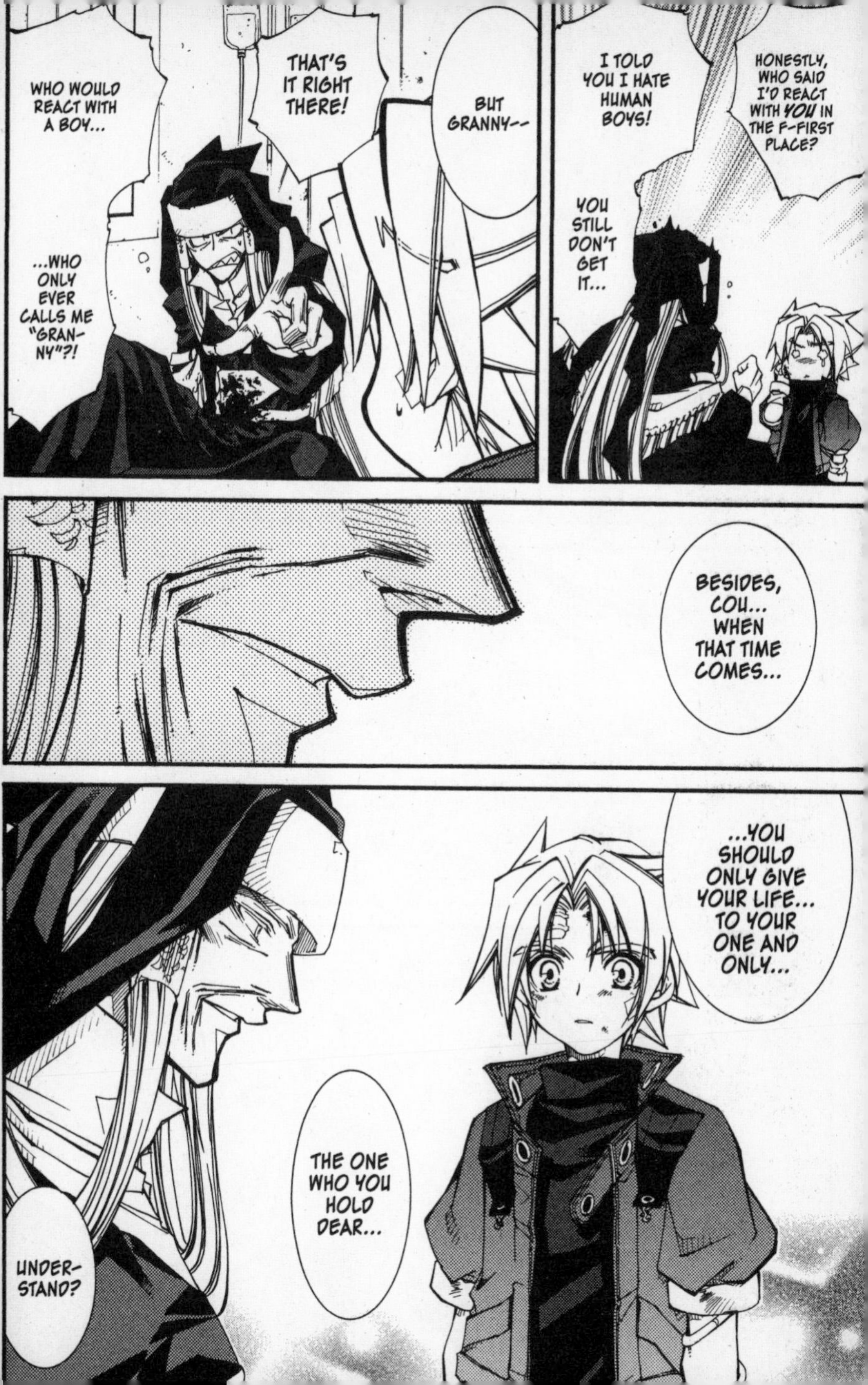
HONESTLY, WHO SAID I'D REACT WITH YOU IN THE F-FIRST PLACE?
I TOLD YOU I HATE HUMAN BOYS!
YOU STILL DON'T GET IT...
BUT GRANNY--
THAT'S IT RIGHT THERE!
WHO WOULD REACT WITH A BOY...
...WHO ONLY EVER CALLS ME "GRAN-NY"?!
BESIDES, COU... WHEN THAT TIME COMES...
...YOU SHOULD ONLY GIVE YOUR LIFE... TO YOUR ONE AND ONLY...
THE ONE WHO YOU HOLD DEAR...
UNDER-STAND?

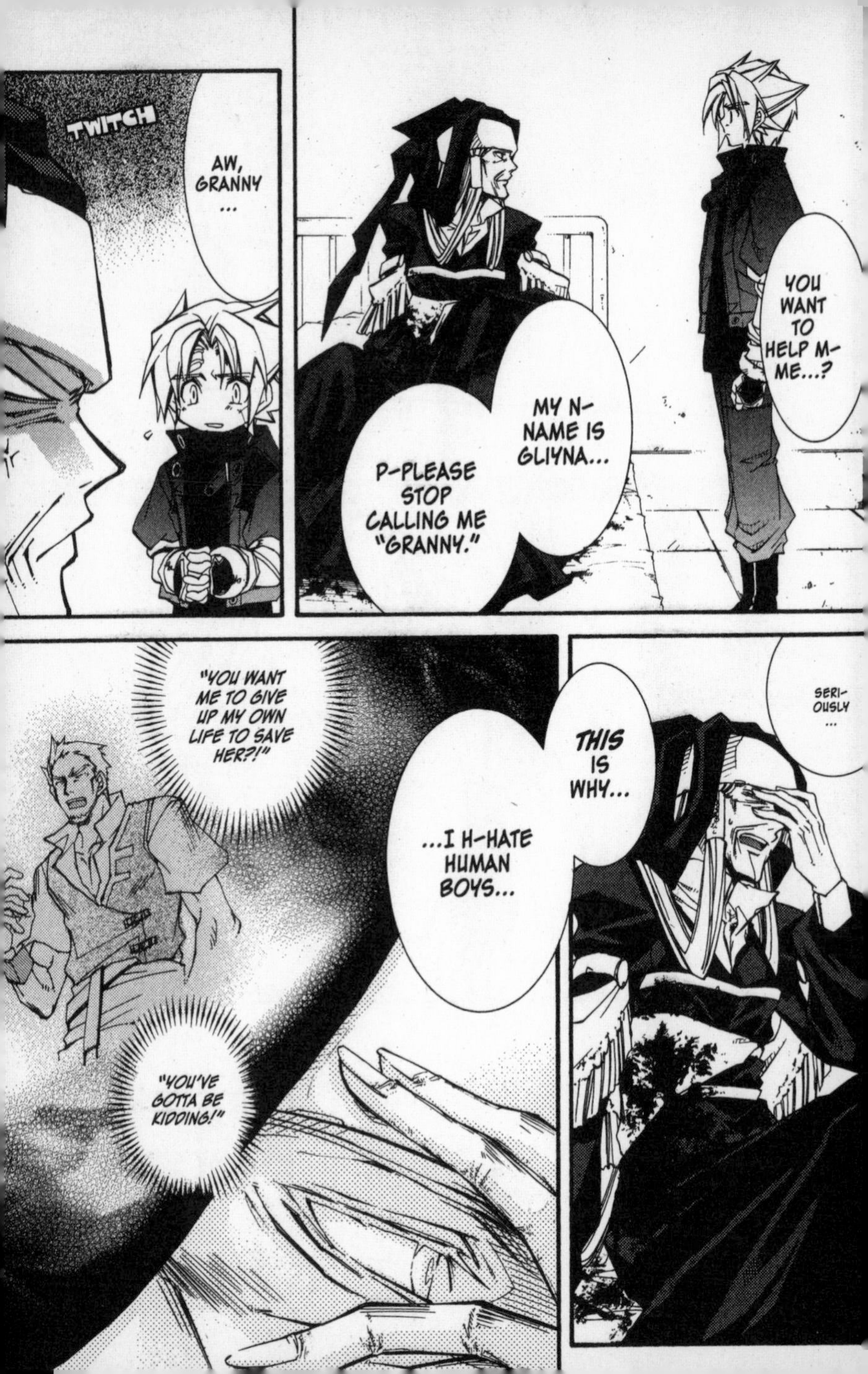
YOU WANT TO HELP M-ME...?
MY N-NAME IS GLIYNA...
P-PLEASE STOP CALLING ME "GRANNY."
AW, GRANNY ...
TWITCH
SERI-OUSLY ...
THIS IS WHY...
...I H-HATE HUMAN BOYS...
"YOU WANT ME TO GIVE UP MY OWN LIFE TO SAVE HER?!"
"YOU'VE GOTTA BE KIDDING!"

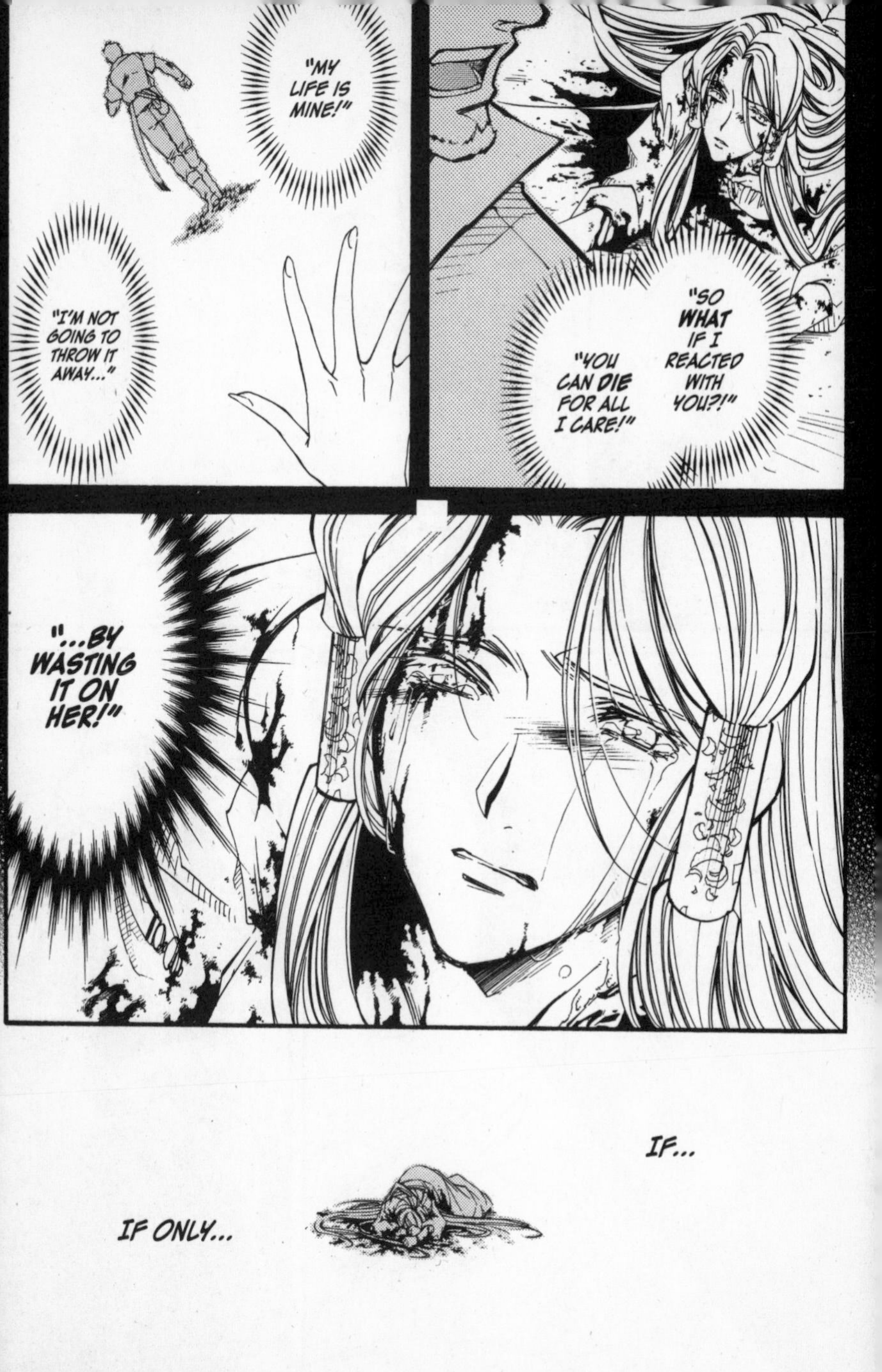
"SO WHAT IF I REACTED WITH YOU?!"
"YOU CAN DIE FOR ALL I CARE!"
"MY LIFE IS MINE!"
"I'M NOT GOING TO THROW IT AWAY..."
"...BY WASTING IT ON HER!"
IF...
IF ONLY...

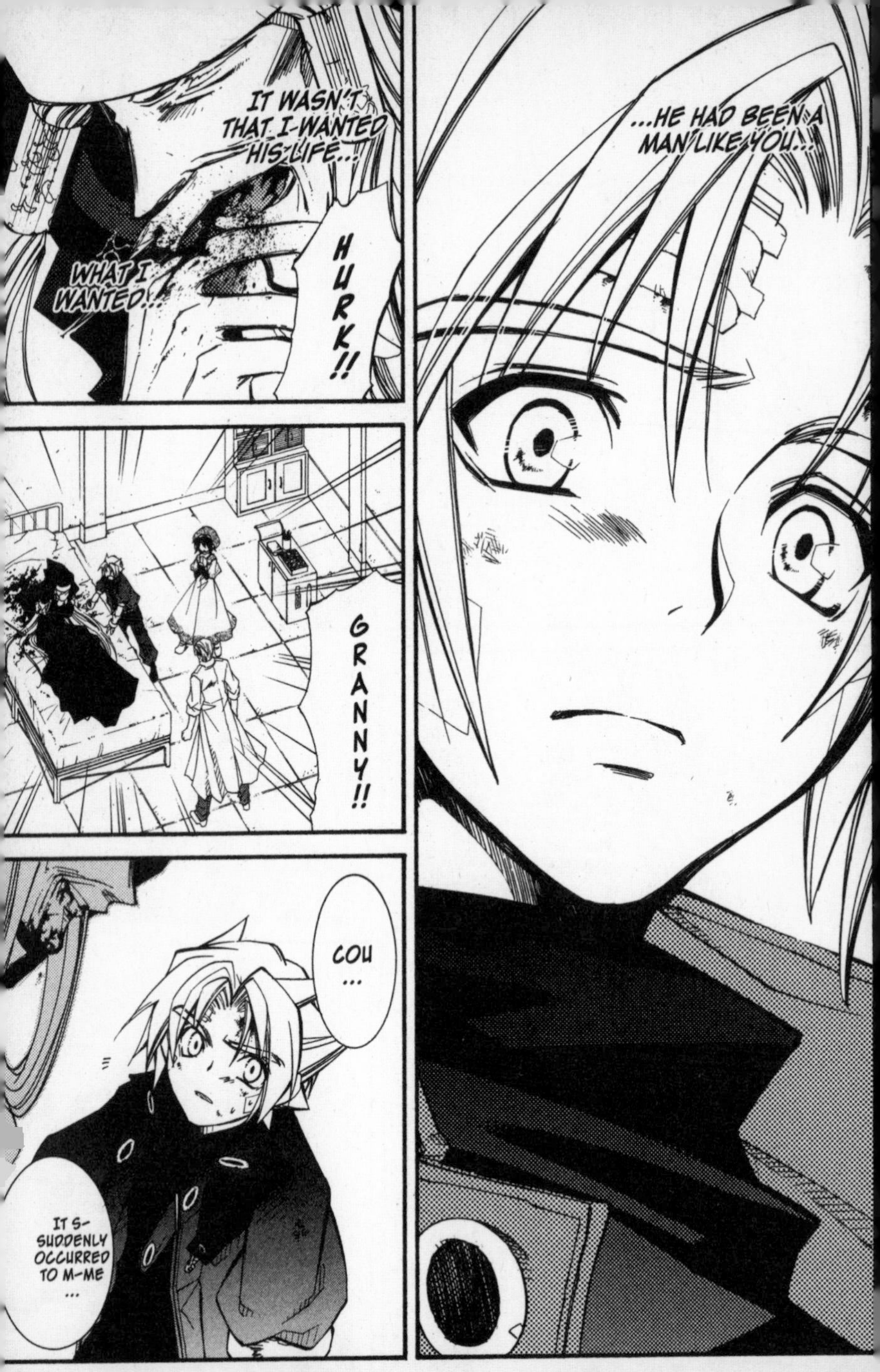
...HE HAD BEEN A MAN LIKE YOU...
IT WASN'T THAT I-WANTED HIS LIFE...
HURK!!
WHAT I WANTED...
GRANNY!!
COU...
IT S-SUDDENLY OCCURRED TO M-ME...

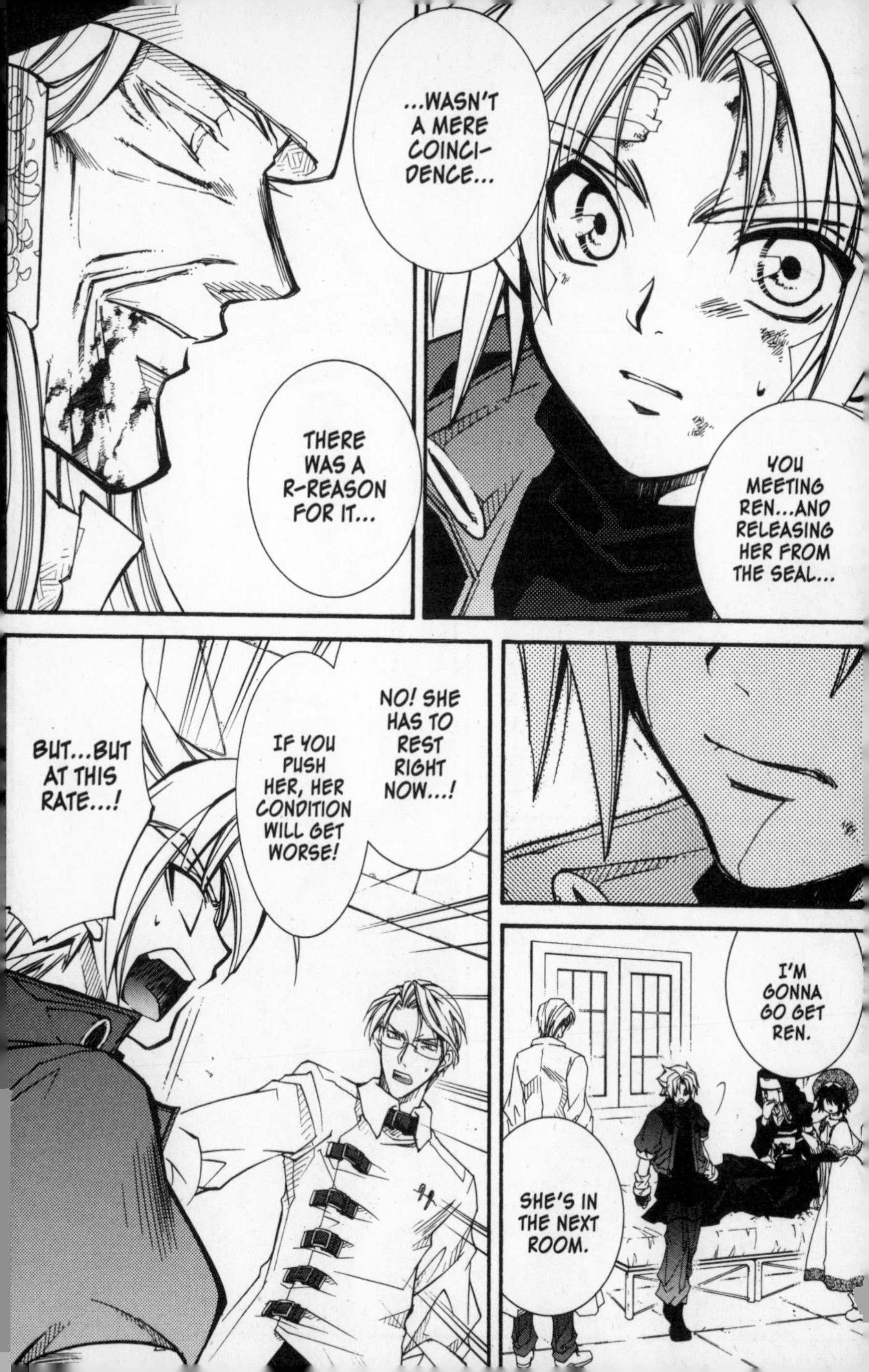
YOU MEETING REN...AND RELEASING HER FROM THE SEAL...
...WASN'T A MERE COINCI-DENCE...
THERE WAS A R-REASON FOR IT...
I'M GONNA GO GET REN.
SHE'S IN THE NEXT ROOM.
NO! SHE HAS TO REST RIGHT NOW...!
IF YOU PUSH HER, HER CONDITION WILL GET WORSE!
BUT...BUT AT THIS RATE...!

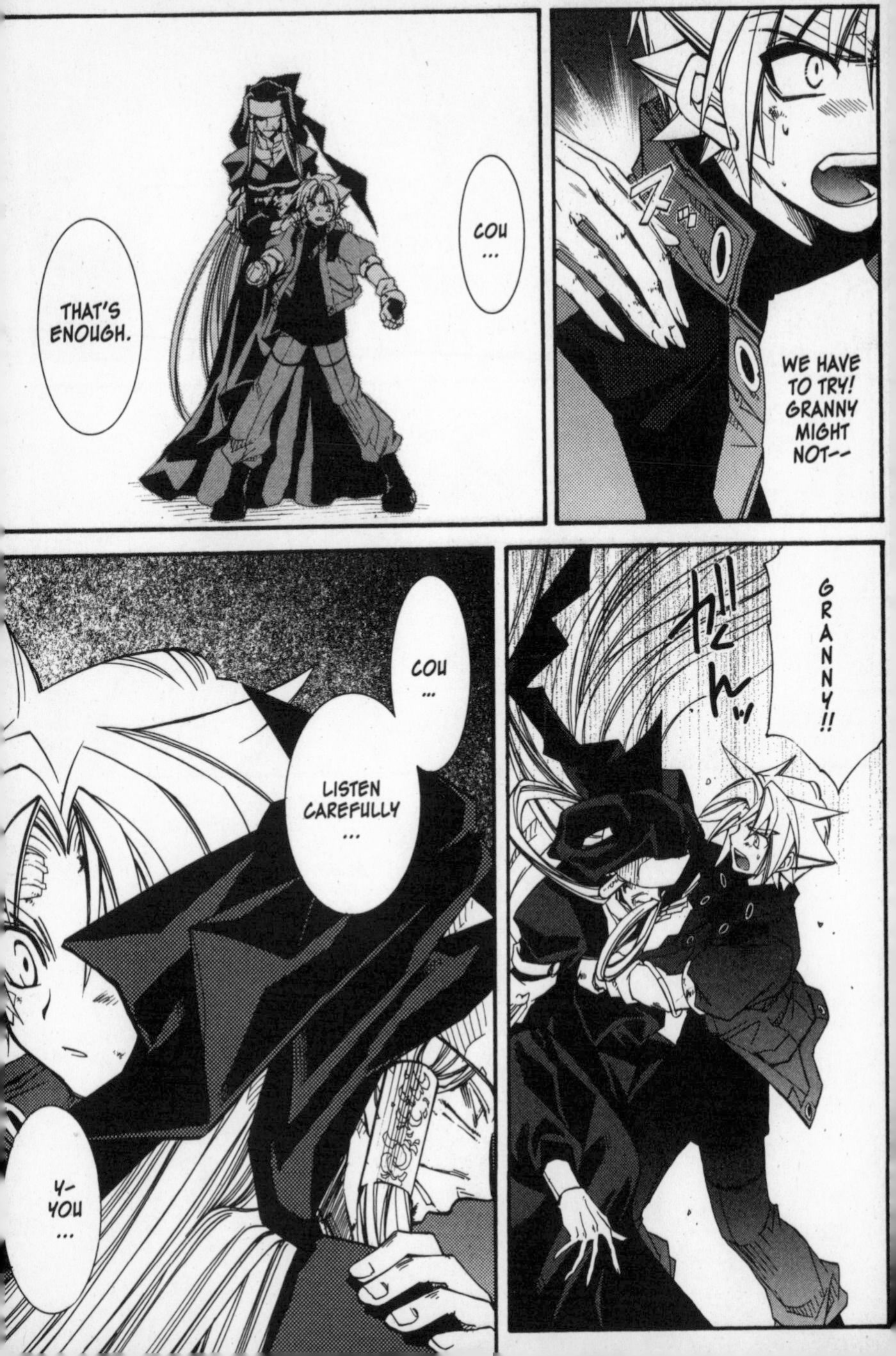
WE HAVE TO TRY! GRANNY MIGHT NOT--
COU ...
THAT'S ENOUGH.
GRANNY!!
COU ...
LISTEN CAREFULLY ...
Y-YOU ...

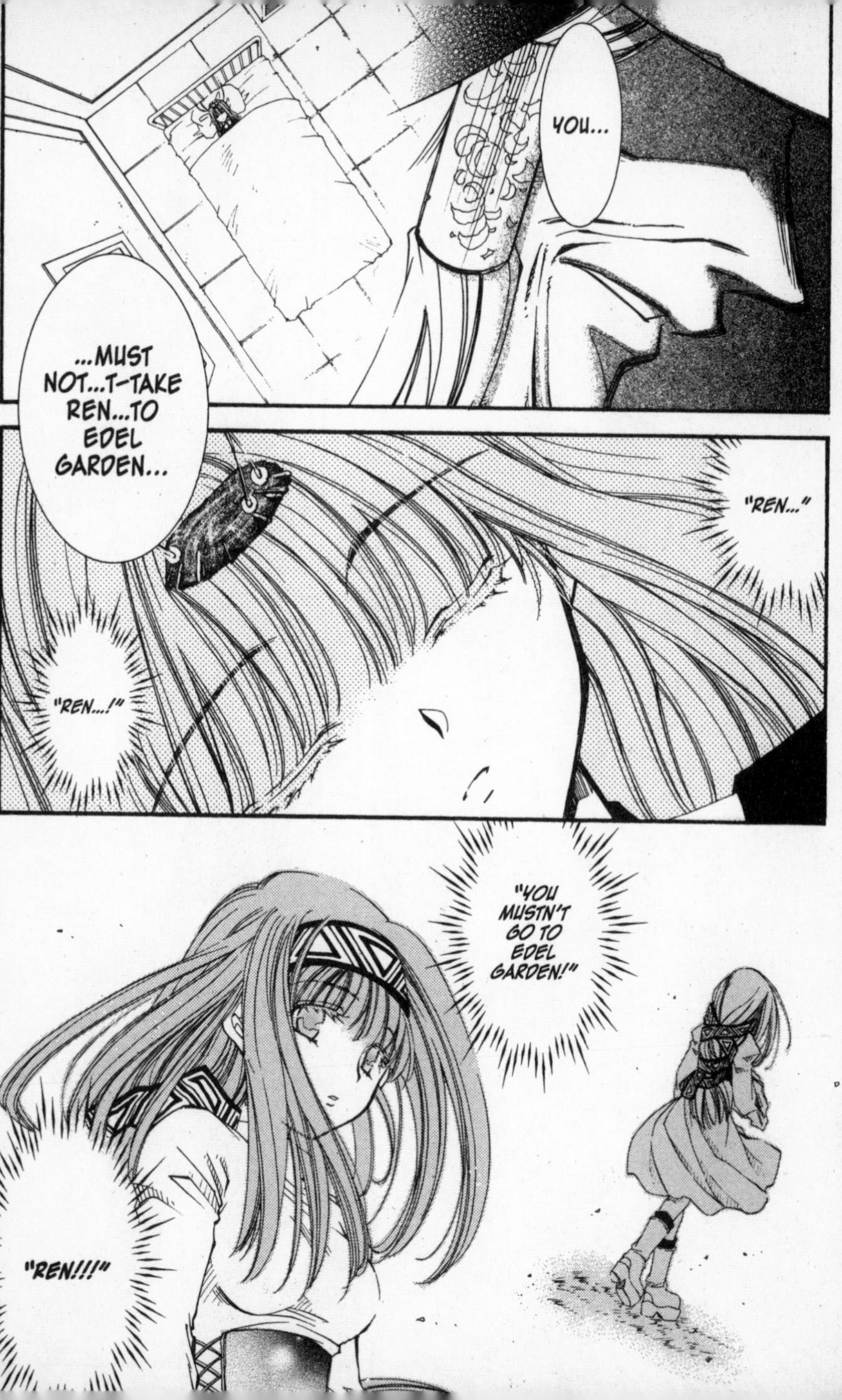
YOU...
...MUST NOT...T-TAKE REN...TO EDEL GARDEN...
"REN..."
"REN...!"
"YOU MUSTN'T GO TO EDEL GARDEN!"
"REN!!!"

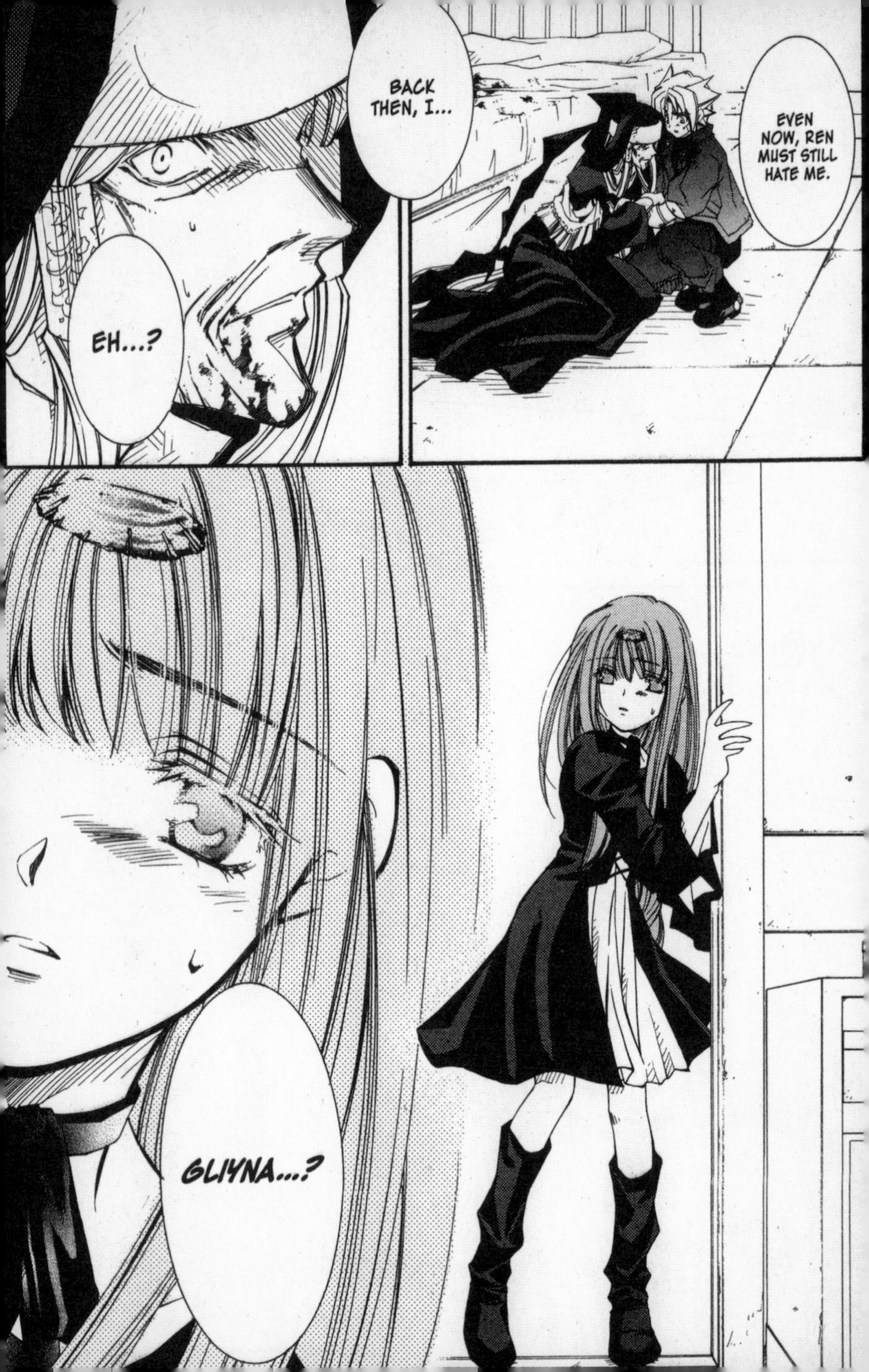
EVEN NOW, REN MUST STILL HATE ME.
BACK THEN, I...
EH...?
GLIYNA...?

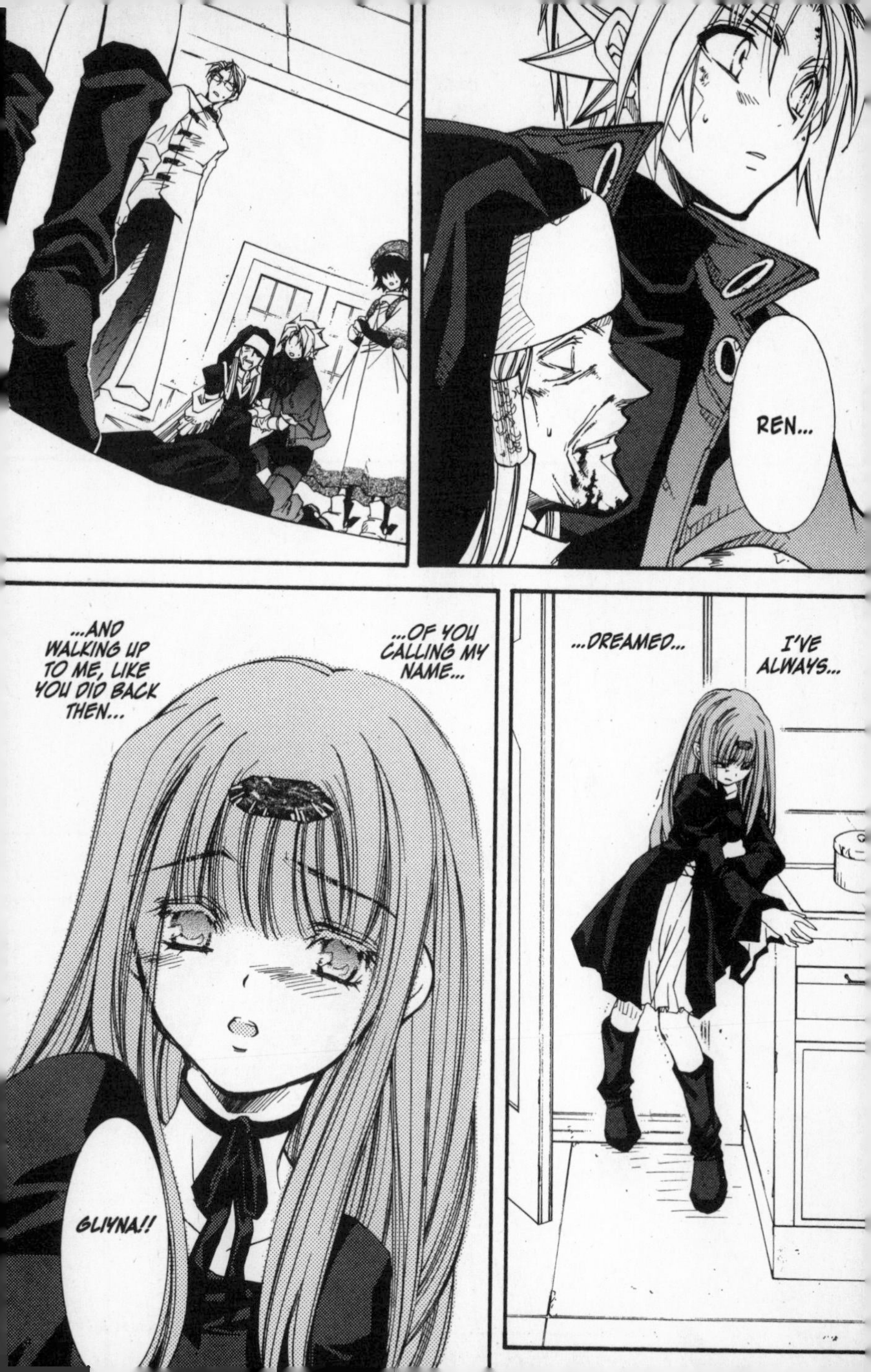
REN...
I'VE ALWAYS...
...DREAMED...
...OF YOU CALLING MY NAME...
...AND WALKING UP TO ME, LIKE YOU DID BACK THEN...
GLIYNA!!

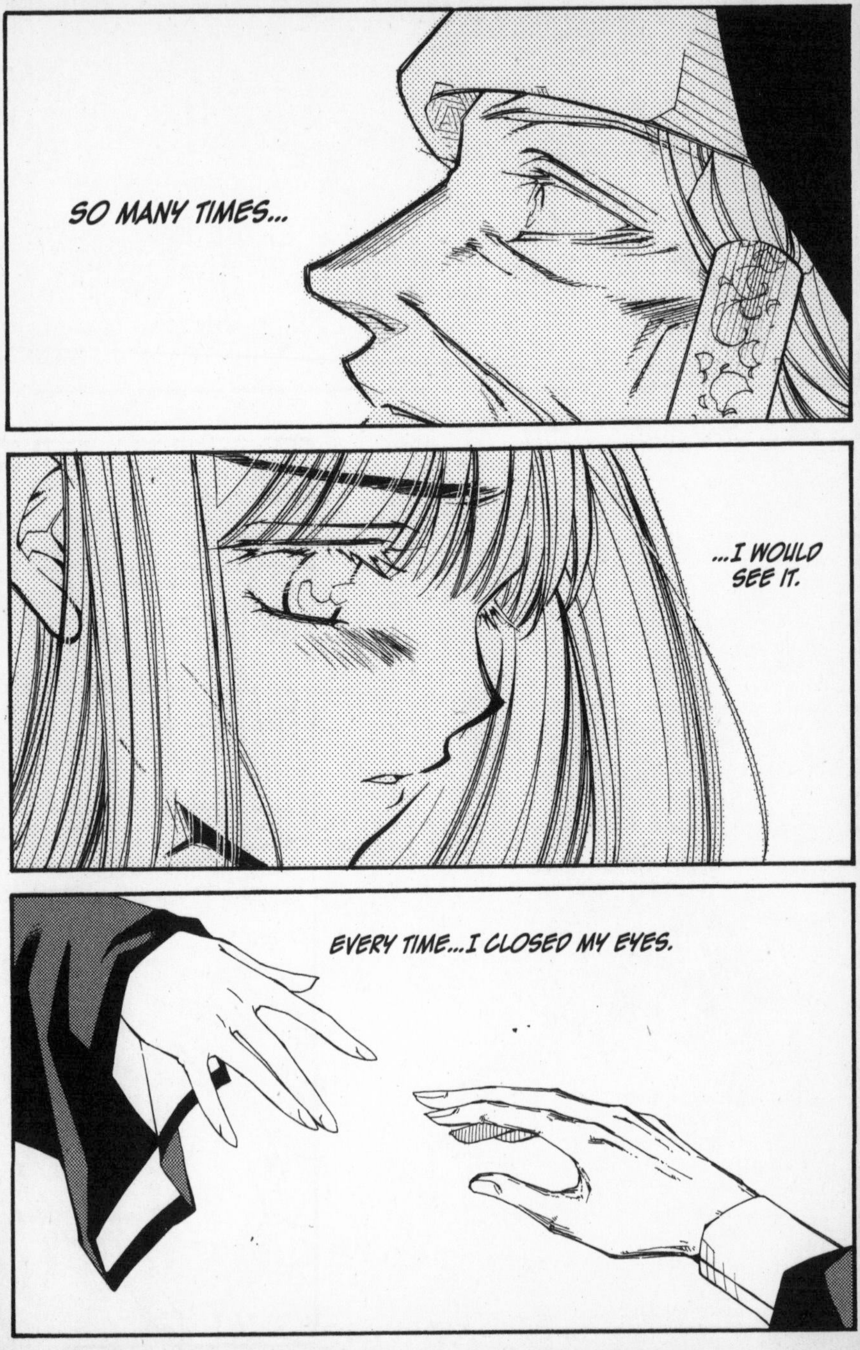
SO MANY TIMES...
...I WOULD SEE IT.
EVERY TIME...I CLOSED MY EYES.

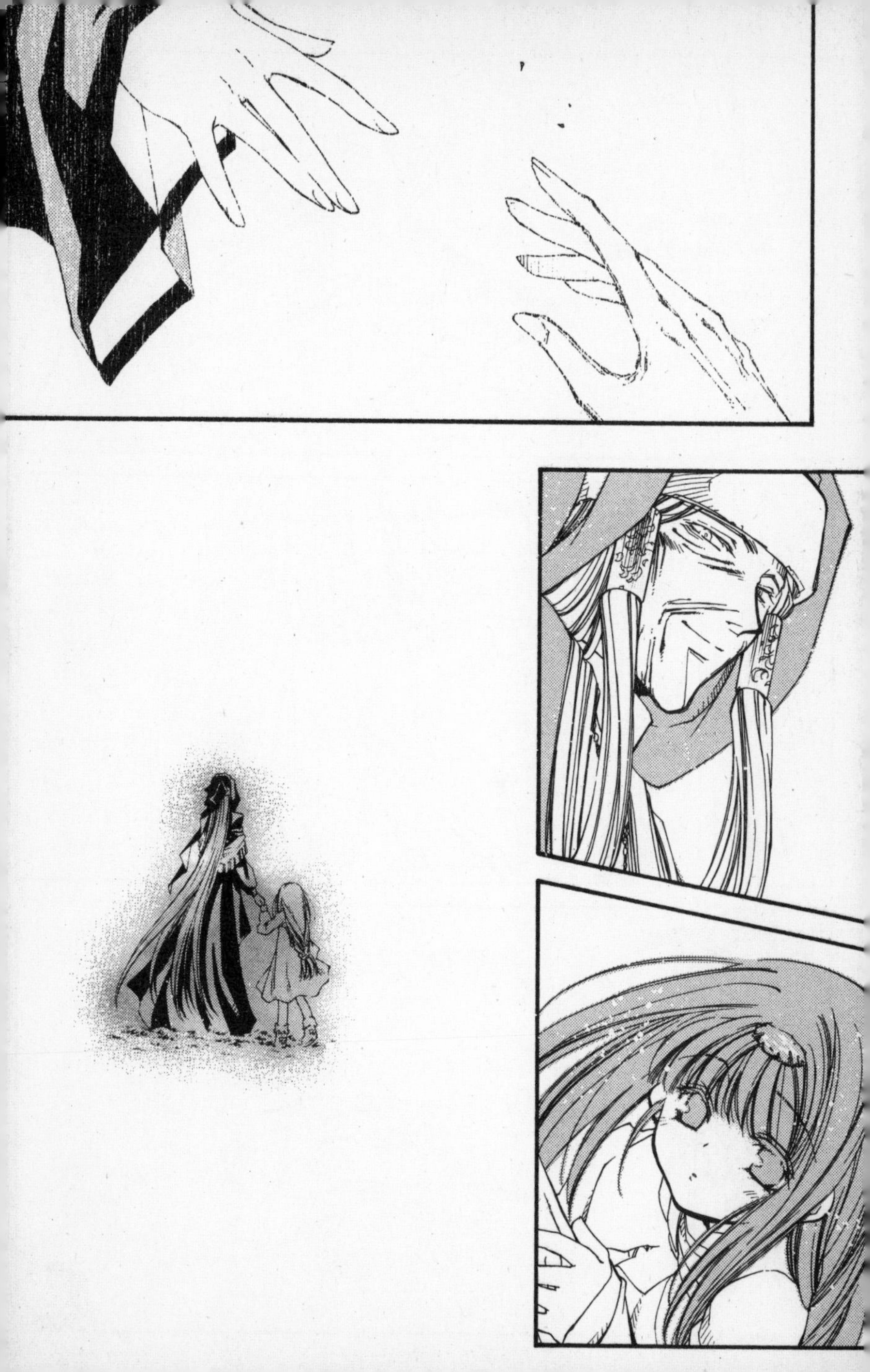

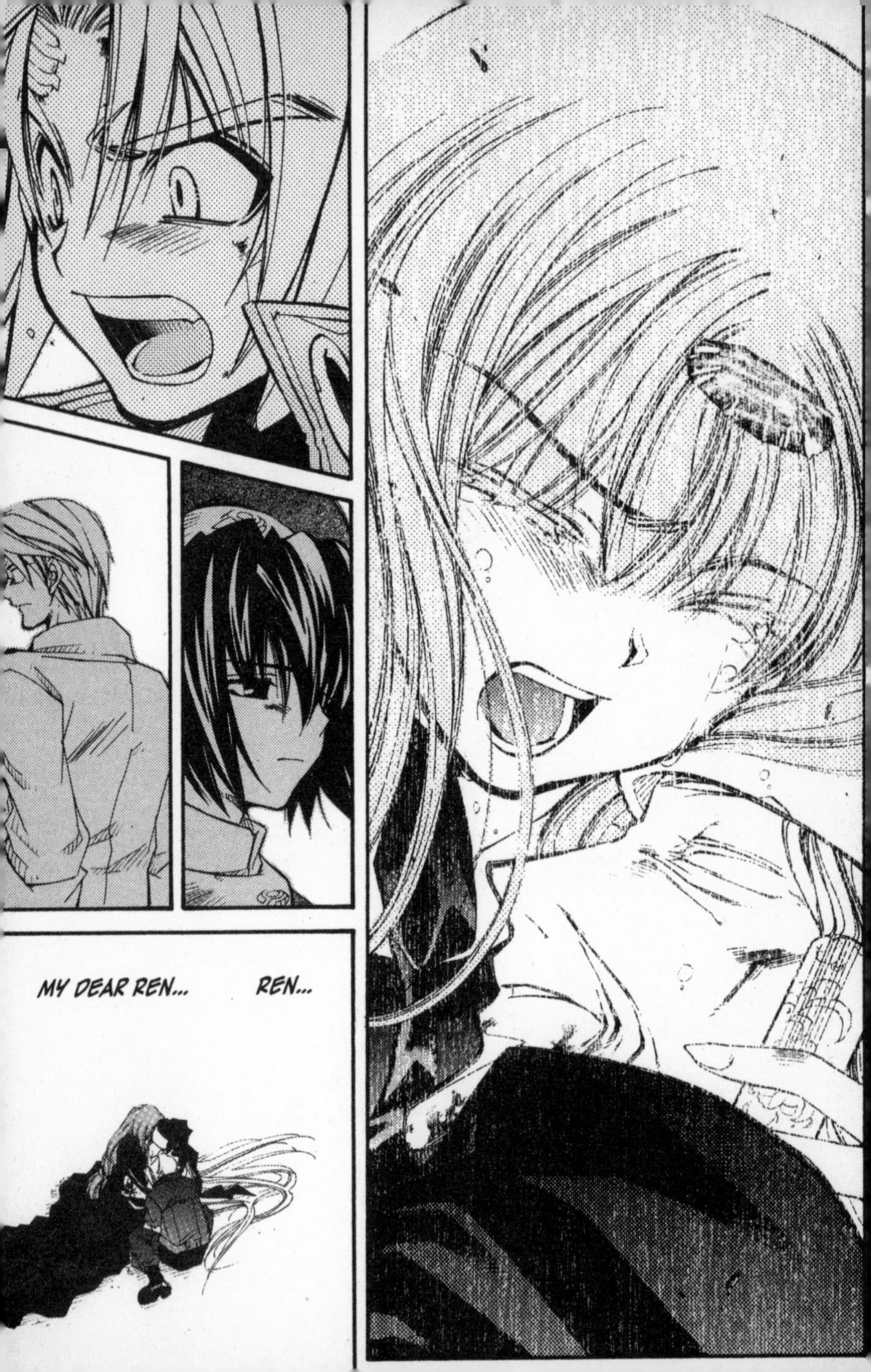
REN...
MY DEAR REN...

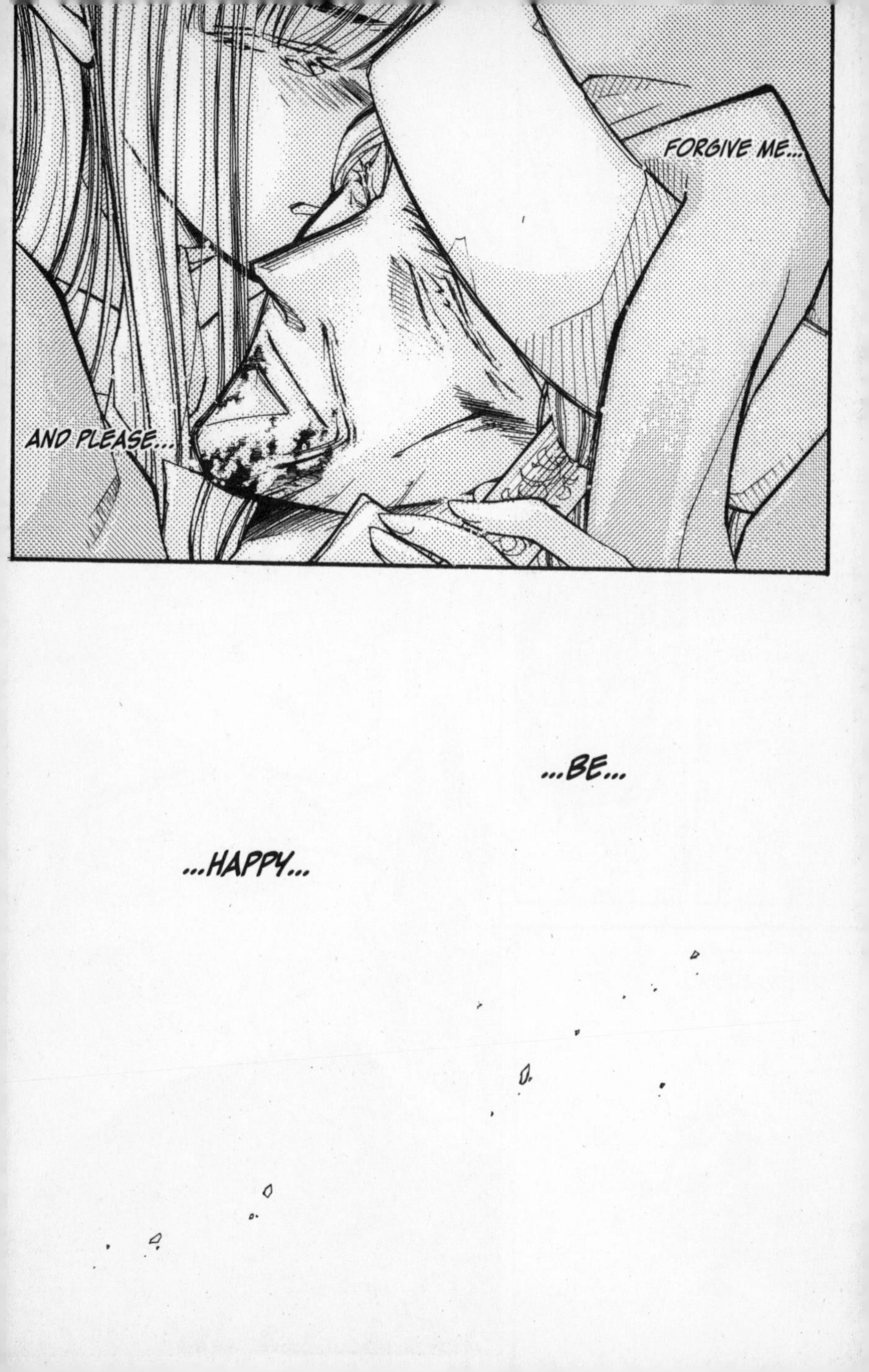
FORGIVE ME...
AND PLEASE...
...BE...
...HAPPY...

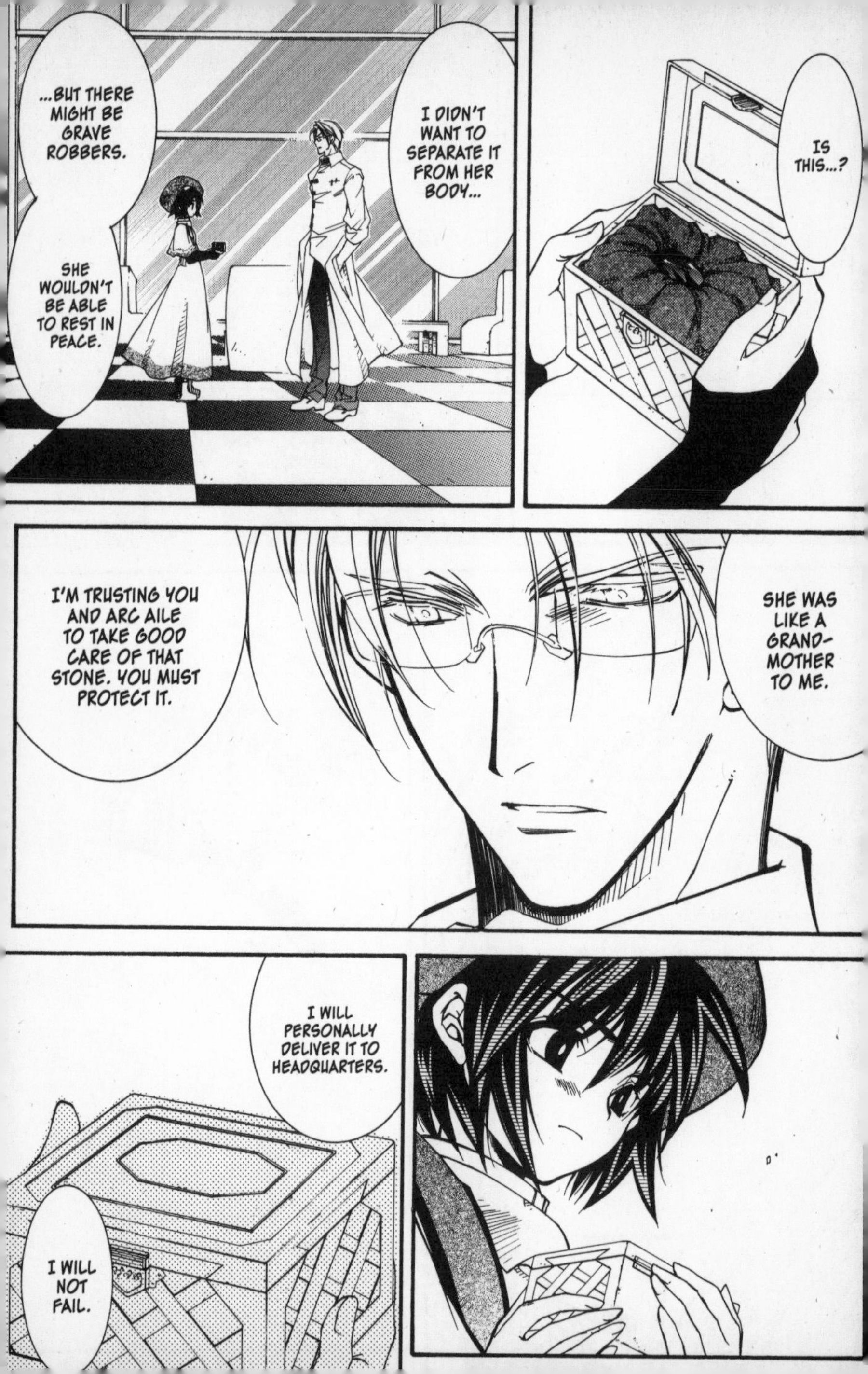
IS THIS...?
I DIDN'T WANT TO SEPARATE IT FROM HER BODY...
...BUT THERE MIGHT BE GRAVE ROBBERS.
SHE WOULDN'T BE ABLE TO REST IN PEACE.
SHE WAS LIKE A GRAND-MOTHER TO ME.
I'M TRUSTING YOU AND ARC AILE TO TAKE GOOD CARE OF THAT STONE. YOU MUST PROTECT IT.
I WILL PERSONALLY DELIVER IT TO HEADQUARTERS.
I WILL NOT FAIL.

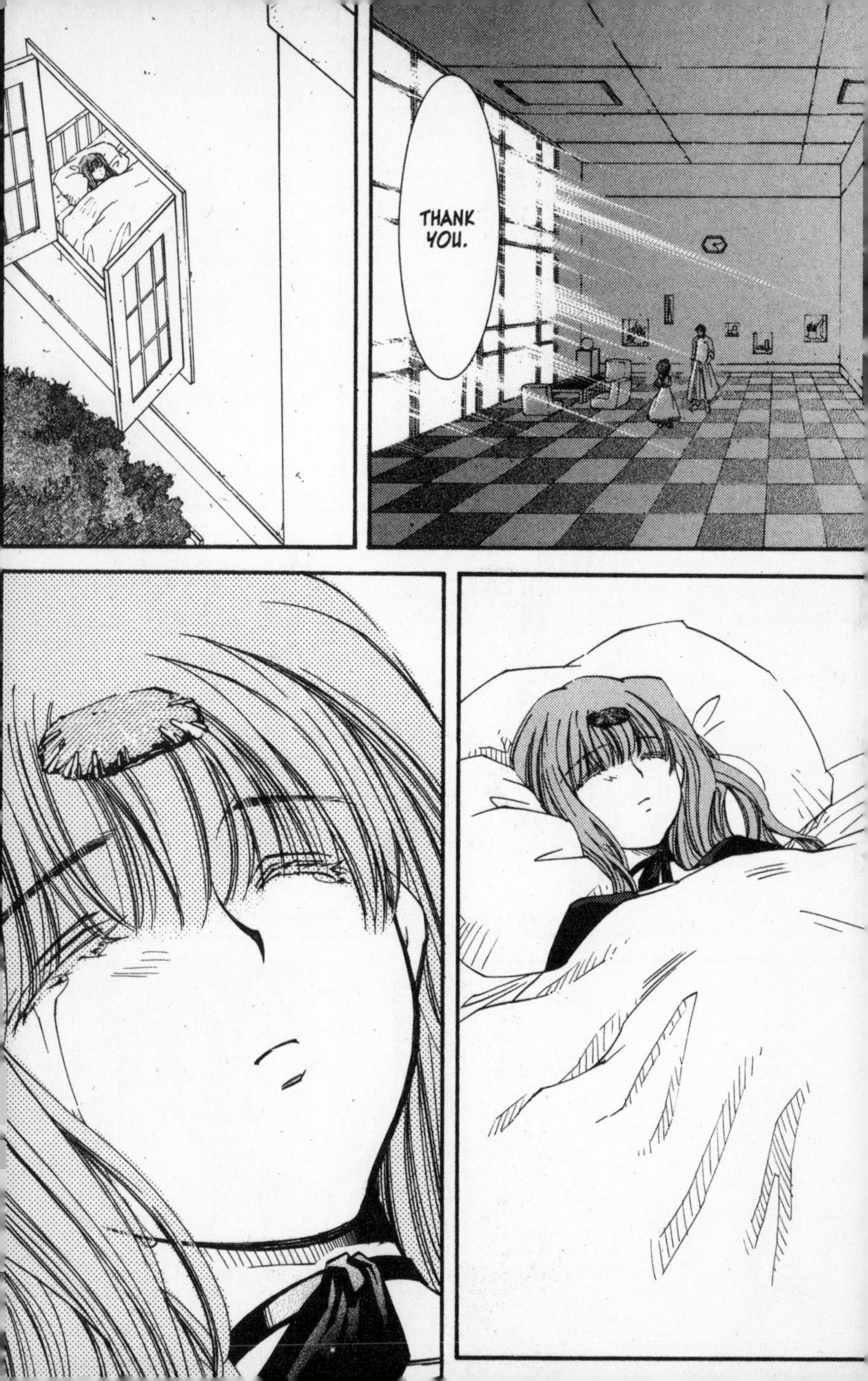
THANK YOU.

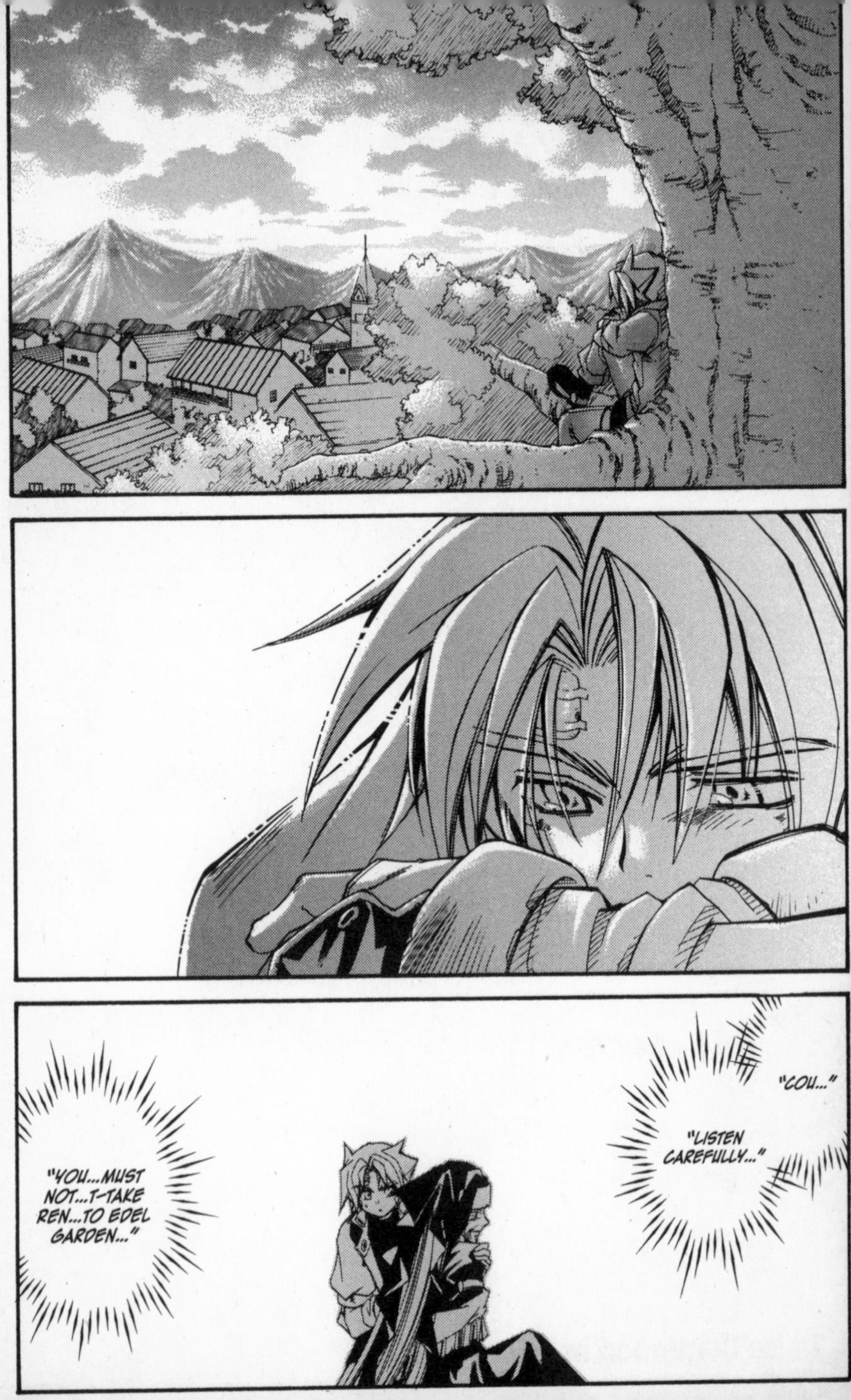
"COU..."
"LISTEN CAREFULLY..."
"YOU...MUST NOT...T-TAKE REN...TO EDEL GARDEN..."

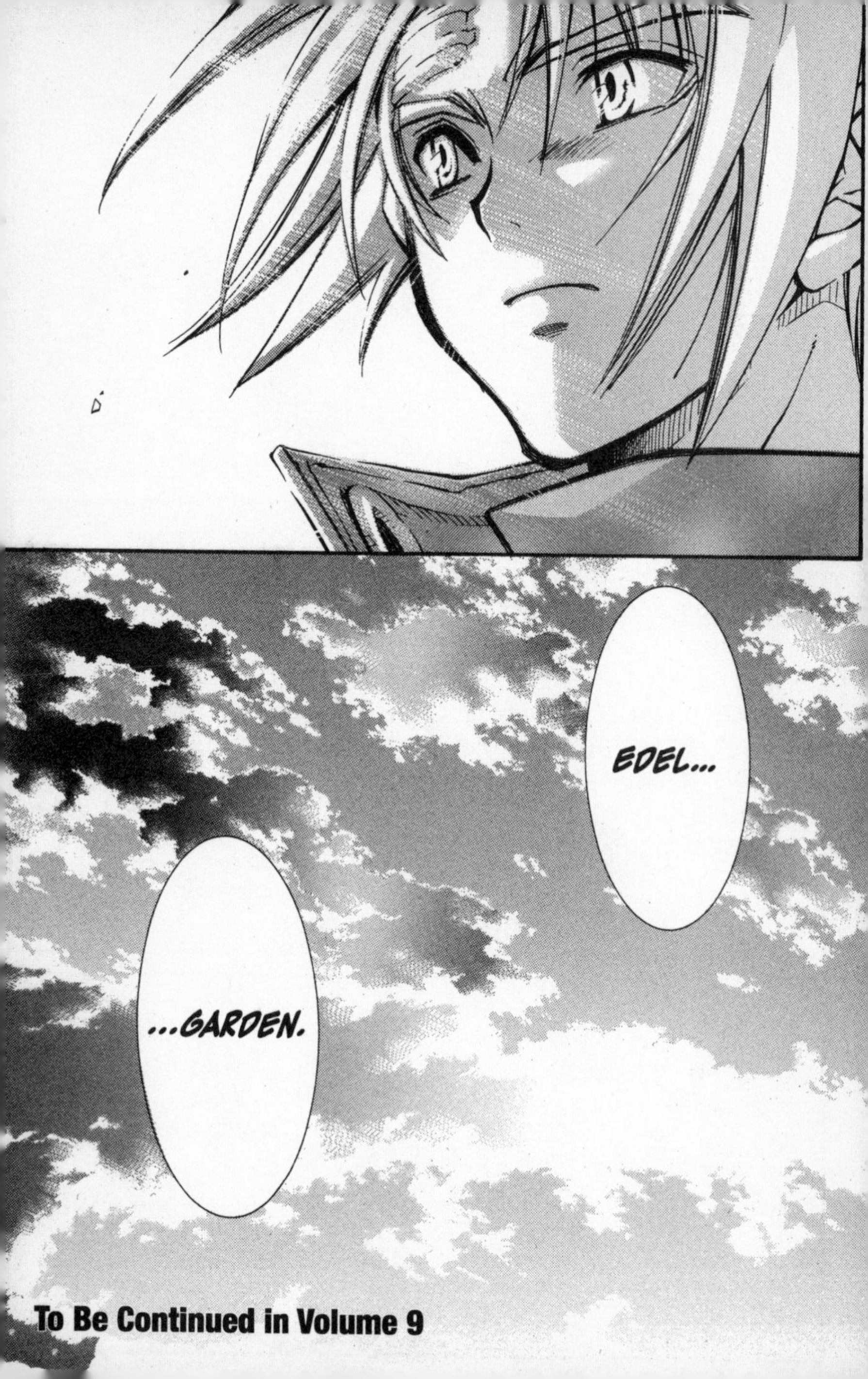
EDEL...
...GARDEN.

To Be Continued in Volume 9

In The Next Volume of

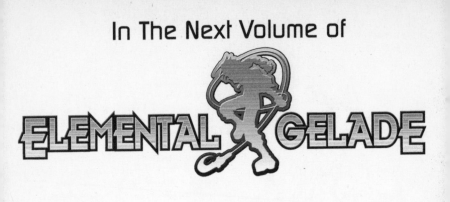

ELEMENTAL GELADE

WHILE THE COUD AND COMPANY MAKE THEIR WAY
TO THE TOWN OF TOLO DYLE, MORE AND MORE
MEMBERS OF ORGANITE ARE LEARNING ABOUT COUD
AND HIS POSSESSION OF THE SHICHIKO-HOJU.
MEANWHILE, CISQUA, COUD AND THE OTHERS ATTEND
THE TORO FEST AT TOLO DYLE. BUT THE PARTY IS
SOON CRASHED BY THE SWEET ANGELS, A GROUP
OF TWELVE EDEL RAIDS, ALL WITH DIFFERENT, BUT
DEADLY, ATTRIBUTES. CAN COUD AND REN TAKE
OUT THESE ANGELS OF DEATH? OR WILL OUR
TWO HEROES BE THE ONES PLAYING
THE HARP WHEN THE DUST SETTLES?

FIND OUT IN THE NEXT
THRILLING VOLUME!

Grayarts

I wanted to have more scenes with him singing....

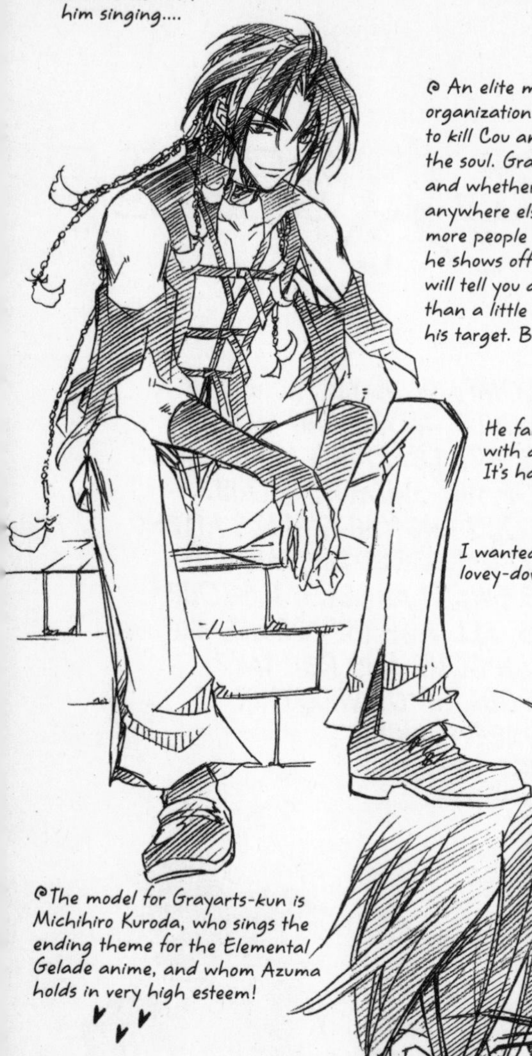

@ An elite member of the mysterious organization Organite, he was under orders to kill Cou and take Ren. He sings songs of the soul. Grayarts-kun loves to stand out, and whether he's on the deck of a ship or anywhere else, he's on stage (laugh). The more people there are around him, the more he shows off his skill! He is too generous, and will tell you anything free of charge. More than a little careless, he often misidentifies his target. But that's kinda his charm.

He failed at his mission and met with an ow ow ow owie fate (cry)! It's hard on Azuma, too!!! Waaaah!

I wanted to draw more of him being lovey-dovey with Coco-tan... Sniffle...

@The model for Grayarts-kun is Michihiro Kuroda, who sings the ending theme for the Elemental Gelade anime, and whom Azuma holds in very high esteem!

♥ ♥ ♥

He's a rock 'n' roll star.

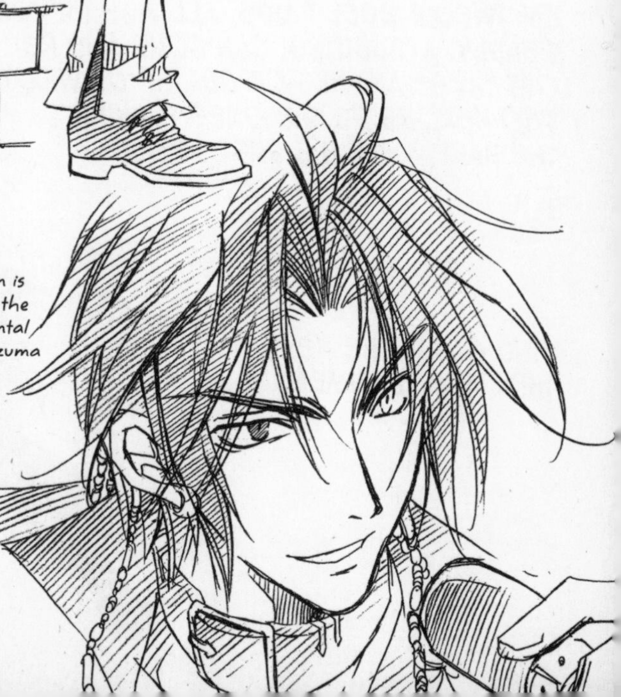

@The model for Cocovet is an adorable girl who I saw in a fashion magazine.

Her eyes are...Lum-chan? Datcha!!

Cocovet
(Cicoria Cor Wetvie)

@As Grayarts-kun's Edel Raid, Coco-tan loves Grayarts-kun. They're lovey-dovey! Unlike Ren-chan and the others, Coco-tan is a support Edel Raid, whose attacks are meant to strengthen her Pleasure's abilities--which is why she powers up Grayarts-kun's singing voice! Because Coco-tan is a strengthened Edel Raid (like she's been remodeled), if her strengthened core stone is taken out or broken, she dies. Sniffle... Sniffle...

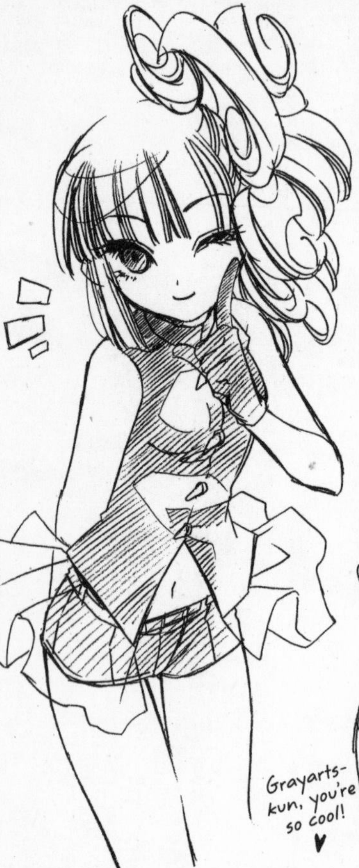

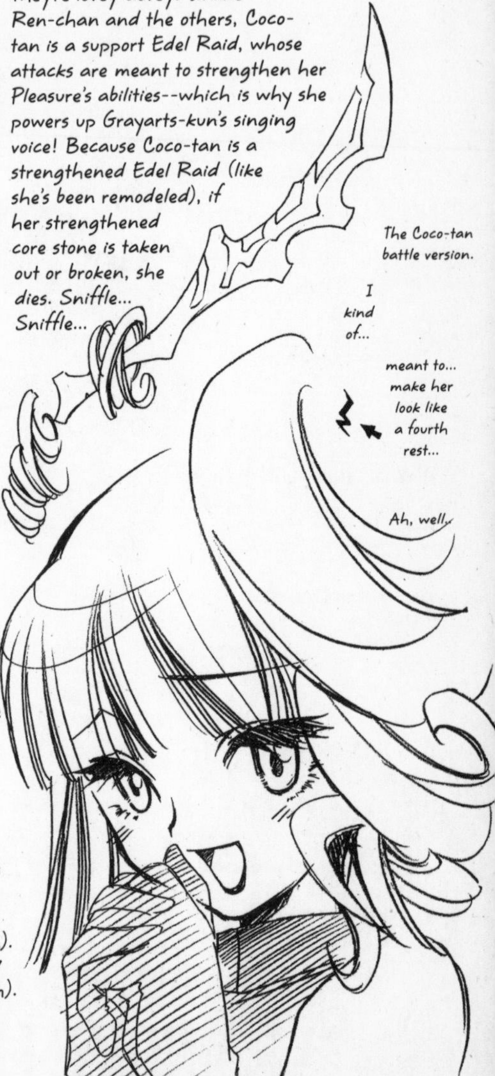
The Coco-tan battle version.
I kind of...
meant to... make her look like a fourth rest...
Ah, well..
Grayarts-kun, you're so cool! ♥

@Coco-tan's core stone is red-violet. It's on the right side of her chest. The way she recovers her Edel Raid power is through "wild enthusiasm" (being a fan). If she just flares up and says, "Kyaaa ♥ Grayarts-kun ♥" she can recover (laugh). It's very economical...just like Tickle!

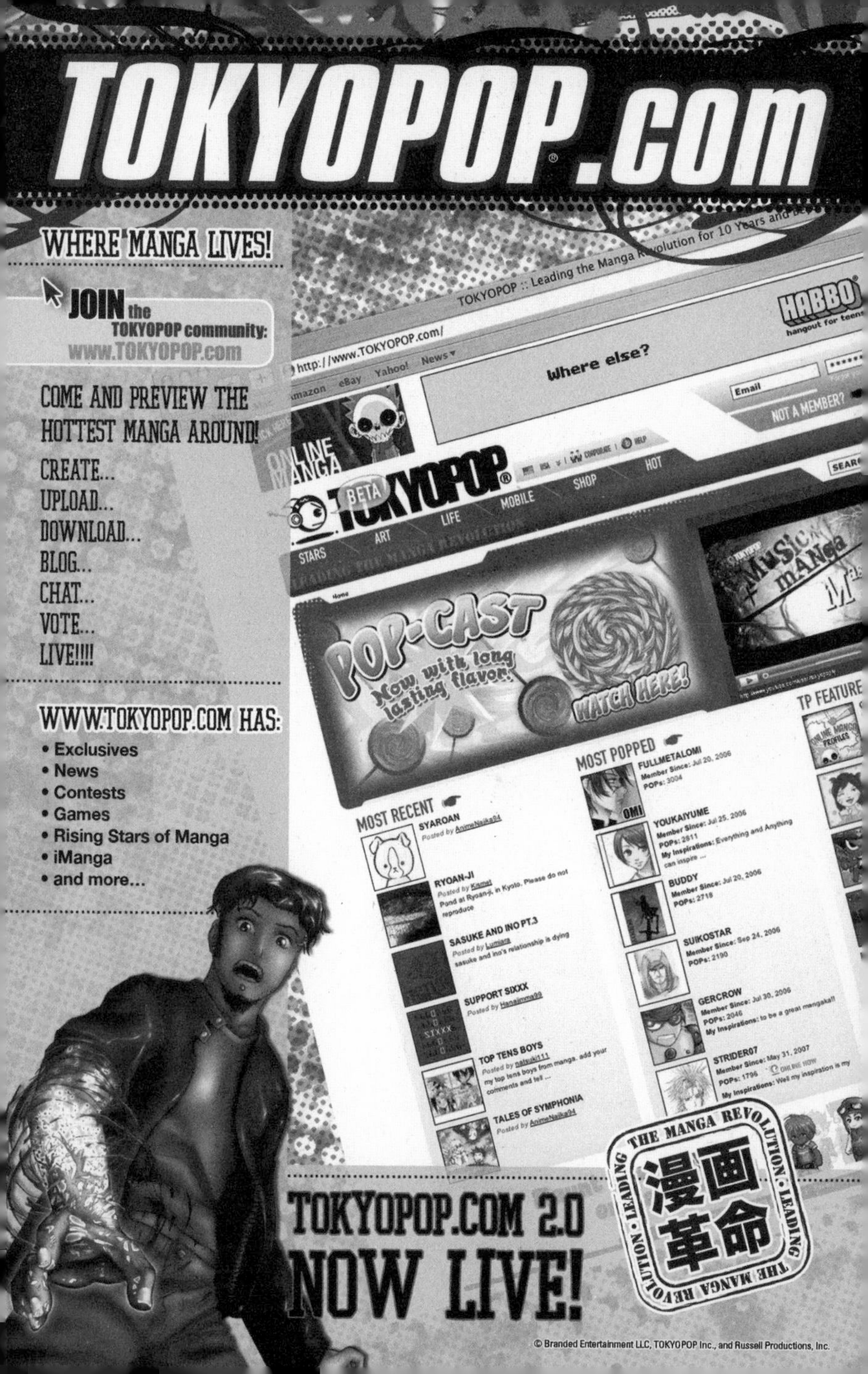
TOKYOPOP.com
WHERE MANGA LIVES!
JOIN the TOKYOPOP community:
www.TOKYOPOP.com
COME AND PREVIEW THE HOTTEST MANGA AROUND!
CREATE...
UPLOAD...
DOWNLOAD...
BLOG...
CHAT...
VOTE...
LIVE!!!!
WWW.TOKYOPOP.COM HAS:
• Exclusives
• News
• Contests
• Games
• Rising Stars of Manga
• iManga
• and more...
TOKYOPOP :: Leading the Manga Revolution for 10 Years and
http://www.TOKYOPOP.com/
Where else?
TOKYOPOP
STARS
ART
LIFE
MOBILE
SHOP
HOT
POP-CAST
Now with long lasting flavor.
WATCH HERE!
MOST POPPED
MOST RECENT
TP FEATURE
TOKYOPOP.COM 2.0
NOW LIVE!
THE MANGA REVOLUTION · LEADING
漫画
革命
© Branded Entertainment LLC, TOKYOPOP Inc., and Russell Productions, Inc.

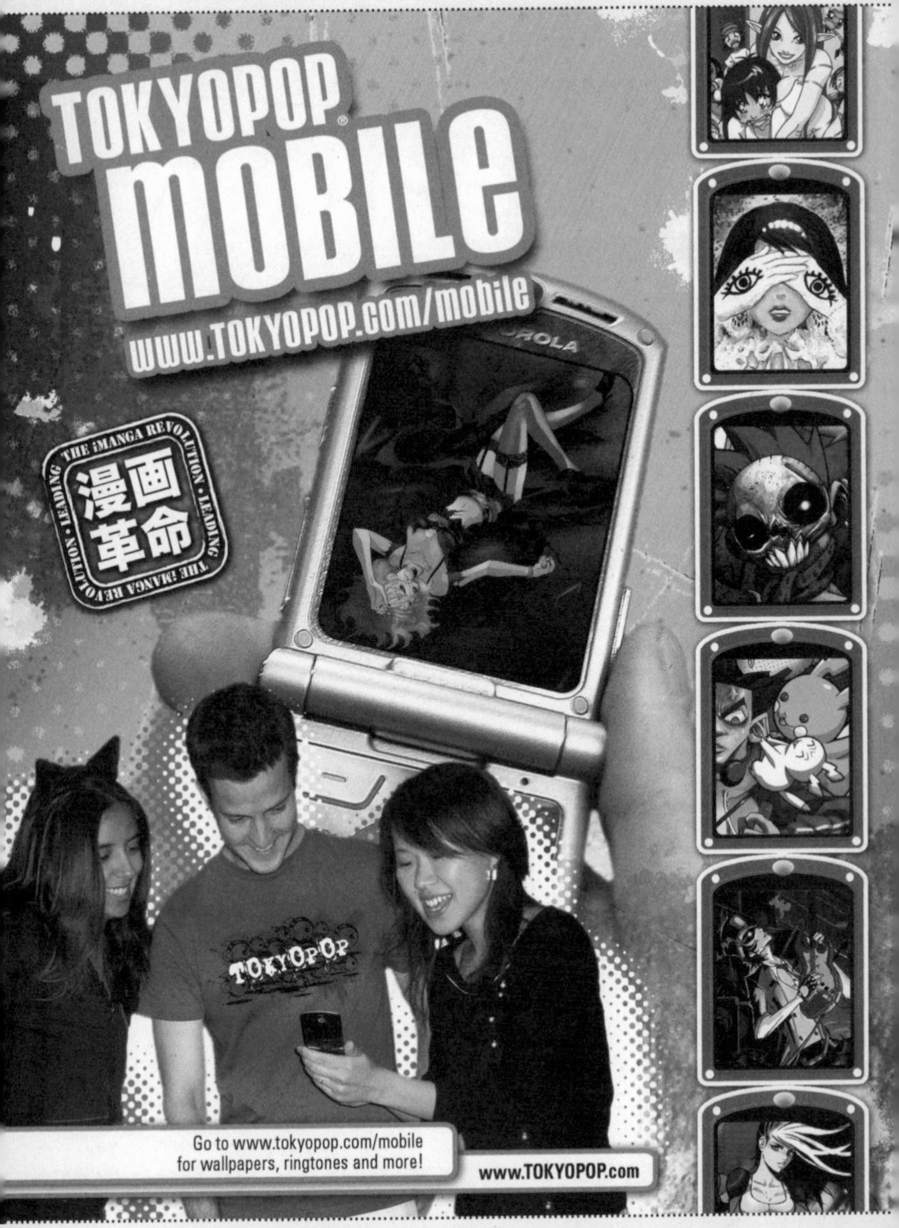
TOKYOPOP
MOBILE
www.TOKYOPOP.com/mobile
THE iMANGA REVOLUTION · LEADING · THE iMANGA REVOLUTION · LEADING
漫画革命
TOKYOPOP
Go to www.tokyopop.com/mobile
for wallpapers, ringtones and more!
www.TOKYOPOP.com

FOR MORE INFORMATION VISIT: WWW.TOKYOPOP.COM

TOKYOPOP MANGA SUPPLEMENT

From the creator of *Peace Maker*

ヴァッサロード

+

Nanae Chrono

The Vatican has employed a new assassin who's a vampire, *and* a cyborg. If you think he sounds nasty, wait `till you see his master! When these two hot guys collide, the good times and carnage will roll like a head off a guillotine!

© NANAE CHRONO/MAG Garden

FOR MORE INFORMATION VISIT: WWW.TOKYOPOP.COM

TOKYOPOP MANGA SUPPLEMENT

SUPER HYPER
AUDIOTISTIC
SONIC REVOLUTION!!!

www.myspace.com/tokyopop

www.TOKYOPOP.com

TOKYOPOP RECORDS

Available at the iTunes Music Store
and everywhere music downloads
are available. Keyword: TOKYOPOP

New releases every month!
Check out these great albums
AVAILABLE NOW!!!

©2007 TOKYOPOP Inc.

FOR MORE INFORMATION VISIT: WWW.TOKYOPOP.COM

TOKYOPOP MANGA SUPPLEMENT

AS SEEN ON CARTOON NETWORK

TRINITY BLOOD ™

Trinity Blood Volume 7
While lost in the city, Ion and Esther meet a
strange young tea-seller who reveals that
Radu may be alive…but not before a fight for
their survival against Dietrich's vampire
zombie soldiers!

ACTION   OT OLDER TEEN AGE 16+

LET THE BLOODLETTING CONTINUE

THE SOURCE MATERIAL FOR THE ANIME AND MANGA

THE ADVENTURES CONTINUE IN THESE EXCITING TRINITY BLOOD NOVELS

Trinity Blood
Rage Against the Moons
Volumes 1, 2 and 3

Trinity Blood
Reborn on the Mars
Volumes 1 and 2

POP FICTION

Trinity Blood Volume 7 © Kiyo KYUJYO 2006 © Sunao YOSHIDA 2006 / KADOKAWA SHOTEN
Trinity Blood: Rage Against The Moons, Volume 3 © Sunao YOSHIDA 2001 / KADOKAWA SHOTEN
Trinity Blood: Reborn on the Mars, Volume 2 © Sunao YOSHIDA 2000, 2001 / KADOKAWA SHOTEN

FOR MORE INFORMATION VISIT: WWW.TOKYOPOP.COM

TOKYOPOP MANGA SUPPLEMENT

Hotel AFRICA™

Hotel AFRICA
VOLUME TWO
By Hee Jung Park

Anything can happen at the Hotel Africa

Tales of heartbreak, irony, and redemption are in store when you check in a second time to the Hotel Africa. Continue along with Elvis as he reveals more tales of the desolate hotel and its strange guests.

INCLUDES ORIGINAL COLOR ART!

ART NOT FINAL

hee jung park's
fever

one

Also available from Hee Jung Park
Fever

Once you go to Fever, you will never be the same...

Too Long

A girl who attracts suicide victims, a shy record store customer, and the star of a rock band... what could these three have in common? Find out in this moving collection of short stories.

© Hee-Jung Park

FOR MORE INFORMATION VISIT: WWW.TOKYOPOP.COM

ARE YOU TRULY ALIVE?

In the collapsing world of the afterlife, two guardians face the ultimate question: Thaddeus yearns for answers, while Mercutio seeks his true love. Will they be able to find it all before it's too late?

ART BY ROB STEEN AND STORY BY STORMCROW HAYES

A MEDITATIVE AND BROODING EXPLORATION INTO THE ENDLESS POSSIBILITIES OF THE AFTERLIFE.

FANTASY

OT OLDER TEEN AGE 16+

© Sam Hayes, Rob Steen and TOKYOPOP Inc.

READ AN ENTIRE CHAPTER FOR FREE: WWW.TOKYOPOP.COM/MANGAONLINE

TOKYOPOP MANGA SUPPLEMENT

THE QUEST TO SAVE THE WORLD
CONTINUES IN THE BEST-SELLING
MANGA FROM TOKYOPOP!

VOLUMES 1-4 AVAILABLE NOW!

ORIGINAL MANGA COMIC BY SHIRO AMANO / ENTERBRAIN, INC. © DISNEY.
CHARACTERS FROM FINAL FANTASY VIDEO GAME SERIES © 1990, 1997, 1999, 2001, 2002 SQUARE ENIX CO., LTD. ALL RIGHTS RESERVED.

FOR MORE INFORMATION VISIT: WWW.TOKYOPOP.COM

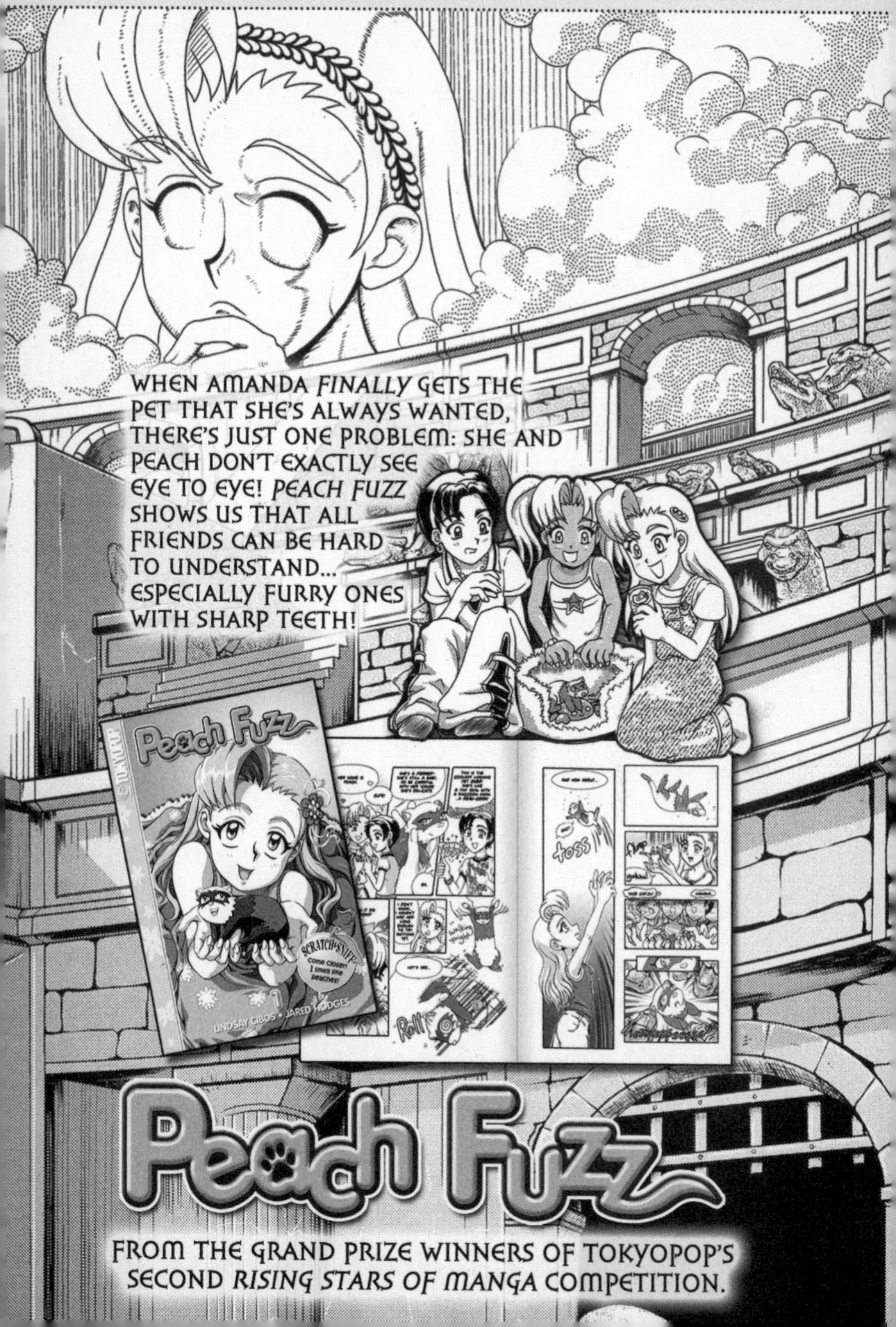
WHEN AMANDA *FINALLY* GETS THE PET THAT SHE'S ALWAYS WANTED, THERE'S JUST ONE PROBLEM: SHE AND PEACH DON'T EXACTLY SEE EYE TO EYE! *PEACH FUZZ* SHOWS US THAT ALL FRIENDS CAN BE HARD TO UNDERSTAND... ESPECIALLY FURRY ONES WITH SHARP TEETH!
Peach Fuzz
TOKYOPOP
1
LINDSAY CIBOS • JARED HODGES
toss
Roll
Peach Fuzz
FROM THE GRAND PRIZE WINNERS OF TOKYOPOP'S SECOND *RISING STARS OF MANGA* COMPETITION.

PEACHFUZZ

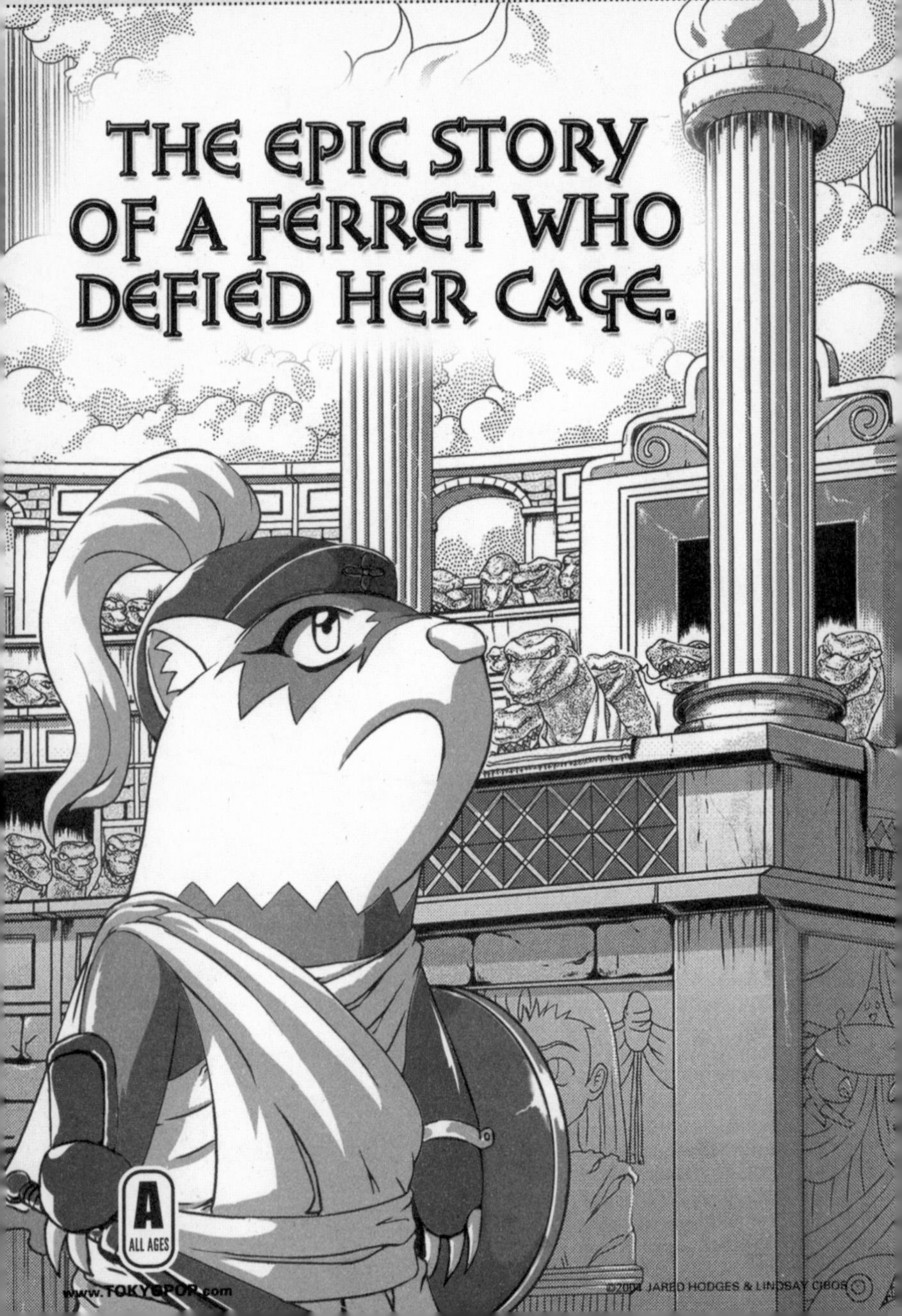
THE EPIC STORY OF A FERRET WHO DEFIED HER CAGE.
A ALL AGES
www.TOKYOPOP.com
©2004 JARED HODGES & LINDSAY CIBOS

ROADSONG

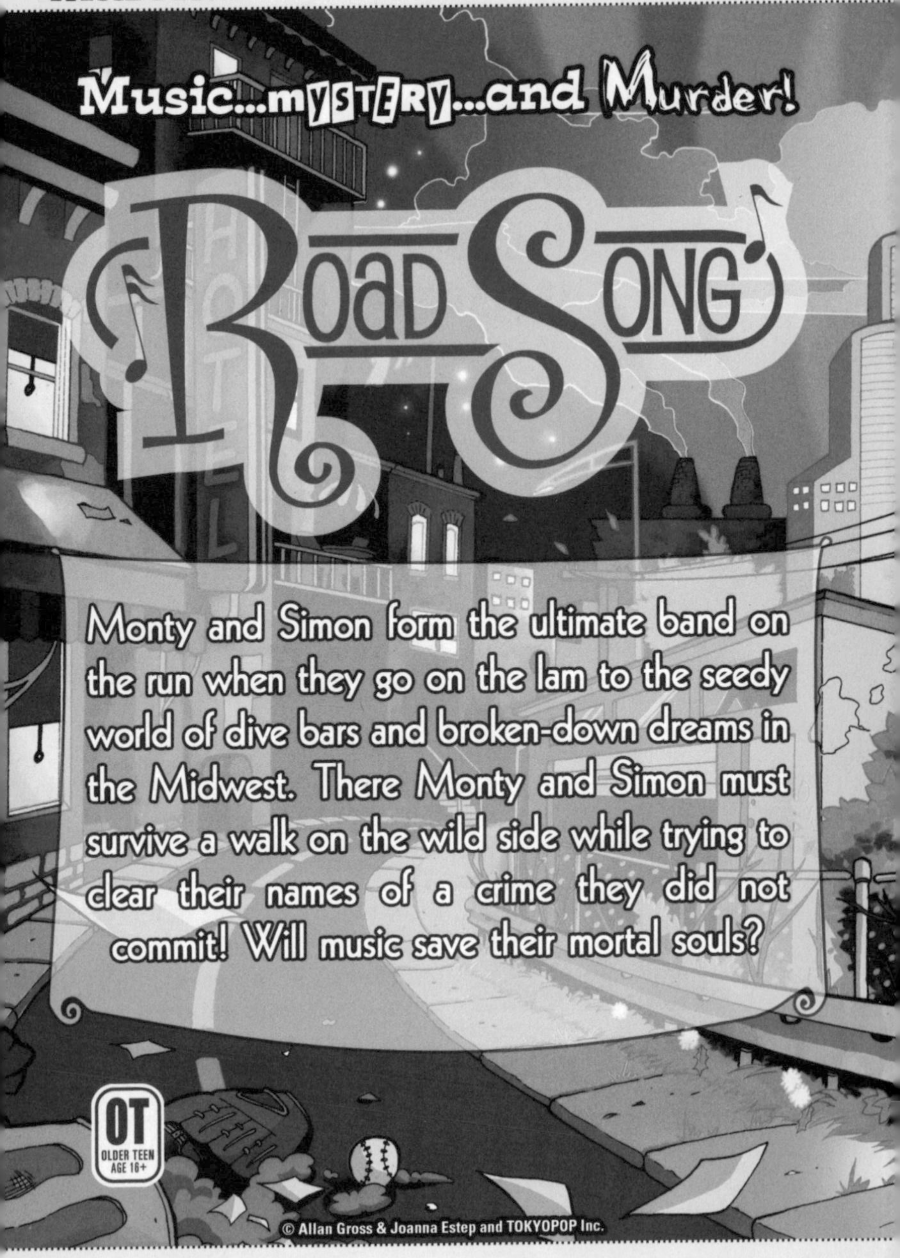

Music...mystery...and Murder!
RoadSong
Monty and Simon form the ultimate band on the run when they go on the lam to the seedy world of dive bars and broken-down dreams in the Midwest. There Monty and Simon must survive a walk on the wild side while trying to clear their names of a crime they did not commit! Will music save their mortal souls?
OT
OLDER TEEN
AGE 16+
© Allan Gross & Joanna Estep and TOKYOPOP Inc.

READ A CHAPTER OF THE MANGA ONLINE FOR FREE:

STOP!

This is the back of the book.
You wouldn't want to spoil a great ending!

This book is printed "manga-style," in the authentic Japanese right-to-left format. Since none of the artwork has been flipped or altered, readers get to experience the story just as the creator intended. You've been asking for it, so TOKYOPOP® delivered: authentic, hot-off-the-press, and far more fun!

DIRECTIONS

1
2
3
4
5
6
7
8
9
10

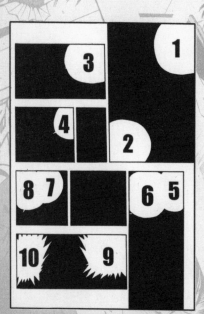

If this is your first time reading manga-style, here's a quick guide to help you understand how it works.

It's easy... just start in the top right panel and follow the numbers. Have fun, and look for more 100% authentic manga from TOKYOPOP®!

THE MANGA REVOLUTION · LEADING
漫画革命

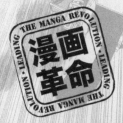